An Annotated Digest of

Will Book A

Guilford County
North Carolina

1771–May Court 1816

Jane Smith Hill

HERITAGE BOOKS
2007

IHERITAGE BOOKS
AN IMPRINT OF HERITAGE BOOKS, INC.

Books, CDs, and more—Worldwide

For our listing of thousands of titles see our website
at
www.HeritageBooks.com

Published 2007 by
HERITAGE BOOKS, INC.
Publishing Division
65 East Main Street
Westminster, Maryland 21157-5026

Copyright © 2005 Jane Smith Hill

All rights reserved. No part of this book may be reproduced or transmitted in any form or by any means, electronic or mechanical, including photocopying, recording or by any information storage and retrieval system without written permission from the author, except for the inclusion of brief quotations in a review.

International Standard Book Number: 978-0-7884-4438-8

ACKNOWLEDGEMENTS

Entirely too long ago the Guilford County Genealogical Society decided to rework Mrs. Webster's publication: GUILFORD COUNTY, NORTH CAROLINA WILL ABSTRACTS 1771-1841. The Staff of the North Carolina Collection of the High Point Public Library in High Point, NC cooperated with the Publications Committee and the work began, using photocopies made from the North Carolina State Archives microfilm reel # C. 046.800001. These copies were delegated to the volunteers from the Society, and the abstracting began.

Due to the faintness of the ink, the size of the wills, and other problems with the actual film, we began to utilize copies of the original wills housed in the North Carolina State Archives in Raleigh, North Carolina.

Since we had access to copies of the original wills, it seemed a good idea to include the signatures of the Testators and these are in a group.

As the wills were abstracted, they were handed to me to input into my computer and I began the process, but it soon became apparent that an abstract did not do justice to the men and women who made these wills, and so it became a Digest. My knowledge of the people in these wills, learned over 30+ years of research in the records of Guilford County, made it imperative that I use all this knowledge in the finished product.

Due to the illness and death of my husband and some health problems of my own, work on the Digest has been sporadic and slow, but it is now ready for the printer.

Mrs. Webster's book contained Will Books A, B, & C along with some unrecorded wills. I have chosen to include the unrecorded wills that fit into the time frame of Will Book A.

All these wills are housed in the North Carolina State Archives in Raleigh, North Carolina and photocopies are available for a fee.

My deepest thanks go to those who gave their time to abstracting these wills. They are: Gail Lawson, Bobbie Redding, Jean May, Faye B. Willard, Alice Matthews, Martha Powers, Judy Millikan, Betty L. Brown, Pamela D. Jones, Sue Bishop, and Ken Baldwin. Those of the staff of the North Carolina Collection include Jackie Hedstrom, Yvonne Bell Thomas, Rousie Hobson, and Heather Forbis Marks.

Jane Smith Hill
February 2005

FOREWORD

How many people read any part of a genealogy book except the index? If you are seeking Guilford County ancestors, it might be of inestimable value to read this foreword.

Guilford County was settled, beginning about the 1750s by a mixture of people with a mixture of religions; 18th century Germans with their Lutheran and German Reformed churches. The Scots-Irish, those lowland Scots who settled in the Plantations in Northern Ireland who were mostly Presbyterians, although the sect was different from the modern group. The English Baptists; the English who were members of the Religious Society of Friends, known as Quakers; the English who were members of the Anglican Church, i.e. The Church of England; the French Huguenots who were Protestants, and the un-churched.

The 18th century Germans were soon to begin changing their names and to begin to become Americanized. Intermarriage with their English-speaking neighbors hastened the process. The names began to be anglicized as soon as they landed in America; the English clerks had to accommodate the names to something the clerks could manage. Although most of the 18th century Germans were literate in German they did not learn to write English until much later.

Not only were the German names misspelled, but those of the English were also misspelled because few of them could read or write. When the English clerks wrote the names they heard, those names had to be understood by their owners when the clerk called them out. It was an oral society and spelling was up to the person doing the writing.

Incidentally, very few of the within wills were written by the Testator; most were written by a neighbor or someone called in to write for them. The wills in the will books were recorded by the Clerk of Court when the original was brought to court for probate. The originals were filed away, and it is wonderful how many have survived.

The date the will was written was not the date the Testator died. The Testator died between the date the will was written and the date the will was brought to court for probate. Court was held four times each year and was known as the Court of Pleas and Quarter Sessions. If a person died between sessions of Court, the will could be brought before a Justice and the probate could begin, and the probate data was not always registered at the next court, so there are no probate dates on some of the wills.

If you will sound out the names in the index, you will find that great license was taken with spelling. The name Sullivan is a good example. There are also some extremely unfamiliar names whose origins are not known to me.

Revokes is a form used in the writing of most wills, even though a particular testator did not revoke a will. It was impossible to determine whether the revoke was a form or a real happening, so I have added the word "revokes" after each will which contained the word, leaving the reader to make the decision of its validity.

Codicil is an addition to a will and there are several in these wills. Forgetting something while dictating the will or changes in the family circumstances might call for a codicil.

Another interesting thing is the beginning of a will. Most wills began with the words "In the name of God, amen". That seems to have been a standard for most wills. But if your ancestor was a Quaker, or was from the New England colonies, or from another place or religion, you might see the following: "Be it remembered", "know all men by these presents", "I, ----- -----", "whereas I -----", "In the year of God".
All these represent a person from a different background and should be investigated.

Quakers did not swear an oath, they affirmed, so if you see affirmed you probably have a Quaker.

Among the very interesting words and phrases found among these wills there are several I want to share with you.

"Ly down mistress & rise up master" is a new expression to me and I have not found it in any of the reference books. It might mean that the wife went to bed as the mistress, but due to the death of her husband, she arose as the master of the farm.

Wife to is wife of. Beaver hat is just that; one made of beaver skin. Spring coult is a colt born in the spring.

A Cardinel is a short hooded cloak. Originally of scarlet cloth; worn by women in the 18th century. The bequests of clothing to the heirs may sound odd to us, but remember that most all clothing was raised from the ground up from flax, wool and some cotton, to the finished product and was thus quite important.

The word Jurat occurs in these wills and the Jurat is the witness who went to Court to prove the will for probate.

Beast is a creature, usually a horse creature.

Seal is always on the document and in the olden days was a blob of wax placed on a document and with a signet ring of raised design pressed into the warm wax. The word seal was often written with lots of special effects when a real ring was not used by the person. Very few of the settlers had seal rings. It indicates that he signed his name or made his mark. Seal was necessary for legality.

Puter is Pewter. There will be lots of phonetic spelling, so do not let it confuse you. Sound out the words and the meaning will come to you.

A riding chear is a riding chair, but I have been unable to determine just what form the chair took. The explanation of a Barshir plow still eludes me. Nowhere have I found out just what it was like.

Bed and furniture, what was involved? The bed, of course, plus pillows, sheets, covers and possibly bed curtains. That may not sound like much of a legacy but it certainly was to our ancestors.

Remember, Guilford was on the frontier and stores were few and far between.

Also, Guilford County was erected in 1771 from the eastern part, about 4 miles, of old Orange County and from the western part of old Rowan County. In 1771 it contained not only itself, but also Rockingham and Randolph counties. Randolph County was taken off the southern part of Guilford in 1779, but Rockingham was not taken from Guilford's northern part until 1785, so some of these wills and people may now be in Rockingham County. Counties have parents just a people do and it is a wise genealogist who remembers this.

Another interesting item is the Battle of Guilford Court, fought March 1781 between our General Nathaniel Greene and Britain's Charles, Lord Cornwallis. Although Greene retreated leaving Cornwallis in command of the battleground, Greene so devastated the British Army that they could not pursue the Rebels. The first ten years of the Court Minutes were lost or destroyed during this conflict and their loss is devastating to researchers. The Court House was just north of present Greensboro and the Battle Ground itself is well maintained.

Other definitions you might want to see can be found in several books, two of which are: NORTH CAROLINA RESEARCH, Edited by Helen F. M. Leary, published by the North Carolina Genealogical Society, and WHAT DID THEY MEAN BY THAT? B\by Paul Drake, J.D. There may be WEB sites that will help with these older words and phrases.

Jane Smith Hill

SIGNATURES OF DEVISORS

[signature]

ROBERT BREDEN

[signature]

PETER COBLE

[signature]

JAMES COOTS

[signature]

ELIAS COWEN

Charles Deatherage

CHARLES DEAR

Phil: Deatherage

PHIL: DEATHERAGE

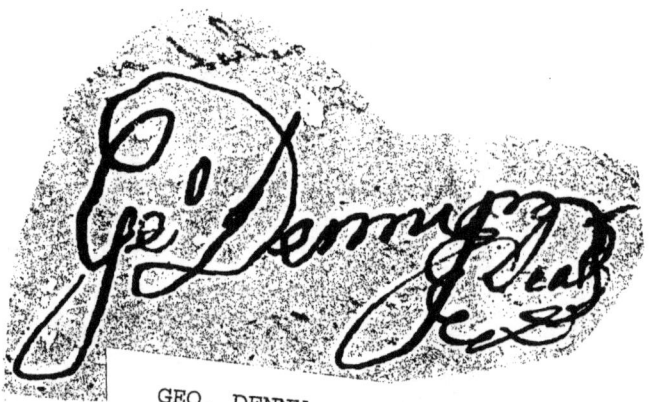

GEO. DENNY

James Denny

JAMES DENNY

PATRICK DIAMOND

WILLIAM DICK

DANIEL DILLON

JAS. DOAK

ABRAM ENDSLEY

JOSIAH FINLEY

ELISHA FLACK

DANIEL FISHER

WILLIAM FORBES

WM DOAK

ROBERT DONNELL

ROBERT DOUGHERTY

ROBERT DWIGGINS

[signature]
JOHN FORBIS

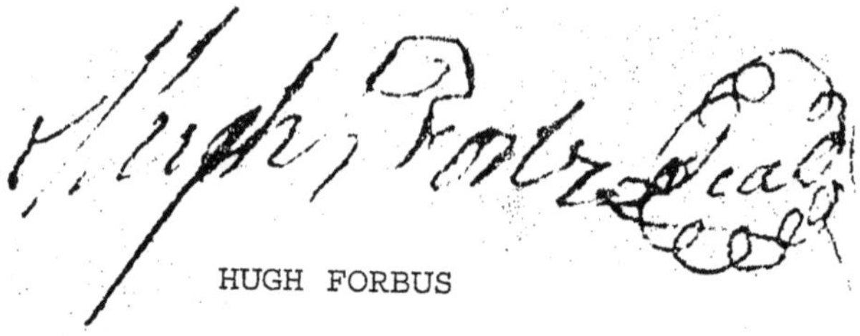

[signature]
HUGH FORBUS

[signature with text: "testament in the time of signing and sealing"]
DAVID FOREHAND

[signature]
ARTHUR FORBUS

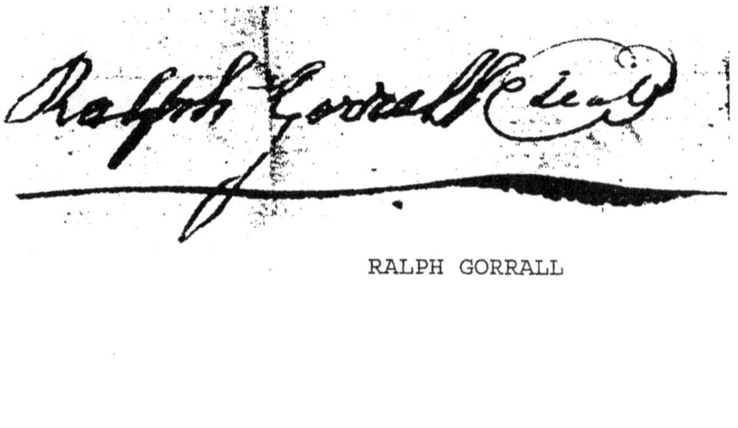

[signature]
RALPH GORRALL

WILLIAM GOWDY

EDWARD GUILBERT

ROBERT GWIN

JOHN HAMILTON

FRANCIS HARTLEY

JOHN HEALY

ISAAC HILL

JOSEPH HINDS

DAVID HODSON

WILLIAM HOGGATT

JOSEPH HOSKINS

JABEZ HUNT

JOHN HUNT

WILLIAM HUNT

CHRISTOPHER HUSSEY

DAVID JACKSON

JAMES JACKSON

JAMES JOHNSON

JOHN KALLUM
[His signature was written over the work SEAL]

JAMES KIRKMAN

PETER KIRKMAN

DAVID KERR

ELIZABETH KERR
[Elizabeth signed her name, but the ink had faded too badly to make a copy]

THOMAS LANDRETH

EDW'D. LONEY

ADAM LEAKY

HENRY LEE

ROBERT LINDSAY

WM. LOMAX

SAM'L. LORIMER

JOHN McBRIDE

JOHN McCALL

signature JAMES McADOW

signature JOHN McCLEAN

signature MOSES McCUISTON

signature SAMUEL McDILL

signature CHARLS McDORMAN OR McDARMON

signature PATRICK McGIBBONEY

JAMES M'GREADY

JOHN McMURREY

JOHN McMURRAY

JAMES McMURRY

WILL. McNAUGHT

ABEL McKNIGHT

JOHN McKNIGHT

ENOCH MACY

DINAH MACY

HENRY MACY

MATTHEW MACY

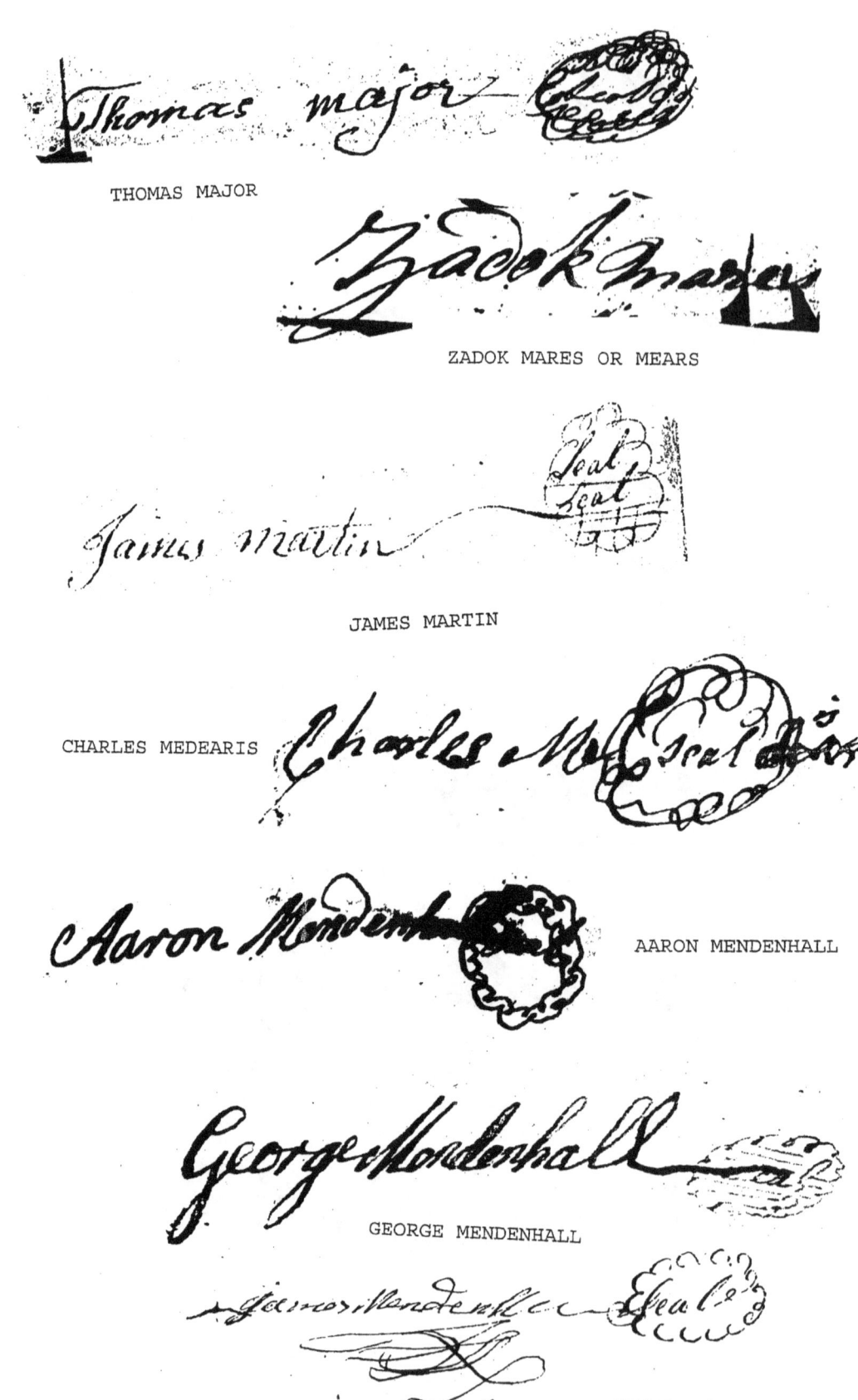

MORDECIA MENDENHALL

MOSES MENDENHALL

THOMAS MENDENHALL

WILLIAM MERONEY

WILLIAM MILLS

WILLIAM MONGOMMERY

WILLIAM MONTGOMERY

THOMAS MORELAND

EDWARD MULLOY

ROBERT NEELEY

GEORGE NELSON

JOHN PEASLEY

JEHU PEEPLES

CALEB PERKINS

JOSEPH PERKINS

DAVID PHILPOTT

HENRY PORTER

JAMES PORTER

JAMES PORTER

EZEKIEL PRTICHETT

WILLIAM QUAIT

HANNAH RANKIN

JOHN RANKIN

ROBERT RANKIN

signature WILLIAM RANKIN

signature WILLIAM REA

signature HENRY REED

signature DAVID REYNOLDS

signature JOHN RHODES

signature JOHN RHODES, JUNER

signature WILLIAM REEVES

signature JOHN ROSS

signature JOHN ROSS

JOSEPH RUCKMAN

JOHN RUDDUCK, SENIOR

WILLIAM RUSSELL

HEZEKIAH SANDERS

JOEL SANDERS

JOHN SANDERS

ROBERT SAPP

JOSEPH SCALES

JOHN SCOTT

REBECKAH SCOTT

ROBT. SCOTT

WM. SCOTT

WM. SEARCY

JOSEPH SHARBROUGH

WM. SHAVER

WM. SHAW

JAMES SHELLY

JOHN SHELLY

RICHARD SIMPSON

HENERICK SIGFRED

JACOB SOUTS

GEORGE STALKER

GAYER STARBUCK

MATTHEW STARBUCK

WM. SPRUCE

GEORGE STALKER

SHADRACH STANLEY

BENJ'N. STARRATT

FINLEY STEWART

JOHN SULLEN

NICHOLAS TALLEY

EDWARD TATUM

SIMEON TAYLOR

JAMES THOMAS

HENRY THOMPSON

SAMUEL THOMPSON

THOMAS THORNBRUGH, JUNER

JAMES THORNBURG

THOS. THORNBURGH

JONAS TOUCHSTONE

lEVI TUCKER

JOHN UBANKS

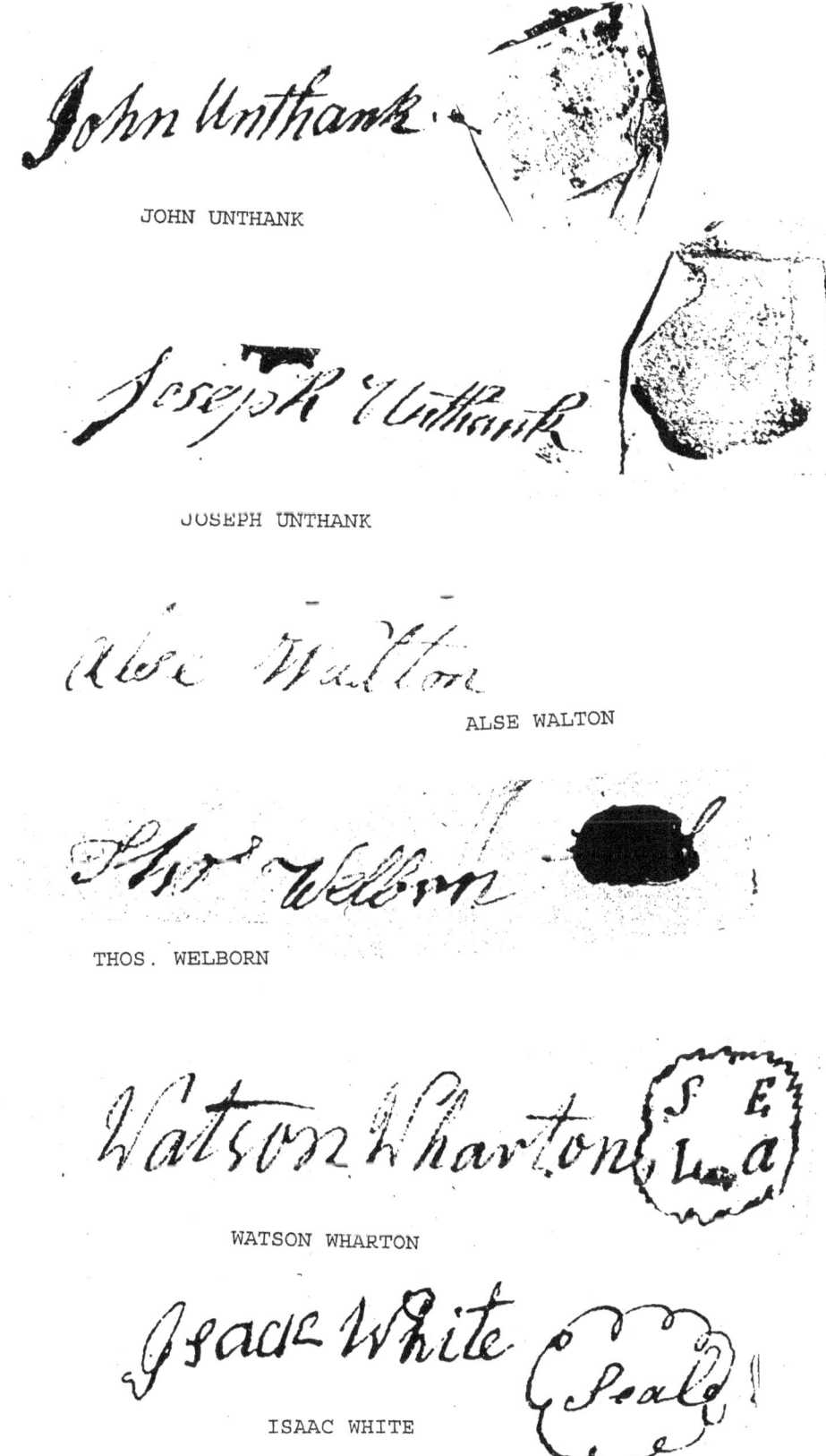

JOHN WHITE

WILLIAM WHITE

DAVID WILEY, SR.

THOMAS WILEY

EDWARD WILLEY

MICHAIEL WITT

ARTHUR WOODBURN

WILLIAM WOODBURN

JOHN WOODSIDE

JOHN WORK

JOHN WORK

Francis Worth (Seal)

FRANCIS WORTH

James Wright Jr. (Seal)

JAMES WRIGHT, JUN.

MARKS BY TESTATORS AND WITNESSES

Can anyone identify the four Coble men whose names are above that of Tobias Clap? Just think what a time the Clerks had with the German signatures and/or marks.

The mark that resembles an up right with three horizontal marks through the stem is an old letter and is used interchangeably as an " I " or a " J ".

Charity Dillon could write the letter "C". Phillip Glass/Gless tried to make a "P" for his first name.

Hannah Knight made her initials as her mark. Palliser Iseley made an "E" because his name in German is Eisley.

The name above that of Joseph McDowell is a German name. Anyone want to give it a try? John Nation made a letter "J" for John, and William Raper made the letter "W" for his first name.

William Shannon made an interesting letter "S" for his mark. Thomas Taylor appears to have made a "T" for his mark.

Jane Smith Hill
February 2005

Boady Hannah

John $\underset{mark}{\overset{his}{\mathbf{I}}}$ Alexander Sr. (Jurat)

Sind in the presents
of John $\underset{mark}{\overset{his}{\mathbf{I}}}$ Canady) Jurat
John Wilson

Anthony $\underset{mark}{\overset{his}{\times}}$ Coble

Rachel Cummins

her $\underset{mark}{\bigstar}$ Seal

Daniel Daugherty (his mark) {seal}

Charity Dulley (her mark)

Signed in the presents of
William Eken (his mark)
Jeremiah Shelly } Swrat

Philip R. Gless (his mark) {seal}

George {his H mark} Hodgson [seal]

John {his ✠ mark} Maynard [seal]

Joseph {his ✠ mark} Hogg[...] [seal]
mark

Hannah {her H mark} McKnight
mark

his
Palmer E Scoley +
mark

his
John L Laurence his Echols
mark

his
Joseph D McDowell
Mark

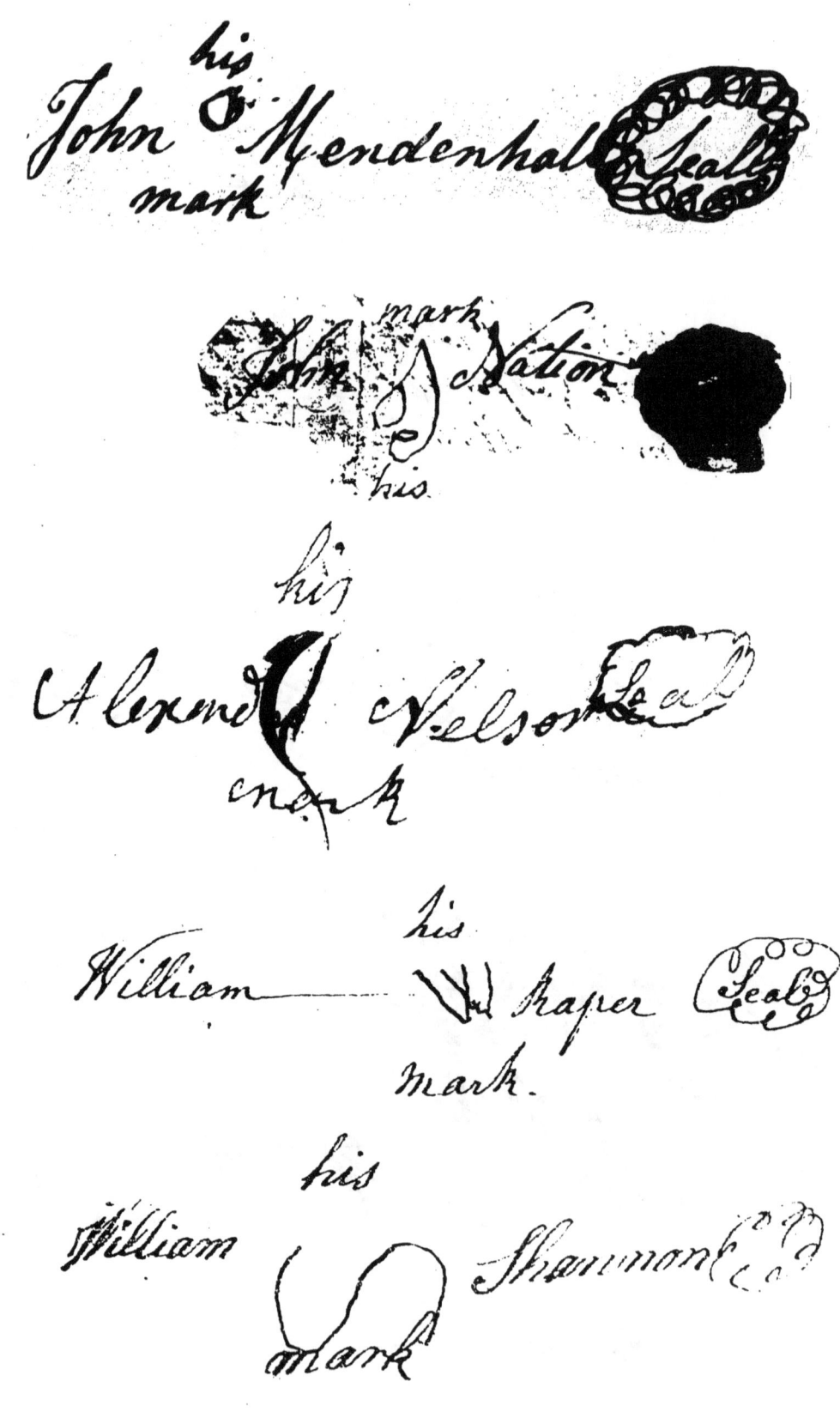

his
John X Sharp
mark

Richard Proctor [Seal]

Shemuel Hartford

his
Andrew X Shatterly
mark

his
John X Smith
mark

Joseph X Sharp [Seal]

her
Sarah X Starnes
mark

John {seal} Hon[?]

his
Thomas Taylor {seal}
mark

Allon his D wilson {seal}
mark

AN ANNOTATED DIGEST OF WILL BOOK A, GUILFORD COUNTY, NORTH CAROLINA

AN ANNOTATED DIGEST OF WILL BOOK A, GUILFORD COUNTY, NORTH CAROLINA

APRIL COURT 1771 - MAY COURT 1816

THE DIGEST

A:001 pp:1/2 JAMES ARCHER   2 Jan. 1799   Aug. Ct. 1799
Son: David Archer 150 acres of land whereon he now liveth & 1 Negro girl Phillis.
Wife: Catherine Archer all remaining part of my land & plantation during her life or widowhood, also 5 Negroes: Jack, Peter, Dick, Jacob & Jenny; Dau: Sarah to share in this bequest.
Dau: Sarah to inherit land & plantation with wife, but at death or remarriage of wife Catherine, Dau: Sarah to have 2 Negroes namely Dick & Jenny.
Wife: Catherine & Dau: Sarah to have half the stock of my cattle & sheep, also my waggon & 4 waggon horses, all my plantation tools, household & kitchen furniture during her life or widowhood; then to Dau: Sarah Archer 3 cows & 6 sheep, 1 bed & furniture, 1/2 of the pewter, one waggon horse to her & her heirs forever.
Sons: John Archer & David Archer to have the remaining part of the sd tract of land to be equally divided between them.
Son: John Archer 1 Negro boy named Isaac, also 1 boy after wife's death named Jacob.
Dau: Mary Hamilton 1 Negro woman named Jude.
Son: Thomas Archer 20 sh besides what he has already had as part of my estate.
Dau: Elizabeth Hamilton 20 sh besides what she has already had as part of my estate.
All remaining estate, real & personal, to be divided between my 6 children; Thomas Archer, John Archer, David Archer, Elizabeth Hamilton, Sarah Archer, & Mary Hamilton.
Seal: James (his x mark) Archer
Exes: John Hamilton, Robert Linzey, Carolus Judkins
Wits: Carolus Judkins (Jurat), Joel Judkins (Jurat), John Stevens
"revokes"

A:002 pp:2/3 JAMES ANTHONY 25th of 1st mo 1796   Aug. Ct. 1799
"I James Anthony..."
Wife: Mary Anthony 1 old bay mare that she was wont to ride, 2 cows with all my hogs, 1/3 part of all the linen we have made since we was married & £5 in hard money to her & her heirs forever.
Son: Obed all my right of a tract of land on the waters of Hickory Creek which he now lives on with 1/2 of all farming tools, cart, plows, chains &C at my wife's decease I give my son Obed my clok [clock] but if he dies without any lawful heirs my will is that my son Jonathan to have my clok I also give Obed all my wearing apparel to him & his heirs forever.
Son: Jonathan all my tract of land I bought of John Wilson that my son lives on containing 140 acres & 1/2 of all farming tools, cart, plows, chains, etc.

AN ANNOTATED DIGEST OF WILL BOOK A, GUILFORD COUNTY, NORTH CAROLINA

Dau: Lyda 5 silver dollars.
Dau: Ruth 1 brown mare four years old, 1 cow to her & her heirs forever.
Wife: the clok as long as she lives, at her decease as per above.
5 Daus: remaining estate: Charlotta, Phebe, Merab, Ruth & Judah equally, to them & their heirs forever.
Seal: James Anthony
Exes: son Obed Anthony, & friend Stephen Gardner
Wits: Abigail Gardner, Stephen Gardner Jr., & Stephen Gardner (Jurat)

A:003   pp:3/4   ISAAC ARMFIELD   20th 12th 1784   no probate date
"Whereas, I Isaac Armfield..."
Wife: Elizabeth Armfield the plantation whereon I now live & all my personal estate except such a part as will pay my just debts during the time she remains my widow.
Eldest Sons: William & John Armfield my tract of land whereon I now live containing 200 acres equally divided between them at death or marriage of my widow.
Dau: Sarah Armfield the 1st colt that shall be foaled from my stock.
6 Children: Sarah, Isaac, Ann, Joseph, Jacob, & Elizabeth Armfield all remaining part of my personal estate at the death or marriage of my widow to be divided between them.
Seal: Isaac Armfield
Exes: son William Armfield & brother William Armfield
Wits: Enoch Macy, William Armfield, Nathan Armfield [Jurat not named]

A:004   p:4   JONATHAN ARMFIELD   24 Jan. 1801   Feb. Ct. 1801
Wife: Elizabeth 1 Negro girl Lier [Leah?], 1 Negro man named Cug, 2 other Negroes, 1 woman named Hannah, one child named Sarah to be sold to the highest bidder & the money put to interest during her life or widowhood to be appropriated to her use & all but one tract of my land to be sold.
Bro: Solomon Armfield tract purchased from John McBride, all other property to be sold, just debts paid & the money to be put to interest 7 years & the interest arising therefrom during that time with £100 of the principle I bequeath to Sarah Stanley son Jonathan Standley & if my wife should be pregnant at this time to heir to all the rest of my property.
Seal: Jonathan Armfield
Exes: wife Elizabeth Armfield & Solomon Armfield
Wits: John Rosier [Rossen?] (Jurat), Henry Stuart, & Thomas Newlin

A:005   p:5   CHARLES ADEAR   16 Jan. 1785   Feb. Ct. 1786
"be it remembered that I Charles Adear..." "farmer"
Wife: Margaret Adear all goods & chattles with the plantation whereon I now live at her discretion during her widowhood to raise my children upon & afterwards to be equally divided among my 8 children namely Mary, Charles, Elisabeth, Sarah, William, Jane, John, & Margaret Adear. only my land be equally divided among my 3 sons Charles, William & John Adear.
4 children by my first wife, namely Ester, James, Ellinor & Cathren have 5 sh each of them to be paid by my Exes.
Seal: Charles (his x mark) Adear
Exes: wife Margaret Adear & John Ruddock, Jr.
Wits: John Ruddock (Jurat)   Joseph Brown
"revokes"

A:006 pp:5/6 MARTHA ALLISON   23 June 1810   Feb. Ct. 1811

Negro woman Lucretia Martin to Major Jeremiah Forbis & his heirs under the following restrictons, viz. that he shall pay Isabella Finley wife to John Finley $100 & unto Martha Wilky wife to James Wilkey $100 & it is my will that they may severally have a right to collect the above donations at any time after my decease or their heirs.
Samuel Allison & his heirs 1 Negro boy by the name of Sam.
John Allison & his heirs 2 Negro boys named Martin & Walker his choice of remaining Negro boy to be sold or valued & his price or value to be paid or given to Isiah Allison's son & dau. Samuel & Martha equally as they come of age.
to Esther Grimes' dau. Jain Allison all money remaining after burial charges are discharged together with the price of one clock that I will to be sold.
remainder of my goods & clothing to be equally distributed amongst the above named legatees.
Seal: Martha (her x mark) Allison
Exe: Samuel Allison
Wits: Isaiah McDill & Joseph McBride
CODICIL: 9 Dec. 1810
Jane Britton 1 habbit [habit] & 1 silk handkerchief.
Ann Shard [?] 1 habbit & 1 silk handkerchief.
James Allison 1 pr. double blankets.
Esther Grims $25 or whatever money is left after my burying expenses except 3 pieces of gold now in my pocket which I give to Martha Allison d/o John Allison, also my Bible, & one habbit.
Mary Forbis all my beds & bedding & table cloths.
Jane McDill my black bonnet & check apron, & all the rest of my property to be equally divided between Elisabeth Allison, Mary Allison, Ann Allison & Mary Forbis.
Seal: Martha (her x mark) Allison
Wit: Robt. C. Gilmer (Jurat)
[the first part -- body -- of this will is noted to be a "soiled document" & is illegible. Codicil is legible. MB]

A:007 p:7 JOSEPH ALEXANDER 28 Mar. 1799   May Ct. 1799

Wife: Martha Alexander the plantation I now live on containing 150 acres adj. Andrew McGee on the East, Robert Galbreath on the North, Thomas Landreth on the West, John Doak on the South, with all farming & blacksmith tools, 5 head of horses, all my stock of cattle, hogs, & sheep & all household property to remain in her possession during her natural life & all the perishable property to be at her disposal at her death & the land to be given unto my son George Alexander.
Seal: Joseph Alexander
Exe: wife Martha Alexander
Wits: Robt. Hannah Sr. & John Doak (Jurat)
"revokes"

A:008 pp:7/8 JOHN ALLEN, SR.   8 Feb. 1780   Aug. Ct. 1781

Son: Daniel all the land that I now possess & to maintain my wife Sarah during her natural life. If sd. wife sees cause not to live with Daniel then to her 1/3 of my estate according to law.

AN ANNOTATED DIGEST OF WILL BOOK A, GUILFORD COUNTY, NORTH CAROLINA

Son: Daniel to maintain all my daus: viz, Sarah- Ann- Jemima Mary & Keziah.
when daus. marry or leave son Daniel to give each of them 1 cow & calf which I bequeath to each of them for their part of my estate.
Son: Benjamin Allen 1 cow & calf.
Sons: John & Joseph Allen 5 sh besides the land that I gave to son Daniel & all estate not bequeathed above.
Seal: John Allen
Exes: friend Josiah Settle & William Clark
Wits: Daniel Allen, Joseph Clark, Rebecca Clark, Wm. Clark, (Jurat) John Allen, Jr.

    A:009 pp:8/9 JEREMIAH ANDREWS 19 Dec. 1799   May Ct. 1800
Wife: Mary Andrews 1 feather bed & furniture, 1 dish & 2 basons, 7 plates, 1 saddle & bridle, 6 cows, 3 yearlings, 1 chest & trunk, 2 pots & 1 [oven?], 1 flax wheel & reel.
Son: Benet all balance of estate excepting what property is at Roger Willis.
Granddaughter: Mary Willis 1 feather bed & furniture, 1 bason, 1 dish & 3 puter plates.
Seal: Jeremiah (his x mark) Andrews
Exes: wife Mary & Roger Willis
Wits: Jonas Touchstone, (Jurat)   Burgess Delay

    A:010 pp:9/10 WILLIAM AKEN 27 May 1799   Aug. Ct. 1799
"Know all men by these presents..."
Son: William 358 acres of land on the North end of my plantation including the dwelling house & other houses & all my personal property but what shall be here mentioned to John & the girls that shall be married at my decease.
Son: John 200 acres of land on the South end of the plantation only with this proviso, I order John to live with his brother William, if William will take sufficient care of him & give a sufficient obligation for his maintenance during his life the 200 acres of land mentioned to John shall be William's.
If William will not comply with what is here written the 200 acres of land shall be for his maintenance as the Executors shall think fitted to dispose of it for that use.
Son: John 1 feather bed & bedclothes & my boddy clothes to be divided betwixt John & William.
as for my daughters [not named] that is unmarried at my decease each to get 1 good feather bed & bed clothing, 2 good cows & calfs, 1 good puter dish & 6 puter plates, 1 good walnut chest, 1 spinning wheel & 1 good horse & saddle.
Son: Robert & each of my daughters [not named] that is married at my decease I leave each of them £3.
Seal: William Aken/Ekin
Exes: Thomas Wiley, John Thom
Wits: John Thom (Jurat), James Sloan
"revokes"

AN ANNOTATED DIGEST OF WILL BOOK A, GUILFORD COUNTY, NORTH CAROLINA

A:011 pp:10/11 WILLIAM ARMFIELD, SEN'R 28 Mar. 1804 May Ct. 1812
"Whereas I Wm. Armfield, Sen'r..."
Wife: Lidia Armfield all my estate real & personal while she remains my widow.
Son: Wm. Armfield £10 of my estate to be paid on 1 year after the death or marriage of my wife.
Children: Mary Brown, Nathan Armfield, Solomon Armfield, Ann Field, David Armfield 20 sh each to be paid out of my estate in one year after the death or marriage of my wife.
Son: Joseph Armfield all rest of my estate, both real or personal at the marriage or death of my wife.
Seal: Wm. (his x mark) Armfield Lidia (her x mark) Armfield*
Exes: wife Lidia & son Solomon Armfield
Wits: Wm. Armfield (Jurat) Joseph Armfield
*There are several instances in these wills wherein the wife signed her name/mark, reason not known. In this case Lydia was a second wife. JSH

A:012 pp:11/12 BENJAMIN AYDELOTT 3 Sept. 1813 Nov. Ct. 1813
Wife: Tabithy Aydelott full use & benefit of the tract of land whereon I now live & 1 Negro man named Pompey, 1 horse called Jack, 2 cows & calves, 1 sow & pigs, 1 bedstead, 1 feather bed & furniture, 1 fine chest, 1 wallnut table, 1 _barshir*_ plow, 1 set of harrow hoes, 1 pr. drawing chains, 1 leather collar, 1 weeding hoe, 1 faling [felling] ax during her natural life & at her decease to be disposed of in manner hereafter mentioned & for her support the present & ensuing year I allow her out of the crop of corn 30 barrels, 500 wt. of blade fodder, 600 wt. of hay, 800 wt. of pork, & 8 bu. of wheat.
Son: Parker Aydelott 20 sh to be paid 12 months after my decease.
Dau: Shaday Spence 20 sh to be paid to her 12 months after my decease.
Son: Shadrach Aydelott the tract of land whereon he now liveth.
Son: Leven Aydelott 10 sh to be paid to him 2 years after my decease.
Dau: Lucy Aydelott 1 Negro girl named Venis, 2 feather beds & furniture & 2 bed steads.
Dau: Sarah Aydelott 1 Negro girl named Tamor, 2 feather beds & bedsteads & furniture.
remainder of any estate to be sold at public sale & the money arising from same to be applied as far as it will go to the discharge of any lawful debts.
at decease of wife what remains to be sold & out of that money I give to my son Shadrach Aydelott $280, & the remainder to be equally divided between my two daus. Lucy Aydelott & Sarah Aydelott.
Seal: Benjamin Aydelott
Exe: son Leven Aydelott
Wits: Daniel Donnel (Jurat) John Hancock (Jurat)
*barshire plow: we have found no clue as to what type of plow this may have been. JSH]
"revokes"

A:013 pp:12/13 JAMES ANDERSON 25 Nov. 1814 May Ct. 1815
Wife: Sarah all property of every kind that she was possessed of when she became my wife, also a Dutch oven, a kittle, a small pot, a fire shovel, a pr. of Steelyards, my spectacles, knives & forks, 300 wt. of meat, 25 bu. of grain per year, to have my plantation to live upon & all

emoluments & rents of sd. plantation during her widow-hood, a cow & 1 horse or mare.
Son: Isaac Anderson 1 cow.
Son: John Anderson one bed & the plantation at the expiration of the life or widowhood of my wife Sarah.
Dau: Sarah Sullivan my chest & 600 -----[?].
Son: William Anderson 1 bed.
All my children balance of my property not mentioned in this will to be equally divided among them.
Seal: James Anderson
Exes: wife Sarah Anderson & William Harvey
Wits: John Finley (Jurat) Elizabeth (her x mark) Finley (Jurat)
"revokes"

A:014 pp:13/14   JOHN BLAIR 22 Sept. 177[9 crossed out,7 added]   28 Sept. 1778
"planter"
Wife: Jean Blair a good horse & saddle, her bed & spinning wheel over & above that 1/3 part or whatever the law allows; and also that so long as she shall remain a widow to have her living & subsistance out of my lands & tenements, that she live with my children & school & bring them up in a Christian manner.
4 Sons: Thomas, John, Andrew, & Jonathan Blair all my lands to be equally divided among them, that each to enjoy the same when they arrive to the age of 21 years respectively, without let or molestation, their mother living while a widow only excepted.
2 Daus: Jean & Martha Blair £50, a horse & saddle, a bed & furniture.
Seal: [none found]
Exe: [none]
Wits: [none]
Probate: 28 Sept. 1778 This day came before me the subscriber one of the Justices of the County aforesaid William Gowdy, Thomas Blair & Hugh Blair and made oath that the above instrument of writing was the sentiments of John Blair as his last will & testatment except that Thomas Blair was not present at part of section first & that Hugh Blair did not hear any part of section second Sworn to before me William Dent} Thos. Blair, W. Gowdy, Hugh (his x mark) Blair

A:015 p:14 ALEXANDER BREDEN 26 Oct. 1793   Nov. Ct. 1793
Wife: [not named] 2 horses, use of the plantation & tools, a bed & furniture, a wallnut chest, her saddle & a cow, in consideration of which she is to raise & give my children a christian education.
Oldest Daus: [not named] a bed & furniture to each.
Son: William, the land when he is of age, from which he is to support his mother as long as she bares my name; I allow him a new saddle, my large Bible and my shop tools.
My books to be equally divided amongst my heirs.
Remainder of property to be appraised by freeholders on oath, my wife to take her 1/3 part of said appraisment, the rest to be sold & equally divided amongst my daus: & in case my wife dies or changes her name her part is also to be divided among my daus.
Seal: Alexander Breden
Exes: Daniel Gillespie Sen'r. & John Donnell
Wits: Rev. David Caldwell (Jurat) & John Orr

AN ANNOTATED DIGEST OF WILL BOOK A, GUILFORD COUNTY, NORTH CAROLINA

A:016 p:15 JOHN BEALS   21st of 4th mo 1809   May Ct. 1809
"I John Beals..."
Wife: Susannah Beals use & profit of plantation whereon I now live during her widowhood & no longer also with the privilege of my personal estate, 1 feather bed & furniture, 1 cow & the black mare during her life.
Son: John Beals 100 acres of land whereon he now liveth with all the privileges there unto belonging.
Son: Caleb Beals 100 acres of land whereon he hath lately built ajd. John Beales.
Son: William Beales 100 acres of land on the tract of the other two just mentioned on the south side of Deep River.
Son: Jesse Beales 100 acres of land whereon I now live with all the improvements thereon belonging.
Son: Eleazar Beales 50 acres of land off the south side of this tract I now live on joining Bethuel Coffin & Isaac Cook & 1 year old mare colt.
Dau: Sarah wf. of John Carter $5.
Dau: Margaret wf. of Benjamin Millikan $5.
remaining part of estate equally divided among all my children.
Seal: John Beales
Exes: son John Beales & Bethuel Coffin
Wits: Joshua Dicks (Jurat) "by affirmation" Nathan Dicks

A:017 p:16 BENJAMIN BARNARD 7th of 9th mo 1792 Nov. Ct. 1792
"Whereas I Benjamin Barnard..."
Wife: Eunice all estate both real & personal as long as she remains the widow of my body- if she marry my will is that she have 1/3 part of my estate.
Son: Timothy £8 worth of my stock & 1/5 part of my household furniture.
Sons: Libni, Frederick, Shubal & Elisha all my land to be equally divided between them, the remaining part of my horses, cattle, sheep, & hogs to be equally divided between them provided that they equally take care of & support in a decent manner my dau. Eunice if either of them decline or don't take care & provide for her maintainance my will is that they or either of them shall have but one half as much of my estate as them that will take care & provide for her.
Dau: Eunice my best bed & furniture - at her decease to my son Elisha.
Daus: Mary, Lyda, Lusinda, & Matilda each 1/5 part of my household furniture.
Dau: Matilda the west end of my house as long as she lives single.
Son: Timothy all my wearing apparel.
Seal: Benjamin Barnard
Exes: wife Eunice Barnard & son Libni Barnard
Wits: Stephen Gardner (Jurat) [affirmed] Abigail Gardner

A:018 pp:17/18 ROBERT BREDEN 12 June 1777 Aug. Ct. 1778
"being very week in body..." "farmer"
Wife: Mary 1 bed & furniture at her choice, 1 milch cow to be always kept for her on the estate, 1 horse & saddle to ride when she pleases, 10 bu. wheat & 10 of corn to her yearly, 100 wt of pork & 50 of beef

AN ANNOTATED DIGEST OF WILL BOOK A, GUILFORD COUNTY, NORTH CAROLINA

well cured salted to her year by year, if she chooses to live in a separate house, to have one built for her on any part of the plantation she shall choose, fuel for her fire constantly found, the aforesaid yearly allowances to be confirmed during her natural life, 1/2 bu flax seed sown yearly for her, & 1 little pot, the pewter dish & 2 pewter plates.
Son: Charles Breden plantation on which I now dwell with all the improvements, 1/3 of my moveable estate except the bequeathments following:
Dau: Margaret Breden the bed she now sleeps on with its furniture & 1/3 of my moveable estate.
Son: Robert Breden 1/3 part of my moveable estate, 100 acres of land off the plantation I now live on, to be laid off by my Executors or 2 other honest neighbors, it is to be laid off on the E side of the plantation & must take in but 1/2 of the bottom & lying on Reedy Branch, to give his mother Mary Breden 100 wt of well salted pork yearly during her natural life, & that he pay 1/3 of the charges of the Deed that is to be taken out for the land.
Son: Alexander Breden £20 to be paid out of my moveable estate before it is divided amongst the rest of the Legatees, & to be paid to him when he stands in need of it or at the discretion of the Executors.
Sons: Robert & Alexander Breden all wearing apparel.
Seal: Robert Breden
Exes: beloved step-son James Donnell & my good friend John Rankin
Wits: John Donnel Thos. Donnel
"revokes"

A:019 p:18 JESSE BEALS   24th of 7th mo 1811   Aug. Ct. 1811
"I, Jesse Beals..."
Wife: Ann Beals use & profit of this plantation I now live on during her widowhood & no longer, & after my mother Susannah Beals has done with it.
I also give my wife Ann Beals all the moveable property that I got with her when I married her; the Black Stud horse to be sold for her use; also 1 cow.
Son: John Beals this plantation that I now live on if he survive my mother, if he should die in minority or without heir of body it is my will that the above mentioned plantation be sold & divided between my 4 brothers, namely John, William, Caleb, & Eleazar.
remainder of my property be sold to help raise my little son with.
Seal: Jesse Beals
Exes: John Hoskins & Bethuel Coffin
Wits: James Thornburg/Thornborough (of Caleb)* [Jurat by affirmation] & John Beals
* "of" was used to indicate a relationship, usually that of parent/child. JSH

A:020 p:19 JOHN BARNETT 1781 [no day or month given] Aug. Ct. 1781
Wife: Elizabeth Barnett 1/3 of all my estate allowing her the use of my Negro called Glassgow during her life or widowhood & then Negro to be sold & his price equally divided amongst the children; that is after my wife receives her third of all my estate, then the rest to be equally divided between my beloved daugher Margaret Barnet, & my son John & dau. Mary Brown & Anne, & Elizabeth & Son William & Son <u>Jas.</u>[?] after

allowing son Joseph my silver watch over his share or the price thereof to be left in William Barnett's care.
Seal: John (his x mark) Barnett
Exes: William Barnett & James Robinson
Wits: William Plunket & Elinor (her R mark) Robinson [no Jurats given]

A:021 pp:19/20 WILLIAM BARNHILL 23 Sept.1791 Nov. Ct. 1791

Wife: Sarah Barnhill 2 horses & 2 cows her choice; 4 sheep, her choice of the flock & household goods & 14 acres of land to contain the plantation whereon my son William now lives with firewood and rail timber [for fences] sufficient to be hers during her lifetime; all the rest of my stock & property to be sold & my lawful debts paid & the rest if any to be given to my wife Sarah.
Dau: Mary Stuart 1 cow, 2 sheep to take her choice after her mother, & in case my dau. Mary should live longer than her mother she is to have the afsd. plantation as long as she lives in full part of her portion & at her death the afsd. 14 acres of land & plantation to fall back to the old track.
Son: William Barnhill the remaining 200 acres of land whereon I now live & he is to give his mother yearly while he keeps the plantation & land 40bu. of corn & 20 bu. of wheat, & if he sells the land & plantation he is to give her £20 of the money; also I give to my son-in law William Jenkins £30.
if William sells the plantation he is to give William Jenkins £20 out of the price.
Robert Barnhill's son William Barnhill £5.
Sarah Barnhill d/o my son William Barnhill my young Bay mare.
all the rest of my stock & property to be sold, my lawful debts pd. and the rest if any to be given to my wife Sarah.
Seal: William Barnhill & Sarah Barnhill
Exes: Robert Hannah & Thomas Landreth
Wits: George Forbis (Jurat) Isaac Hays (Jurat) Margaret (her x mark) Blaise
"revokes"

A:022 pp:20/21 WILLIAM BEARD 11th of 9th mo 1794 May Ct. 1795

"I William Beard..."
Wife: Levina Beard all estate real & personal during her widowhood except what is reserved for my children; if she should incline to marry she to have no more of my estate than one good feather bed, the best my house affords & furniture 1st choice of my horses & a good woman's saddle & bridle.
Son: David Beard all the interest that is now in possession of which he has merited by his Hatters trade, also all the Hatters Tools & the residue of his time from my death till he arrives to the age of 21.
Son: Benjamin Beard all that tract of land I bought of Richard Glover 88 acres with all the privileges thereto belonging.
Son: William Beard at his mother's decease or marriage the plantation that I now live on with all the privileges thereto belonging.
Daus: Lidya Beard & Rachel Beard, each 1 good feather bed & furniture, 1 cow & calf & woman's saddle provided each should marry up before my wife deceases or marries.
At wife's decease or marriage all residue of estate be equally divided among my children namely David, Benjamin, William, Lydia & Rachel, & if

any of my sons should decease in minority it is my will that his or their part of my estate shall devolve to my other son/s; also if either of daughters should decease in minority, their part of my estate devolve to the other.
Seal: William Beard
Exes: trusty & well-respected Stephen Gardner & Jno Talbot
Wits: Stephen Gardner (Jurat) "affirmed" & Barna[bas] Coffin
"revokes"

A:023   p:22   JOHN BENSON   17th of 9th mo 1793   Nov. Ct. 1793
"I, John Benson..."
2 Daus: Jane Shelly & Ailee Mendenhall all the pewter I own to be equally divided between them besides the equal share of the residue of my clear estate.
The residue of my clear estate to be equally divided among 4 children: Jane Shelly, John Benson Jun'r., Ailee Mendenhall, & Reuben Benson to them & their heirs forever.
Seal: John Benson
Exe: trusty friend George Manlove
Wits: James Caldwell, Richard (his x mark) Glover   (Jurat)
"revokes"

A:024   pp:22/23   NATHANIEL BROWN   1 Jan. 1790   May Ct. 1790
Lands, goods & chattles sold, just debts & funeral charges paid.
Dau: Elizabeth McMurry £15.
Granddau: Mary McMurry £4.
Nathaniel McNeary £4. [No relationship given]
Remainder to be equally divided amongst all my grandchildren [not named]
Seal: Nathaniel Brown
Exes: John Brown & William Brown
Wits: James McMurry   (Jurat)   Thomas Brown

A:025 pp:23/24 RICHARD BORTON Sen'r.   17 Dec. 1799 Feb. Ct. 1801
Wife: [not named] 1 Negro boy named Tom, 1 bed & furniture, 1 mare named Blaze & saddle, 1 spinning wheel, 1/2 dozen house cheers, 1 table, 1 chest, & what cookery ware is belonging to my cubbard, & 1/2 of my pot mettle [pot metal] & 1/2 of my puter, 2 cows & calves, 1/3 of my hogs & 1/3 of my sheep & the half of my working utensils - my wagon excepted.
Son: Richard Bourton 1 Negro boy named Bobb.
Son: William Bourton 1 Negro man named Benn, 1 Negro woman named Hanney, 1 Negro boy named Joe, my wearing apparel & saddle.
Dau: Elizabeth Simons   £20 currency.
Dau: Mary Mileham 1 Negro boy named Sam to her & her heirs of her body forever.
Dau: Dorcas Bourton 1 Negro girl named Nell, 1 horse & saddle named Polley, her bed & furniture, 1 cow & calf, 1 yearling, 1/2 of my pot metal & 1/2 of my puter, the Negro to her & her heirs forever.
Dau: Mileham 1/3 of my land whereon I now live after my wife's death.
3 grandchildren 1/3 of my land whereon I now live: Richard Reaves, Martha Reaves, & Thomas Reaves to enjoy after my wife's death.
personal property to be sold, just debts paid, the balance to be equally divided amongst my children as follows to wit: sons Richard & Willam, & daus. Elisabet[sic], Mary & Dorcas.

AN ANNOTATED DIGEST OF WILL BOOK A, GUILFORD COUNTY, NORTH CAROLINA

Seal: Richard Bourton
Exes: sons Richard Bourton & William Bourton
Wits: Thomas Lowe, John Hallum (Jurat), William Hallum
John Hallum, Esqr. of Rockingham County

A:026   pp:24/25   CATHERINE BOYD   12 Jan. 1783   Feb. Ct. 1783
Dau: Margaret Wason [Watson?], a colt & a cow & calf I called Ugley.
Son: Andrew Boyd rest of my estate & no sale to be made unless for the funeral charges.
Seal: Catrine[sic] (her x mark) Boyd
Exer: Mr. John Hilom "to see justice done to the Legatees"
Robert Boak (Jurat) John Hallum (Jurat)

A:027   pp:25/26   JACOB BOON   17 Jan. 1795   Feb. Ct. 1796
Son-in-law Adam Whitesell 1 tract of land containing 50 acres adj. the lands of Andrew Gibson & Michael Charles.
Dau: Margaret Whitesell my bed & furniture &C. & all belonging thereunto
Grandchildren: Ann Boon, Jacob Boon & John Boon £90 in gold & silver, £30 each when they come of age.
John Boon, s/o Martin Boon, Dec'd. £25 hard money providing he shall give his brothers & sisters an equal part of the land left by his father when he comes of age, & if not, I leave him 5 sh only.
Daniel Boon, Martin Boon, & Catherine Boon, children of Martin Boon, Dec'd. £25 each to be paid as they come of age.
they are to have the above £25 left to their brother John Boon to be equally divided between them providing he doth not give them a equal part of the land left by his father, but if he doth it, then to have his equal part.
And whereas Adam Whitesell my son-in-law hath got £100 of my estate already in his hands, I order that he shall not have any more until the children of Martin Boon, dec'd. have got their £100 & then the remainder of my estate to be sold & equally divided between my daus. & my grandsons & my granddaughters.
Seal: Jacob Boon
Exes: Adam Whitesell & John Boon, Sr.
Wits: Wm. Rainey (Jurat) & Benja. Rainey

A:028   p:26   JOHN BURNEY   22 Aug. 1794   Nov. Ct. 1794
Wife: Catherine, 1 good horse & saddle, 3 cows, her bed & furniture & chest & all that is about the dresser, & her maintinance off the plantation whilst she lives & my negro Jeffrey to work for her; plantation to be at her disposal while she lives.
Eldest Daug: Elizabeth 1 horse & saddle, 1 bed & furniture, 1 chest, & 2 cows.
Dau: Rebekah 1 horse & saddle, 2 cows, 1 bed & furniture & chest.
Son: Robert 200 a. of land where he now lives adj. to my son William's land.
Son: John the plantation whereon I now live at his mother's death.
To my 3 Grandsons: William's John, Robert's John, & John's son William all land after son Robert has his 200 acres
Grandson: William to have Jeffrey at wife's decease.
All remaining estate to be equally divided amongst all my children both men & women, the clock only excepted which is to be Elizabeth's.
Seal: John Burney

AN ANNOTATED DIGEST OF WILL BOOK A, GUILFORD COUNTY, NORTH CAROLINA

Exes: wife Catharine & son Robert
Wits: John Gilchrist, George Denney (Jurat) & William Denney (Jurat)

A:029 p:27 JOHN BLEAR* 8 Oct. 1770 Feb. Ct. 1772
Wife: Martha all & every of my moveable effects by her freely & peaceably to be enjoyed until the day of her death; all that remains after her death to be peaceably enjoyed by my son John forever except: 5 sh Sterling which I bequeath to each & every one of my children [not named] to be levied out of my land & Moveable effects by my wife Martha & son John, Exes.
Seal: John Blear
Exes: wife Martha & son John
Wits: James Cunningham (Jurat) & William Gowdy (Jurat)
* also possibly Blair

A:030 pp:27/28 JAMES BILLINGSLEY 25 Jan. 1776 May Ct. 1776
Married children already provided for: James, Elizabeth, Clarana, Samuel, & John J., each 2 sh & 6d [pence] Sterling money.
Son: William 1 bed & furniture to be reckoned in with his equal part with the following children: Martha, Walter, & Bazil -
Dau: Martha 1 bed & furniture, 1 chest & 1 cow to be in part of her equal share with the last fore [sic] mentioned.
Two youngest sons: Walter & Bazil my plantation when they come of age & that they share an equal part of my moveable estate with other of my sd last mentioned 5 children.
Wife: [not named] during widowhood 1 bed & furniture, 1 horse, 1 mare, 2 cows & calves & my plantation.
If a widow when my sons come of age for her to have her right in the land so long as a widow; this is exclusive of her 1/3 of any moveabale estate.
Seal: James (his *E B* mark) Billingsley
Exec: wife [not named] sole Executrix.
NB I bequeath to my Dau. Clarenca to the value of £3 of my estate exclusive of the above 2 sh 6d sterling. [written below his seal]
Wits: Tidance Lane & William Horner (Jurat)

A:031 pp:28/29 JAMES BLAIR 1 Mar. 1776 May Ct. 1776
"miller"
Wife: Mary a child's part for so long as she continues unmarried & her to have the care of all & to **ly down mistress & rise Master** *[my stress marks] during her life & this house to be hers to sell during her life & the 1/3 part of all the stock & moveables.
Son: John my mill & the land which I now possess with all the tools belonging to the mill & all the tools belonging to the plantation with a good horse & saddle when of age & to pay unto his sister Agnes £50 out of the mill & land above mentioned a child's part of the stock & other moveables.
Dau: Agnes £50 in money off her brother John's estate when she is of age & 1/3 part of moveables & stock to be hers; that is a third part of stock & moveables " N.B. this fifty pounds whats mentioned above in sd John's Estate or part."
Seal: James (his x mark) Blair
Exes: my wife Mary & son John

12

March the 13th   I, Mary Blair do ack. the above will. J. Sapp, Jr.   Mary her (x) mark Blair
Wits: Moses Campbell, Francis McBride, Adam Lacky (Jurat)
"revokes"
*we have been unable to find a definition for this phrase. It could indicate that she is to have command over all the plantation and it's people. JSH

   A:032   p:29   WILLIAM BROWN   10 Aug. 1794   May Ct. 1795
Son: James the tract of land whereon I now live and to my loving wife [not named] during her widowhood.
Son: Elias that plantation whereon my father & mother now liveth after their decease.
Daus: Nancy & Rebekah 1 beast, 1 bed & furniture, & 1 cow & calf each one.
Wife: to have the care & use of all my other property during her widowhood.
Seal: William (his x mark) Brown
Exes: wife [not named] & Edmund Bullock
Wits: George Brown (Jurat), John Endsley, William Gray

   A:033   p:30   WILLIAM BRITTAIN   1 Jan. 1794   Feb. Ct. 1794
"Whereas, I ..."
Son: Henery that part of my land lying on the South West of the branch called Murfries branch & joining Caleb Jonsons & Joseph Unthanks line with the improvements thereon.
Son: Joseph between the sd Mirfies Branch & a line beginning at a post oak corner on my North line on the East side of the Great Road & running a straight course to the corner of William Coffin's field the North corner of sd. field near the maple branch on my line with the improvements thereon.
Son: William all the remaining part of my land with the improvements thereon.
Daus: Hannah Hunt, Mary Witty, Rebekah Robinson, Naomy Robinson, & Cath Brittain, & Anne Brittain each 5 sh.
Wife: Rebekah the remaining part of my estate to be at her disposal while she remains my widow; if she marries it is my will that the remainder part of my estate to be equally divided between my two daus: Ruth Brittain & Anne Brittain.
Wife: Rebecca to have maintanance by the prophets [sic] of my land while she remains a widow of me. if she marries, the remaining part of my estate to be equally divided between my 2 daus. Ruth & Anne.
Seal: William (his x mark) Brittain
Exes: wife Rebekah & trusty friend Joshua Dix [Dicks] to make over by deed or deeds of conveyance the above mentioned land according to law
Wits: Daniel Baldwin (Jurat), Uriah Baldwin (Jurat) [both Jurats affirmed] & Thomas Terry

   A:034   p:31   MATTHEW BROWN   3 Feb. 1787   [May 1787 ?]
340 acres of land lying on both sides of the Reedy fork Creek be sold and the money equally divided amongst my 3 sons, Viz: John Brown, Robert Brown & William Brown.

AN ANNOTATED DIGEST OF WILL BOOK A, GUILFORD COUNTY, NORTH CAROLINA

Son: William Brown 300 acres on the West side of the plantation that I reside upon, with all the improvements, stock of horses, cows, sheep & hogs.
Son: Matthew Brown 340 acres lying on the East end of the plantation I now reside upon, 2 cows & calves, my won bed & furniture.
Dau: Jean Rail 20 sh.
Dau: Margaret Drift 1 doubloon in gold the sum of 20 sh left to Jean Rain & the doubloon left to Margaret Drift together with all my funeral charges to be livied & raised off that part that I have bequeathed to my son William Brown.
Seal: Matthew Brown
Exes: Col. John Peasely son Wm. Brown
Wits: Sampson Stewart Andrew (his x mark) Short (Jurat)

A:035 p:32 ISAAC BEESON   3 Mar. 1802   May Ct. 1802
"Know all men by these presents..."
Wife: Phebe to receive all of the estate both real & personal during her widowhood. in case she should marry she will have only equal with one of my children.
Son: Isaac to receive all land whereon I now live with all the buildings & privileges thereto belonging at the decease or marriage of my wife - likewise one bed & furniture.
Son: Nathaniel the tract of land I now own adj. the land belonging to George Mendenhall.
Daus: Mary, Charity, Phebe, & Martha each 5 sh.
Sons: Benjamin, Samuel, Edward & William each 5 sh.
Two children of my deceased son Richard each of them 5 sh. [not named].
At decease of wife all the remaining part of my estate of what name or nature not mentioned here to be equally divided among all my children now living, not prefering one before another.
John Ades now living with me shall have a horse creature when he arrives to the age of 21 years.
Seal: Isaac Beeson
Exes: Wife Phebe Beeson and son Isaac Beeson
Wits: Hezekiah Starbuck (Jurat) Joshua Haines (Jurat) Benjamin Beeson
Proved in open court by affirmation
NB the words now living was interlined before this was signed & sealed.

A:036 p:33 JOHN BARNES   16 May 1801   May Ct. 1802
Wife: Elisabeth one feather bed & furniture during her natural life.
Son: Jesse Barnes and Son-in-law Purnell Chance the remaining part of my purse and estate to be divided after paying all my debts and that they give one heifer apiece to my 3 granddaughters and Sarah Hutton.
Son: John Barnes 5 sh.
Joshua Gullett, 5 sh.
Son-in-law: Elijah Rawley 5 sh.
Seal: John Barnes
Exe. son Jesse Barnes
Wits: Joseph Glenn, Benjamin Dixon, Benjamin (his mark) Nutter
N.B. names of my granddaughters which are forgot in the above will are Ellisebeth, Aney, & Rodey Swigitt
"revokes"
Caveat: of the within will by Elijah Rawley & Joshua Gullett at August Court 1801 and continued from court to court until May Court 1802 when a

Jury being impanelled &C find that the testator did devise. Then came in Jesse Barnes & qualified.[as Executor]

A:037   pp:33/34   JEAN BARNETT   13 Feb.1804   Feb. 1805
Polly McCulhatton d/o William McCulhatton [McElhatton] my bed & furniture, my spinning wheel & reel and all my wearing apparel & chest at my death.
Polly McCulhatton [McElhatton] wife of William McCulhaton one milch cow at my death.
Seal: Jean (her x mark) Barnett
Exe: dear beloved friend Polly McCulhatton
Wits: L. Dilling, James Coots (Jurat)
"revokes"

A:038   pp:34/35   WILLIAM BALDWIN   11th of 2nd mo 1808   Nov. Ct.1809
Three Bros: John Baldwin, Jesse Baldwin, Daniel Baldwin, my watch, gun, all carpenter & joiners tools, all farming tools, & all my wearing clothes, equally divided as my executors may direct.
Daniel is under age; Exrs. to dispose of his part as they may think for his interest.
Three sisters: Elizabeth Baldwin, Jane Baldwin & Sarah Baldwin all notes & bonds due me from any or all persons to be equally divided.
Father: John Baldwin all residue of my estate.
Seal: William Baldwin
Exes: father John Baldwin, Barnabas Coffin
Wits: John Sanders, Joseph Mills, (Jurat)
"revokes"

A039:   p:35   JAMES BROGDON   17 Jan 1810   Feb. Ct. 1810
Wife: Anne Brogden & two Daus: Patience & Kesia estate excepting one feather bed and furniture and the 3 Negros (that is Charles, Cleria, Allie) the bed & Negro boy Charles I bequeath to my wife Anne to her & her heirs forever - Cleria excepting, her increase I bequeath to Patience.
Allia the youngest Negro girl I give & bequeath to Kesia my youngest daughter with the one half of the increase of both the negro girls when she arrives at woman's age.
the other half of their increase to my other daughter Patience to them & their heirs forever.
Seal: James Brogdon
Exes: John Walker, John Dinkins
Wits: Wm. Brown, John Walker, Jr. (Jurat), William Lucas

A:040   p:36   EDWARD BULLOCK   20th of 1st mo 1813   May Ct. 1813
"Know all men by these presents..."
Six Sons: William Bullock, David Bullock, John Bullock, Edward Bullock, James Bullock, Len Bullock, 5 sh. each.
Four Daus: Elizabeth Ralph, Susanna Loney, Sarah Stafford & Winneford, 5 sh. each.
Wife: Ann dogged [sic] [Doggett?] Bullock the use profit & income of all my estate both real & personal that remains during her natural life.
Son: George Bullock all my estate of whatsoever name or nature both real and personal forever.
Seal: Edward Bullock

Exes: wife Ann dogged [sic] Bullock & my friend William Starbuck, jointly
Wits: Hezekiah Starbuck (Jurat), Latham Starbuck, Joel Hunt
May Term 1813 The execution of the within will was proven in Open Court by the affirmation of William Starbuck one of the subscribing witnesses thereto... *[the clerk has confused the Executor, William Starbuck with Hezekaih Starbuck, the Jurat] JSH*

A:041 p:37 THOMAS COX of Richland Creek, [no date] Nov. Ct. 1771, Thomas Henderson, C.C.

"Whereas I, Thomas Cox..." "yeoman"
Body to be buried by my brother Solomon Cox & William Wierman who I appoint my Exers.
Wife: [not named] fether bed & bed clothes, a side sadle & bridle & the 3rd part of all the remainder of my personal estate excepting only such particular articles as are hereinafter given to particular persons.
Son: Thomas 100 acres of land including the improvements whereon I live.
Son: Joshua 100 acres of land to be laid off for him on the south side of the afsd. tract & joining Solomon Cox.
Son: Daniel 100 acres of land to be laid off for him on the west side of my son Thomas' land.
Son: Abner all the remainder of my lands to be laid off for him where it shall be most suitable to be valuable.
Dau: Sarah a fether bed.
Dau: Martha a fether bed to be made of the benefits of my improvements.
Wife: shall live with my son Thomas as she sees cause as long as she is single.
Son: Thomas £10 proclamation money.
all my children to have larning at least to reed and write.
Son: Abner £15 proclamation money.
remainder of personal estate to be equally divided amongst all my children; sons to possess their parts at age 21; daus. to possess their parts at age 18.
if sons do not live to 21 then his or their part to be sold to the highest bider of his bretheren and the price to be equally divided amongst his brethern.
if sons & daus. do not live to the years above ordered to possess their estates shall be equally divided amongst the living ones.
Seal: Thomas Cox
Exes: Solomon Cox & William Wierman
Wits: Wm. Garner, Stephen Hussey, (Jurat), John Kenworthy

A:042 p:38 THOMAS CRAWLEY 16 Jan 1778 May Court 1778

Son: Thomas Crawley 200 acres of land on the head of Hickory Creek.
Wife: Frances Crawley my whole estate during her life & at her decease to be equally divided amongst my children [not named].
Son: John Crawley 1 sh Sterling.
Seal: Thomas (his x mark) Crawley
Exe: [none named]
Wits: James Jackson, Junior James (his x mark) Jackson, Cenior [senior] (Jurat)

AN ANNOTATED DIGEST OF WILL BOOK A, GUILFORD COUNTY, NORTH CAROLINA

A:043   pp:38/39   MOSES CAMPBELL   29 July 1782   Aug. Ct. 1782
Wife: Rebecca, lends to her third part of estate for life, real & personal.
Sons: William & James (their heirs & assigns) or the survivor of them the third part of the tract of land whereon I now dwell to be equally divided between them; if no heirs, land to be sold and equally divided among the survivors of my daughters [not named].
Remaining two thirds of all personal estate be equally divided among all my children who at that time may be living [not named].
Seal: Moses (his x mark) Campbell
Exrs: Thomas Blair & Peter King, Sr.
Wits: Joseph Dell   Mary (her x mark) Dell   Charles Bruce (Jurat)
"revokes"

A:044   p:39   ELENOR CHAMBERS   2 June 1781   Aug. Ct. 1781
Dau: Sarah Stuart - a pattern of cotton cloth for a gown, one quilted petticoat, one fine apron, one white handkerchief.
Dau: Elenor Mount - half of a thirty-gallon still.
Son: Thomas Chambers - the other half of the above mentioned still.
Son: Frederick Fulkerson and Dau: Mary Fulkerson - all residue of my property equally between them.
Seal: Elenor (her mark) Chambers
Exr: Son: Abram Fulkerson
Wit: Nottey Jordan, (Jurat) Elizabeth (her x mark) Jordan, Levina (her x mark) Ellis

A:045   p:40   JACOB CHRISTMAN   1 April 1779   n.p.d.
"of Reedy Creek,* Province of Guilford County, NC"
Eldest sons: John & Jacob - each £10 currency less of my estate & effects than the remainder of my children.
Wife: Barbara - bedding, large iron pot, 1 tea kettle, cups & saucers, tea pot & such thereto belonging, 1 horse with a side saddle & bridle, 1 of my best cows, two sheep, 1 spinning wheel & my chest, 1 pewter dish & a large pewter plate, 2 pewter plates and 2 spoons & 1/3 part of my moveable estate & household furniture; house & plantation whereon I now live during widowhood; if she alters her condition and not remain my widow, then after her decease the above mentioned articles be divided among my children in equal parts, share & share alike.
Children: Daniel; Balthaser; John George; Abraham; Joseph; Henrich; David; Catherina; Barbara; Elisabeth; Rebecca; & Anna Maria (except my two eldest sons: John & Jacob) they shall receive as above.
Seal: Jacob (his x mark) Christman
Exe: friend Jacob Drog [?**], son Jacob Christman
Wits: John Matthew Mückseh (Dutch name in this place) [sic, the English clerks could not read German handwriting. The name looks like John Henry Wirtburgar. JSH] & Ludwig Meining (Jurat)
"revokes"
*Reedy Fork rises in e Forsyth County and flows e into w Guilford County, ne across Guilford County and into nw Alamance County where it enters Haw River. Mentioned in local records as early as 1755. (Powell. p.408)
**[possibly Trog] JSH

AN ANNOTATED DIGEST OF WILL BOOK A, GUILFORD COUNTY, NORTH CAROLINA

    A:046   p:41   JOHN CAFFEE   19 July 1783   May Ct. 1785
Wife: not named
Children: Michael Caffee, Elizabeth Milford, Nancy Bell, John Caffee, Sophia Barnes, Sarah Beach, Mary Dimon & Rebecca Norman each one sh. Sterling.
Son: Thomas Caffee tract of land on which I now reside, about 220 acres.
Residue of estate equally divided between Thomas Caffee, Margaret Caffee and Lucy Caffee.
Seal: John (his x mark) Caffee
Exe. sons John and Thomas Caffee
Wits: Charles Bruce, David Peoples, Hubbard Peoples (Jurat)
"revokes"

    A:047   pp:41/42   CHARLES CURTIS   3 April 1781   Aug. Ct. 1781
John Morton: one tract of 248 acres in Spotsylvania County, Commonwealth of Virginia.
Wife: Margery, one Negro fellow named Isaac; at her decease Isaac to be divided between my 2 daus. Nancy Johnson & Judy Morris.
Son: Peter Curtis 400 acres of land on South side of Dann River in Guilford County [now Rockingham County] running up and down the said river for his complement.
Grandsons: George Morris & Curtis Morris 240 acres adj. the above land I gave to my son Peter to be equally divided between them.
Wife: remainder of estate real & personal to her & her heirs.
All other children: one shilling each. [not named]
Seal: Charles (his x mark) Curtis
Exes: wife Margery Curtis and George Johnson [Johnston]
Wits: George Peay, Moses (his x mark) Lillard, (Jurat) Wm. (his x mark) Lovil

    A:048   pp:42/43   JEREMIAH CROWDER   28 Jan. 1795   Feb. Ct. 1795
"farmer"
Son: Isaac Crowder one black roan colt.
Wife: Marthy: all my estate during her widowhood; at her decease to be equally divided amongst my children: Sary Pritchett, Fanny Wilson Crowder, Elizabeth Crowder, Patsy Crowder, John Crowder, William Crowder, Anderson Crowder, Jeremiah Crowder.
Son: Pleasant Crowder 5 shillings for his part.
Seal: Jeremiah Crowder
Exes: wife Marthy Crowder and my son-in-law Joseph Prichett
Wits: David Gilliam (Jurat) William Crowder

    A:049   p:43   JAMES CUNNINGHAM   24 Sept. 1791   n.p.d.
"I James Cunningham..."
Two Sons: Jeremiah & Mathew Cunningham, all my lands, a wagon, plantation tools, all horses not hereafter mentioned.
Dau: Isabel Cunningham young sorrel mare & saddle.
3 children: Jeremiah, Mathew, Isabel Cunningham, household furniture, cattle, hogs, sheep, and every other thing not mentioned above to be equally divided.
Son: William Cunningham 5 shillings
Dau: Elizabeth Burney 5 shillings
Seal: James Cunningham
Exrs: sons Jeremiah Cunningham & Mathew Cunningham

AN ANNOTATED DIGEST OF WILL BOOK A, GUILFORD COUNTY, NORTH CAROLINA

Wits: Drury Peeples, (Jurat) Edw. Long (Jurat)

A:050 pp.44/45   ANTHONY COBLE 24 May 1790 Nov. Ct. 1793
Son: George 150 acres the SW part of where I now live on the head springs of Bever Creek, described by deed dated the 10th day of May 1788.
Son: Ludwick Coble 150 acres the NW part of where I now live on the waters of Bever Creek described by deed dated the 10th of May 1788.
Son: David Coble 150 acres the SE part of where I now live on the waters Shockles [Shockless] Creek as described by deed dated the 10th May 1788, all improvements to home tract, the still & its worm.
Sons: George, Ludwig, & David pay unto my 6 daus. £30 apiece in the following manner:
Son George Coble shall pay unto my 2 daus. Barbra Glas & Lisabeth Smith in 4 years from this date, £10 & from that time every year £10 until the 30 pounds each is paid.
Son: Ludwick shall pay £60 to my 2 daus: Eve Glas & Molly Shatterling in the following manner - in 4 years from this date, £10 and from that time every year ten pounds until £30 is paid to each of sd. Eve & Molly
Youngest son: David Coble shall pay £60 to my two daus: Thorely [Dorothea] Graves & Mary Graves in the following manner, £10 in 4 years & from that time in every year £10 until £30 is paid unto the said Thorely & Mary.
Sons: George, Ludwick, & David shall give me yearly so long as I & my wife [Mary Amick] are alive 45 gallons of brandy or whiskey & if one of [sic] die the half, & I will that the sd. 3 sons shall keep me & my wife as long we are both alive 3 cows & 2 horses creatures & if one die only 2 cows & 1 horse or mare & I will that all what other Race [sic] of the stock from sd. creatures shall all belong to sd. 3 sons, & that they pay me yearly 7 bu. of wheat & each 50 wt. of pork & 1 quarter acre of flax & 2 of wool each yearly & as much hay sufficient for sd. creatures & oats & corn likewise & that I have Liberty in my dwelling house & my wf. so long [as] we are a live & I will & order that my youngest Dau: Catarena Cortner shall have £30 out of my moveable estate excepting the above named creatures; any money over & above the above shall equally be divided amongest all my sons & daughters.
Seal: Anthony (his A mark) Coble
Exr: son John Coble
Wits: George Cortner, Jacob Coble (Jurat) David Coble

A:051 pp:45/46 THOMAS CHARLES CRAFT   27 Oct. 1794 Feb. Ct. 1795
Betty, Negro girl, to be sold & such other property to the amount to pay just debts & funeral charges.
Wife: Charlotte 1/3 part of my lands lying in Guilford County for life & 1/3 part of moveable estate also.
Son: John Charles Craft remaining part of land in Guilford County.
Remainder of estate be equally divided among my 7 children:
Marry, Sarah, Nelle, Rebecka, Lydia, Gean Charles   -----[tape covers the words; the original will not in Archives]
Seal: Thomas Charles Craft
Exrs: wife Charlotte & son John
Wits. Robert Donnel (Jurat), James Weatherly (Jurat), Thomas Johnson

AN ANNOTATED DIGEST OF WILL BOOK A, GUILFORD COUNTY, NORTH CAROLINA

A:052 pp:46/47 ABIJAH COFFIN   2nd of 9th mo 1793   Nov. Ct. 1793
"Whereas I ..."
Wife: all the estate that my father may leave to me during her widowhood; sorrel colt & the saddle she rides, 1 feather bed & furniture, 1 cow, 1 4-gallon pot, 1/2 doz. pewter plates, 1 gallon basin, the largest plates, all her wearing clothes.
Dau: Mary all my lands & estate that my father may leave me & also all my personal estate of whatever name soever that I don't hereafter name but if she should die in her minority or without heir of her body I give unto Abijah Coffin son of brother Libni Coffin the land I now live upon but if he die without heirs of his body or in his minority I give said land unto William Coffin son of brother Willam if he die within his minority or without heir of his body it is my will said land be sold and equaly divided between my seven brothers, namely Libni, William, Samuel, Barnabas, Matthew, Bethuel & Levi.
Abijah Coffin s/o brother Libni wearing clothes, hat, & chest at the age of 19.
personal estate be sold & money put at interest for my dau. Mary to have at age 18.
Dau: Priscilla share of land & money equal to my dau: Mary to be equally divided between her & her sister Priscilla in the same manner.
Seal: Abijah Coffin
Exrs: brother Matthew Coffin & friend Allen Unthank
Wits: [no witnesses in Clerk's Copy, but Jacob Rogers, John Howel & Richard Williams proved the within will at Nov. Ct. 1793]

A:053 pp:47/48 BENJAMIN COFFIN   1st of 12th mo 1789   May Ct. 1790
"taylor"
"I, Benjamin Coffin..."
Wife: Elizabeth use & profits of 1/2 of my estate real & personal in North Carolina during her widowhood; reduced to 1/3 if she remarries.
Son: Aaron Coffin estate inherited from my father in Nantucket in New England & what descended from my Grandfather Bathalder Hussey at Winter Harbour.
Son: Adam Coffin my real & personal estate in North Carolina after decease of his mother, or all but 1/3 of each at the end of her widowhood.
Dau: Elizabeth Barnard 1 pot & 1 skillet, 1 pewter platter.
Dau: Phebe Coffin a living or support on home place with brother Adam if single. If married to be fitted out in like manner as sister Elizabeth Barnard.
Dau: Rachel Coffin brother Adam's support at home place while single, after marriage to be fitted out in like manner with her sister.
Seal: Benjamin coffin
Exrs: wife Elizabeth Coffin & son Aaron Coffin
Wits: Daniel Worth, James Dicks (Jurat) Job Worth (Jurat)

A:054 pp:48/49 JAMES CALHOON 29 January 1795   Feb. Ct. 1795
Wife: Jinnet horse & saddle, 2 cows, 2 sheep, stock of hogs, bed & bedding, housel [household] furniture, maintenance on land.
Son: John Jonstone Calhoon, land on which I live.
Son: Sammuel £15 to be paid by my son John J. Calhoon.
Dau: Eleanor Calhoon 200 acres of land lying on the head of Hogin's Creek.

AN ANNOTATED DIGEST OF WILL BOOK A, GUILFORD COUNTY, NORTH CAROLINA

Son: James Calhoon or his heirs the young mair.
Children: Elizabeth Calhoon, Mary Calhoon, Ann Calhoon, Robert Calhoon, Sarah Calhoon, Eleanor Calhoon, Mary Calhoon and their heirs to be equally divided among them all my other estate not mentioned above.
Seal: James Calhoon
Exrs: sons John J. Calhoon & Sammuel Calhoon
Wits: Abner Bowen (Jurat) Samuel Calhoon
"revokes"

A:055 p:49 DAVID COOPER   25 Jan. 1792   May Ct. 1792
"being sick and weak in body..."
Wife: [not named] personal estate, 1 Negro wench named Nell, & during her widowhood 1/3 part of my land.
Son: John 1 year old mare colt.
Dau: Ann 2 cows & calves, a bed & bed clothes, & £5 from each brother's share, amounting to £20 cash.
Sons: John, David, Thomas, & William whole of my lands equally divided & each one has choice according to birth right beginning with the eldest, John, then David, then Thomas & last William.
Seal: David Cooper
Exes: wife [not named] & son John
Wit: John Job (Jurat)

A:056 p:50 HANCE CLARKE   -- [no date] March 1791 May Ct. 1791
Wife: Mary all my lands, goods & chattels except -
Dau: Ann Clarke, 20 sh. & my Bible.
Dau: Mary Clarke, 20 sh. & a Bible.
Dau: Catherine Clarke, 20 sh. & a Bible.
Dau: Jean Clarke, 20 sh. & a Bible.
Seal: Hans Clarke
Exrs: wife Mary Clarke & John Stuart, Senior, blacksmith.
Wits: James McBride (Jurat) "and somebody else" [sic] [the original will shows a name signed in German script]JSH

A:057 p:50 WILLIAM CHARLES 4 April 1796 May Ct. 1796
Sons: William & Solomon Charles each 1 horse worth £14.
4 daus: Sarah, Mary, Anna & Leah Charles each 1 feather bade [sic] & furniture worth £14.
Wife: Leah Charles plantation I now live on during her widowhood & my personal estate. Should Leah remarry she will have an equal share with one of my children.
8 Chil: Ruben, Isaac, William, Solomon, Sarah, Mary, Anna & Leah Charles & their heirs - at the departure of my wife from widowhood, land is to be sold and equally divided.
Seal: William Charles
Exrs: wife Leah Charles & Elijah Charles
Wits: Matthew Coffin, Elijah Charles (Jurat), Tarleton Johnson

A:058 pp:51/52 JOHN PHILIP CLAPP 8 Sept. 1797 Nov. Ct. 1798
Eldest son: Valentine Clapp tract of land on which he now lives on the Alimance containing 200 acres, 10 sh cash.
Son: Adam Clapp 412 acres on the waters of Rock Creek on which he formerly lived, & 10 sh.
Son: John Clapp 200 acres on which he now lives & 10 sh.

Son: Luddowick Clapp 300 acres on which he now lives & 10 sh.
Children of dau. Barbary Swing, deceased, formerly wife to Mathias Swing - 1 Negro wench named Jenny & her increase, 5 sh. cash to each child.
Dau: Christina Albright wife to Phillip Albright 1 negro boy named Franck & 10 sh.
Dau: Molly Hagey wife to Conrod Hagey 210 acres on which they now live & 10 sh.
Dau: Catharine Brown wife to Adam Brown land on which Adam Brown now lives & 10 sh.
Dau: Mary Shaver wife to Jacob Shaver 1 Negro girl named Lydia & 10 sh.
Dau: Eve Burrow wife to Ephraim Burrow 1 Negro girl named Nancey & 10 sh.
Wife: Barbary all remaining estate real & moveable consisting of lands, Negroes, stock of all kinds, household furniture & instruments of agriculture.
Seal: John Philip (his x mark) Clapp
Exrs: wife Barbary & David Cotner, Junr.
Wits: Samuel Lindsay, John Job, Jun. (Jurat) John Cooper (Jurat)
Codicil: Continues to approve will & adds that Exrs. make unto son-in-law Ephraim Burrow a good deed for the tract of land on which I now live containing as supposed 494 acres agreeable to a memorandum of an agreement entered into between me and sd Burrow which memorandum is now in the possession of Samuel Lindsay on sd Burrow's performing the conditions on his part or on his giving bond and approved security to the satisfaction of my sd Exrs. for his well and truly performing all sd. conditions...
29 Sept. 1798.
Seal: John Philip (his x mark) Clapp
Exrs: [same]
Wits: Samuel Lindsay Jacob Goble [Coble] (Jurat) Tobias Clapp

A:059 pp:52/53/54 **WILLIAM COFFIN** 4th of 5th mo 1796 Nov. Ct. 1796
"I William Coffin..."
Wife: Elizabeth my sorrel mare, 1 feather bed & furniture, the loom and utensiles thereto belonging, the 1/2 of my puter, the half of my iron casting [cast iron utensils] that are now in use for housekeeping in my family, a wooden chest & all her wearing aparel, a side saddle, two bed steds, one table, the cradle, the Earthen ware of every kind, 1 looking glass, a teakettle, coffee pot & coffee mill, one half of the chairs now in use in the house my oyl[oil] cloak the fire shovel and fire tongs & £10 current money of this state to her & her heirs forever. to have the use and profits of the plantation whereon I now live with the use of 1 horse the old waggon & gears, plows, & hoes & such other farming utensiles that are now on the plantation that my Exe. may think needful, also the use of my cattle sheep & hogs during the time she remains my widow except she remains a widow until my son William arrives to the age of 21 years, then only the 1/2 of the neat profits arising from the plantation & stock above mentioned & not any more nor any longer than she remains my widow.
Son: William Coffin the tract of land & plantation whereon I now live & the land adj. that I lately purchased of William Britton.
Son: Elihu Coffin the tract of land & plantation which I purchased of John Hunt laying & being on the waters of Brush Creek.

AN ANNOTATED DIGEST OF WILL BOOK A, GUILFORD COUNTY, NORTH CAROLINA

Dau: Esther Coffin 1 feather bed & furniture 1/2 of all my puter half of the iron casting now used in my family, half of the chairs now in use, a good walnut chest, a good new desent suit of clothes including a beaver hat a horse & saddle worth £20 & my silver tea spoons that are now in use to be delivered to her at the age of 18 years or marriage if she marry before she arrives to that age, also the box looking glass that I now have delivered to her soon after my decease all which I give to her & her heirs forever.
Dau: Achsa Coffin feather bed & furniture & £10 current money.
Sons: Vestal Coffin, Nathan Coffin & Job Coffin the tract of land I purchased of Thomas Hunt & the tract of land I purchased of Bethuel Coffin & the tract of land I purchased of Robert Guilbreath with all the appurtenances severally belonging thereunto equally divided among or between them & their heirs forever.
Sons: William Coffin & Elihu Coffin the remainder of my horses, my desk and book case with all my books, my chest & all my wearing apparel my clock & watch, my large silver spoons with all the remainder of my estate both real & personal to be equally divided between them & their heirs forever.
Executors to dispose of all the perishable articles given to my three children: William, Elihu, & Esther Coffin to the best advantage by publick or private sale & that they put the money therefrom arising to interest with good security until the last named children severally come of age that they may then have their money with interst as also their other money & if either of the 3 last named children die in minority the survivor to have the real estate of deceased & the personal to my daughter Esther Coffin & if both of last named sons die in minority the real estate given thereto descend as follows--the one half to my daughter Esther Coffin & the other half to be equally divided between my other four children namely Achsa, Vestal, Nathan, & Job Coffin.
Seal: [none found]
Exes: brother Barnabas Coffin brother Matthew coffin
Wits: [none found]
November Court 1796 Admitted to probate The hand Writen [sic] proven in open Court by William Starbuck, Sam'l Coffin, Jacob Rogers, & Bethuel Coffin by order of Court. Nov. 22nd 1796 Barnabas & Matthew Coffin qualifyed as Exrs. [We believe this will may have been written by William Coffin. Because he neither signed the will nor appointed witnesses to the will, it might have been treated as a holographic will JSH]

A:060 pp:54/55 THOMAS CRANOR 6 April 1795   May Ct. 1796
Wife: Hannah Cranor all my lands & the rest of my estate so long as she remains my widow, except 2 rifle guns & them I bequeath as follows:
Son: Joseph Cranor the gun that was left to me by my father.
Son: Moses Cranor that gun that is now at Henry Ford's that I once bought of Henry Ford.
If wife marries again the estate should be equally divided amongst all our dear & loving children at the time of her marriage otherwise she to keep all my estate as long as she lives and after her death it to be equally divided amongst all my dear & loving children [not named].
Seal: Thomas (his x mark) Cranor
Exe: brother Moses Cranor
Wits: Finsmore Howren, Matthew Macy (Junior), Benja. Trotter

AN ANNOTATED DIGEST OF WILL BOOK A, GUILFORD COUNTY, NORTH CAROLINA

Proved in open court by the oaths of the 3 witnesses.

A:061 pp:55/56   JOHN CLARK   6 Sept. 1790   Nov. 1790
Wife: Mary one half of all my possessions that I possess in this country.
Brother: Charles Clark 5 sh. as a token of my love.
Nephew: John Clark here with me at this present time all the remaining half of all my possessions here as also the whole of my right & claim in **IRELAND** [my emphasis, JSH] to be by him recovered for the sole use of him & his heirs forever & also all my body clothes.
Seal: John (his x mark) Clark
Exes: Andrew Wilson & William Scott
Published as the last will & testament of John Clark, Senr.
Wits: Sarah Ried (Jurat) Hannah (her x mark) Denney
Nov. Term 1790, Sarah Ried swore she saw Hannah Denney sign as a witness at the same time.
"revokes"

A:062   pp:56/57   ABRAHAM COOK   29 April 1792   Feb. Ct.1793
Dau: Rachel Jessop 5 sh.
Dau: Mary Stephens 5 sh as the remainder of her part.
2 youngest daus: Sarah Cook & Ruth Cook all my household goods also cattle & sheep their mother's clothes that is yet remaining with me to be equally divided between them.
Son: Isaac Cook 131 acres & 16 poles of land lying in the SW corner of my tract of land on waters of Deep River to begin at the corner of sd. tract in ORDHOOKS[?] line E 114 poles & corner & from thence N 184 poles for complement.
Son: John Cook 131 acres & 16 poles of land lying in the SE corner of sd. tract & joining to his brother Isaac's part on the W & extending 184 poles N for complement.
Son: Abraham Cook remainder of sd. tract of land lying to the N of his brother's parts & joining them as the plat will show & also I give him my gray horse.
Son: Nathan my plantation I now live on containing 100 acres of land and my sorrel horse.
Seal: Abraham (his x mark) Cook
Exes: trusty sons Isaac Cook & Abraham Cook
Wits: Enoch Macy, Daniel Baldwin, James Thornburg (Jurat) on affirmation
"revokes"

A:063   pp:57/58   SAMUEL COFFIN   4th of 1st mo 1799   May Ct. 1799
Wife: Mary use & profits of the plantation I now live on 4 years (if she continues my widow until that time) also my sorrel mare colt Cate & all her wearing cloths & household furniture that she had when I married her, also the use of 1 bar shear [this may be a type of plow], & harrow & 1 shovel plow also the use & profits of all my cows except what is hereafter given to my children - provided she remain my widow that term of time, but if she should incline to marry my will is as soon as she doth that she have no more but the household goods & wearing cloaths above mentioned with the mare Cate, 2 cows, the remainder of my sheep & all the hoggs (except the boys) to have to her heirs forever, But if she should remain my widow after the expiration of 4 years it is my will that she have the use & profits of but 1/2 of my plantation - the other

AN ANNOTATED DIGEST OF WILL BOOK A, GUILFORD COUNTY, NORTH CAROLINA

half to be equally divided among my 6 sons; John, Samuel, David, Thomas, Jethro, & William Coffin.
Son: John 1/2 of my plantation at the expiration of 4 years except his mother-in-law [step-mother] should marry or decease before that term of time & if so for him to take immediate possession provided he pay to my sons David & Thomas each 1/6th part of the value of the whole of my plantation the valuation to take place at his coming in possession & the payments to be made as my Executors shall direct.
Son: Samuel Coffin the other half of my plantation at the expiration of 4 years as above provided he pays to my 2 sons Jethro & William Coffin each 1/6th part of the value of the whole.
Sons: David, Thomas, Jethro & William Coffin to have the above mentioned 6th part of the value of my plantation when my Executors shall direct
Dau: Mary Coffin 1 good feather bed & furniture, 1 cow & calf, my large looking glass, a half dozen puter plates, half dozen knives & forks, my large iron pot & large Dutch oven, half dozen good common chairs & one good sheep.
Dau: Priscilla Coffin 1 feather [bed].
Dau: Lydia Coffin 10 sh.
Remainder of household goods be equally divided amongst my 3 daughters namely Deborah Starbuck, Mary Coffin & Priscilla Coffin.
Residue of estate to be equally divided among my sons & if any should decease without heir of body the legacy to descend to the others.
Seal: Samuel Coffin
Exes: brother Barnabas Coffin Matthew Coffin
Wits: Jesse Stanley, Abel Coffin, John Stuart (Jurat)
"revokes"
CODICIL: 26th 1st 1799 ratifys & confirms the above last will & testament & do further give unto my daughter Mary Coffin one feather bed that is to say one bed with furniture & one without furniture & it is my will & meaning that she my daughter Mary shall have her home at the house where I now dwell in with every privilege to carry on her business that my Exers. shall think proper & for her to reside there as long as she remains in an unmarried state if she choose to stay.
Seal: Samuel Coffin
Exrs: brother Barnabas Coffin & Matthew Coffin
Wits: Jesse Stanly (Jurat) [in probate spelled Standley]
Deborah Terrell, Anner [Anna ?] (her x mark) Coffin

A:064 p:59 JOSHUA COFFEE   1 Sept. 1797   Feb. Ct. 1798
Son: John Coffee 1st choice of 5 slaves to be disposed of for the purpose of procuring land.
Wife: Elizabeth shall enjoy the land so procured during her natural life, & after her decease the land shall be vested in my son John & his heirs.
Son-in-law: Mr. Harris if he returns such property to my estate as he has received, then the whole estate to be equally divided and distributed between my wife Elizabeth & my 2 children John Coffee & Polly Harris.
At death of wife all to be divided between my 2 children John Coffee & Polly Harris.
Seal: Joshua Coffee
Exes: wife Elizabeth and son John Coffee

AN ANNOTATED DIGEST OF WILL BOOK A, GUILFORD COUNTY, NORTH CAROLINA

Wits: "written by John Starret by direction of Joshua Coffee in his illness of body September 1st 1797 and then signed & delivered by him to John Starret, (Jurat)"

A:065   p:60   LUDWICK COBLE,   17 May 1809   Aug. Ct. 1809
"planter"
Wife: Eve Coble live on & have full power of all my possessions during her widowhood.
Sons: to my 2 sons John & Eli all land equally as she may agree between themselves (after the death of their mother who must inherit it while a widow); however if either of them marries or takes to a way of living of their own I order that John may remain on the improvement with his mother.
Daus: Sarah, Anne Sophia Mary each to have a right to demand & get a good horse or mare as they come of age, also must have of household furniture &C the same or like value as my daughter Mary Clap has got.
All my children may have an equal part of all stock goods or chattels money or property that may be left and to prevent any disputes after my decease I declare that my son David Coble and daughter Mary Clap has each of them got and had what I think a just & equitable part according to what I have named to the rest of my heirs; David & Mary to share in the equal division above named.
Seal: Ludwick Coble
Exes: wife Eve & son John
Wits: George Gobel (Jurat) [spelled Cobble in probate] W. Corsbie

A:066   p:61   NATHANIEL CLARK   15 Nov. 1802   Feb. Ct. 1803
Wife: Ann all my estate both real & personal during her life or widowhood, only she must pay my just debts - if she marry my estate to be sold and equally divided between her and my children that should be then living - if she should die before she marries I desire my land and Negroe woman & her increase if any & all my personal estate to be sold & equally divided between all my surviving children [not named].
Seal: Nathaniel (his x mark) Clark
Exe: wife Ann
Wits: Justain Knott (Jurat) Solomon (his x mark) Warren Nancy (her x mark) Knott
"revokes"

A:067   p:62   THOMAS CUMMONS   2 Sept. 1808   Nov. Ct. 1808
Daus: Rachel & Amy 230 acres of land on waters of Rock Creek divided equal parts.
Dau: Rachel to have Negro boy Auston to be her right & property during her lifetime; 1 bed with furniture belonging to it, & the old bay mare & 1 cow.
Dau: Anny the young bay mare & 1 cow & calf & the Negro Care mine [?] & her 2 children Sally & Thankful to be her right & property during her lifetime & a bed & furniture belonging to it.
Dau: Jane her children 200 silver dollars to be equally divided among them.
Dau: Betsy 100 silver dollars.
Dau: Margareth 1 Negro boy named Isaac.
Dau: Mary 150 dollars.
Step-dau: Betsey Bell 40 dollars.

AN ANNOTATED DIGEST OF WILL BOOK A, GUILFORD COUNTY, NORTH CAROLINA

Sons: Robert Cummons & Samuel Cummons remaining property for them to divide what is over & above equally all my children except Rachel & Amy is to have of the pewter & pots & house & furniture whatever Robert & Samuel see proper to give them.
Seal: Thomas (his x mark) Cummons
Exes: sons Robert Cummons & Samuel Cummons
Wits: Robert Law John Cummons (Jurat) [note: the will was proven by John Christman at Nov. Ct. 1808. Samuel Cummons qualified as Executor at Feb. Ct. 1816]JSH
"revokes"

A:068 p:63   HENRY CAMPLIN   22 Feb. 1805   Aug. Ct. 1805
"Witnesseth, I Henry Camplin..."
Wife: Rebeckah use & rights of all my estate both real & personal during her life or widowhood.
Eldest Son: James at the expiration of my wife's natural life or widowhood £2 & no more as I have given him as much already as I have give to either of my other sons.
Daus: Rebeckah Kelley & Sally Camplin 5 sh to each & no more.
Daus: Dolly Williams & Sophia Williams 5 sh apiece & no more.
Sons: Henry Camplin & Hooper Camplin at the expiration of my wife's natural life or widowhood all that tract of land whereon I now live 100 acres on the S part including the old improvements, - I give unto my son Henry Camplin & the remainder part unto my son Hooper Camplin it being 150 acres whereon I now live & in case that either of those two sons or both should die without leaving issue it is my will that their surviving brothers or brother shall inherit the other part.
Daus: Brittana & Annetta Camplin 5 sh each & no more.
Remainder of estate of every name & nature to my two sons Henry & Hooper Camplin, share & share alike.
Seal: Henry (his x mark) Camplin
Exer: Wife Rebeckah Camplin
Wits: George Swain & James Wilson} Jurats

A:069 pp:64/65 TOBIAS CLAPP, SEN'R   23 Jan. 1800   Feb. Ct. 1800
Son: Daniel all that parcel of land whereon he now liveth, containing 137 acres & also 63 acres to be surveyed adj. the aforesaid land out of a certain tract of land I purchased of Ad[lai] Osbon [Osborne] & to begin at the 2nd corner of my old tract to make 200 acres in the hold [whole].
Son: Valentine Clapp all that piece or parcel of land whereon he now liveth containing 200 acres.
Son: Philip Clapp all that piece or parcel of land whereon he now liveth containing 114 acres, and I value and rate all my land at $2 per acre, and whereas I have not [given] Philip as much land as one of the others of his brothers, I will that the remainder part be paid him in moneys out of my estate at the afsd rate of $2 to make him equal.
Wife: Christina 1/3 of the remainder of my land, viz: of the old tract & of the land I bought of Ad. Osbon the 60 acres excepted I have given to my son Daniel during her lifetime, also 4 cows, one heffer & 1 steer, the choice of all my cattle, also one horse, the choice of all I own, also 12 hogs, the choice of all I own, also 3 beds & bed cloths, & ditto 1 spinning wheel, one plough & gears for 2 horses & my Negro wench Amey & her chld Ishmel I rate at $240 if my wife choose to take them at that

AN ANNOTATED DIGEST OF WILL BOOK A, GUILFORD COUNTY, NORTH CAROLINA

price then they said to be in her part as I will that she shall have an equal part with each & every of my children, & if she doth not choose to take the afsd. Negros, then the said to be sold at publick sale and the afsd. sum to be paid her viz: the rate of the Negros.
Son: Tobias as I have given him no land I will that he have $400 to make him equal with his brothers at the rate of their land. Also the 2-year old horse colt, & all stock of bees.
I value the remainder of Negros as follows: Dick $200; Frank $300; Bill $200; Nelley $200.
4 Daus: Elizabeth, Margeret, Magdelin & Barbary each $400 to make them equal with their brothers agreeable to the rate of their land & if my daus. choose to take the Negros at the afsd. rate to be in part of their portion, if not, then the Negros to be sold at public sale & each to have their portion in money.
Remainder of estate to be sold at publick sale, and after all lawfull debts be paid, & my wife's part & my children's part be paid, & if there be any remainder, to be equally divided amongst my wife and all my children.
Sons: George & Isaac the plantation whereon I now live & the land bought from Ad. Osbon be equally divided in 2 parts & my son George have the choice & my son Isaac to have the other.
Son: George to have my ---- spring coult [possibly a colt born in the spring.JSH]
Seal: Tobias (his x mark) Clap
Exrs: son-in-law Henry Keck & friend Adam Starr
Wits: Adam Starr (Jurat) George Greeson (Jurat)

A:070 pp:65/66 MARY CAMPBELL   4 July 1805   Feb. Ct. 1806
"widow"
Grandson: James Campbell, s/o Archibald Campbell my gold watch.
Granddau: Polley Campbell, d/o James Campbell my best suit of wearing clothes, 2 cows & calves, 6 silver tea spoons, & 1/2 of my cupboard furniture.
Niece: Sarah Covey the other 1/2 of cupboard furniture, all my geese & the rest of my wearing clothes beside the suit left to Polly Campbell.
John Thorpe, s/o Aaron Thorpe the sum of $20.
Aaron Thorpe, my part of the still we purchased between us.
Sons: Archibald Campbell & James Campbell & Nephews: Edward Edwards & Leven Covey each 1/4 of all the rest of my estate, real or personal that I may have any right or interest in, to be sold & divided among them.
Seal: Mary Campbell
Exrs: worthy friends Leven Covey & Abraham Peeples
Wits: J. Moore, Richard Borton (Jurat)

A:071 pp:66/67 THOMAS COOK   1st of 2nd mo 1805   May Ct. 1805
"I, Thomas Cook"
Wife: Mary the use & profits of the plantation that I now live on, all the farming tools thereto belonging, 2 mares, one called Fly & the other Blaze, with 2 cows & calves, her choice during her widowhood, but if she incline to marry, that she have but one feather bed, & common furniture, all her wearing clothes & so forth to her & her heirs forever.
Son: Thomas Cook $10.
Son: Joseph Cook $10.

Son: John Cook the Blacksmith tools that he has now in use & the horse that is now called his, & 1 feather bed & common furniture.
Son: Jacob the mare called Polla.
Son: William Cook the 2 year old horse colt & $50.
Three sons: Zimri Cook, Isaac Cook, & Nathan Cook at their Mother's decease or marriage the plantation that I now live on with every priviledge thereto belonging provided there remains residue enough of my personal estate to pay William the $50, if not for them to pay the $50 equally between then & the remainder I give to them & their heirs.
Granddaughter: Elizabeth Cook 1 feather bed & common furniture.
Dau: Sarah Stuart $10.
If either or any of my sons die in minority or without heirs of body; their parts to devolve to my survivings sons.
Residue of personal & real estate of any kind to be equally divided among the remainder of my sons.
Seal: Thomas Cook
Exes: sons Joseph Cook & Thomas Cook
Wits: Barnabas Coffin (Jurat) John Stuart, Jr. (Jurat) Jonathan Mills

A:072   pp:67/68   JEAN CRISWELL   7 Oct. 1794   Feb. Ct. 1801
Eldest Dau: Margaret Work   5 sh.
Eldest Son: James 1/3 of all my estate.
Youngest Son: William 1/3 of all my estate.
Youngest Dau: Mary the remaining 1/3 of all my estate.
Seal: Jean (her x mark) Criswell
Exrs: sons James & William, & dau: Mary Criswell.
Wits: John Larkins, John Gilchrist (Jurat)

A:073 pp:68/69   SARAH CRANOR   15 July 1797   May Ct. 1801
Grandson: Joseph Cranor, s/o Joshua Cranor 1 cow.
Granddaughter: Mary Lester my linen wheel I spin on & a pair of cotton cards, 1/2 gallon bason, & a pair of tongs & 1 of my newest blankets.
Dau: Elizabeth Ford my riding mare.
Granddaughter: Sarah Ford my bed that I lay on & furniture.
Granddaughter: Elizabeth Ford my new saddle & bridle & a half-gallon bason.
Granddaughter: Prudence Ford my chest & counterpin & a 1-gallon pot.
I bequeath to my beloved son Thomas Cranor's estate 1 silver dollar & the account I have against the estate.
Grandsons: William Ford, Moses Ford & Thomas Ford all the rest of my stock & household property to be equally divided amongst the three.
Seal: Sarah (her   mark) Cranor
Exr: son-in-law Henry Ford
Wits: Winsmore Howren (Jurat), Sarah (her x mark) Howren, Mary (her x mark) Ke ney [this name is unclear in both the original will and the Clerk's copy]
"revokes"

A:074   pp:69/70   FRANCIS CUMMINS   30 Oct. 1792   Feb. Ct. 1800
Wife: Jane Cummins the plantation whereon I now live together with all my stock of horses, catle, sheep & hogs during her natural life or widowhood toward the schooling and bringing up of my sd. children. But if my wife should marry during the minority of any of my children, then the Executors to have the sd. plantation & stock for the schooling &

bring up sd. children. at her marrying or deceasing all my estate to fall into the hands of my children & their heirs & assigns forever as they marry or come of age, except the £5 that shall be at the discretion of my wife to will as she pleases.
Dau: Anna £55 to consist of a hors, sadle, bed & furniture to be [rated] at £25 or if they fall short of that sum to be made up if something else; & if over £25 to be reducted [sic].
Daus: Martha & Thankful £55 to be paid in like manner as dau. Ann & if my sd. Exrs. should not agree or be removed before each child should have their dividend, the legatees shall choose 2 men under good caracter to make such valuation.
Sons: Thomas & Elija all my land to be equally divided at the descretion of my Exrs. in case of death or removal of any of them, each son when arrived to age to choose two men.
Seal: Frs. [Francis] Cummins
Exrs: wife Jeane Cummons, John Foster & Thomas Black
Wits: Thos. Cummins & Col. Daniel Gillespie (Jurat)

A:075 p:71 **PARIS CHIPMAN** 30th of 1st mo 1797 May Ct. 1801
"I Paris Chipman"
Wife: Margaret full use & privilege of my estate during her life time & also that income is to be pd. by my 2 sons, with as much of my stock & Moveables as she sees proper to choose, & £100 in hard money.
Sons: John & Paris to have my land called Farlow, equally divided.
Residue of my estate to be appraised and divided in 3 parts; 1 part to son John, 1 part to son Paris, and the last 3rd to be equally divided between my 2 daus: Hannah Horney & Mary Horney.
Seal: Peres [sic] Chipman
Exrs: sons John & Paris Chipman
Wits: Obadiah Harris (Jurat), Manlove Wheeler, & Henry Wheeler.

A:076 pp:71/72 **WILLIAM COFFIN** 31 July 1803 Nov. Ct. 1803
"I, William Coffin"
Son: Libni Coffin £30 of the currency of North Carolina.
Heirs of son William Coffin 5 sh.
Heirs of son Samuel Coffin £40 of sd. currency to be equally divided among them.
Son: Barnabas Coffin £35.
Son: Matthew Coffin £90.
Bethuel Coffin £25 & as I have made a contract with him in respect to the plantation that I now live on including some other property if he fully comply with sd. contract it is my will & meaning for it to stand valid - but if the contract should by any means fail of being fulfilled, then my Executors with my other sons direct Mathew as they may think most just & equitable.
Son: Levi that tract of land I have a deed of from Michal Mason, a clock, great Bible & concordance & £10 currency.
Granddau: Priscilla Coffin, d/o my son Abijah Coffin, dec'd. £150 of the currency afsd. if she lives to the age of 20 years or marriage, but if she should die in minority or without heirs of her body, then for it to devolve to my son Libni's son Abijah & if he should die without heirs of body then for it to be as a residue of my estate.
Dau: Deborah Terrel 10 sh. with what I have heretofore given her.
Grandson: Libni Hunt £10.

AN ANNOTATED DIGEST OF WILL BOOK A, GUILFORD COUNTY, NORTH CAROLINA

Granddaughter: Miriam Hunt £10 currency. It is my meaning that all the sums of money mentioned shall be of one currency.
All residue of my estate of what nature to be divided according to the legacies for each to rise or fall in proportion as given except my granddaughter Priscilla Coffin, for hers not to rise if my estate amounts to more than the sums mentioned.
Seal: William Coffin
Exrs: sons Barnabas & Matthew Coffin.
Wits: George Hodgson, Ann Hodgson, Thomas White (Jurat)

A:077 p:73   CLAIBORNE CURTIS   16 Sept. 1803   Nov. Ct. 1803
Wife: Sarah Curtis, all of his estate.
Seal: Claiborne Curtis
Exrx: wife Sarah Curtis
Wits: Joshua Underwood (Jurat), James Smith (Jurat) Mary Smith
"revokes"

A:078 pp:73/74   JOHN COE   23 Oct. 1807   Nov. Ct. 1807
Daus: Mary Aydelet, Nancy Causey, Hannah Gamble each 40 sh.
Dau: Hulda Coe 1 bed & furniture, a cow & yearling, 1 mare saddle & bridle which she has in her possession, also 1 10-gallon pot & 1 skillet, 1 cotton wheel & 1 flax wheel, 6 puter plates & $30 in cash.
Wife: Sarah Coe all land & premises whereon I now live during her natural life & also my household goods 1 horse named Black, all my farming utensils, $100 in money, all but the land to be her my sd wife's and at her disposal, & one cow & heifer, 1 wagon & gears, & all pots, ovens, 1 tea kettle, my puter, & 1 wire sifter.
Grandson: John Gamble Coe after the death of my wife the plantation & land whereon I now live 170 acres & 1 bed & furniture.
Wife: Sarah Coe my riding chear [chair] & harness.
Son: Avery Coe $59 to be paid out of a note on Thomas Webb for $1108 & 1/2 to him, his heirs or assigns to make him equal with John Coe who received $775 of Thomas Webb.
Wife: Sarah Coe & Dau: Hulda Coe $70 to purchase meal & corn to support my family 1 year provided they live together.
Son: Joseph Coe $100 in notes.
Son: Every [Avery?] Coe $100 in notes to be assigned to him.
Son: John Coe $60 & the remaining if any to be divided between my 3 sons Avery Coe, John Coe, Joseph Coe and Dau: Hulda Coe.
Seal: John Coe
Exrs: wife Sarah Coe & son John Coe
Wits: Andrew McGee (Jurat) & James Galbreath
"revokes"

A:079 p:75   GEORGE CUMMINS   9 Dec. 1805   Feb. Ct. 1808
Wife: Sarah Cummins all stock of all kinds, household furniture & plantation utensils during her life, also <u>250 acres of land in Cumberland on the waters of a creek called Half Gone. [my underline. JSH]</u>
Son: Joseph Cummins 250 acres more or less on each side of my dwelling house & on both sides of Haw River between Thomas Cummins line & Hugh Cummins lines & Edward Bullock & John Medearis & Wm Ragsdale to him & his heirs forever.

AN ANNOTATED DIGEST OF WILL BOOK A, GUILFORD COUNTY, NORTH CAROLINA

Sons: John, Thomas, George, James, Charles & Hugh - each 5 shillings Sterling.
Daus: Elizabeth, Sarah, Mathew [Martha?] 5 sh Sterling.
Seal: George Cummins
Exrs: John ... [too faint to read in both the original and the Clerk's copy]
Wits: Justain Knott (Jurat), William (his x mark) Anthony, Elisebeth (her x mark) Cummins
"revokes"

   A:080   p:76   MARY COVEY   21st of 6th mo 1799   Feb. Ct. 1807
"Widow, of Rowan County, NC"
To Nowel Sapp my part of the wagon.
Step-daughter: Sarah Sapp 1 little chest or box with wooden hinges & 1/4 part of my wearing apparel.
Sister: Elizabeth Tharp all remaining wearing apparel if she survives me, if not to her 2 daus. equally [not named].
Remaining estate equally divided between the children of my brothers and sisters [not named].
Seal: Mary (her x mark) Covey
Exrs: 2 Bros: Martin Pegg & Valentine Pegg
Wits: Abel Knight ye[the] third, Samuel Couch (Jurat)

   A:081   pp:76/77   JOHN CHAMBERS   8 Apr. 1788   May Ct. 1800
"farmer"
Wife: Elizabeth 1 horse & cow, her choice, one bed & furniture, all household furniture & half of my cash if any remains after paying funeral charges. To have sole use & benefit of my plantation with Negro Ails [Alice?] during wife's life. if said wench should have more than one issue or children before my wife's decease one of them shall be at her disposal.
Son-in-law: Andrew Wilson 20 sh.
Grandchildren by daughter Augness [Agnes?] deceased viz. Daniel, Robert & James Wilson £60 current money; £20 each when they arrive at age 21, survivors to take share.
Dau: Jennet Rankin to have the Negro Ails [Alice?] at her mother's decease.
Son-in-law: William Rankin all that remains of my whole estate from the above bequeaths to be divided by & at the discretion of him among his children which he now hath or may have by my daughter his present wife which distribution whether it respects lands, goods or chattles shall be as valid to all intents & purposes as if I had herein personally named each legatee.
Seal: John Chambers
Exes: much respected son-in-law William Rankin & true & trusty friend William Scott
Wits: Jno. Anderson, Jno. Donnel, (Jurat), Wm. Scott
"revokes"

   A:082   p:78   JEAN CALHOON   10 June 1804   May Ct. 1805
Daus: Elizabeth Flemon [Fleming?], Mary Wheatly, Ann Holliday, Sarah Love, Alse Tharpe & Nancy Read all my wearing clothes equally.
Son: James Calhoon 5 sh. raised out of personal estate.

Son: Samuel Calhoon 1 bed, bed stead & furniture & 1 stone jug by the said Samuel Calhoon paying my burial charges.
Son: Robert Calhoon 5 sh raised out of my personal estate.
Son: John Calhoon 5 sh out of personal estate.
Granddaughter: Easter Calhoon 1 bed, bedstead, cord, bolsters, pillows, 5 sheets, 2 blankets & 2 bed quilts, 4 head of cattle & their increase, 4 head of sheep & their increase, 6 puter plates, 3 basons, 3 puter dishes, 6 puter spoons, 6 knives & forks, 2 iron pots, 1 Dutch oven, 1 table cloth, 1 box iron, 1 flax wheel, 1 pr cotton chards [cards], 1 pine chist [chest] & 1 stone pot, also any remainder of my estate.
Seal: Jeney Calhoon
Exe: Benjamin Barham
Wits: Charles Barham (Jurat), Nathan Barham

A:083   pp:78/79/80   BARNABAS COFFIN   16th of 11th mo 1814   Aug. Ct. 1815
"I Barnabas Coffin..."
Wife: Phebe Coffin use & profits during her widowhood of plantation whereon I now live, (Tanyard excepted), with use of 2 horses & all farming tools, the old waggon, as much of my stock of cattle, sheep & hogs as my Executor thinks needfull for her support, remainder to be disposed of to the interest of my estate. If wife remarries she to have 1 horse saddle & bridle, one feather bed with common furniture, 1 cow & calf, & all her wearing clothes.
Son: Jospeh Coffin $100.
Son: Abel Coffin that last piece of land I bought of Joseph Mill containing 4 acres including the house whereon he now lives joining a tract formerly bought of sd. Mills. To him my four books of arts science.
Son: Barnabas Coffin $200 with what I have heretofore given him. Also 1/3 part of the residue of my books, my clock (at his mother's decease or marriage), 1/2 my wearing clothes (that is for them to be equally divided between him & my son Stephen) and my desk.
Son: Stephen $300 & 1/3 part of my books. My books to be equally divided between my 3 sons Joseph, Barnabus & Stephen, but for their mother during hew widowhood to have the use of the large Bible & other Friends Journals that she may choose.
Son: Stephen 1/2 of my wearing clothes, the new waggon he took to the western country & all the money & property he took therein.
Dau: Huldah Stanley $150.
Dau: Phebe Hunt $150.
Dau: Elisabeth Hunt $150.
Dau: Priscilla Coffin the feather bed that is now called hers, also the table, chest and trunk looking glass, all her cloaths &C & $130.
At wife's decease or marriage all household goods be equally divided among my surviving daughters.
3 Grandsons: Barnabas Hunt, Barnabas Coffin, & Barnabas Stanley, each one common family Bible, and one Testament.
All other grandchildren: 1 dollar.
Son: Barnabas, & Son-in-law Jesse Stanley, [I]relinquish all rights of claim on all notes, bonds, debts, or demands on them.
4 sons: Joseph, Abel, Barnabs [sic], & Stephen, all the residue of my estate, 2/3 to be equally divided among them;

the other 1/3 to be equally divided among my 4 daus: Hulda Stanley, Phebe Hunt, Elisabeth Hunt & Priscilla Coffin
Sister: Deborah Tarrell [Terrell?] to have her home & room at my house so long as she chooses, with every privilege she now receives.
Wife: all household goods the Exec. think needful during her widowhood & for my daugters to have the remainder if she choses to keep the desk with the clock let her have it.
Seal: Barnabas Coffin
Exrs: brother Bethuel Coffin & 2 sons Joseph Coffin & Abel Coffin
Wit: Matthew Starbuck (Jurat)

A:084 pp:80/81 SIMON CHRISTOPHER [no date] Feb. Ct. 1812
"late of Franklin County, VA at this time at the house of my friend Aleazer Kersey, sick & low in body..."
Exrs: to pay expenses of my sickness and burial, and to make demand on my son Garett Christopher and my wife Nancy Jarrell the property I lately left in their hands:
1 mare saddle & bridle, two hundred weight of manufactured tobacco & 454 pounds of hand tobacco & that they make publick sale of the above or all that they can get in their hands at the credit of 6 months with all my other property that they can lawfully get in their hands.
All money arising from the above I hereby direct my Executors after expenses, to apply in discharging my just debts which are as follows:
Walker Carter £5.9 Virginia currency
Robert Coaling £7.10 the like currency.
Seal: [no signature]
Exer: [none named]
Wits: [none named]
Feb. Term 1812. The foregoing paper writing being offered to the Court for probate which on proving the hand righting sufficiently was according[ly] done.
Test: John Hamilton CC By J. Davis DC
[this may be the proving of a will by a "*parity of hands*]JSH

A:085 pp:81/82 THOMAS CUMMINS 31 Aug. 1813 Nov. Ct. 1813
Wife: Elizabeth plantation with all my lands while she remains my widow. my grey mare, yoke of oxen, 4 hogs her choice & as much of the crop as will be sufficient for her year's support, and wife to pay my mother Jean Cummins 40 bu. corne & 4 bu. of wheat & 60 weight of Porke & 1000 weight of hay yearly as long as my mother lives or til my widow shall marry.
Sister: Ann Mayben [Mebane] my part of all the books that uncle Thomas Cummins left to me & her.
Remainder of estate to be sold & if my wife is with child and the said child shall live to the age to receive said estate that the sd. child have all the reminder of my estate, and if the said child shall die before it comes of full age that my estate shall be equally divided amongst the children of my brothers & sisters.
Seal: Thomas Cummins
Exrs: worthy friend David Mayben & my wife Elizabeth Cummins
Wits: J. Mills (Jurat), Jane Ozment, Joel Sullivan

AN ANNOTATED DIGEST OF WILL BOOK A, GUILFORD COUNTY, NORTH CAROLINA

A:086 pp:82/84   HENRY COPP [COBB]   13 Dec. 1809   May Ct. 1812
Wife: Catranina [sic] $200 raised & levied out of my estate, her joys [choice] of my horses & sattle [sic] & bridle, 2 cows & the best of my beds with all the furniture belonging to a bed, 2 iron pots & the tea kittle, 2 putter basons, 2 putter dishes, 1/2 doz. putter plates & putter spoons as many as she pleases, 10 bu. wheat yearly to be levied off the plantation & full posation [sic] of my haus & garden & meadow or feed as will suport the two cows & 100 wt. of pork yearly during her lifetime.
Daus: Elizabeth, Dorely [Dorothea], Magdalena, $200 each to be raised & levied out of my estate.
Son: John Cobb $40 to make him in an even balance with the rest of my sons in the land.
Dau: Margaretha [Margaret] $200 to be raised & levied out of my estate.
Sons: Henry Cobb sener [sic] & Felty [Valentine] Cobb since they have each received from my estate to the amount of $200 in land [he does not complete this statement].
Daus: Barbara & Elanor [Hana in the original will] $200 to be raised & levied out of my estate.
Son: Jacob Copp 150 acres of land on the S side of my plantation in lieu of $200.
All property over & above is & shall be equally divided among my children by their name as follows: Elizabeth, Dorley, Magdalena, John, Margaretha, Henry, Felty, Hany, Barbara, & Jacob Copp.
Seal: Henry Copp
Exrs: son John Copp & David Whitesel
Wits: John Crisman (Jurat) Felty (his x mark) Waggoner
"revokes"

A:087 p:84   JOHN COBLE   3 March 1813   Nov. Ct. 1815
Son: Martin Coble 125 acres of land, my waggon, a cow & a bed.
Dau: Mary Coble the balance of my tract of land I live on & 2 cows.
Seal: John (his H mark) Coble
Exrs: son Martin & son-in-law Elisha Bennett
Wits: Jon'n. [Jonathan] Hadley (Jurat) Andrew (his x mark) Shatterly

[2 blank pages in Will Book]JSH

A:088 pp:87/88   JAMES DENNY   26 Sept. 1774   Nov. Ct. 1774
My father's last will be punctually fulfilled.
Wife: Mary, negro Tom & full third part of all my moveable effects, negro Dina at my mother's death; use of house & plantation until my sons James & William be of age in order to Rause [raise] and school them in a Christian manner, & the use of the house I now live in during her widowhood.
Debts & dues discharged & the remainder to be for the use of my sons when of age, but if my wife be now with child if it is a son the same to have equal privilege with the 2 above, & if a dau. the same as above & a childs part of all moveable effects when of age.
Sons: James & William the plantation I now live on, the East end to James, & if my wife is now with child if a son he is to enjoy the improvements I now live on & my son William the middle part (all 3 to have equal part); if there is a dau: James & William to have the land equally, James to enjoy the East part.

AN ANNOTATED DIGEST OF WILL BOOK A, GUILFORD COUNTY, NORTH CAROLINA

If no child of mine lives to enjoy the plantation as above then 1/2 the land to be my wife's property during her life as my widow, & the other sold & divided equally between my brother William & my 3 young sisters,[not named] but if my wife marry another man, the whole land divided as above, that is the money arising from the sale thereof.
Seal: James Denny
Exrs: wife Mary Denny, Alexander Caldwell, & William Gowdy
Wits: Abraham McElhatton (Jurat), Alexander Breden, James Wilson.
"revokes"

    A:089 pp:88/89   PHILEMON DEATHERAGE   24 Jan. 1778   May Ct. 1778
Wife: Elizabeth in the Room and Steade of what the Law allow's here 1/3 part of all my real and personall Estate after paying of my debts during ther Naturall Life, and the
Remainder to be Equally divided between my dearly Beloved Children.
I will George, Sarah, Bird, Schiles, Solomon, James, and Mary Deatherage and that the before mentioned divisions be made when my Executors shall think Necessary after my Eldest Son shall come of age, or my Wife shall alter her Condition by Marriage, and should my said Executors find it most Expedient for the payments of my debts and the more equall making the said Divisions to sell the Tract of Land Whereon I now Live, or part thereof, they are hereby Authorised and Impowered to make a good Right to purchase or Purchasers and further my [desire?] is that my said Executors do not Neglect to cause my Children to be Learned to Read and write and so much Arithmetic as will Enable them to do Common Business as-----------n [paper creased and torn]JSH
Boy John Davis, alias John Hand that is now Bound to me or my Heirs be br----- [paper creased and torn]JSH the same Manner and if any of my sons shall Misbeheave and will not be Governed by their Mother, my Will is that they or Either of them be Bound to a good Trade or Some well disposed Person till they arrive at the age of Twenty Years.
I give and Bequeath to my said Childeren above Named that shall be a live at the decease of my Belove Wife all that part of my Estate both Real and Personal that shall be left at her Death, which I have herein before Bequeathed Equally Amongst them or survivours of them and I do hereby make and Ordain my Beloved Brother George Deatheage and my well beloved son George Deatherage and my Friends Joshua Smith and James Joyce Executors of this my Last Will and Testament, and also Appoint Friends Alexander Martin and Charles Gallaway, Trustees of this my Last Will and Testament to see the same performed according to the True Intent and meaning thereof In Witnes whereof I the said Philemon Deatherage have to this my Last Will and Testatment Set mt Hand and Seal the day and year first written above.
Seal: Philemon Deatherage
Exrs: brother George Deatherage, son George Deatherage, friends Joshua Smith, James Joyce
Wits: James Cook, Alexander Smith, James Gallaway (Jurat)
also appoints friends Alexander Martin & Charles Gallaway Trustees of this my last will and testament.
"Revokes"

AN ANNOTATED DIGEST OF WILL BOOK A, GUILFORD COUNTY, NORTH CAROLINA

A:090 pp:89/90 THOMAS DAVIS 16 Mar. 1780 see minute docket no. 2, p. 27
"cordweaver"
"I, Thomas Davis..."
Wife: Hepzibah Davis use of all my estate both real & personal during her widowhood; if she incline to marry again she to have no more than 1/3 part of the use & profits of my estate.
Daus: Deborah, Lydia, & Elisabeth to have 1/3 of my estate divided equally among them if wife marries.
If wife remains a widow, then at her decease all my household goods be equally divided amongst my three aforesaid daus.
Sons: John, Tristram, Peter & Thomas all the residue of my estate at my wife's marriage or decease.
Seal: Thomas Davis
Exr: wife Hepzibah Davis
Wits: Nathaniel Macy, Paul Macy, Wm. Coffin [Jurat not known]

A:091 pp:90/91 THOMAS DENNIS 24 June 1774 Feb. Ct. 1775
"I, Thomas Dennis..."
Grandson: John Dennis s/o Edward Dennis, dec'd. £1 proclamation money to be paid to him at 21 years of age.
Wife: Sarah Dennis all my household utensils with the beds & furniture, also in partnership & conjunction with my son Thomas Dennis the use & profits of all my other estate both real & personal.
Seal: Thomas (x) Dennis
Exr. son Thomas Dennis
Wits: Jeremiah Reynolds, Benjamin Beeson, Abraham Elliot (Jurat)

A:092 pp:91/92 DANIEL DAUGHERTY 28 Aug. 1786 n.p.d.
[this will was too confusing to abbreviate, so it is copied as written. [JSH]
In the Name of God Amen I Daniel Daugherty of the County of Guilford being Sick & weak in Boddy but of Perfect mind and Memory thanks be given unto God calling unto Mind the Mortality of my Body and knowing that it is appointed for all Men once to Die do make and Ordain this my Last Will and Testament, That is to say principally and first of all I give & recommend my Soul into the Hand of Almighty God that gave it, and my Boddy I recommend to the earth to be Buried in a Decent Christian Burial at the discretion of my Executors nothing doubting but at the General Resurection I shall receive the Same again by the Mighty Power of God and as Touching such Worldly Estate wherewith it has pleased God to Bless me in this Life.
First I give and bequeath unto Elizabeth my Dearly beloved Wife a Mantenance of the Estate & her Room in the House during her life. I give to my well beloved Sons William and Daniel Daugherty whom I likewise constitute name & Ordain the Sole Executors of this my last will & Testament all and Singular my Lands Messuages and Tenements by them freely to be Possessed and enjoyed and I do hereby utterly disallow revoke & disannul all and every other former wills & Testaments I further give & bequeath to my Wife & Daughter Hannah to be equally divided all the Cows except two which I give to Daniel & William each One - I give to my son John Daugherty the Sum of £8 to be paid out of my real & personal Estate the Steers Bulls & Hogs I give & allow for the Use of the house the big pott I give to Daniel & William & the remainder

of the Household furniture I give to my Wife & Daughter Hannah the Coult of the Sorral Mare I give to Daniel & other Sorrel Mare I give to Hannah & the Black Horse I give to my Wife the other Horses being the property of Daniel & William - I give & Bequeath unto my son James Daugherty the sum of one shilling Sterling his whole Legacy, the repairs of the House & plantation I allow to be paid out of the real & personal Estate & I do here by revoke and disannull all and every other former Testaments Wills Legacees & Bequests Ratifying this & confirming this & no other to be my last Will & Testament In Witness whereof - I have hereunto set my Hand & Seal this Twenty Eight - day of August A D One Thousand Seven Hundred & Eighty Six ---
Signed Sealed published & pronounced & declared by the said Daniel Daugherty as his last will & Testament in the presence of each other have hereunto subscribed our names --
NB before signing my Wearing Apparrell I give to my Son John Daugherty
In presence of
Adam Holker   Daniel Dillon Jr   Joseph Thornbrough Juner
Seal: Daniel (his   mark)   Daugherty
Exrs: sons William Daugherty Danial Daughtery
[there is no probate information on this will]JSH
Seal: Daniel (x) Daugherty
Exrs: sons William Daugherty & Daniel Daugherty
Wits: Adam Holker [?] Daniel Dillon, Jr. [Jurat or Junior?], Joseph Thornbrough, Juner.
NB "before signing my wearing apparel I give to my son John Dougherty."
"revokes"

A:093   pp:92/93   ROBERT DWIGGINS   6 Feb.1789   May Ct. 1789
Wife: Lydia all my estate during her widowhood excepting 400 acres of land of a tract bought of Jean Netherly, the sd Lydia to give good bonds & security to the returning of the above estate to the 7 children: Sarah, Elisabeth, Daniel, Ann, Robert, Joseph, & Mary at death of wife.
Son: John Dwiggins 200 acres of land to be given to him at his bequest. If sd. John Dwiggins dies without an heir the sd. land to be divided between the whole of his brothers & sisters. John to pay unto Daniel Dwiggins £20 in money when the sd Daniel comes of age to take it on himself. Sd. land to be on the North side of Netherly Tract, & the horse John now calls his to be his property..
Son: James 200 acres left to him at age 21; he paying unto Robert Dwiggins when he shall come of age the sum of £20 in money. Sd land to join his brother John's land it to join the Netherly tract. If James Dwigons dies without heirs of his body sd. land to be divided among his brethern & sisters. to have a yearling colt called Shaver & my saddle.
Son: Samuel Dwigons all the rest of my land at his mother's death 135 acres of an elder survey where I now live on, a small resurvey unplatted sd. to be 20 acres or upward & 50 acres bought of Netherly tract. said Samuel Dwigins to pay to his brother Joseph Dwigins £20 in money when he the sd. Samuel shall come of age to take it on himself. Samuel dying without heirs of his body sd. land to be equally divided between his brothers & sisters.
My stud horse shall be sold after the 20th day of December next insuing the date hereon. Also the bond of £20 against Will Dobson be continued & the interest be applied to the schooling of the children. the money

AN ANNOTATED DIGEST OF WILL BOOK A, GUILFORD COUNTY, NORTH CAROLINA

or assets arising from the sale of sd. horse or use of sd horse to be applied as the other parts of my personal estate.
Daus: Sarah Dwigins, Elisabeth Dwigins to have £20 each at their marriage.
Seal: Robert Dwiggons
Exrs: Wife Lidia & son John Dwigons, Jun'r.
Wits: Edmond Bowman, John Dwigens, (Jurat) James Dwiggins, (Jurat)
NB: "the words interlind in the gift to John - in money next to his son Samuel tract & sd. Samuel".
NB: "Next in the moveable estate the words Will'm. Dobson".
"revokes"

A:094   pp:94/95   JAMES DENNY   10 Dec. 1790   Feb. Ct. 1795
"farmer"
Married children: Mary Duck, Ann Bass, Mary Anne Peasly, George Denny, Jane Hamilton, Agness & Elizabeth Donnell & James Denny 1 dollar.
Son: James the loan of £5 for 8 years without interest & at the end of sd term I allow him to pay sd. sum to my grandson James Denny, son of George Denny.
Dau: Hannah her horse & saddle, 2 cows & 6 sheep, 1 bed & furniture, 1 chest, 15 pounds of puter & 1 iron pot.
Wife: Agness & Son William to have an equal interest during her life & at her decease I allow her part to become his property with the plantation on which I now live with its appurtenances to son William.
If wife chooses to live with any other of her children I allow her to have her Mare & saddle, her bed & wheel & £5 in money each year during her life & if any money remains after my debts are paid it shall be hers & at her death she may leave these articles to whom she will.
Seal: James Denny
Exrs: son William Denney   son-in-law John Donnel.
Wits: Charles Wheeler, (Jurat) who saw John Rankin become a witness at the same time, & Joseph McGaughy.
"Revokes"

A:095   pp:95/96   FREDRICK DEAN   15 Mar. 1798   May Ct. 1798
"I, Frederick Dean..."
Wife: Frances all my estate both real & personal during her life but if she should marry again she is to have only an equal part with my children.
My 2 sons Thomas Dean & Solomon Dean & my 2 daus: Mary & Elizabeth Dean each 5 shillings.
Daus: that are not married, Sarah, Fanna, Rebeckah, Nansa, Charity & Jean Dean each at the time of their marriage 1 fether bed & furniture, 1 cow & calf, £3.17 sh currency my household goods & moveable property.
Sons: Isaac Dean & Frederick Dean when they arrive to age 21, to each of them a horse worth £25 currency & the place whereon I now live at my wife's decease or marriage if they are of age at the time.
Remaining estate not herein disposed of at the time of my wifes decease or marriage to be publickly sold and equally divided among all my children, not preferring one above the other, & in case any of my children die without lawful issue his or her parts shall be equally divided among the survivors.

AN ANNOTATED DIGEST OF WILL BOOK A, GUILFORD COUNTY, NORTH CAROLINA

Seal: Frederick (x) Dean
Exrs: wife Frances & son-in-law Richard Bowman
Wits: Hezekiah Starbuck, (Jurat, affirmed) William Gray (Jurat affirmed]
James (x) Whicker

A:096   pp:96/97   ABRAM DUFF   6 Mar. 1781   May Ct. 1791
Wife: Mary young bay mare & her own saddle & bridle, her choice of 2 of my best milch cows & 2 calfs, & 2 ewes & lambs, & 2 beds & their furniture & all the pewter & pott which belongs to me.
Nephew: Abram Duff, s/o my brother Samuel as much money or other property as would have purchased one cow six years ago.
Brothers: James, William, Samuel, John & Robert the remainder of any estate to be divided equally among them.
Seal: Abram Duff
Exrs: William Duff & my father Samuel Duff
Wits: Ralph Gorrell, (Jurat), Thomas Brown, Ann (x) Kerr
"revokes"

A:097   p:97   PETER DILLON   15th of 5th mo 1796   Aug. Ct. 1796
"I, Peter Dillon..."
Daniel Dillon, Juner my riding horse, saddle & bridle & all my wearing apearel.
Wife: Charity tract of land whereon I now live 67 & 3/4 acres as also the remainder of my estate.
Seal: Peter Dillon
Exrs: wife Charity & Daniel Dillon Juner
Wits: Witness [sic] Strangeman Stanley & Prefect* Benoni Mills (Jurats)
*Prefect is a term used in some English schools and seems to indicate a supervisor. JSH

A:098   p:98   PETER DICKS   13th of 11th mo 1795   Nov. Ct. 1796
"Know all men by these presents..."
Son: James Dicks my land that lies East of Polecat & Davis' Creek.
Grandson: William Dicks land in the NW corner lying where Lambs line crosses the creek running North to Coffins corner then SE with Coffins line to John Beals corner stone then West to the creek then up the creek to the mouth of the branch below the mill then up sd. branch 6 rods then NW to the beginning.
Wife: Elizabeth Dicks all the remaining part of my land whereon I now live during her natural life & at her death to my Grandson Peter Dicks with all the appurtenances thereunto & also all my personal estate during her life; at her decease I give unto my grandson Peter Dicks my desk & clock.
Seal: Peter Dicks
Exrs: son James Dicks & grandson Peter Dicks
Wits: Salathiel Stone (Jurat) Zacharias Dicks (Jurat)

A:099   pp:98/99   ROBERT DOAK   24 Sept. 1796   Nov. Ct. 1796
Wife: Hannah the plantation whereon I now live & 1 Negro girl named Sisley & 1 still to her & for the use of the family, 1 waggon, 1 brown mare, & 1 sorrel mare & 1 roan horse with all the gearing & plantation utensils with my stock of cattle, hogs, & sheep, & her choice of 2 feather beds & furniture during her life or widowhood.

Son: John Doak 150 acres of land lying in the County of Guilford, part of a tract purchased of James McCuiston to be divided & the sd. John to have first choice of sd. land & 1 Negro boy named Ned at the Expiration of 3 years after date; 1 black horse named Jack & 1 bed & furniture.
Son: James Doak 150 acres of land the balance of sd. McCuiston lands & 1 Negro boy named Jam & 1 horse which is already secured [named in the original will] to sd. James Doak & 1 bed & furniture.
Son: Robert Doak 100 acres of land on the Alamance during his life & in case he dies without issue the tract not to be divided & 1 Negro man named Jonas & 1 bed & furniture & 1 black filly.
Son: William Doak 100 acres of land on the Alamance & in case Robt. dies without issue the sd land to William & 1 negro woman named Mol & the sd William Doak is to give his sister Hannah Doak the first live Negro child that sd. wench has & his sister Elizabeth the 2nd living child & 1 bed & furniture & 1 colt to sd William that is named.
NB the sd. Negro woman is to suckle the children 1 year each at least.
Son-in-law: Robert Gorrell the sum of 1/2 Johannes [money].
Son: Daniel Doak the above mentioned property to sd. Hannah Doak my wife at her Marriage or decease.
Dau: Mary Doak 1 Negro girl named Luse & 1 sorrel filly, 1 bed & furniture & chest & all her wearing apparell & $50 in cash & a saddle.
Dau: Hannah Doak 1 bay filly, 1 chest with all her wearing apperal, 1 bed & furniture, 1 saddle, & $50 in cash.
Dau: Elisbeth Doak 1 colt, 1 bed & furniture, 1 saddle, & $50 in cash.
Seal: Robert Doak
Exrs: John Gillespie, John Doake wife Hannah Doak
Wits: Wm. Doak, (Jurat) James Doak (Jurat) Anne Doak
"revokes"

A:0100 pp:100/101 **WILLIAM DENNIS** 20 Feb. 1791 May Ct. 1791
"I, William Dennis..."
3 sons-in-law: Obediah Calloway, Jonathan Calloway & Matthias Dennis 75 acres of land it being part of a tract of land I bought of James Barrom lying on Mears Fork joining Thomas Brown which is to be taken off the South end of sd. tract by an East & West line on the South side of sd tract.
Sons: William Dennis & Daniel Dennis remainder of my lands to be equally divided between them.
Wife: [not named] possession of the above mentioned land, house & plantation (my sd. sons-in-law portions excepted) & all household furniture of every kind & all my stock namely horses & hogs with all & every kind of household or plantation implements or ----------- [?] during her widowhood & if she should marry I will & desire all the possessions & furniture & stock above named to be equally divided among my 4 youngest children: namely Leah Dennis, Wm. Dennis, Daniel Dennis & Levinah Dennis.
Seal: William Dennis
Exrs: none named
Wits: Matt'w. Brown William Rayle Aaron Mendenhall (Jurat) "affirmed"
"revokes"

AN ANNOTATED DIGEST OF WILL BOOK A, GUILFORD COUNTY, NORTH CAROLINA

A:0101 pp:101/102 PATRICK DIAMOND 24 Oct. 1790 n.p.d.
"sick and weak in body..."
Wife: Sarah 1/3 of all lands & 1/3 of my other personal estate & likewise sustain a certain bound child named Sarah Medlen.
Son: John Diamond 5 sh Sterling
Son: John Thommeson 5 sh Sterling
Son: Stuard Diamond 1/3 of my personal estate.
well beloved [son in the original will] William Pritchett 5 sh Sterling
Dau: Mary Diamond 5 sh Sterling
Son: William Diamond 2/3 of all my lands & at the decease of wife all my lands & 1/3 of all my other personal property.
Seal: Patrick Diamond
Exrs: Sons Stuard Diamond William Diamond
Wits: Valentine Mileham Walter Mileham
"revokes"

A:0102 p:102 ROBERT DAUGHERTY 15 Feb. 1804 May Ct. 1804
"being in a low state of health..."
Samuel Stuart: the lands I bought of him.
William Daugherty, Samuel Dougherty, & Noble Covey: land on waters of Spring Creek in Wilson County, TN [my underline] to be equally divided.
Bro: Samuel to receive my share in the land of my father's estate.
Mother: Jean Daugherty $100.
Sister: Susan Flack $60.
Bro: John Daugherty my sadle.
Sister: Betsy Daugherty all the remaining part of my property.
Seal: Robert Dougherty
Exrs. Brother John Dougherty
Wits: John Starrat, John Alcorn (Jurat) Benjamin Wilson

A:0103 p:103 WILLIAM DOAK 5 Sept. 1807 Nov. Ct. 1807
Wife: [not named] 120 acres of land including improvements whereon I now live to be taken off the South end of the land where I now live while she remains my widow & then to be given unto my youngest son Jonathan forever likewise 1 feather bed & furniture, 2 cowes & the Mark [sic] mare saddle & bridle & the Negroes during her lifetime & then the Negroes to be equally divided between my 3 youngest sons Roddy, Josiah & Jonathan, but Jonathan to have £100 worth of the Negroes more than Roddy or Josiah.
Son: John $10
Son: William 200 acres of land of the tract I bought of Robert Anderson & the sorrel mare [name not readable] saddle & bridle, 2 cowes & bed & furniture.
Son: Robert 200 acres of land it being part of the land bought of Anderson & the bay colt Sweeper, saddle & bridle bed & furniture & 2 cowes.
Son: Roddy 100 acres of land adj. the old improvement 1 bay colt Madly saddle & bridle 2 cowes & bed & furniture.
Son: Josiah 100 acres of land the remainder of the old tract 1 horse saddle & bridle bed & furniture & 2 cowes and the aforesaid 120 acres of land after wife's decease or marriage.
Son: Jonathan 1 horse saddle & bridle 2 cowes bed & furniture.
Dau: Mary £50 hard money 1 good horse saddle & bridle bed & furniture 2 cowes.

AN ANNOTATED DIGEST OF WILL BOOK A, GUILFORD COUNTY, NORTH CAROLINA

Dau: Martha £50 hard money horse saddle & bridle bed & furniture 2 cowes.
Also $3 to Roddy Hannah's son Bille.
the still waggon smith tools & all the eutenshels [utensils] belonging to the plantation to go to the use thereof.
The stud horse to be sold.
Seal: William Doak
Exrs: wife Ann, son William Robert Hannah Sr.
Wits: Roddy Hannah [the Clerk has added Sr. to his name], John (his x mark) Alexander, Sr. (Jurat) "who saw Roddy Hannah sign as a witness at the same time"
"revokes"

   A:0104 p:104 **JOHN DUNLAP** 27 Jan. 1794 Aug. Ct. 1805
Son: John 106 acres of the unimproved land together with all my working tools of every kind & my wearing cloths mare & saddle & bridle.
Dau: Margaret Dunlap *planishing* *[sic] of every nature & kind 6 head of cattle £100 cash which is in different bonds on Col. John Gillespie & his son Daniel Gillespie the sd £100 to be paid to the sd. Margaret out of the last payments of sd. bonds.
Son: Robert 106 acres of land with the improvements whereon I now live.
Grandchild: Mary Armfield 1 cow.
Seal: John (x) Dunlap
Exrs: John Armfield Daniel Gillespie and Margaret Dunlap
Wits: John Alcorn, Jno. Gillaspie Jr. Col. Daniel Gillespie (Jurat)
"revokes"
*planishing: [definition not known JSH]

   A:0105 p:105 **DANIEL DILLON**   20th of 8th mo 1805   Feb. Ct. 1806
"This 20th day of the Eighth month 1805 of New Garden..."
Youngest son Isaac Dillon all the balance of the old survey on the South side of Reedy Fork & Jesse's line including the old meadow that is not conveyed to others.
Exrs: to sell one tract of land lying on the South side of the Ridge on Heads of the branches above whare Robert Bleckley formerly lived which by deed may fully show it being on the North side of Beaver Crick.
Youngest son: Isaac aforementioned a piece or parcel of land lying on the South side of Beaver Crick it being the SW corner of the ould survey, beginning at Stuart's corner in the grate road running thence Southward along sd. Road to a rock, from thence to the ould corner by the pond thence along the ould line to Stuart's corner on the Ridge thence with his line to the begining in sd. road.
Exrs: to sell the ould Mill Seat with all the land lying on the North side of the Great Road & West of Stuart's line it being the NW corner of West end of the ould survey.
Granddaus: Sarah & Elisabeth Wallace $10 to be equally divided between them.
All cash in hand or to be obtained from bonds notes book acts, &C & moveable & perishable property to be sold, collected and equally divided amongst all my children, namely Martha Nathan Willam Peter Jesse Daniel Patience & Isaac Dillon.
Seal: Daniel Dillon
Exrs: sons Nathan & Peter Dillon
Wits: Silvanus Gardner Jonathan Hodgson (Jurat) William Bunch **"revokes"**

AN ANNOTATED DIGEST OF WILL BOOK A, GUILFORD COUNTY, NORTH CAROLINA

A:0106 p:106 ELIZABETH DONNELL   5 Jan. 1802   Feb. Ct. 1802
Bro: Thomas Donnell all cattle.
Sister: Mary Donnell the 1/2 of the money I lent James Wells & Robert Donnell my bed single blanket coverlid & sheet 1 pot a hat purple petticoat. also to have my knives & forks spoons & pepper box.
Bros: Samuel & Harry puter & books to be equally divided.
Bro: Samuel the other half of the money lent James Wells & Robert Donnell one rug a blanket 2 sheets 2 striped gowns & 1 pot & chest.
Bro-in-law: James Denney all the money George Bruce owes (have his note) my trunk sadle bags meal chest chains big wheel little wheel case of bottles churn tub pale [pail] fire dogs pot rack 2 sheets table cloth & mantle 1 pot & chains & all my yarn.
3 Sisters: Jean Hannah & Mary Donnell the remainder of my cloths not mentioned above.
Seal: Elizabeth (her x mark) Donnell
Exr: Brother-in-law James Denny
Wits: Thomas Denny (Jurat) Jno. Donnell

A:0107 pp:106/107/108 CHARLES DEER   30 Apr. 1811   Aug. Ct. 1811
Son: Bradley Deer part of a tract I live on being the South end of it. beginning at John Maxwell's branch on the West side of the track running East along Bradley's fence inclu. his improvement till it come to his meadow thence up hs meadow on the West side to the forks of the branch thence up the last prong of the branch following the meanders of sd. branch to a maple corner at a rocky fall in the branch on the East side of the track including all his improvements with a quarter of an acre in a square piece on the North side of his Spring & also another track or parcell of land I bought of Greenbury Low but not to possess it til the 1st of Nov. next, afterwards to enjoy it without any further incumbrances, likewise 1/2 of a Negro man named Phill at the death of my wife.
Son: Reuben Deer his horse & saddle & bridle 1 feather bed & furniture 1 black yearling colt 1 cow the 1st choice of the stock 1/2 of the above mentioned Negro Phill at the death of my wife 1/3 part of all the cleared and wood land not heretofore bequeathed also the other 2/3 of my plantation with houses & other apurtanances belonging thereunto at the death of my wife.
Wife: Elisabeth Deer during her natural life 2/3 of my cleared & wood land including my dwelling house & other Buildings & a Negro named Phill & a girl named Violet & likewise all the rest of my property & money & a horse I called Medley & 1 featherbed & furniture & to enjoy the same peacibly without being molested during her natural life & to make use of it as she pleases for her comfort & support.
Dau: Fanny Norman the above mentioned horse Medley & bed & such furniture as my wife sees fit to spare, & I lend to her at the death of my wife the above named Negroe Violet during her natural life.
Grandson: Charles s/o Bradley & Catherine Deer 1 bed & furniture at the death of my wife.
3 Grandsons: Joseph, Hiram & Charles Deer Norman, s/o John & Fanny Norman at the death of their mother Fanny Norman the above named Violet with all the increase that she may have after the decease of my wife to be equally divided amongst them.

AN ANNOTATED DIGEST OF WILL BOOK A, GUILFORD COUNTY, NORTH CAROLINA

3 children: Bradley Reuben Deer & Fanny Norman remainder of estate at decease of wife with the increase of Violet to be equally divided amongst each an equal part.
Seal: Charles Deer
Exrs: sons Bradly, Reuben Deer & son-in-law John Norman
Wits: William Brown (Jurat) Matthew Brown
"revokes"

A:0108 p:108 **JAMES DOAK** 8 Dec. 1805 Feb. Ct. 1806
Wife: Mary & Son: John the land & plantation I now live on with all household furiture stock of all kinds & farming tools to be sold at the discretion of my Exrs: & the profits to be laid out in the payment of my just debts & for the support of the family.
Children: Alexander McKeen & Mary his wife, Thomas Blair & Eleanor his wife, John Doak, Jean Doak, Martha Doak, William P. Doak, Robert Doak, James W. Doak my tract of land in TN on the west fork of Stones river to be equally divided amongst them, reserving to my wife the the first choice of the dividends for her use & benefit during her natural life, & the part chosen by her to be the share that my son James W. Doak is to have of the said tract of land.
Sons: John Doak, William P. Doak, James W. Doak the residue of my real estate or any right or claim I have to any land whatever, to be equally divided amongst them.
Seal: John Doak
Exrs: wife Mary & son John Doak
Wits: William Teas (Jurat) John Moore (Jurat)

A:0109 p:109 **WILLIAM DICK** 22 Jan. 1810 Nov. Ct. 1810
Wife: Rebecca all moveable effects such as household & kitchen furniture all my livestock & also the use of the plantations whereon the widows Hutchinson & Gibson live during her life.
Grandson: William Dick s/o James Dick the plantation bounded by Hance McCain on the North, by the Court House on the West, by the plantation whereon I live on the South containing 240 acres except 3 lots that have been conveyed away & including the house where Obidiah Dick kept store & running agreeably to the original deed.
Son: Samuel Dick $500 the amount of a note I have on my son Obediah Dick or in case of his death to his child/children if he has any lawflly begotton, otherwise the sd. $500 to be equally divided between my 3 sons James, Thomas & Obediah.
Son: Thomas Dick the plantation whereon I live containing about 300 acres bounded on the North by the land I have just divised to my grandson William Dick, Westwardly by Smith Moore's land & Eastwardly by land whereon the Widow Gibson now lives & including my House Barns Orchard & old plantation.
3 Sons: James Thomas & Obediah after death of wife Rebecca to sell the plantation whereon the widows Hutchinson & Gibson now live & the money arising therefrom to be equally divided.
After wife's death any personal estate left to be sold & $100 of the money I give to Polly Dick d/o my son John Dick & the residue to be equaly divided between my 3 last named sons James Thomas & Obediah.
Seal: William Dick
Exrs: sons: James Dick & Thomas Dick
Wits: Walter McCuiston Tos. *Deyhill* [?] Robert McCuiston (Jurat)

AN ANNOTATED DIGEST OF WILL BOOK A, GUILFORD COUNTY, NORTH CAROLINA

A:0110 p:110 CHARITY DILLON   9 Sept. 1797   Nov. Ct. 1811
"I, Charity Dillon, widdow of Peter Dillon..."
Son: Benoney Mills all my land & plantation & the remaining part of my goods & chattles of any kind except...
Granddau: Charity Mills 1 puter dish & 1/2 dozen puter plates.
Seal: Charity Dillon
Exrs: son Benoney Mills & friend Jonathan Hodgson
Wits: Strangeman Standley Hur* Hodgson Jesse Stanley (Jurat)
* an unusual name used in several Quaker families. JSH]

A:0111 pp:110/111 GEORGE DENNEY   29 Feb. 1816   May Ct. 1816
4 oldest sons: James Thomas George & William each $1.00.
2 Daus: Marry Ann Wilson & Peggy Denney each $1.00.
Youngest son: Alven Denney the balance of my sorrel horse to be sold & the money after paying the above 6 legatees to be put on Interest for the use of my son Alven Denney.
Wife: Rebecca all sheep & hogs to be at her desposal & all household [sic] 1 cow & calf.
Seal: Geo [George] Denny
Exrs: wife Rebecca Denney
Wits: Robt. Donnell William Denny (Jurat)
"revokes"

A:0112 p:111 ROBERT ERWIN   24 Feb. 1796   May Ct. 1796
Sons: Samuel & James the land I now live on to be equally divided betwen them.
Son: Samuel 1 bay horse to be disposed of as he shall please.
Son: George £10 after the sale money doth come in.
Wife: Mary all movable property to be sold & the notes lodged in her hands except £10 for son George.
Seal: Robt. (his x mark) Erwin
Exrs: wife Mary and William **Mumgummery** [Montgomery?]
Wits: Richard Hodson (Jurat) Rebekah Mongomery (Jurat)

A:0113 pp:112/113 ABRAHAM ENDSLEY   27 Jun. 1808   n.p.d.
Wife: Sarah 1 roan spotted mare named Spanyard 1 spotted cow 1 feather bed & furniture 1/3 part of all the puter Delph [Delft wear] knives & forks 1/3 part of the potts & ovens & wooden vessels 1 book Title Gospal Sonets 1 small Psalm book 1 flax wheel 1 large looking glass & one Japand [Japanned] sugar box during her natural life & to keep in her possession during her natural life or widowhood my home house, buildings, all household & kitchen furniture & all farming utensils not otherwise devised 1 sorrel horse called fox & as many hoggs as is sufficient for the use of the family & still & tubs wagon & gears untill the present fruit is all distilled & then they are to be sold & the money arising therefrom to pay my lawful debts.
Son: Samuel V. Endsley 180 acres of land on the South side of the plantation I live on also the 3rd part of the brandy made this year provided he distills the same and attends to saving the fruit in a diligent & carefull manner.
Son: John Endsley 180 acres of land running through the middle of my tract adj. my son Samuel on the South & a large family bible.
Son: Abraham 180 acres of land lying on the North of my plantation.

Dau: Ayls [Alice?] Nelson $1.00.
Dau: Hannah McGee $8.00 to buy her a Cardenell [cardinel, a type of short ladies cloak; think Little Red Riding Hood] JSH
Dau: Sarah Endsley 1 feather bed & furniture 1/3 part of the puter 1/3 part of the Delph ware 1/3 part of the knives & forks & 1/3 part of the pots & ovens.
Dau: Elizabeth Endsley 1 feather bed & furniture 1/3 part of the puter 1/3 part of the Delph ware, 1/3 part of the knives & forks 1/3 part of the pots & oven & 1 cow & calf.
Dau: Mahala $40 money of the United States to be paid when she come of age.
Wife: to retain in her hands the present crop that is now growing for the support of my family.
All goods & chattels not devised to be sold & the surplus of money after all just debts to be applyed as follows:
$18 for the schooling of my son Abraham Endlsey.
$12 for the schooling of son John Endlsey.
$12 for the schooling of dau: Mahaly Endsley.
Any balance to be divided between wife Sarah & sons John & Abraham & dau: Mahaly.
$8 each to be paid to my daus: Sarah & Elizabeth.
Seal: Abraham Endsley
Exrs: wife Sarah worthy friend Wyatt Peebles
Wits: Jeremiah Cunningham (Jurat) John Loney John Endsley

A:0114 pp:113/114 JOHN EUBANKS 8 Sep. 1812 Feb. Ct. 1813
Tract of land lying in Orange County to be sold by Exrs. & money applied to just debts.
Son: George the older mare Colt.
Son: John the younger colt.
Wife: Katharine balance of all estate during her natural life or widowhood.
George John Rachel & Catharine may live with their Mother until they come of age or marry & to have as much schooling as the circumstance of the family may admit of.
2 colts to be valued at the time they come of age and sd value to be allowed as part of their legacy.
at death or marriage of wife all estate to be equally divided between my 9 children: Elizabeth Richard Frances Polly Philip George John Rachel & Catharine.
Seal: John Eubanks
Exrs: Joseph McCain & James Hofman
Wits: Henry Hart (Jurat) & (*a name written in German script*)

A:0115 p:114 WILLIAM FORBIS 8 Dec. 1771 Feb. Ct. 1772
Sister: Ann Forbis the sorrel horse I bought of John Smith.
Brothers: John Forbis & Arthur Forbis the remainder of estate & lands equally divided.
Seal: William Forbis
Exrs: Brothers John & Arthur Forbis
Wits: Thos. Morgan John McClean (Jurat) & Thomas Wiley (Jurat)

AN ANNOTATED DIGEST OF WILL BOOK A, GUILFORD COUNTY, NORTH CAROLINA

A:0116   p:115   ARTHUR FORBIS   2 Jul. 1780   n.p.d.
Wife: Elizabeth the whole command of my plantation & family & them to be under her command, direction, & government during her widowhood, but if she marries then only 1/3 of my estate.
Son: John Forbis all lands of the old place together with all my land that lies on the South side of Burch Creek.
Son: Arthur Forbis the plantation I now live on at his mother's death or marriage.
4 Daus: Ann Elizabeth Mary & Marthy all movable estate together with that tract of land that I have entered if obtained to be sold and equally divided among them or among survivors of them.
Seal: Arthur Forbis
Exrs: wife Elizabeth John Forbis, Senior Thomas Wiley
Wits: Michael Burke Matthew Russell (Jurat)

A:0117   pp:115/116   THOMAS FLERE   24 Jul. 1781   Aug. Ct. 1781
"Silver Smith late of Wilmington but now in Guilford County..."
Wife: Jane Flere [elsewhere Jan & Jean] 1/2 of all my moveable estate with all debts & bonds & money with 1/2 of a house & lot in Willmington No. 42 on Front Street with 1 Negro woman named Nancy. wife to bring up daughter clear of expence till she is of age.
Dau: Judith remaining half of all my moveable estate with all debts bonds & moneys with 1/2 of a house & lot in Willmington No. 42 on Front Street with 1 Negro woman named Nancy .
Seal: Thomas Flere
Exrs: wife Jane Flere & James McCuiston Junr.
Wits: William Kennedy Ann McCuiston Thomas McCuiston.
Letters Testamentary on the estate of Thos. Flere Dec'd. filed by Thos. McCuiston (& copied) for him. [sic]
18 August 1781 at a Court of Pleas & Quarter Sessions held for Guilford County, NC... [a letter]
To Jean Flere & James McCuiston Greetings
Whereas Thomas Flere late of Guilford County is dead & hath made his last will & testament in writing a copy of which is hereunto annexed and therein appointed to aforesaid Jean Flere & James McCuiston Jur. Executors of the same --
These therefore are to impower you the said Jean Flere & James McCuiston to enter into and upon all and singular the goods & chattles rights & credits of the said Deceased & the same into your possession take wheresoever to be found and an Inventory thereof on Oath to return into the Clerks Office of said County within ninety days from the date hereof and all Just Debts to pay so far as the estate will extend or amount to Witness Thomas Henderson Clerk of ----- [Court?] the 19th day of November 1781 Thos. Henderson --.

A:0118   p:116   JOHN FIELD   12 Dec. 1787   May Ct. 1788
"farmer"
Wife: Mary the plantation containing 150 acres where I now live, 2 work mares & Tib, 3 cows during her lifetime or widowhood.
Son: William Field £5.
Dau: Elisabeth Field 15 sh & 1 cow.
Dau: Ann 15 sh & 1 cow.

Dau. Hester 15 sh & 1 cow.
Son: John Field a £3 note on John Worthenton.
Son: Thomas Field 1 horse colt named Rambo.
Son: Robert Field £1.
Son: Joseph Field 100 acres of land at the lower end next David & pay sister, Elisabeth 15.*
Son: Jeremiah Field 100 acres of land in the middle of the tract & pay sister, Ann £15.
Son: Jessey Field the plantation containing 150 acres after his mother's death or marriage & pay sister Hester £15.
Dau: Jane Janson [Johnson?] [bequest is illegible]
Mother: Elisabeth Powell [John's mother-in-law JSH] to live here during her pleasure.
Seal: John Field
Exrs: wife Mary Field & trusty brother Jeremiah Field
Wits: William Field Lideah (L) Field
*[the original will was torn and poorly mended with tape, causing loss of some words. The clerk's copy does not clarify the problem at all. There may have been more words lost in these torn parts.]JSH

   A:0119   pp.117/118 ARTHUR FORBUS   10 April 1789   Nov. Term 1790
[name also spelled Forbis, Forbes, & Forbush within the will]
Daus: Lydia Donnell   Elisabeth Forbis & Anne Forbis land to be sold & equally divided.
Dau: Elisabeth to receive a horse & saddle, 1 cow & calf, 1 bed & furniture, & her spinning wheel, & 1 pot & potwracks [pot racks] & puter evenly divided between them.
Dau: Anne a horse & sadle, 1 cow & calf, 1 bed & furniture, & her spinnig wheel, Dutch oven & potwracks & her half of the puter.
S/in/law: Hance McCain & Jennet MaCane [sic] 70 sh. to be levied out of the estate.
4 Daus: Jennet McCane, Lydia Donnell, Elizabeth & Anne Forbes to equally divide all remainder of estate. [note; the name Alise Forbus is crossed out 3 times in the original will].
Seal: Arthur Forbus
Exrs: John & Robert Rankin "my true & trusty step-sons".
Wits: Jno. Anderson (Jurat)   Henry Ross & William Gowdy (Jurat)

   A:0120   pp:118/119   WILLIAM FAIRBANKS   13 Aug. 1797   n.p.d.
Wife: Mary all household property to be peaceably enjoyed & for the raising & maintaining of my children till they come of age; the rest of my property to be disposed of by my Exrs. to be laid out in purchasing a piece of land for my wife & family during her natural life or widowhood, but if wife dies or marries before they are of age, then land to be sold and equally divided between my wife & children Viz.
Dau: Susannah
Sons: David & William.
If wife shoud be with child to me then sd. child to be equally dealt with as the rest.
Wife's Dau: Sarah to have her living free but not to have an equal division with the rest of my children.
Sister-in-Law: Sidney Spence & her son John to have their living free but not to have any divide with the rest of my children unless Sidney & son shall assist in supporting my said family.

AN ANNOTATED DIGEST OF WILL BOOK A, GUILFORD COUNTY, NORTH CAROLINA

Wife: to have my old mare for life or widowhood.
Seal: William (x) Fairbanks
Exrs: wife Mary Fairbanks and son-in-law Nathan Spence & worthy friend Ezekial Duweese.
Wits: Wm. Scott (Jurat) Ezekial Deweese Nathan (x) Spence

A:0121 pp:119/120 DANIEL FISHER 12 Nov. 1797 Feb. Ct. 1798
"planter"
Son: Molloston [sic] Fisher 100 acres out of that tract bought from Levin Wright including buildings, provided that he take into his possession...
Son: John & Dau: to teach son John to read, write and sypher to the rule of three & give him 1 horse & saddle worth £30 at the descretion of the Exec.
Dau: Sarah To be taught to read & write & 1 cow & feather bed when she reaches the age of 18 & £17 10 shillings in lieu thereof.
Son: Jonathan tract of land where I now live with outbuildings and all personal estate not already disposed of, provided that he take into his possession the Devisors 3 sons: David, Theodoris, and Nathan Fisher to teach them to read, write, and cipher to the rule of three, & give them each one a horse & saddle worth £30 when they reach the age of 21.
Sons: David & Theodoris each to receive 1 cow worth £5.
Daus: Mary & Hanner Fisher to be taken by son Jonathan to bring them up with learning to read & write at age 18 each are to receive a feather bed & cow worth £17.
Dau: Mary to have all my wife's wearing apparel, loom & saddle.
Son: Thomas Fisher 50 acres of land bought from Levin Wright located at the North end of said tract running so as to leave the buildings in my son Molloston's part. The Colt that his black mare is with foal provided it lives. If not, he is to have a horse worth £25 and some more learning & to sypher as far as the rule of three.
Seal: Daniel Fisher
Exrs: trusty friends William Starbuck & Strangeman Standley
Wits: Hezekiah Starbuck (Jurat) Michel Stanley Susannah Dillon

A:0122 p:121 DAVID FOURHAND 6 July 1802 Aug. Ct. 1802
Son: Gordin 10 shillings
Son: Garesies [?] 10 sh.
Son: Owing 10 sh.
Dau: Molley [Molly] 10 sh.
Son: John 10 sh.
Wife: Prudence 60 acres of land whereon I now live with improvments; the other 50 acres to be sold and 2 acres of the mill to be sold.
Wife: Prudence all household furniture for the use of her & my last 8 children [not named] 1 sorrel mare named Blase, all the stock of cattle, hogs & sheep & all the farming tools for her lifetime. At her death all the property to be equally divided between my last 8 children [not named] I leave 1 young sorrel mare & colt to be sold & 1 tract of land joining Hugh Sherwood of 86 acres to be sold.
Son: Thomas 1 horse colt.
Seal: David Fourhand
Exrs: Roger Kirkman Nehemiah Causey
Wits: Roddy Hannah (Jurat) David (his x mark) Swift

AN ANNOTATED DIGEST OF WILL BOOK A, GUILFORD COUNTY, NORTH CAROLINA

A:0123 pp:121/122 ELISHA FLACK   18 Jan. 1795   Nov. Ct. 1802
Bro: Elijah Flack should take special care and maintain & grant to my mother all privileges on the place that I now live on during her life. He to have 390 acres of land on the lower part of my land.
Sister: Dorcus Flack be given the value of £18 by brother Elijah.
Sister: Hannah Flack 1 gray horse & 1 feather hatt.
Bro: Andrew Flack 150 acres of the upper part of my land lying along the North and South line adj Sols [sic] Fulton.
Bro: Thomas Flack my saddle and wearing apparel.
Seal: Elisha Flack
Exr: brother James Flack
Wits: Claiborn Curtis Thomas Ross (Jurat)

A:0124 pp:122/123 JANE FLACK   15 Jan. 1802   Nov. Ct. 1802
Son: Thomas Flack 300 acres of land.
Andrew Flack's son Elisha my black horse.
Samuel Daugherty's dau: Jenny my saddle.
Dau: Jenny 2 new coverlids.
John Daughtery's dau: Polly my great pot.
Dau: Dorcas my bed & furniture.
Andrew Flack's dau: Jenny my wheel.
James Flack's son Elisha 1 cow.
Sons: Thomas & Elijah my cattle and sheep to be equally divided between them.
Remaining property to be divided among my children as he may think proper.
Seal: Jane (her x mark) Flack
Exr: James Flack
Wits: Andrew Flack (Jurat) Elijah Flack

A:0125 p:123 ROBERT FLEMING   26 Sept. 1806   Nov. Ct. 1806
"being old"
Daus: Isbel Arnett, Sarah Fleming, Mary Cox 5 sh. each
Son: Silas Fleming's heirs 5 sh.
Son: Alexander Fleming 5 sh.
Son: Robert Fleming 1/2 of my land & a mare & colt.
Son: James Fleming the other half of my land and 1 ---[?] colt & saddle & gun.
2 youngest children: Betsy Fleming and Beniah Fleming the one half the balance of estate to be equally divided between them.
Sons: Robert & James the other half to be divided between them.
Seal: Robert Fleming
Exr: Henry Brannock
Wits: William Brannock (Jurat) Benjamin Sherman
"revokes"

A:0126 p:124 JOHN FORBIS   16 Sept. 1793   Mar Ct. 1806
Wife: Mary sole management of the plantation, smith tools, her choice of a ors [horse], equal share of stock, likewise a bed & bedding & household furniture during widowhood.
Four Sons: Jeremy, William, Eli, & Jessy the smith tools to be divided between them at her death.

Four Daus: Liddy, Rebeckah, Poley & Ann household goods to be divided between them at her death.
Son: Hugh Forbis 100 acres of land lying alongside of his own land on the "Bufflow" waters.
Sons: Jeremy & William Forbis the tract of land which I formerly lived on to be equally divided between them.
Sons: Eli & Jesse Forbis the tract of land whereon I now live to be divided equally between them by a North & South line with Eli to the E end and Jessy to the W end.
Four Sons: Jeremy, William, Eli & Jessy Forbis a horse.
8 Children: Jermey, William, Eli, Jessey, Liddy, Rebeckah, Poley & Ann all remaining part of stock to be divided equally.
Daus: Poley and Ann 275 acres of land adj. Hugh Forbis' land to be equally divided between them.
Seal: John Forbis
Exrs: Hugh Forbis, Jeremy Forbis & William Forbis
Wits: Daniel McMin   Hugh Wiley   (Jurat)

A:0127   pp:125/126 JOSIAH FINLEY   21 Mar. 1801   May Ct. 1810
"being sick and weak of body..."
Wife: Alsey the plantation where on I now live, with timber necessary for the support thereof with rails & firewood for the use of Supporting her and my Children during her natural life or widowhood - 1 young bay mare 3 years old, 1 saddle & bridle, 1 chist of drawers, 2 beds & furniture, 1 black walnut table with a falling leaf & 2 milk cows, 1 Negro girl named Poll, all farming utensiles, pots, knives and forks dishes plates and all the wheels and 2 looms and all other during her natural life or widowhood.
Sons: George, James & if wife that now be with child and it is a male child also my Land containing about 370 acres Equally divided by North and South lines to them their heirs and assigns forever subject only to the 2nd paragraph in this will.
Wife: Alsey 1 Negro Garl named Poll during her natural life or widowhood.
Dau: Betsey Finley the above sd Negro Garl named Poll after the death or marriage of my wife Alsey Finley to her my sd dau. her heirs & assigns & 1 bed & furniture.
My will and desire is that all my farming utensils to go with the plantation to my wife Alsey Finley during her Natural life or Widowhood.
5 Daus: Betsey Finley Rachel Finley Lettis Finley Polley & Abigal Finley 1 cow each after my wife have her first choice, 5 dau: to choose according to age.
Dau: Abigal Finley 1 bed & furniture.
Wife: Alsey hogs for support of my family & her, pots forks dishes plates & all the wheels & 2 looms & all necessary things for housekeeping for purspos of supporting my family during her Natural Life or Widowhood.
Son: George 1 large black walnut chist [chest]
Son: James 1 pine chest.
Dau: Betsey 1 small black walnut chist & 1 spinning wheel.
Dau: Polley 1 Bible.
Dau: Abigal 1 preyer book & Harvey's Meditations.

AN ANNOTATED DIGEST OF WILL BOOK A, GUILFORD COUNTY, NORTH CAROLINA

Rest of my Books to my children Viz Bettsey George James & Lettis Finley to be equally divided between them.
Sons: George and James my wearing apparrel when Exrs: may think proper.
Remaining part of estate shall be sold at Discretion of Exrs: and Money divided amongst all the before mentioned children.
Seal: Josiah Finley
Exrs: wife Alsey   trusty friend John Cunningham [continued]
Wits: John Coe Sen'r.   George Findley   Aaron Causey

A:0128   pp:126/127   WILLIAM FIELD   24 Mar. 1815   Aug. Ct. 1815
Wife: Nancy 1/3 part of land, Negro wench named Leah for her lifetime, 1 black mare, her own saddle which she claims, 1 feather bed & furniture, 1 loom & harness, 1 flock of geese, all household & kitchen furniture except beding [sic], all hogs except 5 & all the sheep.
Dau: Jane Hanner 20 sh. to be paid 1 year ofter my death.
Son: Jeremiah 1 Negro woman named Dinah that Jesse Hanner has in his possession & 20 sh. in money.
Son: Jonathan remaining 1/3 of all the land that is now in my possession & after wife's death all the land now in my possession 1 Negro girl named Pats & the first child that Leah has after this, 1 bay horse 1 bay colt that he now claims 2 cows out of flock, 5 hogs 1 year old & all my farming utensils.
Dau: Nancy 1 Negro named Beck 2 feather beds & furniture 2 cows 1 horse & saddle worth $60 to be paid out of Jonathan's property.
Family that is with me at home: use of wagon and gears.
Balance of my property to be sold.
Seal: William Field
Exrs: wife Nancy and brother-in-law William Armfield
Wits: Nathan Armfield   (Jurat)   Jeremiah (his x mark) Field

A:0129   p:128   EDWARD GUILBIRT [GILBERT]   1 Oct. 1782 Nov. Ct. 1782
Wife: [not named] house, Negro wench name Nice & her maintenance while she remains a widow, a mare & saddle, bed & furniture, & 4 cows at her disposal.
Sons: John & William the land, remainder of horses & cattle, & plantation utensils to be equally divided between them.
Son: John the desk & liberty to distill his own grain in the still & the upper end of the land.
William: the still & to have the plantation whereon I now live & to take care of his mother.
Dau: Elizabeth the Negro Nice at death of her mother.
Grandchildren: Jean, Mary & Elizabeth -----[?]
Seal: Edward Guilbirt
Exr: Robert Marley
Wits: Robert Marley (Jurat)

A:0130   pp:128/129   WILLIAM GOWDEY   15 Nov. 1786   n.p.d.
Sons: James & William the land I live on --------? deed of 560 & 90 acres to be divided between them including all improvements.
If sons, William & John incline to learning ---- of them & the Rev. David Caldwell, William Scott & Henry Ross shall think that part of ---- collect their sufficient to pay the expense let it be done only with

promise that William shall ----- Roberts Part & Robert have his to his heirs to prevent James ? from being encumbered with a bad neighbor.
Sons: Robert & John Gowdy the ----- Russell's branch to be divided between them agreeable to quantity.
Dau: Sarah my 4 sons to pay her £20 within the term of 3 years ------- come to the full possession of the land as above of their parts sold as mentioned and of any if my sons die & have no heirs of their own that part to be divided among my children male & female.
Two sons: William & John if they decline to learning ---- of them & the Rev. David Caldwell, William Scott & Henry Ross shall think that part of ----- collect their sufficient to pay the expense let it be done only with promise [?] that William shall ----- Robert's part & Robert have his to prevent James [?] being encumbered with a bad neighbor.
Son: James to have the horse Toney.
Son: Robert to have the mare sorrel.
Dau: Elisabeth Billinsley the black mare & a cow & calf.
Dau: Sarah the mare Phinix & her saddle & the bed I sleep on.
Son: William the horse Jack.
Son: John the 2 youngest colts.
4 sons & dau: Sarah the rest of personal [property] to be divided among them only so much thereof to be --- will pay my debts & burial otherwise disturbs the rest to have ----- part laid off to them & let them separate from those that are peaceable & industrious ----- of personal estate that belongs to sons Robert & John to be sold to the best advantage ---- money reserved for their use.
Seal: William Gowdy
Exrs: James Gowdy   William Scott   Henry Ross
Wits: none found   Proven by J. Henderson   William Scott   Henry Ross
CODICIL: [no notice appears on record of the codicil accompanying the will. This will was in terrible condition]JSH

A:0131   pp:129/130   **JONATHAN GIFFORD**   17 Feb. 1793   Nov. Ct. 1793
Wife: Eunice 1/3 of personal estate & 20 acres during her widowhood. If she marries the 20 acres to be divided among son Jonathan and 2 youngest daughters.
Son: William 153 acre tract of land bought from Joshua Chadwick provided he pay my 2 daus: Sarah & Eunice £12 each to be paid in ----- [?] money or useful property that my Executors think best and most convenient.
Son: Jonathan the tract of land that I now live on (exclusive of his mother's site during her widowhood) containing 100 acres of land more or less, & a large Bible.
Both Sons: tools & wearing clothes to be equally divided between them.
Four Daus: Sarah, Eunice, Mary & Hannah to each a good ewe sheep.
All Children: residue of personal estate of what ever name or nature equally divided among them.
Seal: Jonathan Gifford
Exrs: friends William Bourland   Barnabas Coffin
Wits: Obadiah Harris   Barnabas Coffin (Jurat)   Phebe Coffin
"revokes"

A:0132   pp:131/132   **WILLIAM GRAY**   10 June 1794   Aug. Ct. 1794
Eldest Son James Gray: the land whereon he now liveth beginning at my old line 50 poles from Samuel Beeson's corner on sd line & running S 50 poles, thence E along his line 212 poles to a black oak then N 113 poles

& 1/2 to a black oak corner of the old line thence a straight course by degrees to a big rock on a branch then running down the courses of the branch to the mouth of his spring branch then up the spring branch to the old line then along the line to the beginning.
Son: William Gray 100 acres whereon he now lives according as it's laid off.
Son: Isaac 110 acres whereon he now lives as it is laid off.
Son: John 50 acres of land beginning at Abraham Cook & William Bullard's [Ballard's ?] corner black oak & running N for complement of 50 acres of land it being part of 159 acres I got from Williamson Brown.
Son: Jesse 120 acres of land whereon he now lives but not to take any land on the westering side of his spring branch.
Son: Joseph 100 acres of land as it his laid off for him.
Son: Thomas the land lying between William, Isaac & Joseph not crossing the back field branch.
Son: Samuel the remainder of my land with all my improvements after the widowhood of his mother.
Wife: [not named] her part of the land for her use & benefit for her maintenances during her widowhood with the use and benefit for her said support.
2 Daus: Elizabeth Raper & Mary Brown 5 sh. each.
Youngest Dau: Lydia when she comes of age 2 cows & calves a good feather bed & furniture & a young horse creature.
Youngest Sons: Joseph & Samuel each a cow & calf when they get married.
Seal: William Gray
Exrs: sons William and Isaac Gray
Wits: George L. Brown (Jurat) Williamson Brown (Jurat) Wm. Simmons
"revokes"

A:0133 p:132 GEORGE GULLET   14 May 1796   Aug. Ct. 1796
Grandson: Isack Jester £26 which he is already possessed of.
Dau: Nancy Smith £26 which she is possessed of.
Dau: Margaret Clifton £10 which she is possessed of.
Rest of children: [not named] are to have an equivalent sum with those that has already received. Personal & real estate to be equally divided among the hole [sic] of my children.
Seal: George (his x mark) Gullet
Exrs: Sons John & George Gullet
Wits: Aylett Buckner (Jurat) Thomas Buckner Stephen (his x mark) Huddleston
"revokes"

A:0134 p:133 CHARLES GREEN   20 March 1798   May Ct. 1798
"Know all men by these presents..."
Bro: Jehu my mare saddle bridle & all my hoggs.
Neare Cousin: John Beeson my still & all my tubs a new saddle that is in Peter Searsbuck's [Starbucks's?] hands & all my wearing clothes.
Bro: John Green & John Beeson here behind [sic] to pay all my just honest debts.
Seal: Charles Green
Exrs: John Green Jehu Beeson
Wits: Benjamin Beeson (Jurat) James Sanders (Jurat)

AN ANNOTATED DIGEST OF WILL BOOK A, GUILFORD COUNTY, NORTH CAROLINA

A:0135 pp:133/134 STEPHEN GOUGH 1 Dec. 1798 Feb. Ct. 1799
Wife: Jean 1 horse bridle & saddle cow & calf & 1/3 of all lands & moveable estate.
Son: Daniel 5 sh.
Son: James 100 acres of land where he now lives.
Son: Samuel 100 acres of land that I cleared last year.
Son: Stephen balance of my land.
Daus: Nancy & Polly each a feather bed & furniture, a cow & calf.
After willed articles are settled out of the estate, any extra money to be equally divided among children.
Seal: Stephen (his x mark) Gough
Exrs: wife Jean Gough and Thomas Kirkman
Wits: Jonathan (his x mark) Tatum (Jurat) Charles (his x mark) Spence (Jurat)
"revokes"

A:0136 pp:134/135 ROBERT GWYN 10 Sept. 1801 Nov. Ct. 1801
Wife: Rachel 1 Negro named Sali, 1 grey mare saddle & bridle, her choice of beds & bedding. My wife is with child & if a son the land is to be divided
Son: John my tract of land & 1 Negro named Luce & 1 boy named Ben.
Dau: Isbel Gwyn 1 Negro named Easter.
Dau: Nelly Gwyn 1 Negro named Grace.
Dau: Pollyley Gwyn 1 Negro named Patce.
If now my Beloved Wife is now with a son that then the Land is to be divided & if a Boy he is to have what Land lise at t'other side of Buflo
If a gal she gets non but gets a negro boy named Draper
if a boy gets said Draper, too
Also my beloved wife remains my widow she is to have the manage of the Land & negros til my childer comes of age when my son John comes of age if my wife remanes a wido still she is to have the third of all the clear land & houses during her life time if at any time she seath proper to Mary She is to get the Land & an overseer put over the negros til my childers come of age My Exrs. To put a good overseer over them I also allow my Exrs. To make a small vendue I alow them to sell the old cob mare and too bey horses, sadles & colts & the sorel colt and 2 cows & four and twenty hed of hogs & 1 negro boy named Pompey until my Debts is paid I alow my Childer to be well choold and what horses I alow my children to have a good hors and sadel when at age in witnes of I how set my hand and seal the day and year above
Seal: Robert Gwyn
Exrs: wife Rachel Gwyn John Cunningham
Wits: Patrick McGibboney (Jurat) John Cunningham (Jurat)

A:0137 pp:135/136 JOHN GILLASPIE 13 June 1806 Aug. Ct. 1806
Wife: Elizabeth Gillaspie the plantation on which we now live farming utensils Negro girl named Nance the old black mare, 2-yr old filly 4 head of horned cattle choice of flock her feather beds & furniture with all the other household & kitchen furniture & $50 in money.
Son: Daniel $300 in cash Negro woman Pat & 2 head of cattle.
Son: James S. $300 in cash bay horse called Dunc year-old bay colt 2 head of cattle.
Dau: Betsy Starrett $150 in cash & 3 head of cattle.
Dau: Anna Hannah 1 Negro woman named Mill $150 in cash 3 head of cattle.

AN ANNOTATED DIGEST OF WILL BOOK A, GUILFORD COUNTY, NORTH CAROLINA

Nephew: Rev. John Gillaspie $100 in cash.
Grandson: John s/o Daniel at death of wife to have the tract upon which I now live.
Grandson: Charles Joseph s/o James a tract of land lying on both sides of the Muddy branch & adj. the tract on which I now live.
Grandson: Alfred Hannah 100 acres of land adj the lands of John Hannah & Jessie Weatherly & the tract on which I now live.
Exrs: to sell a tract of land adj the lands of Thomas Crouch, funeral expenses & debts paid & money to be divided equally among the children.
Seal: John Gillaspie
Exrs: son James S. Gillaspie, Esqr. son-in-law John Hannah
Wits: Thomas Black (Jurat) Daniel Gillaspie Margaret Gillaspie
Codicil: whatever species of property may remain is to be at the disposal of by my Exrs. to be apportioned as is above directed.
"revokes"

A:0138 pp:136/137 JAMES GOWDY 22 Jan. 1809 May Ct. 1810
To: James Billingsley s/o Henry Billingsley and Joel Murry the tract of land I now live on to be divided as follows: to begin in the middle of the spring I now make use of & run a due North & South line from the middle of the sd. spring to the out lines of my land the West side to James Billingsley and the East side to Joel Murry.
Sister: Betsy Billingsley my white cow.
To: Rebekah Murry d/o Joel Murry one cow named Starry.
To: Rebekah Ros [Ross] d/o John Ros [Ross] my desk.
Bro: Robert Gowdy my rifle gun.
Bro: John Gowdy my watch & sleve buttons.
Sister: Sarah Anderson my large and small Bibles.
Balance of property to be sold, Exr. to appropriate $20 to the use of Thomas Wilson s/o Archibald Wilson for schooling for him and any balance to be divided amongst Henry Billilngsleys children excepting James Billing [sic] and Jean Murry as they come of age.
Wearing apparel to William Billingsley except my Regmental ---[coat?; uniform?] which I allow to James Billingsley.
Seal: James Gowdy
Exr: Hance McCain
Wits: John Thompson (Jurat) Archer (x) Wilson (Jurat)

A:0139 pp:137/138 NATHAN GLADSON 21 March 1810 August Court 1810
Wife: Ann the plantation houses & stock excepting such things hereafter disposed of to be at her disposal during her natural life.
Eldest son: Daniel 5 shillings.
Four sons: Leven Gladson, John Gladson, Joshua Gladson and Nathan Gladson all my land & improvements at their mother's death to be divided between them...
Two Daus: Minte [?] Gullett & Elizabeth Hacket moveable estate at their Mother's death.
I allow my new wagon, two horses and a quantity of whiskey and a parcel of -----[?], one bed and furniture one cow & calf to be sold to pay my debts.
Seal: Nathan Gladson
Exrs: William Killingsworth Leven Gladson
Wits: John Dinkins (Jurat) Edward Weatherly (Jurat) John Gilchrist

AN ANNOTATED DIGEST OF WILL BOOK A, GUILFORD COUNTY, NORTH CAROLINA

A:0140 pp:138/139 ROBERT GWIN   14 Nov. 1771   Feb. Court. 1772
Wife: Isabella Gwin 1/3 part of all my estate, use of land while she is unmarried & she keeping & raising all my children & Scholing them to reed the byble properly free of all charges until they arrive at the age of Sixteen years each & the whole use of all farm buildings or any she seeth proper to make --- [ink blot] [changes?] on Sd Premises During her Widow hood & may son Robert Gwyn not being of the age of -----[ink blot] but at his age of 21 years he is to have possession of his part & my beloved wife if she remains then my widow is to have the third of all the buildings & clear land during her Life time & Widowhood & if at any time She seeth proper to marige She is to Acquit the Land & it is to be Rented at the discretion of my Exrs. & sd rents to be for the Use Schooling & maintaining Each Child Alike as my Exrs. Seeth they Stand in need Until all be at the age of Sixteen & then all alike Schooled to Reed the Byble Properly if the Sed Rents will be suficient to Pay the Expence & if not, the Interest of the Remaining Part of the money of each Childs part or so much of it as is Necessary for the Aforesaid uses for --- Expended & my Exrs. [will torn]JSH
Son: Robert Gwin at age 21 to be put in possession of his part.
if my beloved wife is now with a son then then the Land is to be Divided & the Division Line is to begin on the top of A Stony ridge that is near Christian Lights house thence West across [?] the tract & my son
Robert Greer to have the North part and my youngest if a boy the other part & if a Girl she is to pay as much money to her as is remaining for each of the other 2 my daughters when she is of age by law & of my estat to be equally divided to each whern of age.
Robert Gynn Porter s/o William Porter living in the Hollow when he is of age, £5.
Son: Robert Negro Lucy when he is of age.
Wife: Negro named Grace.
Dau: Martha £50.
Bro: James Gwyn one of my best suits of apparel.
Mentions other children who have left him.
Seal: Robert Gwyn
Exrs: wife Isabel Gwyn   Henry Work
Wits: Henry Work (Jurat) William Wallace David Morrow
"revokes"

A:0141 p:140 PHILIP GLESS [GLASS]   17 Feb. 1773   May Court 1774
"farmer"
Son: George Gless the tract of land with the mill whereon he now liveth containing 260 acres.
Son: Powel [Paul] Gless the tract of land whereon he now liveth containing 160 acres.
Grandson: George Gles s/o Christen Gles deceased a tract of land on Alemance containing 200 acres formerly inhabited by Christen Gless.
Dau: Catren wife to Jacob Coble £30 currency out of a bond from my son George to me dated Feb. 17th 1773.
Dau: Barbrey £30 currency of the aforesaid bond.
Dau: Mary wife to Tobies Clap £30 currency out of a bond all to be paid when sd. bond comes due.
Dau-in-law: Philpenah Gless widow of Christen Gless the sum of 2 shillings curence [currency].

Wife: Mary Gles all ready money I have on hand, 1 bay mare called Hutch & 1 brown horse named Jack & 2 cows, and to have a free and peaseble portion of my dweling house so long as she shall live.
Son: Philip remainder of my estate real & personal only reserving 20 bushels of wheat and 100 waight of beaf & 10 lbs. shugar & 1 Baril of ----- Licquer fiveteen lbs. of flax & 20 shillings in money to be paid to my wife Mary yearly while she lives for her suport by my son Philip.
Seal: Philip (x) Gless
Exr: son Philip Gless
Wits: James Hunter (Jurat) Jacob Gobel Tobias Clap and three or four other names written in German [sic] [and who may be neighbors, close relatives, or sons-in-law. JSH]

A:0142 p:141/142/143 RALPH GORRELL 31 August 1812 May Court 1816
[Note: this unusual will is herein transcribed in its entirety with original spelling and punctuation. The preamble was standard wordage at that time. JSH]

"In the Name of God Amen I Ralph Gorrell of Guilford County in one of the United States of America Called North Carolina being a little indisposed in body, but of Sound mind & Memory thanks be given to God, calling to mind the mortality of the body & knowing that it is appointed for all men once to die, do make & ordain this my last will & testament, that is to say principally & first of all I give & recommend my soul into the hands of Almighty God that gave it, and my body I recommend to the earth, to be buried in a decent Christian burial at the discretion of my Executors, nothing doubting but at the general resurrection I shall receive the Same again by the mighty power of God, and as touching such worldly estate as it pleased God to bless me with in this life, after the payment of my Just debts which I believe are few, I give & dispose of therein the following manner & form,
first, I give & bequeath to Mary my beloved wife the whole of the Land whereon I now live together with all the farming utensils whilst my son James & two daughters live with her but should my Executors see proper & my son James be inclined to live separate from his mother I allow them to let him have one half of the land & the west end of the dwelling house his mother lives in & part of the farming utensils I also leave my Negroes Ishmael Tena Darcus Smith & Tom a child, the one fourth also of all my household furniture with my three children not yet married; I also allow my wife to have one fifth of Stock in the State bank of forty two shares belonging to me at my death, with my two sons David & James & Daughters Catherine & Margaret. I also leave & direct that all the male children Darcus a Negro woman of mine may have after my death my wife Mary may have to leave to any of my children She pleases
Item: I leave & bequeath unto my son William one hundred Dollars to discount out of the debt he owes my Estate in full for his Share.
Item: I give & bequeath unto my son David my Negro Bob and that tract of Land four hundred & fifty acres laying on both sides of South Buffaloe, joining Weatherly, Gillaspie & others,
Item: I give & bequeath unto my son Robert fifty Dollars & order my Executors to Discount what he owes me also.
Item: I give & bequeath to my Son Ralph living in Ireland that freehold & tract of Land which I purchased of my Brother Robert situate in the Kingdom of Ireland in the County of Donegall on the waters of Louck

AN ANNOTATED DIGEST OF WILL BOOK A, GUILFORD COUNTY, NORTH CAROLINA

Swolly Called the Crannock freehold named Lurgy Brack Drown Hazel and Corouch Lea as may more fully appear from the original tract & conveyance already recorded & in his possession there I also leave him, my Son Ralph fifty Guineas which I gave him when he went away last from here & order my Executors to discount his receipt with me to be in full for his legacy.

I give & bequeath unto my Son James Gorrell (after the death of his Mother) all the land adjoining me whereon I now live except such as I may give now to other legatees, the one half of the land improved & Dwelling house after he arrives of that age as my Executors may think it prudent to have it laid off in his mothers life time, should they disagree. Also my Negroes Peter Smith Hary [?] & Tom a child, also I leave him that tract of Land adjoining Greensboro containing 594 acres he allowing my Son David the privilege to cut timber of pine for building a house, also my watch, Desk & book case After the death of his Mother, with all the land She enjoyed and Negroes males & females (except the males that Darcus may have after my death), as aforesaid; he my son James dying without lawful Issue, I allow my son David & his son Ralph, to have the whole of the land & Negroes left to him.

Item: I give & bequeath unto my oldest Daughter Elizabeth Forbes a Negro girl named Hannah & five pounds in full for her legacy.

Item: I give & bequeath unto my Daughter Catharine that piece or tract of land where I lately have built a new house containing 250 acres all of which John Kerr [?] in his life time owned & all that land that lays west of it to run west from James Matthews old corner in the head of a branch or glade full of bryars, the corner being now rotten and about thirty poles S. W. of an outer field on another tract of land, to run west through that tract of land until it comes to the line of that land which a few years ago I purchased of John Doak, then to run South with that land to Doaks old tract estimated to contain 60 acres more or less, also two Negroes Bill & Lea a child, a bed & furniture her desk a horse saddle & bridle in value worth 150 dollars, three head of cattle & her one fifth Share of money my stock in the State bank as afore said with her Mother & others, all of which She & her heirs to hold & enjoy forever,

Item: I give & bequeath unto each of my two Daughters; namely Mary Maxwell & Agnes Stewart two hundred & fifty Dollars each.

Item: I give & bequeath to my Daughter Ann Tom three hundred & twenty dollars & also I order her to have 25 acres of land to be laid out of that tract by Joab Weatherlys, dividing that tract by a line N & S (Except other ways conveyed during my life) dividing that tract betwixt her & her Sister Margaret in equal parts beginning on James Ozments line and running South my Daughter Ann to have the east part to her & her heirs forever.

Item: I give & bequeath unto my youngest Daughter Margaret the remainder of that tract of land adjoining to her Sisters and Joab Weatherleys estimated to contain 250 acres, whereon the improvement is also a Negro girl named rose, her bed & furniture, a desk a horse, saddle & bridle worth at least 120 dollars three head of Cattle & her 5th part in money in the State bank with her Mother & brothers, namely David & James & Sister Catharine to her & her heirs forever.

Item: I give & bequeath unto my grand Son Ralph Gorrell Son of William that tract of land on Reedy fork Whereon his father lives conveyed to me for 300 Acres; also I allow my Executors to pay him fifty dollars.

Item: I give & bequeath my grand Son Robert Gorrell Son of Robert that tract of land I purchased in part of John Doak except what will lay South of a line to run West from Doaks as now goes north west corner whiteoak to James Ozments line; also my Negro fellow called Pomp & fifty dollars to him & his heirs forever

Item: I give & bequeath to each of my Grandchildren in America named Ralph that I have not before left a legacy namely, Ralph Forbes Robert's Ralph David's Ralph Mary Maxwell's Ralph & Agnes Steward's Ralph fifty dollars each. I also give and bequeath unto my Grandson Ralph Gorrell son of David that tract of land whereon Henry Fisher now lives containing 200 acres and a full share of the remainder of my Estate with my wife & each of my children that may be living at my death, after the sale of whatever [----- ?] whether store goods, or other & the collection of my debts; but no Sale to be made of any farming utentials or waggon Stage clothen, Saddles, books, unles my wife pleases; to be left to her to Divide as She thinks proper, Should any of my Land be left out and not be disposed of by me in my lifetime, I leave the one half of it to the first Son of my Daughter Ann Tom may have named for me the other half to my Grand daughter Mary Stewart.

I also constitute & ordain [the remainder of this line is blank] all of Guilford County to be my Executors of this my last will & testament & I do hereby utterly disallow, revoke, & disanull all & every other testaments wills legacys bequeaths and Executors by me in any wise named willed & bequeathed ratefying & confirming this & no other to be my last will and testament in Witness whereof I have hereunto Set my hand & Seal this 31st day of August in the year of our Lord one thousand eight hundred & twelve"

Signed Sealed, published pronounced & declared by the Said Ralph Gorrell as his last will & testament in the presence of us who in the presence of each other have hereto subscribed our names}

Signed: Ralph Gorrell

Exr: none named

Wits: S. [Simion] Geren J. H. Starrett, Joseph Davis

Post Script before Sealing

In my last devised Legacy where it is left to two grand children namely a male & female it is my will and pleasure that the same together with other female grand Children in America named Mary should have an Equal share of my lands not heretofore willed or sold before my Death with them two, & that my Daughter Margaret shall have one hundred and fifty acres of land adjoining her land left her to the East part of said Tract [7 words crossed out] and the ballance of Anns part which is Estimated at about one hundred & fifteen acres I leave & bequeath to my grand son John Gorrell son of my son Robert Gorrell.

P.S. the words enterlined in the sixth line, with th--n two enterlined before signed and also the words erased in the ninth line, the ballance of that after my Margaret, all done before Signed.

The 31st day of Augt. 1812   Ralph Gorrell

Wits: S. Geren (Jurat) J. H.[?] Starrett, Jo. Davis (Jurat)

State of North Carolina Guilford County} May Term 1816

The Execution of the within Will was proven in open Court by the oaths of Simeon Geren & Joseph Davis two of the Subscribing witnesses - on motion ordered to be recorded, no Executors being appointed in said will Administration with the Will annexed was Granted to David Gorrell Samuel

Thom & John Stewart who qualifyed as such accordingly. Test; John Hanner CCC [Clerk of County Court]

Mr. Hannah will first Copy the Will, & then say "And at a Court of Pleas & Quarter Sessions began and held for the County of Guilford on the third Monday of May 1816. the Said Will was proved by the Oaths of Simeon Geren & Joseph Davis the subscribing Witnesses thereto and Ordered to be recorded: and therefore Administration of the estate of the said Ralph Gorrell Deceased, with the Will aforesaid annexed, was granted to John Stuart, David Gorrell, and Samuel Tom, who entered into Bond and qualified [paper torn away here & several words missing] of the Court of Pleas & Quarter Sessions for Guilford County do hereby certify that the foregoing is a true Copy of the last Will & Testament of Ralph Gorrell, Deceased, and of the Record of its Probate and the granting of Administration with the Said Will annexed - In Testimony Whereof I have hereunto set my hand & affixed the seal of said Court this 25th October 1816 J. Hanner, by A. - Murphy.

A:0143   pp:144/145   MOSES GORDY   24 Oct. 1795   Aug. Ct. 1802
"distressed condition of body"
Wife: Eunice Gordy all my moveable estate only such exceptions as may be hereafter made and my plantation I now live with the house & improvements during her natural life or widowhood wholly to be at her disposal. If she marry I allow the house and plantation --------[sic] into the possession of my son Moses but not before he is twenty one years of age.
Eldest son: Moses 75 acres of land with the house & improvements on which I now live.
Youngest son Isaac 75 acres of land on the South of Moses land.
Daus: Elizabeth Oliphants, Nansey [Stewart?] and Priscilla Elliott no part or portion of my present estate they having received theirs already.
Dau: Polly 1 cow & 1 ewe.
Seal: Moses Gordy
Exrs: wife Eunice   John Gilchrist
Wits: Joseph Elliott   John Gilchrist   Edward McGlamery (Jurat)

A:0144   p:145   MATTHEW GRIER   13 July 1802   Aug. Ct. 1802
"of Alamance settlement Guilford County"
Wife: Mary house, 1/3 of land, 1/3 of cows, her own bed & furniture, 1/3 of all other household furniture which is to be at her own disposal at her death the land only excepted.
Son: Thomas the sum of 5 shillings.
Son-in-law: 5 shillings.
Dau: Nancy Gannon 1/3 part of my land taking in the house & improvements where she now lives to her & her heirs forever.
Dau: Eleanor the other 1/3 part of my land adjoining my dwelling; at death of wife Mary her 1/3 is to fall into the hands of Eleanor & the remainder of cows horses hogs sheep and household furniture.
Farming tools left in common for use of plantation.
Eleanor to furnish wife a horse for wife to ride.
Seal: Mathew Grier
Exrs: Thomas Hamilton of Buffloe   Thomas Grier
Wits: S. Stewart (Jurat)   Thomas Greer **"revokes"**

A:0145 P:146 CRISLEY GLESS [GLASS]   7 Dec. 1771   Feb. Ct. 1772
Wife: [not named] 3 cows, 2 mares, bed & furniture.
Son: George 100 acres of land with the improvements.
"Residue [of the land] to the other that my wife now carries; if it lives it [the land] lying in the county of Guilford"
Seal: Crisley Gless
Exrs: Wife [not named]   Peter Julian
Wits: Jacob William Davis   Jacob Coble (Jurat)   Philip (his P M mark) Mire [Wire?]   (Jurat)

A:0146 pp:146/147 SAMUEL GILCHRIST   5 March 1816   May Ct. 1816
Eldest Son: John all land on the East and North of the branch I now live on & the land upon the county road & my Negros to be equally divided between him & his brother according to their value when he arrives at the age of 21 & further I allow the paper money I have now in hand to be kept to schooling my two sons and my hard money to be kept by my Executors to be equally divided between my two sons.
Second Son: Patrick Davidson Gilchrist all my land that lies on the of the branch I live on and an equal division in all and in every thing before mentioned with his elder brother John Gilchrist that is to say all my Negroes monies and the sale of my moveable property.
N. B. I do appoint for my Executors my brother Robert Gilchrist and Thomas MacNeely to see this my last will and testatment executed.
Seal: Samuel Gilchrist
Exrs: brother Robert Gilchrist & Thomas MacNeely
Wits: Wm. Gilchrist (Jurat) Delilah (x) Heath Sarah (x) Heath

A:0147 p:147/148 JOHN HUNTER   29 Aug. 1777   Feb. Ct. 1778
Son: Edward Negros Charles, Juba, Jerepta, Moll, Fillis, Alex, Dorcas, & Fanny best of stock & household furniture during his & his wifes natural lifetime & then to be divided so that if there are any more children that their estate be made equal to the rest of the children.
Gr. Sons: John & Alexander Hunter, sons of Edward, land I now live on with the mill tract with the two old Negroes Sesar & Fame [?].
Daus: Allay Tate Elizabeth Walker to have their corn ground free at the mill.
Dau: Allay Tate Negroes Cate & Jenny & their increase.
Dau: Elizabeth Walker lends to dau: Negroes Tom, Ross, Cisley, & Isham to be given to her heirs as she thinks proper.
Gr. Son: John Hunter Walker s/o John & Elizabeth Walker 1 Negro which I formerly lent his mother.
David Walker, Joel Walker & William Walker, sons of John & Elizabeth Walker 3 Negro children in possession of John Walker Sen'r. and their increase.
Dau: Sarah May the following Negros: Lucy, Nathan, Sukey, now in her possession to bequeath as she pleases.
Sister: Jane Mackie 1 Negro girl Pheby.
Gr. Children: Robert John Elizabeth & Frances Lee 2 mulatto girls Lucy & Judy; their increase to be equally divided among them & also a debt due me from their father of £58.9.10 Virginia Currency.
Alexander Martin: one Negro boy Ben.

AN ANNOTATED DIGEST OF WILL BOOK A, GUILFORD COUNTY, NORTH CAROLINA

Exrs: to make a deed for that tract of land I received of Mr. Battlesey to whom Col. George Carrington thinks proper.
Residue of estate to children of Edward Hunter.
Seal: John Hunter
Exrs: Alexander Martin, James Martin, James Hunter John Tate & Edward Hunter
Wits: Geo. Peay (Jurat) Giles Carter (Jurat) Agnes Hoggatt

A:0148 pp:148/149 GEORGE HODGSON 5th of 6th mo. 1764 Aug. Ct. 1774
"Whereas I, George Hodgson of Center in Rowan County"*.
Wife: not named.
Son: George Hodgson 200 acres of home plantation & improvements I bought of Robert Lamb, a young Sorrel house called Sorrel, a Dark Bay mare & her colt, 2 cows & calves, both young cows of their first calves.
Sons: Robert & Joseph remainder of said tract including their improvements. Robert & Joseph to pay the cost & charges accruing upon the whole tract to obtain a deed out of the land office for the same, it being only yet entered & surveyed, Robert to pay his own part & Joseph to pay the cost for his own and George's parts. Tract of land adjoining William Ozbun be sold and money given to Robert & Joseph to pay for the deeds mentioned above.
Son: John 5 shillings.
Dau: Sarah Hiett w/o Jno. Hiett 5 shillings.
Dau: Susanna Hiett w/o William 5 shillings.
Sons: George & Joseph any remaining money from the selling of the above-mentioned tract.
Wife & Son Joseph: remaining estate to be equally divided & wife have peacable possession and benefits as long as she remains my widow.
Seal: George his (H) mark Hodgson
Exrs. "trusty friends" Robert Lamb Nathan Dicks
Wits: Thomas Wilson Jeane (her lll mark) Wilson Margaret her (x) mark Williams (Jurat)
"revokes"

*[Center was not a town but rather an area of settlement that took its name from the Quaker Monthly Meeting of that name. The area was in Rowan County at the time the will was written, but fell into Guilford when that county was erected from Rowan in 1771]

A:0149 pp:150/151 JOSEPH HINDS 14 April 1772 Aug. Ct. 1772
"yeoman"
Wife: Susanna all estate both real & personal while she remains my widow. if stock of creatures is too large for my wife to keep she may dispose of them as she shall think needful, but if she marry another man I order and it is my will she should possess my estate no longer.
Son: Joseph 5 shillings proclamation money and [another word or words that are illegible]JSH
Wife: liberty to give her daughter Ann McConnel 1 cow & calf next fall and not before.
Prudence Roberts 1 cow & calf if she lives with wife until the age of 18.
3 Sons: Simon Levi & John Hinds after wife's death or marriage all my estate both real and personal, share and share a like.

Seal: Joseph Hinds
Exrs: wife Susannah Hinds, "friend" Jeremiah Reynolds Isaac Beeson "of Guilford County"
Wits: Edward Norton (Jurat) Joseph Chamness (Jurat) John Wood **"revokes"**

  A:0150 pp:151/152 **CHRISTOPHER HUSSEY** 1st of 4th mo 1773 May Ct. 1774
"Whereas I..."
Exrs: to take out a deed for a tract of land where Samuel Hendrix now lives provided that if the same can be obtained upon an entry made by me before the Land office was shut. if said deed is obtained my Exrs. to make a deed for part thereof to Robert Hodgins Sen'r if said Robert Hodgins will pay half of all costs that have already and shall be made, otherwise my Exrs. shall be under no obligation to make a deed to the said Hodgins. It is my will that my Exrs. shall make a division line between the place whereon I live and the place where my son Stephen formerly lived in such a way as to be most profitable to both places & to make up in my son Stephens old place with an addition of the north end of the ----- [?] survey 200 acres of land. Exrs. to sell this land at a sale & take their pay out of the price for their trouble.
Remainder of the land to be equally divided in 4 parts between -
Son: Stephen Hussey & Daus: Elizabeth Comer, Naomy Cox & Anne Hodgins.
Wife: Anne 1 fether bed & furniture & 1/3 part of all the remainder of my personal estate to be divided off.
Son: Christopher 1 fether bed & furniture & remainder of my personal estate, & tract of land whereon I now live & he shall not debar my wife of the benefits of her 1/3 part during her lifetime.
Seal: Christopher Hussey
Exrs. son Stephen Hussey Solomon Cox Joseph Comer
Wits: Will Weirman (Juror) Samuel Hendrix Mary (her x mark) Hendrix
"revokes"

  A:0151 p:152 **THOMPSON HARRIS** 15 Oct. 1775 Nov. Ct. 1775
Son: Robert Harris 1/2 the land where John Sanders lives.
Son: John Harris the other half of same land.
Son: Thompson Harris 1/2 the land where I now dwell.
Son: Christopher Harris other half of same land.
Wife: Hannah Harris my stock.
Children: all the rest of my household furniture divided equally.
Seal: Thompson (his x mark) Harris
Exrs: wife Hannah Harris son Robert Harris George Vaughon
Wits: Jacob Will--, ---- Thompson John Mount (Jurat) Mary (x) Vaughon
 [note: the name of Jacob --------- in both the Clerk's copy and the original will are impossible to read, and there seems to be an additional name ------ Thompson, in the original. It may be possible to clarify this by seeing the original in the NC State Archives. JSH]

  A:0152 pp:153/154 **WILLIAM HOGGATT** 5th of 9th mo 1771 Nov. Ct. 1771
"Be it remembered..." "yeoman"
Wife: Hannah all my moveable effects both in Doors and out during her widdowhood, and the third during her natural life for the bringing up of my children.

AN ANNOTATED DIGEST OF WILL BOOK A, GUILFORD COUNTY, NORTH CAROLINA

Sons: William, Joseph, & Stephen all my moveable effects equally divided between them except what is hereafter reserved to my other children.
Sons: Joseph & Stephen 320 acres of land 1/2 to each from the South end of the survey I now live on by an East West line and afterward devided by and North and South line Joseph to have his part on the West and Stephen to have his on the East.
Son: William 300 acres of land it being the remainder of my land.
If wife marries again my son William's part of land should be let out and the profits arising therefrom to be my said son's when he is of age.
Dau: Margaret 1 horse and side saddle 1 cow & calf, 1 ewe lamb & £10 in money.
Son: John 1 horse & Saddle, 2 cows and calves, 2 ewes & lambs & £20 in money.
It is my will that case Siphence [?] West that now lives on 100 acres of land which I have lying on great Pee Dee above the mouth of Hand [?] Creek be divided among all my children.
Seal: William Hoggatt
Exrs: brother John Hoggatt, John Beals, Jr.
Wits: Michael Swaim (Jurat) Stephen Cessney [also seen as Sisney] James Land [?]

A:0153 p:154 ISAAC HILL   28 Feb. 1781   Aug. Ct. 1781
Wife: Elizabeth 1/4 part of my estate both real & personal to her own use and discretion forever.
Three Children: Sarah Hill, Richard Hill & Isaac Hill remainder of estate.
Seal: Isaac Hill
Exrs: friends Arch'd. Yarbrough, John Dabney
Wits: Susanah (her x mark) Thrift, Abraham (his x mark) Thrift. [While checking the Clerk's copy of this will against the original will, I found an Inventory of Isaac's Estate and have included it here. JSH]
"October 1st 1781   [Do = ditto]

Those who bought	Names of the items	£. Sh. d.
Ben. Parrott	3 plains	12. 6.
Colo. P. Perkins	2 do & a joiner	12.
Thomas Wilkerson	2 do Cornish do	11.
Colo. P. Perkins	3 do & 1 auger	10.
Thos. Wilkerson	3 do & 3 Chizels	13.
Colo. Perkins	4 do & 4 Guages	8.
Thos. Wilkerson	3 do & 6 Chizels & etc.	16.
Drury Pulliam	1 Glew pot, Chizel & compass screw	1. 5.
Do Do	3 iron dogs & augers	19.
Colo. Perkins	3 augers & 3 Chizels	6.6
Thos. Wilkerson	8 tapes & center Bitts & 1 stick	1. 7.
Drury Pulliam	1 tenon saw	17.
John Dabney	1 hand saw	1.14.
Colo. Perkins	1 howel 1 ro shaw 2 crozes 1 ax 1 compass	1. 1.
John Dabney	10 plain irons & steel trap	1. 4.
Arch'd. Yarbrough	1 x cutt saw file	5.6

Drury Pulliam	1 flatt rasp	4.6
John Dabney	1 flatt file	5.
Arch'd. Yarbrough	1/2 in round rasp	4.
Stephen Williamson	2 gimbletts	2.8 [continued]
William Moss	2 files	.6
John Dabney	1 flat do	5.9
Ben. Parrott	1 whet stone	2.
Colo. Perkins	1 whipsaw file	2.
Arch'd. Yarbrough	1 saw rest	3.
Colo. Perkins	1 chizel 1 file a --- compase	3.
Continued	Brought over	
Holon Sumner	3 sturrips	4.
Drury Pulliam	1 hammer & Bayonet 1 spur & etc.	9.
Arch'd. Yarbrough	a parcel of Glew	9.
Drury Pulliam	1 Rifle Barrel	1.12.
Colo. P. Perkins	1 Shott Gunn	1.0.
Ditto Ditto	1 whip Saw	4. 0.0
Arch'd. Yarbrough	1 whip saw file [no price entered]	
Colo. Perkins	1 sett Horse Phlegms	3.6
Arch'd. Yarbrough	1 Razor	11.
John Dabney	1 Razor	12.6
Hollom Sumner	1 Bay Stallion	70. 0.0
Colo. Perkins	1 Bay Gelding	62. 0.0
Thomas Wilkerson	35 # of Iron @ 17d	2.11.8

Total amt. £158.8.7 E E* amt of Sale of Isaac Hill Dec'd. 1701
List of articles sold Belonging to Estate of Isaac Hill Dec'd. & Executors [the meaning of *EE is not known]JSH

A:0154 pp:155/156 PHILIP HOGGATT 9th of 9th mo 1763 Feb. Ct. 1783
"of Deep River, Rowan County and Province of North Carolina" *
"whereas I..."
Wife: Mary to have income and priviledge of 1/2 of all my improved land & house & household furniture while she is my widow. After decease of wife all personal estate be equally distributed between my 4 youngest sons and dau: Jean.
Eldest Son: Philip Hoggatt 5 sh. to be paid by my Executors upon his giving a full Discharge against my Estate.
Second Son: David 5 sh. as above.
Dau: Jean widow of Henry Meiner £10 & my Bible.
Third Son: William 5 sh. as above.
Fourth Son: John a pair of cart wheels & a rifle gun barrel, both of which are now in his possession & 5 sh.
Fifth Son: Anthony a pot now in his possession & 5 sh.
Youngest Son: Joseph my plantation with all the land adj. which I am in possession of or have a right to, only making a reserve for the support of my wife during her life or widowhood. Also 3 heifers of 2 years old & three steers of same age & 1 steer of 3 years old, & 3 ewes, 1/2 of all my swine & 1 stallion colt named Buck.
Wife: Mary to have a mare called Sorrell & her own sadle.
Whereas I have a patent for a tract of 200 acres of land in Albemarle County in Virginia on the head of Phils creek a branch of the great Bird

AN ANNOTATED DIGEST OF WILL BOOK A, GUILFORD COUNTY, NORTH CAROLINA

[my underline.JSH] it is my will that my Execs. dispose of the same in the best manner & divide the money among my 5 last mentioned children.
Seal: Philip Hoggatt   [continued]
Exrs: 3 sons William, Anthony, & Joseph Hoggatt
Wits: Walter (his x mark) Thornburgh, Henry Thornbrugh, (Jurat), Nathan Dicks
"revokes"
Deep River was not a town, but rather an area of settlement named for both the Deep River and the Quaker Meeting of the same name. The area was in Rowan County at the time the will was made, but fell into Guilford when that county was erected in 1771. JSH

A:0155 pp:156/157 WILLIAM HAMILTON 26 May 1785 24 Feb. 1786
Wife: Mary house & plantation, tools & 1 Negro girl named Hanna, 1 negro named David & 1 named Luse, waggon, horses, 1/2 of the cattle & half of household furniture, 1 set of Smith tools during her widowhood. If she chooses to move to Cumberland [my underline JSH] to have her choise of 200 acres of my land if she remains my widow.
Brother: Thomas Hamilton's son George Hamilton the land I now live on after the marriage of his aunt Mary Hamilton, and the half of my land in Cumberland.
Sister: Joanna Griers' dau. Rebecca Grier the half of my land in Cumberland.
Brother: John Coots dau. Hannah Coots £5.
Seal: William Hamilton
Exrs: wife Mary Hamilton.
Wits: John Cluts,[Klutts] Joseph Hamilton
"revokes"
Caveat: a suit against Gawin Hamilton.

A:0156 p:157 NATHAN HIATT 6th of 10th mo 1786 20 May 1787
"farmer" "Whereas I..."
Wife: Mary Hiatt my bay mare & side saddle & bridle & 1 year old heifer with all my household furniture not herein after mentioned & all my hogs.
Son: Christopher Hiatt my thred stockings & black silk hankerchief my neck stock & buckle, plus money raised from the sale of my great coat thick cloth coat & jacket worsted & lining [linen?] coat & jacket pair of leather breeches, cotten & lining [linen ?]coat Jack coat & breeches furr hat & cotten & wool coat & all my other property...
Wife: all other wearing cloths.
Seal: Nathan Hiatt
Exrs: Uncle William Hiatt, brother-in-law Joseph Thornbrugh
Wits: Jesse Williams, Joshua Dicks, (Jurat) Asher Hiatt (Jurat)
"revokes"

A:0157 p:158 FRANCIS HARTLEY 19 Dec. 1788 August Ct. 1790
Wife: Sarah Hartley all my personal estate during her life or widowhood. At her death I give and devise into my friend Charles Bruce and his heirs my said estate of every kind.
Seal: Francis Hartley
Exrs: Charles Bruce
Wits: Jane (her x mark) Seprall [?], Purnel (his x mark) Blizard
"revokes"

AN ANNOTATED DIGEST OF WILL BOOK A, GUILFORD COUNTY, NORTH CAROLINA

A:0158 pp:158/159 PETER HARRIS   29 July 1790   Nov. Ct. 1790
Three sons: [not named], lands equally divided.
Wife: Hanna to have her living of the clear land while she remains my widow.
Stock of horses & cattle & hogs & sheep sold at the discretion of my executors and to be made use of for raising of my children.
Dau: Nelley one large bason.
Five Dau: [not named] to divide household furnishings.
Seal: Peter (his x mark) Harris
Exer: wife Hanna & George Rayl
Wits: James McMurry (Jurat) James Barham, Henry (his x Mark) Mitchell.

A:0159 pp:159/160 PATRICK HAYS   17 Aug. 1790 Nov. Ct. 1792
Wife: Rebekah all lands & household goods, etc. during her life or widowhood, then to be divided between Rubin Land & Dorcas Denny.
Son: John 5 sh.
Seal: Patrick (his x mark) Hays
Exrs: John Love
Wits: Robert Calhoon (Jurat), James Calhoon (Jurat), Alex. (his x mark) Griffin
"revokes"

A:0160 p:160 THOMAS HOULSTON   25 Sept. 1792   Feb. Ct. 1793
Wife: not named. All land & all other goods to my wife during her widowhood; if she should marry the land with two thirds of the moveables to be secured by my Executors for John, Jonathan, and Moses Stuart, sons to my wife, which estate I will shall be equally divided among said boys.
Bro: Solomon the soral horse to be delivered to him the 20th of December next.
Seal: Thomas (his x mark) Houlston
Exrs: Leven C. Charles
Wits: Bartholomew Williams (Jurat), John (his x mark) Ferguson, Jeremiah Shelly

A:0161 pp:160/161 CHRISTOPHER HIATT no date   February Term 1793
"Be it known that Christopher Hiatt of the State of North Carolina and the County of Guilford deceased leaves the following as his will viz:..."
I desire in the first place that my just debts be paid and my will and desire is that all my land be equally and properly divided into four parts for the best advantage and conveniency for four of my sons and that my son John Hiatt may have the improvement whereon I now live and I will that my dear wife Lydia Hiatt may have her maintenance with him while she remains the widow of me and I desire that my son Asher Hiatt may have the Corner whereon he now lives and there being three sons more and but two parts of land there fore it is my will that two may have the land and that Asher John and the two that have the land should make up fifty pounds to the one that has no land being supposed to be equal in value to the one part of land John ---- [?] they paying one third

AN ANNOTATED DIGEST OF WILL BOOK A, GUILFORD COUNTY, NORTH CAROLINA

and the other three an equal part of the remainder and Amos Hiatt my son being the eldest [?] of the three last mentioned is to have his Choice of the one part of land or the fifty pounds and Mordicai Hiatt the next eldest in like manner to have his choice and Christopher Hiatt my son to have the remainder Either money or land and it is my desire that my Dear Wife shall have her horse bridle and saddle during life and one large Chest and oval table and one large pot to her during her widowhood and then the oval table and pot is for my Dauther Esther Hiatt and the Chest to my Daughter Lydia Hiatt and it is my desire that my Daughter Esther should have a good feather bed and furniture and the youngest horse colt and white cow and calf and itis desire that my son Christopher Hiatt shall have the hand irons and the said Testator also desired that his wife and son Lydia Hiatt and Jehu Hiatt to be Executors this estate."
Seal: no signature
Exrs: wife Lydia Hiatt son John Hiatt
Wits: William (his x mark) Hiatt (Jurat) Jesse Evans (Jurat) Joshua Dicks (Jurat)
[this will was transcribed as written because it was too confusing to be accurately abstracted. jsh]

A:0162 pp:161/162 JACOB HOFHAINS 24 July 1793 Aug. Ct. 1793
Wife: Mary Elizabeth my dwelling house and the little yard, the spring house & still & still house with all thereunto belonging, bed & bedstead with all thereunto belonging, 1 press & all the womens close, 1 iron pot, 2 pewter basins, 6 pewter plates, one dozen spoons, 1 teakettle with cups & saucers, 1 flax hekel, the large Bible, the Farming Book, & one book called -----[unreadable] 1 riding horse or mare, a saddle & bridle, 2 cows her choice & the ready money in hand by first discharging my just debts or demands.
Son: Jacob Hofhains 150 acres of land it being the West end of my land including the improvements where I now live on these conditions paying £35 good and lawful money of North Carolina in four parts, that is the first year £5 & then £10 per year til paid, and also give of the land yearly 12 bushels of wheat & 6 bushels of corn 150 lbs. pork 50 lbs. Of beef 10 lbs. of sugar 3 gallons of molasses, 5 gallons of brandy 10 lbs. of Hackeled flax 5 lbs. of wool 1/2 lb. Of pepper 1/2 lb. Of spice 1/4 of ginger keeping and feeding the horse or mare & the 2 cows & paying the above named articles yearly & for every year during your mothers life.
Son: David Hofhains the remainder 100 acres of land it being more or less the East end of my land including the improvements where Jacob Hofhains lives now, on these conditions that the sd David Hofhains is to pay £35 good and lawful money of North Carolina to be paid in four ----[?] that is the first year £5 and then £10 until paid.
Son: Christian Hofhains £70 of good and lawful money of North Carolina to be paid by my 2 sons Jacob Hofhains and David Hofhains unto Christian Hofhains this is my will and meaning that all and every part of this my will be truly executed to give to the above named Mary Elizabeth my beloved wife and to my son Jacob H. & son David H. And son Christian Hofhains their part as it is stated to be their part and no more of my estate.
All Children: viz. Daniel, Philip, Mallena, Christina, Barbara, & Elisabeth the remainder part of estate of goods and chattels to be

equally divided by the appraisal of three free holders among my childering here named to one and each of them equal share.
Seal: Jacob Hofhains
Exrs: wife Mary Elizabeth son Daniel Hofhains
Jacob Christman John Ozeas/Osias [?]

A:0163 pp:163/164 SETH HUDDLESTONE 3rd of 7th mo 1791 Nov. Ct. 1794
"I, Seth Huddlestone..."
"yeoman"
Wife: Lydia use of all my estate until my son Jonathan arrives to lawful age, if she remains my widow. If she marry to have as a free gift one feather bed & furniture, her choice, her chest & 1 iron pot.
Son: Jonathan 1/2 my real estate to possess at age 21. He to provide suitable firewood cut at the door. All rest & residue of my estate not otherwise mentioned.
6 Daus: Sarah, Levinah, Mary, Elizabeth, Hannah & Rachel to equally divide 1/2 of my real estate at death or marriage of my widow, & to live in my dwelling house until they marry, & all indoor moveables with loom & weaving gear of all kinds.
Seal: Seth Huddlestone
Exrs: wife Lydia Huddlestone, William Beard
Wits: Philip Horney, George Mendenhall, Eliab Gardner (Jurat)
"revokes"

A:0164 p:164 JAMES HILTON 5 Aug. 1796 Aug. Ct. 1796
Wife: Mary Hilton 100 acres of land with improvements during her widowhood.
Son: Stephen the 100 acres at death or marriage of wife.
Son: Elaxander 25 acres of land where he now lives.
Sons: John, Abraham & Daus: Hannah, Priscilla & Ann Alexander 200 acres of land equally divided.
Sons: William, Peter, James £5 each.
Son: John the rifle gun
Seal: John (his x mark) Hilton
Exrs: wife Mary & Michael Wilson
Wits: John Hilton (Jurat), Hezekiah Gardner (Jurat), Michel Wilson Mary Hilton

A:0165 p:165 NAOMI HARGRAVE 14th of 4th mo 1799 May Ct. 1799
Son: Samuel & Dau: Martha all my land, money and moveable estate to be equally divided.
Other sons and daus: [not named] $1 each.
Seal: Naomi Hargrave
Exrs: son Samuel & dau: Martha
Wits: George L. Brown (Jurat) Jesse Hargrave

A:0166 pp:165/166 JOSEPH HOSKINS 24 July 1799 Aug. Ct. 1799
Wife: Hannah 1 mare & saddle, 1 feather bed & furniture, 1 cow, 1 small pot, 1 spinning wheel & $40 forever, and the use & profits of the plantation while she remains my widow & not to sell or dispose of the timber except that needed for the plantation.
Dau: Elisabeth 1 mare colt 2 years old blaze faced, 1 feather bed & furniture, 1 side saddle & bridle, 1 iron kettle, 1 spinning wheel.

AN ANNOTATED DIGEST OF WILL BOOK A, GUILFORD COUNTY, NORTH CAROLINA

Son: John 100 acres of land joining to & on the south side of Thomas White, 1 3 year old horse colt, 5 head of sheep, 1 grind stone, 1 shot gun & my riding saddle.
Dau: Hannah 1 cow, 1 tea kettle, 1 spinning wheel, & $75.
Son: Eli $300 and that he be put to a trade such as he may chose at the discretion of my Executors.
Dau: Ann Hoskins $80 & 1 large pot with hooks & pot rack & half a dozen puter plates.
Sons: Joseph & Ellis all the tract of land whereon I live to be equally divided by my Executors in the best manner for the convenience of both & that Joseph have the part including my dwelling place & each to have $52.
Dau: Mary Hoskins $100.
Seal: Joseph Hoskins
Exrs: friends Thomas White & Jesse Williams
Wits: Thos. Benbow (Jurat) Jesse Evans (Jurat) Phebe Stanley

A:0167 p:167 ARNOLD HOSKINS 10 June 1797 Nov. Ct. 1799
Wife: Elisabeth whole use & all my land during life or widdowhood. At her death or marriage whole personal estate divided equally among my heirs.
Sons: Arnold & Joseph at wife's decease or marriage land be equally divided.
Dau: Neley young black mare.
Dau: Jean 1 side saddle, 1 cow & calf, 1 bed & furniture which is called her own & 6 pewter plates.
Seal: Arnold (his o mark) Hoskins
Exrs: trusty friends John McMury James Tharp
Wits: John McMury James Tharp (Jurat)

A:0168 p:168 JOHN HENDERSON 28 March 1800 May Ct. 1800
"whereas I..."
2 Youngest Sons: Daniel & Thomas 200 acres of the tract of land I now live on including the plantation to be equally divided between them and for the support of my wife during widowhood.
Sons: John & William the remainder of my land equally.
Dau: Rebeca her mare & saddle & 1 feather bed & furniture.
Wife & 5 children: personal property be sold except 2 horse creatures for farming & equally divided between my wife & 5 children. Also the tract of land joining Harper & Bark, which is to continue on the place until she marries.
Seal: John (his x mark) Henderson
Exers: friends John Rudock Samuel M. Millican
Wits: John Murdock (Jurat) James (his x mark) Smith

A:0169 p:168 DAVID HARRIS 18th of 7th mo 1800 Nov. Ct. 1800
"I David Harris..."
Honored Father: Obediah Harris the horse, bridle & saddle I bought of him.
Sister: Elizabeth all the residue of my estate.
Seal: David Harris
Exrs: father, Obediah Harris Barnabas Coffin
Wits: Joseph Mills (Jurat) Hannah Mills Elisabeth Baldwin
"revokes"

AN ANNOTATED DIGEST OF WILL BOOK A, GUILFORD COUNTY, NORTH CAROLINA

A:0170 pp:169-170 STEPHANUS HAWORTH 16th of 4th mo 1804 May Ct. 1804
"I, Stephanus Haworth..."
Wife: Elizabeth a home or place of residence in my Dwelling house & her maintainance out of my land during her Widowhood if she require it, which my son Richard is to do or cause to be done, on receiving her above mentioned Devise, 1 mare & saddle, 1 feather bed & furniture, 4 iron pots, a Dutch oven with all my puter dishes, Delf ware & cullenary ware to be disposed of among my 3 Daus. Rachel, Jane & Hannah as she may see proper.
Dau: Rachel a saddle called her saddle & bed & furniture.
Son: Solomon an anvil which is now in his possession.
Son: Richard my tract of land whereon I live 200 acres with all farming tools, gears & implements of husbandry, a hand ax, Broad ax, adz, Drawing knife, 2 Chissles & 4 augers, 1 an inch and a quarter, 1 an inch, 1 three quarters and 1 a half, a cow, a fether bed & furniture thereto him belonging.
Dau: Jane 1 Saddle, 1 feather bed & furniture.
Dau: Phebe $1 above that what she hath already received.
Dau: Hannah 1 Saddle & 1 featherbed & furniture.
Children: Rachel, Richard, Jane & Hannah all my horses, cows, sheep & hogs etc. be sold at public vendue & the money arising therefrom to be equally divided between them.
Seal: Stephanus Haworth
Exrs: friend John Howell & son Richard Haworth
Wits: Micajah Haworth (Jurat) George Haworth (Jurat) Mary (her x mark) Haworth

A:0171 pp:170-171 JOHN HODGSON 3rd of 5th mo 1804
"Whereas I ..."
Wife: Mary the house I now live in with all the furniture of all sorts & her choice of my horse creatures & 1 cow & £15 & sufficient maintenance of the farm.
Son: Joseph all my land and working tools.
Dau: Sarah Lovet $10 or a cow worth than much money.
Rest of his living children that is alive [not named].
Seal: John (his   mark) Hodgson
Exrs: sons John & George Hodgson
Wits: Joseph Thornbrugh (Jurat) William Thornbrugh (Jurat)

A:0172 p:171 LEWIS HOLTON 27 Dec. 1800 Aug. Ct. 1805
Grandson: Lewis Rannolds [Reynolds?] $12 & 1/2.
Dau: Dinah to be supported by as much of my estate as necessary, the money being paid to the person who keeps her.
Friend: John Coe, Sr. £10.
3 Daus: Sally Cessency, [Sisney?] Nancy Rannolds [Reynolds?] & Rachel Bartley & Granddaughter Hannah Holton alias Coe all the remaining part of my personal estate.
Seal: Lewis Holton
Exrs: loving friend John Coe, Senior
Wits: James Doak William Doak, Jr. (Jurat)

A:0173 pp:172/173 CHARLES HARDIN 7 May 1806 Aug. Ct. 1807

73

AN ANNOTATED DIGEST OF WILL BOOK A, GUILFORD COUNTY, NORTH CAROLINA

Wife: Jean a mare called Nance & a saddle & her living of the plantation during her life or widowhood.
Dau: Rebecca a 1 year old sorrel colt, saddle & bridle & $50 in cash.
Son: Stewart 120 acres of land including his improvements.
Son: John 190 acres of land.
Son: Charles 190 acres of land & a young mare called Sall.
Dau: Catherine Hardin 1 year old horse colt & her saddle & bridle & $25 in cash.
Daus: Rebecca & Catherine the Chicasaw mare & what notes I have in my possession & their living off the plantation as long as they remain single.
Sons: John & Charles equal shares in a black mare called Jance to be kept on the plantation & my waggon.
All other property not mentioned I leave at the disposal of my sons --- [?] and Charles Hardin & what they think proper to give to Rebekah & Catherine Hardin.
David Pritchet [no relationship given] have $5 out of my estate if he thinks proper to go to himself before he is of age & if he stay his time out ... [would this be an apprentice?]JSH
Son-in-law: David Briggance $5.
Seal: Charles Hardin
Exrs: son John & Charles Hardin
Wits: Thomas McCulloch, Senr. Thomas McCulloch, Junr.
"revokes"

A:0174 p:173   JOHN HUNT   21 Sept. 1809   n.p.d.
Wife: Polly her maintenance of my plantation during her life or widowhood, 1 bay mare, all household furniture except 1 fether bed & furniture, 1 cow & calf & 1 sow & pigs.
3 Sons: Jacob, Stuard & William plantation I now live on to be divided equally also the --- [?] acres lying on Joseph Brittain meadow branch to be diveded in the same manner.
Dau: Sally 1 fether bed & furniture, 1 chest and 4 [?]acres of land lying on Moon's Creek joining James Harris' land on the lower.
All moveable property not willed away is to sold and the money used to Shool [sic] my fore Children Jacob & Sally & Stuard & William.
3 Sons: to be put to some trade at 19 years old if it is their desire.
Seal: John Hunt
Exrs: Jehugh Stuard Wm. Brittain
Wits: Nathan Canaday (Jurat) Hannah Hunt Henry (his + mark) Esterig
"revokes"

A:0175 pp: 174-175 GEORGE HUTTON 17 Sept. 1810   Nov. Ct. 1810
"Revoking all similar arrangments made previous to this date"...
My moveable or personal property to be sold to the Highest bidder & the neat amount to remain in the hands of Arnold Hutton as Executor.
Sd amount to be equally distributed amongst the children of the sd Arnold Hutton that is to say Mary Hutton Elizabeth Hutton William Hutton Jemima Hutton Ruthy Hutton James Hutton & Lydia Hutton as soon as the said Lydia Hutton shall arrive to the age of 18 years until when the amount is to remain with him free from the payment of any interst
as to my landed property which I suppose to be 213 acres in 2 tracts I will that my Executor or his survivor make publick sale of the same Land immediately after the afsd Lydia Hutton shall have arrived at the afsd

AN ANNOTATED DIGEST OF WILL BOOK A, GUILFORD COUNTY, NORTH CAROLINA

18 years & make an equal distribution of three amount of such sale amongst the afsd children of Arnold Hutton & until such period shall arrive my Executor the said Arnold Hutton is hereby requested to take particular Care of the same and pay the publick Taxes which may yearly become due for his Expenses in this and all other Respects in executing this my last will and Testament I wish the Court to make the proper allowance. I hereby declare this to be my last Will and Testament Revoking all others In witness Whereof I hereunto set my hand and affix my seal this 17th day of September 1810
Seal: George (his X mark) Hutton
Exer: Arnold Hutton
Wits: Sam Lindsay John Elliott (Jurat) William Grimes
"revokes"

A:0176 p:176 JOHN HARVY   2 Aug. 1811   Aug. Ct. 1811
Wife: Nanney all my land & personal estate of every kind during her natural life to dispose of as she may think proper.
Cousin: Isaac Lamb: at her decease I give & devise to him my land.
Seal: John Harvy
Exrx: wife Nanny Harvy
Wits: John Howell Samuel Lamb (Jurat) Robert Lamb (Jurat)

A:0177 p:176 WILLIAM HITCHCOCK, SENIOR 22 Aug. 1806 Aug. Ct. 1811
Wife: Hannah to pay all my lawful debts & funeral charges & all the residue of my estate to my beloved wife at her own disposal to wit -- all my horses, cattle, hogs, & sheep & all my household furniture & also my farming tools.
Seal: William (his x mark) Hitchcock
Exrx: wife Hannah Hitchcock
Wits: William Piggott (Jurat) David (his x mark) Insley

A:0178 pp:177/178 JABEZ HUNT 28th of 9th mo 1812 Feb. Ct. 1813
"Be it remembered..."
Wife: Priscilla Hunt all my estate real and personal during her widdowhood excepting only my interest in a tract of Land lately purchased by me in co-partnership with my Father Nathan Hunt from Josiah Gilbert which land I Bequeath Wholy to my Father Nathan Hunt by his paying unto my Estate $100 for the same.
At expiration of wife's widdowhood that my dau: Semira Hunt shall have all my Estate Real and Personal (excepting the Legacy to my father of the co-partnership land)
Wife: all household furniture.
If Dau: Semira Hunt die without Heirs that my Beloved Wife Priscilla Hunt enjoy 1/2 of the property belonging to my Dau: Semira during Life Excepting $25 I Bequeath to Springfield Monthly meeting for the use of the Poor and Building a Meetinghouse; and the other Part of the Legacy to my Daughter Semira.
I bequeath to my Beloved Father Nathan Hunt Except the $25 to Springfield Monthly Meeting and it is my will that there be no publick sale of my Property only at the Discretion of my Executors and Lastly I do ordain and appoint my father Nathan Hunt My father-in-law Mathew Coffin Zebulon Hunt and Phenias Albertson my Executors.
Seal: Jabez Hunt
Exrs. Father-in-law Mathew Coffin Zebulon Hunt Phenias Albertson

AN ANNOTATED DIGEST OF WILL BOOK A, GUILFORD COUNTY, NORTH CAROLINA

Wits: David Worth   Joshua Moore (Jurat)

A:0179   pp:178/179   GEORGE HODSON   1st of 1st mo 1808   Feb. Ct. 1813
"living on waters of Pole Cat [Creek]"
"Whereas I George Hodson ..."
Wife: Rachel Hodson her maintenance of my land & plantation during her widowhood. If she marries again she to receive 1 horse beast worth $40 & 1 cow and calf & her bed & furniture forever.
Daus: Phebe Ozborn, Mary Ward, Ruth Bennett, 5 sh. each.
Sons: William Hodson, George Hodson, 5 sh. each.
Dau: Susannah Hodson 1 cow or the value thereof & bed & furniture now called hers.
Dau: Rachel Hodson 1 cow or the value thereof with the bed & furniture now called hers.
Dau: Deborah Hodson 1 cow or the value thereof with the bed & furniture now called hers.
Son: Isaac Hodson 50 acres of land on the North end of my tract.
Son: Zachariah Hodson the remainder part of my land be the same less or more.
Remainder of estate to remain in the hand of my wife without any interruption or sail or other while my widdo; at her marig or death then to my Sons Isaac & Zacharia land to be at their disposal.
Seal: George (his x mark) Hodson
Exrs: sons William & Isaac Hodson
Wits: Job Worth   John (his x mark) Williams (Jurat)

A:0180   p:179   JOHN HEALY   31 Dec. 1809   Feb. Ct. 1813
Aaron Rich [no relationship stated] 150 acres of land joining Talton Johnson's land.
Wife: Phebe Healy all I possess during her life & at her death Jesse Healy is to have the home plantation, Negro Sam & Ned, corner cupboard, clock, bed & furniture.
Mary Healey: Jacob
Pheobe Healy,, to Mary Healy, Negro Mary to Phebe Healey Hugh Healeys daughter my wach & Rifle Gut to Patrick Healy, Hugh Healey $10 Dollars in money   Harry to Aaron Rich & the Ballance for Phebe my wife to do with as she sees proper, except I leave John Brown the Bay colt, sadle & Bridle.
NB If Phebe Healy should die before Jesse Healy comes of age the land & Negroes is to be let out & the money put to Jesse [?] use and like the Negroes Coming to his sisters,. [Sic]
Seal: John Healy
Exrs: none named
Wits: Manlove Horney (Jurat)   Samuel Horney

A:0181   p:180   WILLIAM HIATT   30th of 6th mo 1814   Aug. Ct. 1814
" I make & ordain what followeth..."
Wife: [not named] to have her maintenance of the land I now live on while she remains my widow & also the grain for her & the family.
Son: Aaron 55 acres of land where I now live.

3 Oldest Sons: Joel, Bennajah & Isom balance of tract adj. Amos Kersey on the waters of Deep River to be sold & money divided equally among three sons.
Dau: Rebecca 1 fether bed & furniture & 1 cow & calf.
Remainder of estate to be equally divided between my wife & my daughters. [not named]
Seal: William (his x mark) Hiatt
Exrs: sons Bennajah and Silas
Wits: Richard Williams (Jurat) Jesse Evans Samuel Kellum (Jurat)

A:0182 p:180 PHILIP HAM --- [sic] 4th mo 1814   Aug. Ct. 1814
"I Philip Ham..."
Son: Hezekiah 5 sh with what he has already received.
Son: John all the land that I now live on provided he pays & takes up a note of mine of $100 that is in the hands of Isaac Beason. I also give him 1 feather bed with common furniture & my large Bible.
Daus: Elizabeth Johnson & Ann Johnson all the residue of my estate to be equally divided among them.
Seal: Philip Ham
Exrs: son Hezekiah Ham & son-in-law William Johnson.
Wits: Barnabas Coffin Eleazer (his x mark) Hunt (Jurat)
"revokes"

A:0183 pp:181/182 JOSEPH HOGGATT 3 July 1803 Aug. Ct. 1815
"Planter"
Wife: Pheby Hoggatt a maintenance of my plantation during life or widowhood, also 1 bed & furniture. 1 mare called Snip & saddle.
Oldest Son: Stephanus Hoggatt $1.00.
Sons: Philip, Joseph, William, Nathan, & Mahlon Hoggatt $1.00.
Son: Zimri Hoggatt all the lands I now possess.
Son Isaiah Hoggatt 1/2 of the $128 & profits of that money put in the store & the other half of that money and prophets to be divided between Pheby Newby & Sarah Hoggatt
Oldest Dau: Pheby Newby 1 3-year old Heiffer.
Dau: Sarah Hoggatt 1 mare known by the name of Blaze & saddle, 1 cow & calf, 4 head of sheep & her bed and furniture.
Ballance of all household furniture & stock at the Death or Marriage of my wife to be equally divided between all my children.
Seal: Joseph (his + mark) Hoggatt
Exrs: Zimri Hoggatt Isaiah Hoggatt
Wits: Thomas Moore Samuel Hunt (Jurat)
"revokes"

A:0184 p:182 SMITH HAITH [Heath]   18 July 1805   Feb. Ct. 1816
Wife: Tabitha Haith my plantation house & moveable estate during her life or widowhood, also my stock during the said term but in case of marriage I allow my moveable estate to be equally divided between my children & I also allow my grandson Thomas Dick an equal share of the moveables.
Three Sons: Henry Heath, John Haith & Samuel Haith land divided as it now stands.
Son: John 60 acres including the improvement where he lives on the East side of the little poplar branch.

Son: Samuel 60 acres at my wife's decease or marriage including the improvement I now live on.
Son: William Haith 1 horse creature to the value of $60, also my bed & furniture.
N.B. Son: Samuel 1 horse to be given him at my death.
N.B. there is one bed in my possession which was given to my daughter Elisabeth by her grandmother which I lay no claim to nor desire it to be cancelled in my will.
Seal: Smith (his x mark) Haith
Exer: wife Tabitha Haith   John Haith
Wits: Jn. Widows   James Criswell   (Jurat)

A:0185 p:183 WILLIAM HEATH, Senior   16 Feb. 1816   Feb. Ct. 1816
Wife: Delilah my whole estate of which I am now possessed of at present.
Seal: William (his x mark) Heath
Exrs: wife Delilah   friend James Priden
Wits: Samuel Gilchrist   Robert Gilchrist   (Jurat)

A:0186 p:184 GEORGE HIATT   2 Jan.1793   Nov. Ct. 1793
"Whereas, I..."
Dau: Ruth Dicks my big iron pot & hooks.
Dau: Ursley [Ursula] Stephens my other iron pot called the middle size pot & hooks.
Granddaughters: Susannah Hiatt d/o John Hiatt, dec,d the little pot. To her sister Martha Hiatt the dutch oven.
Wife: Martha Hiatt all the rest of my estate for her to dispose of as she thinks proper.
Seal: George (his x mark) Hiatt
Exrs: Wm. Armfield, Senior   Wm. Hiatt to carry on a lawsuit depending between me and Thomas Archer
Wits: Wm. Armfield   James Wilson (Jurat)   Wm. Armfield 2nd

A:0187 p:184 JOSHUA HANES [HAINS]   21st of 7th mo 1813   Aug. Ct. 1813
"Know all men by these presents..."
Wife: Hannah use profits & income of all my estate both real and personal while she remins my widow, but in case she marries again my will is she shall then have the use of only of an equal share with my children and at the decease or marriage of my wife I give to my
Son: Joseph Hanes fivety [50] dollars.
Son: Jeremiah $10 a year for every year he takes care of and improved the plantation for his mother.
Bound Boy and Bound Girl: Jonathan Miller & Rebekah Gesford serve out their times and the requisitions of the indentures be complyed with.
I will that my buildings be repaired out of my estate as they now stand in need.
5 Sons & 2 Daus: John, Joseph, Jacob, Jobe, & Jeremiah Hanes & Elizabeth Hanes, Sarah Eddins all the remainder of my estate both real & personal equally divided among them.
Seal: none
Exrs: none
Wits: none
August Court 1813   Hezekiah Starbuck & Hannah Hains proved [the] within will in open Court and on motion admitted to record. Then came in the Executors herein appointed and qualifyed as such.

AN ANNOTATED DIGEST OF WILL BOOK A, GUILFORD COUNTY, NORTH CAROLINA

A:0188 pp:185/186 ROBERT HODSON 7th 4th mo 1813 May Ct. 1813
"I, Robert Hodson..."
Sons: Richard, Jonathan, David, Thomas, Robert, & Jesse the sum of 5 sh. each for their use & benefit.
Five Daus: Elizabeth, Rachel, Rebecca, Mary & Martha the sum of 5 sh each for their use & benefit.
Wife: Sarah all the property which I obtained with her to be at her own disposal forever, & while she lives & remains my widow she to be intitled to my house & 1/3 of the products of my land & stock.
Son: Hur & Dau: Sarah the remaining 2/3 for their use & support.
Dau: Sarah if she marries to have 1/3 of the stock & remainder of my household furniture & 1 side saddle.
Son: Hur to have the rest, with my clock & all my farming utensils, Smith tools, & 1 feather bed & furniture, 2 iron pots & an oven, my rifle gun.
Seal: Robert Hodson
Exrs: wife Sarah & William Harvey
Wits: Thomas Swain Paul Beard (Jurat)
"revokes"

A:0189 p:186 DAVID HODSON 8 Mar. 1816 May Ct. 1816
Wife: Hester house and Lands during her Natural Life & Widdowhood, 4 beds & furniture, 1 pare dressers & furniture, 4 cows & 1 calf, 2 pots and 1 dutch oven, 1 skillet, 1 flat iron, 1 shovel, 1 pr fire tongs, 8 head of hogs, 6 head of sheep, 1 horse, 1 case of bottles, 1 small chest, 1 table, 6 cheres, all the farming utentials, $50 in cash, 30 bu of corn, all the wheat in hand & all the wheat I have growing, all the Cotton & Flax, 1 Real [Reel], 1 Loom, 2 spinning wheels, 1 big wheel, 1 pare of cotton Cards, 1 pr of wool cards, 1 looking glass.
Dau: Rachel $4.
Dau. Axey [possibly Achsa] $5.
Dau: Margaret $4.
Dau: Charity $4.
Dau: Hester $30 & 1 chest.
Dau: Elizabeth $30.
2 Sons: David and Simmeon all lands to be equally divided among them. Remaining Estate to be sold and the money divided between them.
Rest of the property be sold & the money to be equally divided between my 2 sons, & the balance of Money in Hand or to collect to be Equally divided between them.
Seal: David Hodson
Exrs: wife Hester Jesse Hodson
Wits: N. Millis Joash Reynolds William (his x mark) Harvey (Jurat)

A:0190 p:187 JOHN HALL 5 Mar. 1816 May Ct. 1816
"Farmer"
Son: James all my lands, wagon & all farming tools, all clothing large bibel [Bible] & all unwilled property.
Two Daus: Agnes & Becky all their mother's wearing apearel & 3 counterpins, [a bed cover] the needle wrough one for Becky, one stencil the other white for Agnes, and 2 stands of bed curtains one for each of them, & $5 each out of my son James Hall's part.

All three children: James, Agnes, Becky the rest of my bedding and clothing to be equally divided, all my pewter, and all my stock of horses, cattle, hogs my chest and pots to be sold and equally divided amongst them. All money after my just debts are paid to be equally divided, & my books also.
Seal: John Hall   continued
Exrs: son James Hall   Robert Gillespie
Wits: John Pritchett   (Jurat)   Eli Hall   (Jurat)

A:0191 p:188 JOHN HEATH   11 Feb. 1816   May Ct. 1816
Sister: Elizabeth 1 cow & heifer only.
Wife: Charlotte all my land & moveable property during her life or widowhood, my land to be divided from the W fence of the plantation a due NS course & likewise the Westend of the same to Dau: Nancy & the East end where I now live to my Dau: Levina.
Daus: Nancy & Levina all of my moveables to be equally divided between them.
Seal: John Heath
Exrs: wife Charlotte Heath   Moses Gilchrist
Wits: Joseph Braley   William Burney (Jurat)

A:0192 p:189 SAMUEL HEATH   --- Mar. 1816   May Ct. 1816
Wife: Jestin Heath my plantation & my moveable estate during her natural life or widowhood.
Son: John Heath my land & plantation when he arrives at the age of 21, but as his mother is now pregnant and if it should be a son, I allow him to have half of my land.
3 Daus: Mary Sarah & Kesiah an equal divide of all my moveable property at their mother's death or marriage. If the child be a girl it is to have an equal share with its sisters.
Bro: Ralph Heath all my Smith tools.
Seal: Samuel (his x mark) Heath
Exer: wife Jestin Heth   brother Ralph Heath
Wits: Robert (his x mark) Heath (Jurat)   Delilah (her x mark) Heath   John Gilchrist

A:0193 p:189 JACOB HEATH   22 Mar. 1816   May Ct. 1816
Wife: Mary all moveable property with my plantation during her natural life or widowhood and the care of her father & mother I commit to her also.
Eldest Son: Samuel the land he now lives on.
Two Sons: Robert Heath & Ralph Heath the tract of land whereon they now live to be equally divided between them & to pay their brother Samuel Heath $50 each one of them.
Eldest Dau: Ede Pilkington $300.
Daus: Keziah Heath & Rebekah Heath $300 each, to be given to them at their mother's decease or marriage or sooner if their mother pleases to do it.
If estate should not be sufficient to afford them $300 apiece they must put up with less but each to receive an equal share.
All children if estate should amount to more it is to be equally divided between them.
Seal: Jacob (his x mark) Heath
Exrs: wife Mary Heath   son Ralph Heath

Wits: Delilah (her x mark) Heath (Jurat)   Levin Woollen   John Woollen
John Gilchrist

A:0194 p:190 LODWICK ISLEY, JUNIOR 26 July 1788 n.p.d.
Wife: Elizabeth all estate real & personal during her woodyhood [sic] or till my oldes chald comes to lawful age & then I order my estate to be Ekule [equal] & pay them as they come of age but if my wife should marry before any of them come of age I order a Vandue [vendue] to be ------ and all my Estate sold off and to give my wife the third part of my Estate & the Remainder to be devided among my Chaldren [not named]
Seal: Lodweek (his LE mark) Isley
Exrs: Peter Summers Christian Isley
Wits: Andrew Gibson Palliser (his E mark) Isley (Jurat) & a signature in German [sic]

A:0195 pp:191/192 GEORGE INGLE, SENIOR 17 Sept. 1797 Feb. Ct. 1801
Wife: Margaret 159 acres of land it being the lower part of my old tract during her widowhood. At her death or remarriage to revert to youngest son Adam.
Wife: all money on hand 2 horses 2 cows 2 head of sheep all stock of Hoggs & farming instruments 1 bed & furniture & wagon 6 pewter plates 6 knives 6 forks 2 iron pots & other kitchen furniture.
Eldest Son: Barnabas tract of land on which he now lives 200 acres.
Sons: George & John a tract of land lying on the South & East sides of the old tract on which I now live 108 acres with saw & grist mills.
Son: Jacob 100 acres to be struck off the upper part of my old tract.
Son: Ludwick tract of 165 acres the right to which is now disputed. Should land be taken away by an Older claim, then each heir to pay Ludwick enough to make his part of my estate equal to the others.
3 Daus: Philpena Lovena & Sophia each, 2 cows & calves, 2 sheep, 1 bed & furniture, 1 chest, 2 iron pots, 1 frying pann, 1 spinning wheel, 2 pewter dishes, 6 pewter plates, 6 common pewter spoons.
Dau: Margaret, wife to ------ Christo [sic] £5.
Dau: Matlena £5.
Granddaughter: Eve Swing, d/o my dau. Barbary Swing deceased £5 paid in cash to her father George Swing.
Daus: Catherine Huffman w/o John Huffman, Mary Clapp w/o John Clapp, Christina Fipps w/o Aaron Fipps, Turley [Dorothea] Greeson w/o Isaac Greeson, Philipena, Lovena & Sophia residue of estate.
Seal: George (H) Ingle
Exrs: wife Margaret old Friend Jacob Coble, Sr.
Wits: Sam'l. Lindsay (Jurat) Jacob Clerk [?] & (a signature in German) [sic]

A:0196 pp:193/194 THOMAS JENKINS 18th of 3rd 1770 Nov. Ct. 1771
"yeoman"
Wife: Lettis [Lettice?] 1/3 part of all my estate goods & chattels & her bed & furniture & her wearing clothes.
Son: Hur remaining part of estate.

AN ANNOTATED DIGEST OF WILL BOOK A, GUILFORD COUNTY, NORTH CAROLINA

Children: Ann Smith, David Jenkins, Martha Cox, & Thomas Jenkins, 1 shilling each.
Son: John Jenkins all remaining part of my estate.
Seal: Thomas (his x mark) Jenkins
Exrs: sons John Jenkins Thomas Jenkins
Wits: Joseph Ozbun Samuel Ozbun (Jurat)
"revokes"

A:0197 p:194 MICHAEL JORDAN   8 Mar. 1775   May Ct. 1775
"Innholder"
Wife: Mary her heirs & assigns forever a house & lot in Wilmington, improvement & house in Guilford County near the Court House, money stock, furniture, goods & chattles & all estate real & personal.
Seal: Michael Jordan
Exrs: wife Mary
Wits: Waightstill Avery, Esqr. (Jurat) Robert Archibald Robt. Agnew Jacob Mayer
"revokes"

A:0198 pp:195/196 ALEXANDER JOYCE   3 Mar. 1778   May Ct. 1778
Wife: Jane Joyce lend [sic] of three Negroes; Ned, Sue & Pegg, 240 acres of land including the plantation whereon I now live to be laid off in the NE corner runing down the river & out to the line which land my son Robert to have when he arrives at full age & 2 Negroes to wit: Harry & Cate & £1.
2 children belonging to the Negroe Pegg to be lent to my wife Jane be kept & enjoyed by my said wife & all the future increase of both Negroes lent as also all their increase be sold & the money arising from the sale be equally divided amongst all my sons which shall at home be living. Also 1 black mare called Tibb & saddle & bridle. Also a still & its belongings jointly occupied with son Elijah.
Son: Thomas £10
Son: Joseph £100
Son: John 526 acres of land lying in Pittsylvania County in VA on Sandy River, also Negros Dick & Jenny
Son: James 1 Negroe man named Will & £100
Son: Elijah 200 acres of land to be laid off in the SW corner of the land I now live on running down the river & 1 Negroe woman named Hagar.
Son: Alexander £100 & 1 Negroe boy named Ceasar.
Son: Elisha 1 entry or tract of land including the mill, 1 Negroe woman named Jude & £100, & 1 horse saddle & bridle.
Son: Andrew 200 acres of land part of the tract I now live on the lower end lying on both sides the river, 1 Negroe boy named Sam & £100 & 1 horse saddle & bridle.
Dau: Sarah 1 Negroe woman named Nan, her increase & £10 & 2 cows now in her possession.
Dau: Margarett 1 Negroe girl named Amy, 1 horse & saddle, 1 bed & furniture & 1 spinning wheel.
Dau: Esther 1 Negroe girl named Dinah, 1 horse & saddle 1 bed & furniture 1 spinning wheel.
Dau: Elizabeth 1 Negroe named Jenny, 1 horse & saddle 1 bed & furniture & 1 spinning wheel.

Dau: Mary 2 Negroes Jacob & Agnis 1 horse & saddle 1 bed & furniture & 1 spinning wheel.
Wife: Jane & Son: Elijah my still & whatever is thereunto belonging to them jointly.
All residue of my estate of every kind not herein devised be sold at public auction by my Executors & the money arising from the sale (after reserving £100 thereof for the education of my little children: Elisha, Andrew, Robert, Margarett, Elizabeth & Mary) be equally divided amongst my sons: John, James, Elijah, Alexander, Elisha, Andrew & Robert Joyce.
Seal: Alexander Vernon (Joyce) [sic]
Exrs: son Thomas Joyce Elijah Joyce trusty friend Patrick Hamilton
Wits: James Holderness Charles Gates (Jurat) James Vernon (Jurat) Alexander Smith
"revokes"

A:0199 p:197 PLEASANT JOHNSON   8 June 1787   n.p.d.
Wife: Elizabeth all & every part of any real & personal estate during widowhood for to raise my children, if wife should marry, then to be sold & the money set out on interest & equally divided among my surviving children [not named] as each comes of age.
Seal: Pleasant (his x mark) Johnson
Exrs: Claiborn Curtis
Wits: Joel Johnson (Jurat) Nicholas (his x mark) Smith Mary (her x mark) House
"revokes"

A:0200 p:197 JAMES JACKSON   24 Mar. 1785   May Ct. 1789
Sons: 2 eldest James & David all my estate to be equally divided between them at or after my decease.
Son: Gabril, youngest son 100 acres of land whereon he now lives except such a part of my estate as will discharge any just debts & funeral expenses.
Seal: James Jackson
Exrs: William Armfield s/o Isaac Armfield Joseph Thornburg, Jr. [?]
Wits: William Armfield (Jurat) John Armfield Nathan Armfield (Jurat)

A:0201 p:198 WILLIAM JACKSON   1 Oct. 1792   Nov. Ct. 1792
Son: Andrew Jackson to him & his heirs all real & personal estate of lands, horses, chattels & hogs & all other moveables & things.
Wife: Margaret if she lives after me shall be keeped & maintained by my said son, Andrew, as long as she lives, & to live with him, & the charges of her & my funerals to be discharged by my son Andrew.
Son-in-law: Joseph Summers 10 sh to be paid out of the estate by my son Andrew Jackson.
Seal: William (his x mark) Jackson
Exrs: George Wilson, Esqr.
Wits: James Willson (Jurat) Mary (her x mark) Ross (Jurat)

A:0202 p:199 ALEXANDER JOHNSON   23 Dec. 1790   Nov. Ct. 1793
Dau: Elizabeth Johnson 8 head of cattle, 4 cows, 2 heffers & 2 calves which is her own claim, 8 head of sheep, 1 cow of my claim named Bless, 1 mare called Bonney & her colt.
Son: John Johnson 1 guinea [money].

AN ANNOTATED DIGEST OF WILL BOOK A, GUILFORD COUNTY, NORTH CAROLINA

Dau: Mary Johnson my own bed & furniture & 1 mare colt that came of Pol [Pol is the name of the mare that foaled the colt]JSH
Son: Thomas Johnson 1 guinea [money].
Dau: Sarah Johnson $1.
Dau: Margarett Beard 1/2 Joe [money].
Dau: Agnes Alexander $1.
Dau: Jennett Johnson 2 cows & 1 calf that she claimed & 1 two year old Heffer [sic] of my claim and 7 head of sheep & 1 mare called Fly.
Dau: Esbell [Isabel?] Johnson 2 cows & 1 calf of her claim, my cow Daisy & 9 head of sheep & my roan colt called Jack.
Son: George 2 mares, 1 horse colt of his own claim & my dwelling, plantation 1 waggon & gears & all plantation using tools 1 cow & calf of his own claim 4 head of sheep & 1 cow of my claim called Gentle & is to pay my 3 daus: Elizabeth, Jennett, & Esebell Johnson £15 each as he can raise it. Also my saddle to be kept for my gran[d]son to ride on long as he stays with him.
Grandson: Joseph Alexander 1 heffer calf.
Other: my desire is that 4 steers & all my hogs and all household furniture should be for the use of the house as long as my 4 children lives together and if they part to be equally divided between Elizabeth, Jennett, Esebell & George Johnson.
Seal: Alexander (his   mark) Johnson
Exrs: son George Johnson
Wits: Daniel Sherwood (Jurat) John Stephenson (Jurat) Samuel Sherman [?]
"revokes"

A:0203   pp:200/201   GEORGE JAMISON   21 March 1794   Aug. Ct. 1796
Wife: Elisabeth 100 acres of land lying & being in the County of Guilford for her life, likewise all other goods & chattles to her & at her disposal at my decease.
Seal: George Jamison
Exrs: wife Elizabeth Jamison   friends Joseph Hiatt   James Dunning [?]
Wits: Joseph Pearce   Silas Pearce (Jurat)   Joseph Hiatt   James Deviney

A:0204   p:201   DAVID JACKSON   7 April 1800   May Ct. 1800
Bro: James Jackson 1 brown cow or the value thereof in money.
Bro: Gabrel Jackson 1 dark brown mare (which he received some years ago as a lone [loan], which I have not yet received nor any value for her) & $5 in cash.
Bro: Gabrel's son Joseph Jackson 1/2 of the tract of land I now live upon & that to be laid off at the descretion of my Exrs.
Bro: Gabrel's son David (if any such should be named previous to the date of this my will), the other half of the tract of land with as much of the improvement as the Exrs: think most advisable.
David Jackson (if any such there is) the 1/2 of all my stock of horses, cows, sheep & hogs - and if there should not be any of my Brother Gabrel's children named David the land and stock which he the said David was to possess shall be equaly divided among by brother Gabrel's children.
Remainder of all estate to be divided among my bro: Gabrel's children as my Exrs. think most advisable for the benefit of the children.
Seal: David Jackson

AN ANNOTATED DIGEST OF WILL BOOK A, GUILFORD COUNTY, NORTH CAROLINA

Exrs: Maj. Patrick McGibbony   Daniel Gillaspie
Wits: William (his mark) Jenkins   Col. Daniel Gallispie (Jurat)   Patrick McGibony (Jurat)
"revokes"

A:0205 p:202 WILLIAM JACKSON   16 Sept. 1804   Nov. Ct. 1804
Wife: Sarah all my stock & household furniture during her life & at her death all to my son John.
Son: Joseph a certain piece of land beginning at Elijah Manship SE corner running North 50 poles then turning & running East to Joseph Jackson own line.
Son: John Executor of this my last will & testament & all the rest of my lands messuages & tenements be him freely to be possessed & enjoyed.
Seal: William Jackson
Exrs: son John Jackson
Wits: James Fraizer   Nickoson Millia (Jurat)   Andrew Williams
"revokes"

A:0206 p:203 JAMES JOHNSON   11th of 7th mo 1800   May Ct. 1809
"I, James Johnson..."
Sons: Joshua & Caleb Johnson wearing apparel, wagon & all necessary implements thereto belonging & crosscut saw be equally divided between them.
Son: Solomon $10.
Son-in-law: John Beals & his wife Susanna my cutting boxes, duch [Dutch] knife & 10 sh currency.
Heirs of Dau: Margaret Clark 10 sh currency.
Heirs of Dau: Eleanor Williams 10 sh currency.
5 Children: Joshua Johnson, Caleb Johnson, Sarah Whickersham, Hannah Howell & Mary Hiatt residue of estate not otherwise disposed of, all book debts, notes & bonds be sold and the money equally divided among them.
Seal: James Johnson
Exrs: worthy friends Caleb Johnson   Allen Unthank   John Howell
Wits: Robert Brattain (Jurat)   Joseph D. Barnett (Jurat)   Reuben (his x mark) Beard

A:0207 p:204 EPHRAIM JENKINS   2 Sept. 1811   Nov. Ct. 1811
All estate to loving friend Hans Pettersen.
Seal: Ephraim (his x mark) Jenkins
Exrs: Hance Petersen
Wits: Jos Gibson (Jurat)   William Ray

A:0208 pp:205/206 JAMES KIRKMAN   24 March 1790   May Ct. 1791
Son: George Kirkman 1 cow & calf in full part of his portion.
Son: William Kirkman in tread/trade [?] in full part of his portion.
Son: Elijah Kirkman 1 Negro Boy named Charles in full part of his portion.

AN ANNOTATED DIGEST OF WILL BOOK A, GUILFORD COUNTY, NORTH CAROLINA

Son: Elisha Kirkman 1 Negro Boy named Daniel in full part of his portion.
Daughter: Mary Hendrick's son James Hendricks 60 acres of land it being part of a parcel of land purchased of William Dick lying to the East of John Forbises black jack corner & joining with sd Forbises land, 1 Negro girl named Senah & sd land and Negro to be in "possetion " of the sd Mary Hendrick during her life and then to be delivered to the sd James Hendricks her son & £20 in tread/trade [?] to her in full part of her portion.
Sons: Thomas Sherwood Kirkman & Rodjer Kirkman all that tract of land whereon I now dwell containing 400 acres, likewise 100 acres joining the same tract purchased of William Dick to be equally divided between them share & share alike land & premises, all money after my just debts & funeral charges are paid equally divided, all the rest of the Negros & the reminder of estate after their mother's death.
Son: Thomas Sherwood Kirkman 1 Negro man named Isaac, 1 horse & feather bed.
Son: Rodger Kirkman 1 Negro boy, 1 horse, & 1 feather bed with furniture to them both.
Wife: Mary the dwelling house & the third part of the cleared land with firewood and real timber sufficient to support her during her life.
Seal: James Kirkman
Exrs: wife Mary Kirkman   Hendnay Hendricks   Robert Hanna
Wits: John Forbis (Jurat) Daniel McMuir (Jurat) Catherene (her mark) Ludenum (Jurat)

A:0209 p:207 **PETER KIRKMAN**   23 Nov. 1800   Feb. Ct. 1801
Wife: mare & saddle 2 cows & her own bed & furniture, use of plantation for the support of her and my children so long as she remains a widow or until the boys come of age.
Dau: Sarah my other Bed & furniture, desk & $20 in money.
Wife & Dau: remainder of household furniture to be equally divided between them when she comes of age.
2 Eldest Sons: John & George the plantation whereon I now live.
Other 2 sons: William & Peter the remainder of estate to be equally divided between them.
Seal: Peter Kirkman
Exrs: brother William Kirkman   wife Eleanor
Wits: W. Jackson (Jurat) James Millis William Adams (Jurat)

A:0210 pp:207/208 **DAVID KERR**   19 Nov. 1802   May Ct. 1804
Wife: Catherine dwelling house and all the household furniture, a Negro woman named Sall & her 2 children, her choice of all my stock of horses or mares, her saddle, 2 cows, 10 bu. of grain her choice of each every year during her life, the animals to be kept on the plantation, & the sd. Negro woman, Sall, & her 2 children & animals to be at her disposal at her death as she shall think proper.
Son: William Kerr the plantation where I now live, all working tools and $100.
Sons-in-law: Ralph Gorrell, John Tom, David Wiley, Thomas Brown, William Wiley, & George Donnell $100 each.

AN ANNOTATED DIGEST OF WILL BOOK A, GUILFORD COUNTY, NORTH CAROLINA

After each legetee [sic] is discharged according to what I have above mentioned, my wife is to have the disposal of it as she thinks most proper and equitable.
Seal: David Kerr
Exrs: wife Catherine Kerr, Ralph Gorrell John Tom
Wits: George Donnell   Thomas Wiley   John Thom   (Jurat) William Wiley (Jurat)
"revokes"

A:0211 p:209 JOHN KILLAM, SENIOR   29 Sept. 1804   Aug. Ct. 1805
Sons: Custus & Samuel all lands to be equally divided between them; Custus to have the lower part & Samuel the upper part.
Son: Henry & if either of these my two sons should dye without lawfull heir his part of said land to fall to my son Henry Kilam & the colt that my mare is with.
Sons:& Daus: Custus, Samuel, Elisabeth, & Ester my 4 feather beds.
10 children: residue of estate to be equally divided among Joshuway Kellam, Shadrick Killam, John Kellam, John Tumbleston, [sic] Sary Oaks, Ester Killam, Elisabeth Killam, Henry Killam, Custus Kellam, Samuel Killam.
Seal: John Killam
Exrs: son John Purnel Kellum
Wits: Henry Potter, (Jurat) Mary Potter (Jurat) Zadock Potter (Jurat)
"revokes"

A:0212 p:210 ELIZABETH KERR   9 Sept. 1809   n.p.d
Dau: Margaret Kerr 1 bed & furniture, 1 pine chest, 6 delf plates, 1 woman's saddle, & crop of cotton now growing to be divided between her & the rest of her younger sisters.
Son: David Kerr 1 horse colt, half the crop of corn now growing & all fodder & 1 gun.
Dau: Isbell Kerr 1 bed & furniture.
Son: James Kerr 10 sh.
Dau: Mary Ross 10 sh.
Daus: & Son: Catharine Kerr & Elizabeth Kerr & William Kerr all the rest of property to be sold to pay my just debts; any balance is left to be divided between them.
Seal: Elizabeth Kerr
Exrs: John Whorton [Wharton]
Wits: Andy Weatherly (Jurat)

A:0213 pp:210/211 ABEL KNIGHT   9th month 1804   May Ct. 1810
"I, Abel Knight..."
Son: Abel Knight 125 acres of land lying at the SW corner of my tract, the sd. land not to come to farther that the brink of hill above the Great Road for complement.
Grandson: Samuel Knight 100 acres of land lying in the SE corner of my tract which is already run off.
Eldest Son: Thomas Knight the plantation of which I now live and all reminder part of land & my will is also that I shall have the house I

now dwell in & I appoint my son Thomas Knight "to support me with what is needful during life"
Son: Jonathan Knight: £60 in lew of land.
Seal: Abel Knight
Exrs: grandson, Abel Knight son of Thomas Knight & William Hunt son of William Hunt Deceased.
Wits: Joel Hiatt   Andrew Knight (Jurat) "affirmed"

A:0214   pp:211/212 CATHERINE KERR   25 July 1807   May Ct. 1816
"widow & relict of David Kerr, deceased"
Son: William Kerr $50. William's dau: Kettren to have my little neggro winch caled Gillet. If it should please God to call of Kettren by death before she is of age then I leave Gilet to his daughter Jean.
Son-in-law: Ralph Gorral & his wife Marey my bed with the furniture belonging to it and to their dau: Kettren my little Negro winch called Eals.
Son-in-law: John Thom & his wife Ellenor my Negro winch called Sal & 1 cow now in their possession.
Son-in-law: William Willey & his wife Ann little Neggro winch called Rous & 2 cows now in their possession.
Son-in-law: Daved Willey $20.
Son: John Kerr's heirs $10.
Son: Daved Kerr's heirs $10 & his son Daved Kerr $50.
Son-in-law: Thomas Brown & his wife Agnes $50.
Son-in-law: George Donnal & his wife Isabella $50.
Son: William & all my daus: any money belonging to my estate after paying off the sums mentioned above to be equally divided.
All Daus: my wearing clothes to be equally divided.
Seal: Catherine   (her x mark) Kerr
Exrs: Ralph Gorrell   John Thom
Wits: William Wiley   John Thom   (Jurat)
"revokes"

A:0215   pp:212/213 WILLIAM LOMAX   4 August 1772   Feb. Ct. 1773
"carpenter"
Wife: Ann 1 feather bed & furniture, 1 pewter dish, 1 pewter bason, 6 plates, 1 pot, 1 frying pan, 6 spoons, 1 cow & calf.
Son: William half my working tools.
Dau: Ann Harrington 1 heifer called Pretty.
Son: Thomas 1 cow & calf and half my working tools.
Son: Terrence 1 roan horse & colt & £3 in money.
Wife: Ann 1/3 estate, 2/3 between Robert Lomax, James Lomax, & Elizabeth Lomax, my sons & dau.
Likewise if my Sons: Robert & James will not live with their brother I do will & order that the Exers: bind them to some trade till they arive at the full age of 21 years.
Seal: Wm Lomax
Exrs: wife Anne & son Thomas Lomax
Wits: Samuel McCracken (Jurat)   Samuel Cowan   (Jurat)
"revokes"

AN ANNOTATED DIGEST OF WILL BOOK A, GUILFORD COUNTY, NORTH CAROLINA

A:0216   p:213   SAM'L LORIMER   [date of will not given]   May Ct. 1774
doctor's charges and funerall charges to be taken out and the remander to be devided as I may think proper.
Two oldest boyes named James & Hugh land equally divided between them.
Wife: Mary to have a child's share of all moveable goods & her lifetime on the land if she do not marry but still an equal devid with the fore youngest childering. [not named]
Seal: Sam'l. Lorimer
Exrs: wife Mary Lorimer & son Hugh Lorimer
Wits: John Nelson   (Jurat)   Alex'd. McKeen

A:0217   p:214   PHILLIP LEWIS   25 May 1797   Aug. Ct. 1797
Wife: Mary Elizabeth 1/3 of my land at her choice as long as she liveth & after her death it is to fall to son Phillip Lewis.
Dau: Barbary my wife to endeavor to pay her as much as one of the others receive for their portion.
Son: Phillip Lewis 2/3 of my land to enjoy at his choice & after the death of his mother he is to enjoy all of the land.
Seal: Phillip (his x mark) Lewis
Exrs: wife Mary Elisabeth & John Swisher
Wits: John Starr   Jacob Swisher   (Jurat)   Joseph Winegardner (Jurat)
"revokes"

A:0218   p:215   JOHN LAKEY [LACKEY]   19 Jan. 1794   Feb. Ct. 1794
"sickly condition"
Wife Rachel dispose all and singular whole estate goods & chattles
After her death to leave it in such manner to my children that is my own children to be equally divided amongst them.
Seal: John Lakey
Exrs. Wfie Rachel Lakey and son William Lakey
Wits: William Byfords (Jurat)   Hezekiah Wheeler   (Jurat)   Quillar (his x mark) Byfords   Isaac (his x mark)   Freer/Frees [?]

A:0219   pp:215/216   DAVID LOW   17 May 1787   Nov. Ct. 1794
I will & have positively given to my sone Samuel a deed for 250 acres excepting 5 acres which I give to the Meeting House [Lows Lutheran Church] which stands on sd tract of land & value sd Land to £300 & the Negro [w]inch which I value to £100 & I Exipt in the Hous -ether ---[?] Son Samuel now Lives the Little Rume [Room] in the corner where the Little Chemly [chimney] is too [toward] the Sun Rice [Rise] with the Rumes [Romes] above and below as long as I live or any year five shillings from the time I from the time I [sic] moved out of the Hous & I except all my Housen Goods wich hed [had] not ben [been] Sold or weld [willed] at the time when I moved from sd Hous & I will and order that my Sone Samuel is to give his Sester [sister] Lesabeth £100 lawful money out of the Estate which I have given to him for I have given my Doughter Lesabeth only 50 acres Land & pd £25 todes [?] Land & 1 ould Negro Linch [wench?] wich I valued to £40 & I will and order that my Doughter Eve shall have to her Heirs & assigns 100 acres of Land from the tract where I now Leves on along the South Side With the Medew [meadow] that Leys [lies] on the Waders [waters] that Runs into Stinking Quarter and I will

& order that my Son Cunrod is to maintain my wife after my death if alive without any Lawful Complaint & he shall have for him & his Heirs & assigns 200 acres of sd tract on the North Side with medow & Imbrovement wich Lay on the Waders that makes [flows] in to Bever Kreek wich is my ould quarter & I will & order that after mine and my Wife Death my Estate What is left be Equal Devi amongst my 2 children Eve and Cunrod and I do apint [appoint] my beloved Nibuers [neighbors] Adam Starr and Jacob Clapp Executors of this my Last Will & Testatment to see avry thing Equilly Devidet amongst my 2 children namely Eve and Cunrod after mine & my Wife Death

In witness whereof I have here unto set my Hand & a fixed my Seal this 17th Day of May in the year of our Lord 1787

Sealed and declared by the above Named David Low this to be his Last Will & Testament in the Pre sints [presents] of us

Geo Cortner (Jurat)   Christopher (his x mark) Lockman   (Jurat)   Peter (his o mark) Cortner

Probate: George Cortner, Esqr. & Christian Lockman proved the will Nov. Ct. 1794

[note: Both the Clerk's copy and the microfilmed original will were impossible to read. The above was taken from a photocopy of the original will housed in the NC State Archvies in Raleigh. The signature of George Cortner is very like the handwriting in the will. It is possible he was the writer, particularly because he was styled Esquire [Justice of the Peace, a Court official] in the probate data, and it is likley he was literate for the times, and wrote the sounds he heard. Part of what he heard was the German accent coming through some of the English words. i.e. waders/waters; housen/household. It was the sound of English spoken by some of our people. JSH]

A:0220   pp:216/217   EDWARD LONEY   10 Oct. 1795   Nov Ct. 1795
Wife: Sarah 1 feather bed & furniture, all kitchen necessaries, her living of the plantation, 1 mare, saddle & bridle, the third part of cows, sheep & hogs, as long as she remains my widow and no longer. If she marries, I allow all that I have given to her to be divided between
Daus: Sarah & Mary, except her mare & saddle that I allow her to keep.
Son: John 150 acres of land, 1 horse, saddle & bridle, 1 cow & calf, 6 sheep, 1 sow & pigs and half of all farming tools.
Son: James 150 acres of land, with 1 good horse, saddle & bridle, with sufficient apparel for a youth to wear, 1 cow & calf, 6 sheep, 1 sow & pigs, also the half of all my farming tools. "I allow him to be larned to reed write & scypher as far as the Rule of three" his learning to be taken out of the whole of my estate the above property and larning I allow him to have again he arives to the age of 21 years"
Dau: Sarah a certain mare that now is called hers with 1 saddle & bridle, 1 cow & calf, 4 sheep, 1 sow & pigs, 1 flax wheel.
Dau: Mary 1 horse to the value of £15, 1 saddle & bridle to the value of £5, 1 cow & calf, 4 sheep, 1 sow & pigs, 1 flax wheel "likewise I alow her to be larned to reed & write her larning to be taken out of the whole of my Estate".
Dau: Elisabeth Cumton 1 cow & 1 flax wheel.
Seal: Edw'ed Loney
Exrs: wife Sarah Loney & son John Loney
Wits: Jeremiah Cunningham (Jurat)   Abner Endsley
"revokes"

AN ANNOTATED DIGEST OF WILL BOOK A, GUILFORD COUNTY, NORTH CAROLINA

A:0221 pp:218/219 THOMAS LANDRETH 18 June 1800 Nov. Ct. 1800
Eldest Son: Francis Landreth 100 acres of land off the west end of the plantation where I now live.
Son: Thomas Landreth the whole of that tract of land (210 ac.) purchased of Isaiah Weatherly.
Son: John Landreth 92 1/2 acres & 32 rods purchased of John Doak, together with 10 or 12 acres off the said East corner of old place Beginning at the SE corner running on the West line so far as to come by a North line within 3 or 4 poles of Calamns [?] Branch extending North across the Meadow Branch then East to the old line. 1 young bay horse named Dick. If sd John should marry in his mother's lifetime, I recommend it to her if she can conveniently furnish him the said John with household furniture in the same manner as she hath done her sons who are now married or as near as she can.
Son: Simon Landreth $125 out of an obligation on Bennoni Cleyton [Clayton?]. All his school books.
Son: Jedidiah Landreth the balance of the above named obligation on Clayton and an Obligation on Robert Hanner of $193.50 & an obligation on John Ellette of $50.
Wife: Martha the whole of the plantation where I now live, except what is mentioned in the above will for her & the support of the Family during her Widow Hood at the expiration of which all the movable property not disposed to be disposed of at her discretion for the benefit of the family.
Son: Asa Landreth the plantation is to become his property at the end of her widowhood.
Seal: Thomas Landreth
Exrs: wife, Martha Landreth son, John Landreth
Wits: John Finley John Ellett (Jurat)

A:0222 pp:219/220 ADAM LACKEY 28 Dec. 1800 Feb. Ct. 1801
Wife: Martha Lackey all the Tract of Land I now live on with the improvement yearly & every year during her natural life, 1 Negro girl named Fillis & all Fillis' issue, all household & kitchen furniture, her choice of the 1/2 of all library of books, her choice of 2 head of the best Horses, & farming utenshels to her & her hairs [sic] forever.
Nephew: Adam Leeky, s/o my brother Alexander Lackey, after death of my wife, all & singular the plantation whereon I now live containing 402 acres.
residue to be sold & divided as follows: to Robert Stuart's son named Adam Lackey $50.
Adam Lackey, William Burney's son, grandson to John Burney $50.
Walter McConnel for his friendship & in anticipation of his taking care of his aunt $70.
William Lackey said to be the son of my brother Samuel Lackey 5 sh.
Allimance Congregation $40.
Brother Alexander Lackey's Children, sisters Catrine Burney & Mary Burney; Jane Porter's children equally divided among them.
Seal: Adam Lecky
Exrs: wife Martha Leekey Col. Dan'l. Gillespie (Jurat) Ralph Gorrell (Jurat)

AN ANNOTATED DIGEST OF WILL BOOK A, GUILFORD COUNTY, NORTH CAROLINA

NB: sworne before sealing the cloack [clock?] & cow that I now have after my wife decease I leave to Samuel Burney son of my sister Mary Burney over & above whatever little legacy he may share with the others. **"revokes"**

A:0223 pp: 220/221 JOHN LAURENCE, SEN'R. 20 Feb. 1800 May Ct. 1804
Wife: Ann Laurence 1 feather bed & furniture to dispose of as she thinks proper.
Son: Caleb Laurence the rest of Estate to him & his heirs forever.
Seal: John (his mark) Laurence Sen'r
Exrs: wife Ann Laurence Joel Harris
Wits: Harmon McGee Edw. Tatum Talor (Jurat) Noel Parrish (Jurat)

A:0224 p:221 ANDREW LAW 31 March 1807 May Ct. 1807
Daus: Rachel & Elizabeth $1 each.
Sons: James, Robert, & Andrew $1 each.
Wife: Margaret remaining part of estate in Land, movable & perishable property during her Life to be freely by her possessed & enjoyed with all Benefits arising therefrom; at her Decease the whole to be sold at public sale & equally divided among my 3 children Rachel, Andrew, & Elizabeth.
Whereas a mistake was made in running my son Andrew's land my will request is that the line between him & William Tryon [Tryor? Fryar?] be extended South til his compliment of 130 acres be made up in a parallel line with the divisional line between my sons Andrew & Robert.
Son: James my wearing clothes.
Seal: Andrew (his x mark) Law
Exrs: wife Margaret & nephew John Smith
Wits: Hezekiah Wheeler (Jurat) John Forbis
"revokes"

A:0225 pp:222/223 HENRY LEE 2 July 1803 Aug. Ct. 1808
Son: Henry Lee 1 Negro boy Peter plus what he hath already received, and the Distill [still] during his life & after his death to his children if he has any living, if none living then to be equally divided betwixt my three children Joshua Lee, Elizabeth Harrell & Abigail King.
Son: John 20 sh as I have already given & delivered unto him what ever I intended of my estate for him.
Son: Joshua Lee 1 Negro boy Dick with what he has already received.
Dau: lends to Elizabeth Harrell 3 Negroes which she hath already recieved. 1 Negro girl, Selah, 2 Negro boys Sam & Bob during her life & after her death to her Children to be equally divided amongst them for ever.
Dau: lends to Abigail King 3 Negroes which she hath already received. 2 girls, Dinah & Penny; 1 boy Jacob to her during her life, then to her children to be equally divided amongst them all.
Grandson: Henry King Lee, s/o Joshua Lee 1 Negro girl Creese, which he hath already received.
Wife: Sarah Lee all my living both Negroes & household goods & furniture which is not given away nor sold nor Lent to any of the children during her widowhood on condition that she not wast nor destroy any part thereof. If she should do so, my Executors are to take it out of her hands.

Residue of estate after death of wife to be equally divided betwixt Joshua Lee, Elizabeth Harrell, & Abigail King.
Seal: Henry Lee
Exrs: trusty friends Joshua Lee, William King, David Harrell
Wits: John Dougherty   John Caffey (Jurat)   James Chilcutt   Michael Caffey

A:0226   pp:223/224   ADAM LOMAN, SENIOR   6 June 1814   Aug. Ct. 1814
Wife: Elisabeth 1/3 part of my land including the dwelling house other buildings plantation & orchard along the lines next to the River Reedy fork down to the Rode leading a cross George Wagnor's ford & up said Road towards my son Adam Loman as long as she lives & then to be equally divided between my sons Andrew & George.
Son: Andrew 81 acres of land on the other side of the said Road to plantation where John Coleman Jun'r. settled & now lives.
Son: George 81 acres of land next to my son Adam Loman.
Wife & Children at home: all household property, stock of every kind to raise and support them, except one Gray horse I allow them to sell.
Dau: Sally Hughes 1 cow or the value thereof.
Seal: Adam Loman
Exrs: Adam Loman   John Smith
Wits: William Weatherly (Jurat)   [the other signature appears to be in 18th century German script, as does that of the testator, Adam Loman. Jsh]

A:0227   pp:224/225   ROBERT LAMB   1 Feb. 1814   20 Feb. 1815
Sons: Samuel, Simeon, & John Lam all the lands previously given them to gather with their stock & every piece of property that has been given to them.
Daus: & Grand Dau: Elizabeth White, Deborah Hoggett, Ester Hodson, Ann Reynolds, Margate Bouldin each & every one of them the whole property which had been given them.
Wife: [not named] all household furniture, live stock, during her life & at her death to be equally divided bewteen my 3 sons my 4 daus. & my grand dau.
After all just debts are paid, residue of estate equally divided to my 8 children.
Seal: Robert (his x mark) Lamb
Exrs: friend Zeno Worth
Wits: Daniel Worth (Jurat)   Benjamin Hall
"revokes"

A0228   p:225   SAMUEL MILEHAM   15 Feb. 1795   May Ct. 1795
"whereas I ..."
Wife: Elizebeth 1/3 of my land & a mare called Peg, 1 bed.
Sons: John, Samuel, & Ebenezer the 2 parts of land out of 3 to be equally divided among them. [not named]
Dau: Sarah a good horse & saddle, a good Cow & Calf & bed.
Dau: Nancy a good Horse & saddle, a good Cow & Calf & bed.
All Children: the remainder of my estate to be equally divided amongst all the children.
Seal: Samuel (his x mark) Mileham
Exrs: John Tomlinson Sen'r.   Wife Elizabeth Mileham
Wits: Ezekial Dewese (Jurat)   William (his x mark) Simpson (Jurat)

AN ANNOTATED DIGEST OF WILL BOOK A, GUILFORD COUNTY, NORTH CAROLINA

    A:0229   p:226   JAMES MONGOMERY   26 March 1797   May Ct. 1797
"Whereas...I"
Son: John all my land provided he will pay to my 6 daughters £60 hard money or that which may sute them as well to be paid in the following manner to wit:
Daus: Jane, Elizabeth, Lydia, Charlette, Margret, Mary when each comes of age.
Discharge all just debts.
Son: William my yearling colt.
Family: to stay together using stock and household furniture if they can for their support until dau. Mary comes of age. then the household furniture to be equally divided amongst my 6 daus. & the remains of my stock to go to my son John.
Seal: James (his x mark) Mongomery
Exrs: son William Mongomery son John Mongomery Libni Ba----- [this name is unreadable in both the original and in the clerk's copy]JSH
Wits: Matthew Macy (Jurat) John Walton Nathaniel Walton (Jurat)

    A0230   p:227   **CHARLES MEDEARIES**   15 March 1793   Aug. Ct. 1793
"sadler"
Eldest Son: Thomas Medearis 1 horse & saddle, 1 bed & furniture, 1 cow & calf, £12 current money & all the appurtenances of which he has now in possession.
Son: John Medearies all my lands which I now possess, 1 Sorrel mare named Bet & saddle & bridle.
Wife: Elizabeth all my lands, movable estate & debts, either by bond note or book debt during her life or widow hood to dispose of at her own discretion, then to be sold & equally divided amongst my children.
Son: John Medearis is to give Malchi Medearies Stephen Medearies & William Medearies each one £12 current money of the State of North Carolina they being his three younger brothers when they come of age which gives the said John a full inheritance to the said land.
Seal: Charles Medaris
Exrs: wife Elizabeth   son John Medearies
Wits: Edmund Jean (Jurat) John Dwigans (Jurat) Mary (her M mark) Dwigans
"revokes"

    A:0231   p:227   DINAH MACY   18th of 5th mo. 1796   Feb. Ct. 1797
"Whereas...I" "widow"
Dau: Anna Macy my large looking glass & large Pewter Platter, small tin canister & small leather trunk, large stone picklepot, stone Juge & large walnut chair.
Dau: Abigail Stanton my worsted gown & dark colored linsay Coate, 2 new handkerchiefs 1 checkt [sic] 1 blue checked apron, also cloth for a checkered apron. [The handwriting was very difficult to read] JSH
Grandau: Dinah Macy handirons, fire shovel & tongues [tongs], my Sacred History & Elwoods History, & my low chair.
Dau-in-law: Hannah Macy my duffil Blankit, 1 toe sheet, Round table & bellows.
Grandau: Anna Ozbun 1 Garlick [?] sheet, 1 checkte apron, & my warming pan.
Grandson: Thaddeus Macy 1 Black heffer 4 years old.

Grandau: Hepzabah Russell 1/2 of the fethers out of my bed with 1 bolster & 1 pillow, 1 checkted apron.
Grandau: Mariam Swain 1 checkted apron.
2 Grandsons: Isaac Macy & David Macy all carpenters & farming tools with all remainder of cattle to be equally divided between them. Isaac my large Chest & David the small chest with my coverlid. [coverlet] JSH
2 Grandaus: Abigail Macy & Anna Macy each 1 large silver spoon, 1 feather bed & the remaining part of the other feather bed, iron trammel, quart cup & large teapot to be equally divided between them with my 2 bedsteads & Cord
Grandau: Sarah Macy my pint pewter cup.
Daus: Anna Macy & Dau-in-Law Hanny Macy all remaining part of my wearing appearel & household furniture to be equally divided between them.
Seal: Dinah Macy
Exrs: son-in-law Enoch Macy   dau-in-law Hannah Macy
Wits: Thaddeus Macy   (Jurat)   Dinna Joy

A:0232 p:229   ROBERT MITCHAL   6 Nov. 1775   Nov. Ct. 1775
Wife: Margarate 1/3 part of all lands and tenaments, 1/2 of all my chattles Viz: horses, cows & sheep, & 1/2 all my other movables with the house I now live in during her natural life & at her death to be disposed of at her discretion either to her son Adam or her grandson Robert Mitchel.
Son: Adam the remaining 2/3 parts of my lands.
Daus: Mary Ross & Jean Anderson each £2.
Grandson: Robert Mitchel £18.
Youngest Dau: Rebecca the other 1/2 of my Cattle viz Horses, cows & sheep & movables & 1/2 of all my money & Book debts after my full debts & burial expenses are discharged & the other half to my beloved wife Margarate.
Seal: Robert (his x mark) Mitchel
Exrs: James Denny   Robert Rankin
Wits: Adam (his o mark) Mitchel   Alex'r. Caldwell   (Jurat)

A:0233   pp:229/230   WILLIAM MOUNTGOMERY   14 July 1796   Nov. Ct. 1796
Wife: Hannah Mountgomery 1/3 part of all my movable estate & to have the plantation on which I now live in at her disposal during her natural life or widowhood.
Eldest Son: William Mountgomery, Eldest Dau: Frances Buchanan, Second Dau: Eliazbeth Bailey, Hannah McKnight 1 silver dollar each.
Hannah McKnight 1 silver dollar   [Relationship not stated]
Dau: Mary 1 horse & saddle, 1 bed & furniture.
Son: John Mountgomery all my Smith tools.
Son: David all my lands namely the plantation on which I now live or at his mother's decease or marriage the land I bought of John Gilchrist & the 45 acres I entered between Edward McGlamary, John Gilchrist & myself & sd. David to have all the moveables not willed away already.
Son: David to pay unto his sister Rebekah Child called Jean which I have taken under my care £50 hard money to be paid to sd Jean when she arrives to the age of 18 years. To settle all my accounts both debt & credit out of his legacy.
My Books to Frances Buchanan Mr. Chamocks book upon the Divine Attributes.

AN ANNOTATED DIGEST OF WILL BOOK A, GUILFORD COUNTY, NORTH CAROLINA

Son: John the same author on Regeneration.
Wife: Hannah & Son: David remainder of books to be equally divided betwixt them.
Seal: William Mountgomery
Exrs: William Scott John Gilchrist
Wits: John Gilchrist (Jurat) Samuel Gilchrist Robert Gilchrist
"revokes"

A:0234 pp:230/231 AARON MENDENHALL 19th of 11th mo 1789 Feb. Ct. 1794
"whereas I, Aaron Mendenhall..."
Oldest Son: James 100 acres of land taken off the East end of my tact with a North & South line across the whole tract.
Son: Moses 100 a across the West end of sd tract.
Wife: Miriam during her Widowhood the house & all plantation & the rest of the land for to support her children & household goods & plantation utensils of every kind to be kept in their place Horses Cows Sheap & Hogs under the care of my Beloved Wife and little Fammily to raise grain & support life. She is to sell nothing for he [Aaron Mendenhall?] has debts owing him enough to clear all. If wife marry she to have a feather bed & its furniture, a horse & cow & a child's part for there is nothing meant in any part of this worthy of giveing my right or title to land to my wife but in order as leaving her in peacable possession to portion the children as well as she might be abillitated. [sic]
Son: Aaron: If wife should decease in any short time my will is my land be equally divided between my 3 boys, Aaron to have the middle division comprising the house.
Three Daus: Dinah, Miriam & Charity to share equally in the moveables with the boys, except the Smith tools.
Oldest Son: James the Smith tools for him to learn on, then to be his.
Seal: Aaron Mendenhall
Exrs: wife Miriam Bethuel Coffin
Wits: George Rayl (Jurat) "affirmed" John Thomas Molley (her x mark) Thomas George Rayl
"revokes"

A:0235 pp:231/232 JAMES MARTIN 6th of 10th mo 1793 Feb. Ct. 1796
"Whereas I, James Martin..."
Wife: Mary Martin the use & profit of the whole of my Estate both real & personal during her widdowhood.
Son: John Martin at the death of my said wife 77 akers of land I mean on the N E part of my land.
Son: James Martin 100 acres of land on the SW part of my land it being the same of which he is now possessed & living on.
Son: Henry residue of my land after the death of my aforesaid wife.
Dau: Francis [sic][should be Frances] Martin use of my North Room with her heretofore necessary privileges thereunto belonging with her firewood so long as she remains single.
Daus: Frances Martin & Mary Beeson all household furniture after the death of my said wife equally to be devided between them.
Dau: Hannah Sillivan 5 sh.
Sons: & Daus: James & Henry Martin, Frances Martin & Mary Beeson after my debts are all paid all the residue of my estate part & part alike.

Seal: James Martin
Exrs: esteemed friends Nathanniel Macy & Paul Macy
Wits: Joseph Iddings (Jurat) Samuel Lamb (Jurat) Nathaniel Moore

A:0236 p:232 ZEDOCK MEARS   16 Nov. 1789   Feb. Ct. 1790
Wife: Elizabeth all land & horses & every & all my chattels together with my household furniture shall go to use of my wife during her widowhood & then to be divided among the children [not named] equally as the law directs.
Seal: Zadock Mares [Mares in the original will]
Exrs: none appointed
Wits: Seth M------[there are 2 names unreadable] James Mills (Jurat)
[Wife: Elizabeth was appointed Administratrix of the estate with a copy of the will annexed]

A:0237 p: 233 THOMAS MENDENHALL 8th of 10th mo 1782   Feb. Ct. 1785
"Be it remembered..."
Wife: Phebe all free hold Land house & houehold goods all my plantation impliments all my Shop tools my horses cattle hogs & sheep to hand & hold as my Self during her Life & after her decease I give unto to my
Son: Mordecai Mendenhall 68 acres of land off the West end of my tract deviding it by a North & South line.
Son: Seth Mendenhall 66 acres of land joining unto Mordecais divided off my acres North & South line.
Son: Enos Mendenhall 66 acres of land joining to Seths on the East end of the tract.
Daus: Mary Jane, Ruth, Phebe, Beulah & Asenath all moveables equally divided at of decease of wife.
If one of my Sons should decease under age the land to be equally divided between the other 2, the Elder holding the West end.
Seal: Thomas Mendenhall
Exrs: wife Phebe hole & sole Executor
Wits: Moses Mendenhall (Jurat) Isaac Mendenhall (Jurat) John Mendenhall (Jurat)

A:0238 pp:233/234 WILLIAM MERONEY   14 Dec. 1786   18 Feb. 1788
Son: John 224 acres of land lying on the East side of Rock branch. John to keep my [son?] Isaac Meroney till he is 20 years old & to give him Schooling & a horse worth £20 or the same in money. John to have my gray horse.
Wife: Ruth Meroney may hold the clearing of 30 acres joining the Plantation & timber to support the sd Plantation in during her widow hood & no longer & the bay mare called fancy.
Daus: Rachel Meroney, Elezebeth Meroney & Lyda Meroney each to have a feather bed & furniture & a cow at the age of 16.
George Hampton shall have a cow at age 20. [No relationship given]
Son: Nathan Meroney 5 sh.
Children: remaining part of estate shall be equally divided among them.
Seal: William Meroney
Exrs: son John Meroney
Wits: John Ross   Mary (her x mark) Ross
[no probate information given]

AN ANNOTATED DIGEST OF WILL BOOK A, GUILFORD COUNTY, NORTH CAROLINA

A:0239 pp:234/235 THOMAS MAJOR 13 Jan. 1789 Feb. Ct. 1789
"of Alamance Congregation..." *
"planter"
Wife: Margaret my mare & saddle, all my household furniture & 2 cows.
Grandson: Thomas Peasley £10 lawful money.
Granddau: Elenor Johnson £20 lawful money.
Col. John Peasley & Marshall McLane to put or cause to be put out the above bequathed money out to interest at or before the year 1790 for the use of the above named legatees.
Seal: Thomas Major
Exrs: sons-in-law Robert Peasly George Stuart
Wits: Isaiah McBride
"revokes"
*[probably Alamance Presbyterian Church JSH]

A:0240 p:235 MATTHEW MACY   24th of 5th mo 1804   Aug. Ct. 1804
"whereas I Matthew Macy..."
Wife: Abigail Macy the use and profits of the Plantation whereon I now live with all my Stock farming tools & household furniture during her widdowhood.
Sons: Matthew Macy & George Macy each 5 sh.
Daus: Sarah Springer Abigail Coffin Elizabeth Coffin at death of my wife that my 3 daus. shall have the remaining part of my estate both real & personal to them and their heirs & assigns forever.
Seal: Matthew Macy
Exrs: trusty friends Zaccheus Macy Paul Macy, junior
Wits: Paul Macy (Jurat) Nathaniel Macy (Jurat)

A:0241 p:236 JOHN MENDENHALL 20th of 3rd mo 1794 Feb. Ct. 1800
"I, John Mendenhall..."
Wife: Mary all the household goods she had when I married her, to be at her disposal forever, & the thirds of the profits of my farm during her widowhood.
Son: Moses Mendenhall all the interest of a bond I received of him in the year 1782 for £24.16 sh.
Zachariah Stanley the sum of 5 sh. [no relationship given]
Son-in-law: Nicholas Robinson £2 money of North Carolina.
Dau: Miriam Mendenhall a large bible, Fox's & Chalkleys Journals, also Isaac Penningtons works, & all remainder of household goods & utensils of husbandry, all my horses, cows, sheep & hogs & all & every messuages, tenements & hereditaments whatsoever to her, her heirs & assigns forever.
Seal: John (his o mark) Mendenhall
Exrs: dau: Miriam Mendenhall
Wits: John Howell (Jurat) Joseph Iddings (Jurat) Stephanus Haworth
"revokes"

A:0242 pp:236/237 EDWARD MULLOY 27 May 1796 May Ct. 1801
150 acres of land in Rockingham County be sold to pay Abel Edwards & Thomas Edwards their portions & all other demands against my estate. If not enough in the price of sd land, that all moveables there be as much sold as needed to satisfy the demands against my estate.

AN ANNOTATED DIGEST OF WILL BOOK A, GUILFORD COUNTY, NORTH CAROLINA

Wife & 4 children namely James, Jane, Edward, & Daniel the overplus be equally divided among them.
Wife: Ruth the land whereon I now live together with what moveables left after paying my just debts. All the moveables to be my wife's during her natural life & to be disposed of as she pleases at her death.
Son: Daniel when he arrives at age 21 the land to be sold to the highest bidder & the price divided equally among my wife & children.
Other: If any of my children should predecease their siblings the survivors to share & share alike, & if all die before they come to the age of maturity then the estate to remain in the hands of my wife Ruth during her Natural life & at her decease to be divided equally between Jeremiah Mulloy and James Mulloy, the orphan children of my brother James Mulloy, late of Rockingham County, deceased & if said orphans should die before they arrive to age of maturity, then the estate to devolve on Abel Edwards & Thomas Edwards, the orphan children of Thomas Edwards, late of Chatham County, deceased.
Sons: be bound and apprenticed to some mechanic to learn a trade, each to have his choice of trade. Said boys to be bound at the age of 17 years or sooner if their Mother should find it most convenient so to do.
Seal: Edward Mulloy
Exrx: wife Ruth Mulloy
Wits: John Marris [Morris?]   Levi Coffin (Jurat)   Phebe Anthony

A:0243   p:238   WALTER MILEHAM   1 Sept. 1798   Nov. Ct. 1798
Wife: Ann 1/3 of my land & 1 bed & furniture & the third of the moveable property enduring her lifetime.
Son: Walter Mileham 2/3 of the land & likewise his mother's thirds of the land at her death & 1 horse named Brock & 1 bed & furniture & 1 gun.
Dau: Sarah Mileham 1 feather bed & furniture, 1 heifer named Flower & her mother's third of the moveables at her death.
Dau: Catherine Williams 5 sh.
Sons: Valentine Mileham & Jacob Mileham all my right of land in the Delewer State & other property belonging to me in that State & 5 sh each.
Grandchildren: Susanah Ross, Fracnai [?] Ross, Levy Ross the sum of £10.5 sh hard money to be equally divided between the three.
Son: Samuel Mileham, his heirs, 5 sh.
Seal: Walter (his x mark) Mileham
Exrs: wife Ann   son Valentine
Wits: Ezchiel Dewess   Nathaniel Simpson (Jurat)   John Tomlinson

A:0244   p:239   MORDECAI MENDENHALL   9th of 5th mo 1796   Nov. Ct. 1803
"I, Mordecai Mendenhall..."
Wife: Charity lend to her the plantation & personal estate during her life except what I hear after order otherwise.
Heirs of Sons: Richard, Thomas, Aaron & Dau: Charity Mills 5 sh each.
Son: Isaac the Plantation I now live on containing 334 acres at the decease of my wife to him & his heirs forever.
Sons: Moses, Stephen, Mordicia & Isaac Mendenhall money & notes of hand at the decease of their Mother & all the remainder of my personal estate to be equally divided amongst them.
Seal: Mordecia Mendenhall
Exrs: sons Stephen & Isaac Mendenhall
Wits: Mathew Coffin (Jurat)   Gallant (his / mark) Ayers   Hannah Coffin

AN ANNOTATED DIGEST OF WILL BOOK A, GUILFORD COUNTY, NORTH CAROLINA

A:0245 pp:239/240 ENOCH MACY 22nd of 7th mo 1805 May Ct. 1806
"Whereas I, Enoch Macy ..."
Wife: Anna Macy all my real & personal estate during the time she continues the widow of my body & if in case she marrys I give her 1 feather bed & furniture, 1 horse & saddle, one cow & calf.
Son: Henery Macy 150 acres of land off the South end of my possessions including 50 acres I bought of Henery Cannady at the death or marriage of my wife.
Sons: Thaddeus Macy & Stephen Macy the remaining 140 acres off of the North end of the above tract at the death or marriage of my wife to be equally divided between them.
Dau: Anna Osborn 10 sh.
Daus: Dinah Macy, Miriam Macy & Sarah Macy all the remaining part of my household furniture at their mother's death or marriage to be equally divided betwixt them, except my desk. Each dau: to have 1 cow & calf.
Daus: to have their living off of the plantation with their industry during the time they live single & with the privelege of living in the house that we now live in.
Dau: Dinah the weaving loom with all the gears & £10 & Sewell's History.
Son: Henery my desk provided he furnish his sister Sarah with a Chest worth $6 & half, all Smith & plantation tools with my farming tools, large Bible & waggon.
3 Sons: all the remaining part of estate to be equally divided betwixt them.
Seal: Enoch Macy
Exrs: sons Thaddeus Macy Henery Macy Stephen Macy
Wits: Isaac Gardner Bethuel Coffin (Jurat)

A:0246 pp:241/242 WILLIAM MILLS 17 May 1804 May Ct. 1804
Mother: Cathrine Mills $400 if she is now living & if not alive the said $400 to be disposed of as herein mentioned.
Mrs. Molly Price w/o David Price $50 to be paid to her in cash immediately after my death by my Executors considering it to be my duty for her kindness & attention to me during my illness.
Sisters: Anne Lacy, Mary Morrison & Margaret the rest & all my estate both real & personal to be sold & the money arising from sale with the remaining balance of my cash to be equally divided. Survivors share equally.
Seal: William Mills
Exrs: trusty friends Hance McCain John Moore
Wits: Obadiah Dick (Jurat) William Tease (Jurat)
"revokes"

A:0247 pp:242/243 GEORGE MENDENHALL 3rd of 10th mo 1805 Nov. Ct. 1805
"I, George Mendenhall..."
Wife: [not named] 1 feather bed & furniture, the Tib mare & saddle, 2 cows, her choice of the stock to her & her heirs forever. The use of the tract of land whereon I now live with its appurtanences if she continues my widow until my Son George comes of age & all my household furniture & farming utencils to be at her disposal during her widowhood except such as are hereinafter disposed of.
Son: Nathan £5 in the last payment of his land more than he has had.

AN ANNOTATED DIGEST OF WILL BOOK A, GUILFORD COUNTY, NORTH CAROLINA

Son: Richard the land where his Tanyard is in consideration of his having paid for the improvement to be laid off as allotted & £5 in the last payment of his other tract.
Oldest Dau: Jemima part of the land I bought of William Lane & John Sweet to be divided along the old road & 1 feather bed & furniture & a sorrell colt called hers.
Son: James the land I bought of Isaac Beason & to run North from the NW corner percimon grub til it shall intersect a line running along the South edge of Federal Street & thence as heretofore allotted & the use & privilege of the House he lives in, water & firewood & 1 acre on each side of the land to include some apple trees during the time he may tend the Mills to be laid off at the discretion of my executors.
Son: William a Mill seat that I bought of Samuel Lamb & 25 acres of land off the East end of the tract I bought at Shelley's vendue & 1 a lott in James Town as heretofore allotted & his books.
Dau: Hannah 75 acres of land off the South end of the tract I bought of John Talbert & 1 cow & 1 feather bed & furniture.
Dau: Judith the land on the West side adj. Jemima's & 1 feather bed & furniture or the value thereof.
Dau: Mary 75 acres of land off the West side of the land I bought of David Hoggatt by running a line South to Hannah's land & 1 fether bed & Furniture or the value thereof.
Dau: Abigail the balance of my land joining William & Mary & 1 feather bed & furniture or the value thereof.
Son: George the plantation Bryan Smith lives on to come into possession at 21 years. Previous to that time it to be let out & the profits be applied to his schooling, also the Mills & the plantation whereon I now live to come into his possession at the same age & if he keeps the Mills in repair & if his Mother continues my widow he to give her 1/3 of the profits of the Mills. If George should die without issue then all his quota to descend to his surviving brothers in Co.[mpany?]
Five Sons: the land joining this original tract & Jonathan Huddlestone to be held by my 5 sons in Company with all necessary privileges for the conveyance of water from about the ford of the river at the mouth of the tail race.
All Children: land joinining Isaac Williams, the Lott in Johnsonville, Randolph County, my part of the Whetstone Quarry in Randolph County, & all other property not already disposed of at the discretion of my Executors.
Children: Nathan, Jemema, Hannah, Judith, Mary, Abigail, & George each a lott in Jamestown to be laid off a the descretion of my Executors.
Wife & unmarried children reasonable privileges of the House so long as they live single.
Seal: George Mendenhall
Exrs: sons Nathan & Richard Mendenhall
Wits: Matthew Coffin (Jurat) Thos. Moore James Coffin (Jurat) John Macy
"revokes"

AN ANNOTATED DIGEST OF WILL BOOK A, GUILFORD COUNTY, NORTH CAROLINA

A:0248 p:244 MOSES MENDENHALL 2nd of 9th mo 1804 Aug. Ct. 1805
Wife: Betty Mendenhall all & singular my goods & chattles to support my family during her widowhood, & what she leaves at her death or marriage to be equall divided among my wife & children [not named]; my stock to be disposed of in manner above directed also my just debts & funeral charges paid.
Seal: Moses Mendenhall
Exrs: father Moses Mendenhall
Wits: Moses Mendenhall, Sen'r. Richard Mendenhall, 2nd (Jurat)
"revokes"

A:0249 ABRAHAM MASON pp:244/245 Sept. 1814 Aug. Ct. [no year given]
"planter"
Wife: Rachel the tract of land & premises I own in Guilford County adj the lands of William Raper & others fully to enjoy occupy & possess without molestation of any person whatever during her natural lifetime, & after her death to descend to my 4 children to be equally divided amongst them. Also 1/6th part of all the debts due me by others after all just debts owing me are paid.
Anny Payne: [no relationship stated] $20 to be paid out of my moveable estate.
Dau: Sarah Stanley & Thom Stanley [sic] 10 sh & the remaining 4/5's of all my estate.
4 Children: Reuben Mason, Roda Payne, Lidia Smith, & Mary Jones to them their husbands and heirs forever the remaining 4/5's of all my estate both real & personal, debts & etc. to be equally divided.
Seal: Abraham (his x mark) Mason
Exrs: wife Racheal William Raper
Wits: Solomon Raper Benjamin (his x mark) Payne
"revokes"

A:0250 p:246 JAMES MENDENHALL 21st of 9th mo 1811 Nov. Ct. 1811
"I, James Mendenhall..."
Wife: [not named] the use of the house, plantation & mills by keeping them in repair, to raise & school my children, all household furniture & plantation utensils. If she marry to have a cow & calf, feather bed & furniture & a portion with the girls.
Sons: John & Aaron land to be equally divided between them with an East & West line John having the Mills & Aaron the house at 21 year old.
Daus: Miriam, Ann, Mary & Susannah each to have a feather bed & furniture, a cow & calf, a side saddle & wheel.
Wife & Daus: my riding chair, cotton machine & shop tools be sold & the money put at interest to be equally divided between them.
Seal: James Mendenhall
Exrs: esteemed friends James Thornburgh Haniwel Edwards
Wits: Moses Mendenhall (Jurat) Thomas Thornburgh (Jurat)

A:0251 pp:246/247 WILLIAM MONGOMARY 9 June 1806 Feb. Ct. 1811
Wife: Rebekah 1/3 of all personal estate for ever & also that she has the support of 1 horse beast & 1 cow to be kept by the profits of plantation clear of any expense to her while she remains a Widdow.
Eldest Son: Robert parcel of land where he now lives on the North side of the creek North of my tract where I now live.
Dau: Ruth Hodson $1.

Son: William parcel of land beginning at William's corner black jack running from said corner North to Gardners line including all on the East side of sd line, with his paying my son Irwin 1/3 of what sd piece of land may be valued to.
Son: Samuel 50 acres of land beginning at Williams corner black jack running West to Caldwells line then being confined to follow my original line until it shall be enough to make out the complement of 50 acres on the South side of my land.
Dau: Mary 1 feather bed & furniture & $1.
Dau: Rebekah 1 feather bed & furniture & £10 & 1 side saddle.
3 younger Sons: James, George, & Levi all the remainder part of my sd tract of land where I now live to be equally divided among them.
Sons: Robert, Samuel, James, George & Levi my waggon.
All Children: Robert, William, Ruth Hodson, Samuel, Rebekah, Irwin, James, Georg [sic] & Levi to share in remainder of estate. *[Note: dau. Mary is not mentioned in this list of children in either the clerk's copy of this will, nor in the original]*
Seal: William Mongomery
Exrs: wife Rebekah   son Robert
Wits: Jonathan Parker   William Parsons (Jurat)   James Leonard
"revokes"

A:0252 p:248 HABIKKUK MORGAN   13 Feb. 1816   Feb. Ct. 1816
Wife: Nancy sole use & management of my plantation containing 350 acres with all farming utensils, household furniture, waggon, her choice of 2 horses, all the corn & meat, cows, hogs, & sheep during her widowhood. All that is not consumed by wife Nancy to go to my step-son Samuel Hunter, along with the balance of the money after the Legatees are paid.
Brother: James Morgan 10 sh.
Sister: Charlotte Heath: 50 sh.
Sister: Deborah Right: 10 sh.
Larkin More Casey: $50. [no relationship stated]JSH
The balance of horses and 2 sets of Smith tools & the plantation formerly the property of John Morgan to be sold by Exrs. to pay the money left to the above named Legatees.
Seal: Habikkuk (his x mark) Morgan
Exrs: wife Nancy   Jeremy Forbis
Wits: James Bright   (Jurat)   Margret (her x mark) Bright

A:0253 p:250 JOHN McKNIGHT   12 Aug. 1770   May Ct. 1771
Sons: Robert & William: land to Robert the 1/2 on the East end of my plantation & William the other half on the West with the improvements.
But: if the Child my wife is with is a boy, I allow my land to be divided into 3 equal parts, Robert to have the East end, William the Middle, & ye [the] youngest the West end.
Wife: Catrine 2 work horses, plow & plow irons, & plow hanging & 4 cows, & the use of the land until my youngest son be of age, for which consideration she to give my children a Christian education.
Wife: Catrine & children Elizabeth, Robert, William, Catrine, & Hannah all moveables to be sold except these desposed of above, each to have an equal part. If my wife continues to bear my name she shall have my House

to live in & my youngest son shall keep for her use a horse & a cow & sufficiency of provision.
Seal: John McKnight
Exrs: wife Catrine   Alexander McKnight   Thomas Donnel
Wits: Robert Rankin   James Denny (Jurat)
Catrine McKnight agrees to the above will and as on evidence thererof sets to her hand   Catrine (her x mark) McKnight
"revokes"

    A:0254   p:257   WILLIAM McNAUGHT/McNEIGHT   24 Nov. 1771   Feb. Ct. 1772
Estate be all disposed to publick sale such as my Land Claim of land, clothers, saddle & bridle & all other such things as maybe found belonging to me, & all my lawful debts & demands to be justly discharged & give & bequeath the rest to Brother Hugh McNeight.
Seal: Will McNaught
Exrs: Matthew Scott & William Scott
Wits: Gabreil Scott (Jurat)   Matthew Scott   Thos. Scott (Jurat)   William Scott
NB: "revokes"
NB: Executors not named in the will. Probate record indicates that Matthew Scott & Wm. Scott were appointed "in said will".

    A:0255   p:252   TIMOTHY McCALL/McCALY   25 Oct. 1774   Nov. Ct. 1774
"laborer"
Fill Putall [sic] £50 if to be found. If not to be found I allow 25 to the good of the Parish & the rest to my Executer's sick wife.
Alexander Mood & Thomas Close or their assigns all & singular my whole estate by them freely to be possessed & enjoyed.
Samuel Morrow shall have 1 shirt out of my clothes the white shirt.
Seal: Timothy McCall
Exrs: Alexander Mood & Thomas Clos
Wits: Hannery [Henry?](his x mark) Colston (Jurat)   James (his x mark) Alton   Samuel Morrow (Jurat)
"revokes"

    A:0256 p:253   ALEXANDER McKNIGHT   26 July 1774   May Ct. 1775
Son: Robert all land.
Wife: Hannah the benefits of my Land, house & improvements until my son Robert is of age or so long as she bears my name, bed & furniture, a cow & horse, saddle & the use of the Chest of Drawers during her natural life, & then to be given to my
Dau: Jean or her Heirs in consideration of which she is to give my children a Christian education with provisions & clothing during their minority, 1/3 of all remaining moveables.
Dau: Jean remaining 2/3 of estate, 1/2 silver tea spoons notwithstanding what is mentioned above.
Seal: Alex McKnight   Hannah (her h mark) McKnight
Exrs: Alexander Caldwell   James Donnel
Wits: Robert Donnal   Moses McClean (Jurat)   Mary (her x mark) McClean

A:0257 pp:254/255 JOHN McMURRY, SENIOR   24 Dec. 1789 (1791) [sic]
Wife: [not named] her mare & saddle, 1 cow, her choice, all household furniture & to be maintained during her life or natural widowhood with her son William.
Son & Daus: James McMurry, Betsy Carr, Margaret Brown 20 sh each.
Son: John McMurry 20 sh & 30 acres of land adjoining his own place with the improvements he has made.
Son: William the tract of land whereon I now live with all the necessary utensils exclusive of the 30 acres above mentioned.
Dau: Jean McMurry 1 young mare, a colt from the Bawney mare with a saddle and bridle, 2 cows, 1 feather bed & furniture her mother pleases to give her.
Son: Robert McMurry £100 current money of sd state, to be raised & collected out of the remmaining part of my Estate, 1 stallion colt now in being from the Bawney mare & his boarding fee while he is under the tutition of Rev'd David Caldwell.
NB before perfecting the above will the mare left to my daughter Jean, dyed. I bequeath to her instead thereof my roan Horse likewise after complying with my sd will as above directed any over pluss that may reamain to be given to my son William to be enjoyed by him forever.
Seal: John McMurry
Exrs: friends William Gowdy Henry Ross
Wits: Wm. McAden W. Gowdy (Jurat) Henry Ross (Jurat)
"revokes"

A:0258 pp:255/256 JOHN McCALL   1 May 1780   Feb. Ct. 1796
"of Yourk [York] County in the State of Pennsylvania"
Brother: Matthew McCall £5
Brother: Robert McCall £5
Cousins: Elizabeth Walker & Martha Cochrain £500 each.
Cousin: Samuel McClennan £300.
Samuel McClellans 2 sisters each £100.
My cousin the wife of James Hall £100.
Friend John Lindsay senr £100.
Cousin Mary Willson £100.
Cousin Agnes Carson £500.
Cousin Jenne Mager £100.
If any of my Blood relations that is to say first or second cusns [sic] should come in from Ireland I desire that my Executors should pay each of them £100 out of my Estate proveded there be any surplus in my Executors hand at the time of their arrival.
£1000 to be appropriated to the Relief of the poor to be disposed of at the Discretion of my Executor.
Cousin Robert Lindsay his heirs and assigns forever all that my messueges tenements of Land and the ferry adjoining Lying & being in York & Lancaster counties formerly known by the name of Nelson's Ferry place as reference to deeds of conveyance from my brother Mathey McCall to me will more fully appear.
Seal: John McCall
Exrs: friends Robert Lindsay Robert Cochran, Sr.
Wits: Jonas Littall (Jurat) Daniel Baldwin (Jurat) James (his x mark) Hellon
"revokes"

AN ANNOTATED DIGEST OF WILL BOOK A, GUILFORD COUNTY, NORTH CAROLINA

A:0259   pp:256/257   MARY McCONNELL   21 Nov. 1794   Nov. 1796
Sons: John McConnell & Wm. McConnell who live in Pennnsylvania, to each of them to be paid out of my goods and effects.
Dau: Mary Blayr [Blair ?] 1 gown & petticote & my cloke & 1 pare of bed blankets.
Dau: Martha Leacky 1 petticote wrapper Apron & 1 coverlet & my bed curtains.
Son-in-Law Adam Leacky had & Lost my mare. I make no allowence nor charge for her.
Younger Dau: Linvell McBride 1 of my gowns.
Margarett McBride d/o Francis McBride corded poplin gown.
Martha McBride d/o Francis 1 bed & 1 pair of blanketts & 1 bed quilt.
Leawell McBride, s/o Francis 6 buckles.
Agnes, d/o James Bayr my bonnett.
Son-in-Law Adam Leacky all debts that may be due on note or bond for his trouble in keeping & burying me at my decease.
Seal: Mary (her   mark) McConnell
Exrs: son-in-law Adam Leacky
Wits: Jean (her x mark) Elder   Henry Porter (Jurat)   Ralph Gorrell

A:0260   pp:257/258   JOSEPH McDOWELL, SENIOR   3 April 1797   May Ct. 1797
Wife: [not named] her bed & bed cloths, equally divided in proportion to the beds in the house, her spinning wheel, chest, her wearing cloths, the third of the land with the half of the Mansion house with my daughter Mary.
Son: Joseph McDowell, Junior the sum of 5 sh.
Daus: Elizabeth Duff & Hannah Ferguson 5 sh each.
Dau: Mary McDowell her own bed & bed cloths that she made use of at Mr. Caldwells & her sadle & bridle & all her wearing appparel & bible.
Wife: is to have her third of the property sold & the remainder to Dau: Mary.
Son: James McDowell (if alive) all my lots, son Johns cloths & also the 1/2 of the land I now live on.
Dau: Mary the other half of the sd land & if son James never returns daughter Mary is to enjoy the whole of sd land for ever.
Seal: Joseph (his   mark) McDowell
Exrs: son Joseph McDowell   worthy friend Hance McKean [McCain]
Wits: Wm. Scott (Jurat)   Robert McCuiston   (Jurat)   Hugh Shaw

A:0261 pp:258/259   JOHN McMURY   27 Feb. 1798   May Ct. 1798
Wife: Mary lands that I am seized of with every priveledge belonging to them during her natural life or widowhood. At her death or 2nd marriag sd lands be sold & the money arising therfrom to be equally divided between my 2 nephews: John McMury s/o James McMury & John McMury son & orphan of Robert McMury dec'd.
Brother-inLaw: John Mitchell a negro boy named Will or £50 in money to be optional with my wife which she gives [sic]
Wife: Mary a negro woman Violet with her 3 children named Sall, Tom & Peter to be by her freely enjoyed forever & all debts collected, creditors paid, & the balance of my estate to wit: my house hold

furniture of every kind, my stock, farming and working tools, money, bonds, notes & book accounts to be freely enjoyed by her for ever.
Seal: John McMury
Exrs: wife Mary son James McMury
Wits: James McMurry (Jurat) Robert Johnson Henry Ross (Jurat)
"revokes"

A:0262 pp:259/260 CHARLES McDARMAN 15 Aug. 1799 Nov. Ct. 1799
Wife: Hannah all & every of estate after paying all my just debts the money for which I wish to be raised out of the present crop & my stock of hogs and cattle & 1 still the balance to be hers during natural life or widowhood & then to return to my Son: James McDarmen.
Seal: Charles McDormon
Exrs: trusty friends Isaac Gray Williamson Brown
Wits: Michel McDarmon William Gray (Jurat) Robert Bell (Jurat)

A:0263 pp:260/261 JAMES McADOW 23 Sept. 1799 Feb. Ct. 1800
Wife: Margret all household furniture until daughters come of age if she remains a widow, & then to be equally divided amongst my daughters as they come of age: Mary Sarah and Darcus and Martha.[there is no punctuation between Mary Sarah: they may be two girls or only one]JSH
Wife: gray mare, all plows & gears & axes & hows [hoes] JSH & all farming utensiles 1/3 of my cows & 1/2 the sheep & all hogs, grain, corn & wheat for the use of the family as long as she remains a widow.
Wife: 1/5 of my household furniture to be her choice to be at her disposal forever.
Executors: to sell Bay Mare & colt & to purchase another such as they think will suit my family for their use.
Son: John all my clothes.
$40 of estate be kept & put to the use of schooling children.
Land to be sold but not under 1 year after the proving of this Will & I allow my Executors to take the price of my land & to purchase Land in the State of Caintuck [Kentucky] JSH where they see fit & I allow my wife to keep that land in her possession during her life or widowhood, and then to go to my son Ezrah.
The Wagon that they move into the State of Caintuck to be sold to "purche provision" [purchase provisions] for the use of my Wife and family.
All the money or personal estate that remains to go to the use of Wife & family as long as she remains a widow.
If wife should marry, all the money that remains of personal estate to go to interest & to be equally divided amongst 7 oldest children as they come of age.
Each Son: to have a horse raised from the mares willed to wife and they are to get them as they come of age.
3 oldest sons: John William and David to be bound to some good trade or to the age of 20 years.
Negro Dick to be sold or otherwise if sd Dick can get $250 gave for himself he may go free. [the testator is allowing Dick to buy his freedom]JSH Price of sd Negro to go to Interest & to be equally divided amongst my children as they come of age.
Wife & Children: all books until children come of age & then to be equally divided amongst them at the descretion of my wife the oldest to have first choice.

AN ANNOTATED DIGEST OF WILL BOOK A, GUILFORD COUNTY, NORTH CAROLINA

Son: John best Saddle.
Son William the other saddle.
Brother: John to hire out Negro Dick until the vandue & the money to go to the use of my wife & family.
Seal: John McAdow
Exrs: worthy friends John Huston Levenus Huston wife Margret
Wits: Wm. McAdow (Jurat) W. Ryan (Jurat) Robert Ryan (Jurat)

A:0264 pp: 261/262 MOSES McCUISTON 5 Dec. 1799 Feb. Ct. 1800
Wife: Elizabeth McCuiston during her widowhood the whole of my estate real and personal to be taken cair of by hur & distrubted in the following manner & form.
Daus: [not named] at the time of marriage 1 horse creature & saddle & such household furniture as their Mother shall think fit.
3 Sons at the year of their maturity land as follows:
Son: Robert the part of my land on the North side of Redy fork.
Sons: John & William the South side to be equally divided, but if either of 3 sons should die under age the surviving brothers equally divide his part.
Executors to take an Inventory of the perishable part of estate & record to be made of same and "in case it should apper to my Exacuters that my Estate is a way of Sinking they make make a Sail, of Such estate as appear most profitable to the legetees".
Sons & Daus: the remainder of my estate not heretofore mentioned to be equally divided & they to be raised & schooled.
Seal: Moses McCuiston
Exrs: wife Elizabeth Robert Thompson to be assistant executor
Wits: John Cummings (Jurat) Thomas Blair
"revokes"

A:0265 pp:262/263 MOSES McGREADY 20 Sept. 1800 Nov. Ct. 1800
Son: Samuel R. McGready 100 acres of lands lying on the South & East part of the plantation where I now live the old plantation. He to take full possession of plantation at my decease, & to have all gears & working tools in my possession at my decease. They to be for his help towards the care of his Mother & a bed.
Two Sons: Judah & Aaron 133 acres of land to be divided between them equally by lot.
Son: Judah my mare called Poll & anything left after settling debts.
Son: Aron my gray colt & anything left after settling debts.
Son: James $10.
Son: David $1.
Wife: Jean 1/3 of all my movable property, her living during life & the house I now possess clear of all debts.
Only Dau: Hannah 1/3 of the moveable property cows, hogs, sheep, & household furniture as it shall stand at my decease.
Son: Moses my Cart wheels & other things belonging thereto.
Son: Samuel shall give my son Isaac $40 out of his inheritance.
Seal: James McGready
Exrs: son Moses McGready Samuel Rutherford McGready
Wits: Jonathan Hodgens/Hodgson (Jurat) Isaac Perking (Jurat) Pheriah Perkins.

AN ANNOTATED DIGEST OF WILL BOOK A, GUILFORD COUNTY, NORTH CAROLINA

A:0266 pp:263/264/265   PATRICK McGIBBONEY   2 Jan. 1804   May Ct. 1804
Son: David 1 Negroe boy named Jim & 1st choice of all horse beasts & if it shall be a mare that has a Colt under 1 year old it shall go with the mare, my bed & furniture, all my wearing apparel & my riding furniture, 1 cow & calf, 4 sheep, 1 sow & 6 pigs or shoats, 2 sets of horse gears & as much farming utensils as will be sufficient to carry on the farm to be set off by John Cunningham & Wm. Armfield, the 3rd waggon excepted & all land I possess on the waters of S Buffaloe & 1/4 part of the grain at my decease.
Dau: Margaret Gillaspie $2 & 1/2 to buy her an ax & hoe, & the interest of £100 to be put at interest by my Exrs: & paid to her annually, but if my Exrs: should see that her husband is so reformed that he is likely to do well for himself & family so as to maintain them in a genteel manner then & in that case it shall be in their discretion to give her the principal at the time they may think fit or otherwise let her have the interest during her life & at her death the 1st child she has male or female that has dark hair shall heir the sd hundred pounds.
Dau: Isbel McGiboney only negroe girl named Hannah & her saddle.
Dau: Martha McGiboney 1 bond on Wm. Mills, Jr., Hamilton Hance McCain & Abner Weatherby in lieu of a negro.
Dau: Jean McGiboney negroe boy named Bob.
Friend: Col. Daniel Gillaspie the use of 1 Negroe boy named Isaac during his life & at his death if the County Court of Guilford should deem him worthy of freedom to be set free, otherwise sold & the price equally divided my 4 youngest children.
4 youngest children & Dau: Margret Gilliepies 2nd child (that may have brown hair) all the land I possess in the Tennessee State to be equally divided between them, & if she has no Child of that description viz brown or dark hair, then the above land to be equally divided between my 4 youngest children.
Daus: Isbal McGiboney, Martha McGiboney, & Jean McGibony all the rest of my estate eqqually divided between them except such household furniture as my 3 youngest Daus: may chuse to have valued to them by my Exrs.
Negroe girl named Patience excepted also I leave in the care of my trusty friend John Cunningham untill she arrives at the age of 14 which is left in his descretion to let my Dau: Margaret Gillaspie have her at any time he may think advisable.
James Denny appointed Guardian for youngest Dau: Jean McGiboney.
Seal: Patrick McGibboney
Exr: trusty friend John Cunningham
Wits: Wm. Armfield (Jurat) Thomas Cummins (Jurat)
NB Exr: to make all titles to land that deceased bound to by bond or verbal contract.

A:0267 pp:265/267   JAMES McMURREY   23 March 1804   Feb. Ct. 1805
Son: John whereas I have in my hands $150 of money that was left to my son John McMurry by his Uncle which money I made use of in purchasing the lands whereon I now live, if my son should demand sd money out of my estate I allow my Exrs. to sell as much of my land as will raise said sum to be taken out off the East end of my tract of land by a straight line across sd tract of land.
I allow my Exrs. when my son John arrives at the age of 21 years for to run a line across my tract of land beginning at Mclosses [sic] corner on rock Creek oppisit to the upper corner of the Old Meadow & up sd creek

to the Spring that is now by the fence on the East side of sd creek then due East across my land, but it must be determined whether any is to be sold or not as mentioned in the 2d item ... if he should die before the above mentioned devisions take place I do not allow either of them to be made.
Wife: Elizebeth 1 horse, saddle & bridle her choice, 1 feather bed & furniture, her chest, my buffet & its furniture, my kitchen & dresser furniture, 2 cows & calves, 6 head of sheep, 10 head of hogs & her choice of the different stocks, 1 Negro girl named Mary for her lifetime, at her death Mary & her issue to be sold and the money arising to be equally divided amongst all children then living. Remainder of my lands not mentioned above & their appurtenance's for her life or widowhood. At her death or marriage then to son John McMurry if living, if not to be sold and the money equally divided amongst all children still living.
Wife: Negro man named Will & Negro woman named Ails for 10 years to assist in raising & schooling 3 youngest children & discharging the rent that will be on her land, then they to be appraised & wife to keep them if she chooses, or to sell them & money equally divided bewteen wife & those children still living.
Wife: the money that is yet coming from father-in-laws estate "I give to my wife to be disposed of at her own disreation".
Son: John McMurrey young bay colt called Jed, 1 bed & furniture, 1 ax & 1 mattuck.
Dau: Jean 1 feather bed & furniture, chest.
Dau: Ophelia 1 feather bed & furniture.
Dau: Hanna 1 bed & furniture.
4 youngest children: [not named] to receive money from sale of moveable property not otherwise needed.
Seal: James McMurrey   continued
Exrs: trusty friends William Smith   Joseph Closse   [Close?]
Wits: William Smith   John Smith (Jurat)   Jos. Closs
"revokes"

A:0268 pp: 267/268 JAMES McADOW   8 May 1800   Nov. Ct. 1805
Wife: [not named] 1 bed & furniture, 1 Negro woman called Silve, 2 cows, her saddle & her large seal skinned trunk & her spinning wheel, a horse to ride when she stand in need of one & 1/2 acre of ground sowed in flax every year while she lives by the son she chooses to live with & he must furnish her with firewood her lifetime, & all my cooking utensils & dresser furniture is to be at her disposal & she must have ground for a garden & a cotton patch to her self & I give her the third of my Books & her Negro woman's increase after my death if any is to be divided at a year old as it comes equally between my Sons: David & Samuel & if she don't see proper to live in the house with her son he must build her a decent house convenient to water & he must not let her want for common necessaries of life with food & raiment, & at her death she is to leave her Negro woman & her cows to the son she lived with & the remainder of her Property to who she pleases.
Grand Daughter: Ann Boyd 1 horse, saddle & bridle, 2 cows, 1 bed & furniture, & a spinning wheel.
Sons: Samuel & David the remainder of my estate & Negroes to wit: Gorge, Jerry, Dinah, Nat, Heber, Jacob, Zilph, Peter, Anne, Nancy, Judith & all other Negroes that may fall into my estate before my death & all other

property, cash notes, bonds & book accounts to be equally divided between them.
Son: William to have a deed made by sons David & Samuel for 155 acres of land where they now live on.
Daus: Margaret & Jean each 5 sh.
Seal: James (his x mark) McAdow
Exrs: sons James & William McAdow
Wits: James McAdow   William McAdow (Jurat)
"revokes"

A:0269 pp:268/269 JOHN McBRIDE, SEN'R   25 Jan. 1806   May Ct. 1806
"farmer"
4 unmarried children: Son: James, Daus: Elisabeth, Jean, & Sarah equally among them all the land & stock on it.
Son: John $100.
Dau: Margaret McGaughy's 2 sons David & James McGaughy $30 each to be paid when they come of age. If one or the both dies [it] to go to their mother. 1 cow to her as soon as she desires after my decease.
Grandson: John McBride $100 & 1 middle rated horse & saddle.
"In consideration of the distance of the place of residence of my heirs and to prevent disputes when I am deceased I do hereby prohibit and restrain those my heirs each and every one of them from selling or any way disposing of their particular part or share of sd land until they are all agreed to the same."
Seal: John McBride
Exrs: son James McBride   Samuel Allison
Wits: Samuel McDill   (Jurat)   William Corsby

A:0270 pp:269/270 JOHN MacCLINTOCK   29 Dec. 1806   Aug. Ct. 1807
Wife: Isabella plantation, all lands, houses, Negroes, all stock of every kind, & all household furniture with everything whatsoever Belonging unto me to be at her disposal whilst she lives.
Four Sons: John William Samuel & Robert at wife's decease, land & Anthony, Negro man, to be sold & the money equally divided between them.
Daus: Isabell Dick & Nansey Ballinger $1 each.
2 Negroes Fil & her son Fob to be free & to go where they please at Isabella MacClintocks decease.
Seal: John (his x mark) MacClintock
Exrs: wife Isabella MacClintock   John Gilchrist
Wits: John Gilchrist   (Jurat)   Moses Gilchrist
"revokes"
N.B. Nov. Term 1824 Statement from John Gilchrist relinquishing his executor duty for this will...the said Isabella MacClintock is now dead".

A:0271 pp:270/271 JOHN McCLEAN   15 June 1804   Aug. Ct. 1807
"Know all men by these presents that I..."
Sons: Thomas,   Robert   &   Marshall   each $20.
Daus: Nelly, Margaret, Jean & Polly each $20.
Son John's Son John & Dau: Polly's son John each $10.
Son: Robert land he now lives upon beginning at a hickory at the mouth of a small branch running thence partly a N E course along a marked line to a black oak, then East to a post oak on James Dick's line, then on his line S 7° East to an iron wood bush on the bank of Allamance Creek,

then down the creek to a red oak bush then South 7° East on sd Dicks line to a corner Black Oak on my son Joseph McCleans line then on his line West to Dorcas McCleans line, then making an offset to the right falling on Dorcas McCleans line, then to a post oak corner, then a North course to a hickory on the bank of sd creek, then up the creek to the beginning.
Dau: Jean my bedstead bed & furniture.
Son: Marshall's Dau: Jean my chest.
Son: Marshal the remainder of Land with such proviso hereafter be made, his land to begin at my son Roberts corner black oak, then East to a marked hickory, then North to a black oak on Smiths old line, then West on Smiths line passing the School house to a Stake, then South to a pine on the bank of Allamance, then down sd creek to my son Roberts corner a hickory, then a NE course to the beginning.
Daus: Nancy and Elizabeth each $125, the free use & enjoyment of my dwelling house during the term of their natural life if they choose to keep it so long & at their death it shall go to the use of son Marshal or his heirs.
Daus: all cattle & sheep to be equally divided between them. They to have free use of spring house & cellar, a 3rd part of the garden, 1/4 acre of suitable ground yearly to be plowed & put in good order for Cotton or whatever else they please to put in it & 1/2 an acres of good ground for flax if required. They to have the benefit of as much fruit as may be necessary for their own consumption & if they see meet to keep a horse or a cow apiece, their horse is to have stable room & fed on the best of the hay & their corn, straw or fodder cost free, they shall have firewood brought to them, or liberty to find it themselves anywhere on the plantation they please.
Dau: Nancy 1 black mare & colt & my loom.
Dau: Elizabeth 1 black horse.
Daus: Elizabeth & Nancy all my cattle & sheep to be divided equally between them.
Negro boy Josh if not disposed of before together with my Still be valued by my son Joseph McClean & Isaiah McBride or if sd Negro is Sold his price together with the appraisement of the Still I allow to be divided into three equal parts between Marshal, Nancy & Elizabeth. Yet if Marshal sees meet to keep the aforesaid property at the appraisment I allow him so to do provided he does pay a lawful Interest to Nancy & Elizabeth in Grain at the Current Market price for their part until he discharges the same.
Son: Marshall 1 Eight Day Clock, 1 large Walnut Table as a full Compensation for what he has done toward repairing my house.
Daus: Nancy & Elizabeth all remainder of my household furniture with my Wearing apparel to be disposed of as they see proper, my large Bible I give to Marshal & the remainder of my Books to the two above mentioned Girls.
Dau: Polly what cattle & other property lent her I now give and bequeath unto her.
Other: All Legatees indebted to me either by Note or Book account I allow them to Settle their respective accounts without paying any interest.
Seal: John McClean
Exrs: Joseph McClean, Sr. Isaiah McBride Marshal McClean
Wits: Thomas Greear (Jurat) Joseph McGahey **"revokes"**

AN ANNOTATED DIGEST OF WILL BOOK A, GUILFORD COUNTY, NORTH CAROLINA

A:0272 p:272 GIDEON McKEMMA 30 Jan. 1809 Aug. Ct. 1809
Dau: Marey Bishop 5 sh.
Dau: Elisabeth Hardin 5 sh.
Son: William 85 acres of land.
Son: Shadrach 30 acres of land.
Son: James 30 acres of land.
Wife: Charity all horse, cows, sheep, hogs, & farming utensils, household furniture & her living on the place during her widowhood & at her decease or marriage what property that remains to be at her disposal.
In case she is with child I bequeath it $30 to be raised among all other 3 boys according to their holding of land to be paid unto it when it comes of age.
Seal: Gideon (his x mark) McKemma
Exrs: wife Charity McKemma James Willey
Wits: James Frazier (Jurat) John McKaige (Jurat)

A:0273 p:273 SAMUEL McDILL 19 May 1811 Aug. Ct. 1811
Wife: Jean the free use of 1/2 of the plantation on which we now live, the use or labour of 1 Negro man named Charls, both during her natural life or widowhood with such articles of household & kitchen furniture as she may deem necessary for her own use.
Son: Isaiah McDill 215 acres of land embracing the homeplace under the afsd restrictions & the place whereon John McCann lately recorded, the whole of the balance of my moveable property conditional that he furnish to:
His sister Betsy 1 good feather bed & furniture, 2 cows, 1 good horse, bridle & saddle & pay her $100 in case she thinks proper at any time to leave him.
Seal: Samuel McDill
Exrs: son Isaiah McDill Thomas McCann
Wits: W. Corsbee David Matthews (Jurat)

A:0274 p:274 GEORGE McKENEY 17 March 1801 May Ct. 1801
Son: George McKeney & his heirs 5 sh.
Dau: Jenney Stanford & her heirs 5 sh.
Dau: Lettes/Lettice & her heirs 5 sh.
Wife: Elisabeth negro man Billey, all stock of horses, cattle, hogs & sheep, all household & kitchen furniture & plantation tools during her natural life or widow hood to raise my three young children. Upon her death or marriage what is left to be sold & equally divided between my 3 youngest children: Son: Demsey McKeney and Daus: Polley & Fanny & their heirs.
Son: Jarrat McKeneys children should desire to come in for part I give them 5 sh each.
Dau: Fanney McKeneys Dau: Catey 5 sh.
Seal: George (his x mark) McKeney
Exrs: wife Elisebeth McKeney son Demsey
Wits: Justain Knott John Medearis (Jurat) Patsy (her x mark) Pegram
"revokes"

AN ANNOTATED DIGEST OF WILL BOOK A, GUILFORD COUNTY, NORTH CAROLINA

    A:0275   p:275 **THOMAS MORELAND**   31 Aug. 1792   Feb. Ct. 1793
Wife: Jane during her natural life the plantation with all the improvements thereon to be in full of her dower, also 1 Negro man Jams, 1 Negro woman Sue, 1 Negro girl Hannah & Ben.
Son: William after my wife's death my land on which I now live on in Guilford County, 1 Negro man Peter Amey Ellis - George Ellick & lucy to him & his heirs. [sic]
Son: Francis 1 Negro man Joe Phib Tappley Silvey [sic] & £3 cash.
Dau: Elizabeth [surname left blank] 1 Negro girl Patt during her life then to my son William, she & her increase.
Dau: Mary Ashley 1 Negro man Toney Kitt & Buck [sic] after her decease to be equally divided between all her children then living lawfully begotten.
Son: William to inherit any property left at death of wife.
Joseph -augh [?] all the part of my land on the South side of the Creek on the East side of the Branch down the sd branch as it meanders to Reaves line.
Seal: Thomas Moreland
Exrs: son William Moreland   Hezekiah Bevill
Wits: Thomas (his x mark) Reaves   William Williams (Jurat) William (his x mark) Simpson (Jurat)
N.B. making null & void all former wills...
"revokes"

    A:0276   pp: 277/278 **JOHN NATION, SENIOR** 15 Dec. 1772 May Ct. 1774
Son: Joseph Nation the plantation & tract of land whereon I now live & to enjoy & possess the same & all the appurtenances thereunto belonging immediately after my decease to him particularly.
Wife: Bethiah all moveable estate during her life or widowhood, & in case she should see cause to alter her condition after my decease by marriage then she should be confined to her thirds of my estate. Nevertheless in case of 2nd marriage and she becomes thereby confined to her third that she is empowered hereby do Divide the overplus thereof between my 2 sons John and Joseph Nation. Wife to live on my plantation during her widowhood.
Son: John to have a bed & furniture, Chest & box.
Son: Joseph all the rest of my moveable estate.
Rest of my children to wit: Christopher Nation, Elizabeth Vickrey, Anna Bullar, Bethiah Robins & Frances Robins each the sum of 1 sh sterling and no more.
Seal: John (his   mark) Nation
Exrs: wife Bethiah Nation   son Joseph Nation
Wits: Benjamin Beeson (Jurat affirmed)   Isaac Beeson Juner (Jurat affirmed) Richard Beeson
"utterly revoking & disallowing all other former will or wills...made or done as tho they had never been done."

    A:0277   p:277   **JOHN NOTS/NOTTS[NOTZ]**   15 Sept. 1775   Nov. Ct. 1775
Wife: [not named] the 4th part of my moveable effects, 1 milk cow, 5 pounds of my lands [sic] which I order my 2 daughters to pay as they come to each portion of their land.
Oldest Dau: Catrena the house where I now dwell & 84 acres of land the South side of my land.
Youngest Dau: Barbra the other 84 acres of my land.

I do constitute Malkia Fogelman & Jacob Greeson executors of this my last will and testament and order them to lay my land regular the best way among my two daus: and my moveable property to be sold at publick vendue & the money lent at interest til my daus. come to age.
Seal: Johannes Notz   [John Nots]
Exrs: Malkia Fogelmann   Jacob Greeson
Wits: George Cortner (Jurat)   David Lau   George Fogelman

A:0278 pp:278/279/280   ROBERT NEELLEY   6 July 1787   Nov. Ct. 1787
Money from estate to purchase head stone for the graves of my father, mother, & brother who are buried at the Allimance meeting house.
Wife: Marthy 1 bay mare & colt, the young Bald Eagle mare & 1 bed & furniture & her saddle & bridle, 2 cows & calves, all hogs & all the shelf furniture except such as shall be hereafter devised to my daughter, & all my pot mettle except 1 pot, also all the crop that is or shall be raised on my plantation this year & she to have the use of my plantation during her natural life or widowhood & 1 plow, & 1 hoe unto her & her heirs or assigns.
Dau: Elizabeth Neeley 100 acres of land joining the part that I sold to John Coe, a long square down the East side & South line of my land to her & her heirs & assigns, 6 new puter plates & the largest Puter dish, 1 pot, holding about 3 gallons, 1 black walnut chest & 1 bible.
Son: James Neeley all the remaining part of my land that is not sold laying on the head watters of the Allimance containing 320 acres & in case Watson Wharten should get a Negro for me from Maryland, then he to go to James, all my wareing apparel, 1 desk, my saddle & bridle, all my working tools & the remaining part of my farming utensils, my large Bible & my books.
Executors to lay out as much money of my estate as shall purchase materials & pay workmen to build the house that is begun and make it fit to Dwell in.
Two children: James & Elizabeth all the remaining part of estate, including the balance of money due from John Coe after a just settlement & all other perishable articles sold and money equally divided.
Dau: Elizabeth 1 bed & furniture not to be reckoned as a part of the before Bequeath.
Seal: Robert Neelley
Exrs. Wife Martha Neeley   William Dickey   Thomas Jones
Wits: John Coe (Jurat)   William Dobson (Jurat)   Sarah Coe
"revokes"

A:0279 pp:280/281   ALEXANDER NELSON   24 Oct. 1799   Nov. Ct. 1799
Wife: Jean Nelson her heirs & assigns forever all the land I now live on during her life or widowhood, then to be equally divided between my 2 Sons: James Nelson & Robert Nelson.
Dau: Elizabeth Nelson 1 cow & calf the choice of my stock, 1 bed & furniture.
Dau: Ruth Nelson 1 cow & calf the 2nd choice of my stock, 1 bed & furniture.
Dau: Ezebell [Isabell] Nelson 1 cow & calf the 3rd choice of my stock, 1 bed & furniture.
Wife, Daus:, Sons: remainder of estate sold & equally divided.

AN ANNOTATED DIGEST OF WILL BOOK A, GUILFORD COUNTY, NORTH CAROLINA

Seal: Alexander (his   mark) Nelson
Exrs: wife Jean Nelson   friend Justain Knott
Wits: John Bevill (Jurat) William Bevill (Jurat)   Abraham Endsley
"revokes"

A:0280 p:281 MARY NEWNUM   7 May 1810   Aug. Ct. 1810
Verbal will of Mary NEWNOM taken before me Robert Bell one of the Justices of the peace in and for sd county this 7th day of May 1810, the 9th day after her death:
Son: Edward NEWNOM 1 sorrel mare.
Dau: Sarah 1 sorrel colt.
Dau: Ann 1 puter dish, 1 puter basin, 6 mettle spoons 1/2 dozen puter plates.
Son: Benjamin 1 feather bed & furniture, 1 red cow.
Daus: most of my clothing divided equally except a few things that may suite the boy. [not named]
Administration granted to Edward NEWNOM
Above will proven by the affirmation of Ruth Clark. Robt. Bell, (JP)
Administration granted to Edward NEWNOM August Term 1810

A:0281 pp:282/283 GEORGE NELSON, SENIOR 21 Jan. 1801 Aug. Ct. 1802
Wife: Susanny Nelson free privilege of the plantation whereon I now live to be possessed by her clear of all encumbrances during her widow hood, lends to wife all horses, cattle, hogs, sheep, household furniture, blacksmithy tools, plantation tools, & everything not belonging to said George Nelson until the year 1813 if she continues a widow.
All children: that has not got schooling is to be schooled out of the property that I have lent my wife with what money I may have when I dye.
4 Sons: all lands containing 300 acres.
2 Sons: George Nelson & Jessay Nelson 75 acres a piece.
Son: Joseph 75 acres including the house where I now live not to interrupt my wife or take possession during her widowhood, but he may build on the sd 75 acres to be possessed and enjoyed by him forever.
Son: Alexander Nelson 75 acres of land in the NE corner of my tract.
6 Daus:: Marget, Prudence, Sally, OlleyJan, Betsy, Nansy Nelson 1 cow & calf, feather bed each if it can be spared at their marriage.
10 Children: George, Jessey, Marget, Prudence, Salley, OlleyJan, Betsy, Joseph, Alexander, & Nansy Nelson after the death or marriage of my wife Susanny Nelson to divide my remaining estate.
Executors: after the year 1813 if my wife is then a widow & there is more stock on the plantation than the Exrs. think she can well support, the sd Exrs. may divide such a part of the stock among all my children as equally as they can to be possessed & enjoyed by them forever.
If wife should dye or marry before the year 1813 there may be a division made of the whole of the property among all the children when the Exrs. think best.
Seal: George Nelson
Exrs: Drury Peeples   Jeremiah Cunningham
Wits: Joel (his x mark) Harris (Jurat)   Frederick Peeples   (Jurat)
"revokes"
[note: since the testator mentions the date 1813, that could be a clue to the ages of the children; especially the last one] JSH

AN ANNOTATED DIGEST OF WILL BOOK A, GUILFORD COUNTY, NORTH CAROLINA

A:0282 pp:284/285 SAMUEL OWEN 19 May 1808 Aug. Ct. 1808
Wife: Judith a small bag of feathers, 2 sheets & coverlaid, [coverlid or coverlet] 1 table, 1 oven, 1 straw basket, 1 dresser & the furniture belonging thereto, except 1 pewter dish & 1 pewter bason, 1 pail & washing tub.
Dau: Mary 1 feather bed, 1 coverlaid, 3 sheets, 1 pewter dish & 1 pewter bason & for her to continue with her Mother if they both should live until she arrives to the age of 18 years.
Remainder of estate to be sold, burial expenses paid, any remaining money to be used to school my dau. Mary.
W. Love, an attorney at law has agreed to defend a suit brought against Daniel Leger by me, which the sd W. Love was to have $30 for his service if he gained the suit & nothing if not, & its my desire that my Exr. should attend to this business, & if anything be recovered for it to be considered as my property & be equally divided between my wife & dau.
Seal: Samuel (his x mark) Owen
Exr: trusty friend Harmon Howlet
Wits: Jacob Brassell [Brazell] (Jurat) Ann (her x mark) Howlet J. H. Howlet
"revokes"
[Note: check court minutes for any action on this item] JSH

A:0283 p:286 EPHRAIM POTTER 28 Feb. 1774 Nov. Ct. 1775
Son: Joseph 1/2 of the improvement of land I now live on the lower end lying on Piney Fork a branch of Town Creek & 1/6th of all personal estate.
Son: Abraham 1/2 of the improvement of land lying on Piney fork a branch of Town creek & 1/6th part of my personal estate.
Daus: Alice, Martha, Sarah each 1/6th of personal estate.
Son: John 5 sh sterling.
Wife: Sarah an equal part of my personal estate with my 5 children: Joseph Abraham Alce Martha & Sarah during her natural life or widowhood, & after her death or intermarriage her part to my son Joseph.
Seal: Ephraim (his x mark) Potter
Exrs: William Garratt Edward Stubblefield
Wits: Isham Browder (Jurat) Thomas (his x mark) Norris
[note: this land may have been in present Rockingham County] JSH

A:0284 p:287 JAMES PORTER 1 Dec. 1777 May Ct. 1778
Wife: Ann 1/2 of all I do possess of the moveables & 1/2 of the land during her life.
Dau: Vilet [Violet?] Porter the other half of all & the land to be hers after her mothers death.
James Porter: 1 sorrel colt. [relationship not given]
Seal: James Porter
Exrs: wife Ann Porter Joseph Brown
Wits: Hugh Porter (Jurat) John Hodge
"ratifies this and no other to be my last will and testatment".

A:0285 pp:287/288/289 DAVID PHILPOTT 28 Feb. 1781 Aug. Ct. 1781
Wife: Maryann I lend 1 tract of land laying on the South side of Hogains Creek beginning at a red oak on sd creek turning East 207 poles to a white oak thens North 88 poles to a red oak saplin thens West 62°

AN ANNOTATED DIGEST OF WILL BOOK A, GUILFORD COUNTY, NORTH CAROLINA

North 90 poles to a white sapling then West 30° 90 poles to a poplar on the creek bank & up the meanders of the creek to the 1st station containing 233 acres of land more or less, 2 Negroes 1 named Nathan & 1 Mall, all stock of all kinds & all Household furniture in order to raise & support my children so long as she remains my widow, at her death or remarriage my estate shall be divided amongst my children as per:
Son: Charles 100 acres of land out of my entered [land] that I bought of Capt. John Cook in Caswell County to begin at John McCollams corner tree & run with Johnsons land as the Surveys runs then to Major Dickson land then down with Dicksons land then so far as to strike a cross to John McCollums land then with McCollums to his corner tree so as to make 100 acres of land, 1 cow & calf, & 1 featherbed to be delivered when he shall come of age to 21 years.
Dau: Mary Philpott all the remaining part of my entered land after Charles gets his 100 acres out of it containing 291 more or less, 1 Negro wench named Charity & her increase, 1 cow & calf, 1 feather bed & furniture to be delivered to the age of 16 or marriage.
Dau: Elezebeth Philpott 1 Negro girl named Easter & her increase, 1 cow & calf, 1 feather bed & furniture when she arrive to age 16 or marriage.
Son: Edward Philpott 1 tract of land laying on the North side of Hogans creek beginning at a beech on the creek bank running thece West 74 poles to a hickry thence North 113 poles to a hickry thence East 125 poles to the creek so up the creek as it meanders to the beginning containing 86 acres of land more or less, my afsd tract of land I lent to my wife after her death or marriage, 1 Negro boy named Henry & after the death or marriage of my afsd wife I give to my son Edward Negroes Nathan & Mall, all the rest of personal estate to my son Edward.
If either son Edward or daughters Elezebeth or Mary should die without heir then the surviving party of them three shall inherit estate.
Seal: David Philpott
Exrs: wife Mary Ann brother John Philpott (he to be guardian & trustee over all my children)
Wits: TGR Turner Thomas Weatherford John McCollum
Memorandum that upon the 22nd day of March 1780 Robert Shaw took 2 Bells out of my house in a felonious manner from my wife William Gilmer evidence against Shaw & William Bridges.
Memorandum that upon the 24th day of said month Thomson Heirs Robert Heirs & John Jones took two of my horses & waggon and all my waggon geers, plow gears 1 saddle plowlines 2 bells & bell collars 1 ax in a felonious maner which will be pleased to indite them for, the Evidence is William Reed William Scot Robert Rankin Juner John Rankin
NB my wife went to Capt. William Beathel and asked some of the things from him (as he had the command) but he refused to let her have any of them and so supported them in taking my effects. Now if you think this is inditable please to Indite him likewise
Memorandum that upon the 8th of June 1781 that Francis McNery Shot down my steer in Adam Michals field or cause to be done in a felonious maner for which you will be pleased to indight him for the evidence Henery Reed William Reed James Hunter from William Dick Plaintiff
To Col. Alex. Martin State Attorney.
[notation on the side unreadable - seems to indicate some sort of payment]
[there is no mention of this trouble in the Guilford County Court Minutes of that date. JSH]

AN ANNOTATED DIGEST OF WILL BOOK A, GUILFORD COUNTY, NORTH CAROLINA

A:0286 p:289 CALEB PERKINS   1788   probate date not given
"whereas, I Caleb Perkins..."
Bro: Joseph Perkins, Jr. my saddle & 10 bushel of corn.
Bro: Isaac Perkins 1 cow.
Sis: Mary Perkins 1 cow.
Bro: John Perkins 50 bushel of corn.
Wheat, & oats & the rest of my property not mentioned above to be taken care of my three brothers namely Joseph, John & Isaac, to sell the same & keep the money safe for my two younger brothers: Thomas & Jared, to be given to them when they come of age.
Seal: Caleb Perkins
Exrs: brothers John & Isaac Perkins
Wits: Joseph Perkins   John Thomas (Jurat)   Aaron Mendenhall
"revokes"

A:0287 p:290 WILLIAM PARKHILL   26 Aug. 1789   n.p.d.
"Thy ever blessed and unerring will oh most gracious though offended God be done..."
Wife: Nancy during her life her bed & cloths, lining [linen] wheel & reel, 2 small pots, the furniture that is on the dresser and chest & the whole of my books, 1 cow, 10 bushels of wheat, 10 bushels of Indian corn, & 1 pot rack, & 1/2 of all the profits arising from the sale after debts is paid.
Brother John, Sisters Martha & Meriann, & John Homes, Meryann's son, remainder of estate to be equally divided betwixt them.
Seal: William Parkhill
Exrs: friends William Eken   William Beadey [?]
Wits: William (his O mark) Ekin   Jeremiah Shelly

A:0288 p:291 EZEKIEL PRITCHETT   20 July 1796   Aug. Ct. 1796
Son: Zachariah Pritchet 1 shilling & no more.
Son: Ezekel Pritcher 1 shillng & no more.
Dau: Elezabeth Pritcher 1 sh.
Unity Pritchet 1 sh. [relationship not given]
Isaac Pritchet the plantation I now live on with all its apertenencies containing 247 acres 1 mare named Swallow, 1 white faced heffer & 6 pewter plates. [Relationship not given]
Ezekel Gullet 100 acres of land on which George Forbes formerly lived. If Ezekel Gullet dies without lawful issue the land to fall to my son Isaac Pritchet. [relationship not given]
Zebulon Pritcher 100 acres of land on which John Hood lived. [no relationship given]
Son: Isaac 1 bed & furniture.
My children that are here, sons: John, Zeblon, Isaac; Daus: Hesse & Sarah, remainder of estate to be equally divided.
Seal: Ekel [sic] Pritchet
Exrs: son Zebulon
Wits: Robert Paisley (Jurat)   James Mills   William Paisley (Jurat)

AN ANNOTATED DIGEST OF WILL BOOK A, GUILFORD COUNTY, NORTH CAROLINA

A:0289 p:292 CATHARINE PLUNKET 1 June 1801 Aug. Ct. 1801
Bro: Thomas Plunkett my part of my father's estate which at this time is not a division took place [sic] & all property I now possess.
Seal: Catherine (her x mark) Plunket
Exrs: brother, Thomas Plunket
Wits: William Rose George (his mark) Shoffner (Jurat) Anna Margaretha Shofner [her name written in German script.]JSH

A:0290 p:292 WILLIAM PLUNKETT nuncupative will Aug. Ct. 1801
I allow Caty all the Moovable effects with as much of the fruit every year as she wants & 1 end of the house & firewood & liberty to keep a cow or 2 & a horse creature & liberty to cut hay for them during her plesures & to live in peace without interuption & land for a garden & a cotton patch.
Son: Is [sic] the rest of the land.
Seal: none
Exer: Thomas Plunket
Wits: James Oneal (Jurat) & Samuel Lindsay, Esqr. (Jurat)
"This instrument of writing was proven in Open Court August Term 1801 as the nuncupative will of William Plunket Dec'd. by the oaths of James Oneal & Samuel Lindsay Esqr. & admitted to record; Administration granted with the copy of the will annexed to Thomas Plunket who qualified as such & entered into bonds & etc."

A:0291 p:293 EDWARD PEGRAM 2 Feb. 1802 May Ct. 1802
All moveable property except the slaves hereafter mentioned, shall be sold at public venue.
Wife: Patty 1/3 part of the sale. Lends 1 Negro woman named Fanny & 3 Negro girls named China, Suikey, & Martha for her use during her widowhood & at her death or marriage the aforementioned slaves & their issue to be manumitted & set free from Slavery; 1/3 part of my land during her natural life, lends the whole of land until youngest child comes of age, at which time I will that the whole be sold (reserving her 1/3) & the proceeds divided equally amongst my children. [Not named]
Seal: Edward (his x mark) Pegram
Exrs: wife Patty Pegram friend William Jean
Wits: Travis Jones (Jurat) John Medaris Massey C. Medearis

A:0292 p:294 ELEANOR PRIOR 4 Nov. 1804 Nov. Ct. 1804
Eldest Son: Emmery Dent Prior 1 feather bed & furniture, 1 hair trunk if his guardian if necessity require it.
Son: Paschel Brimajum [sic] Prior 1 feather bed & furniture, 1 chest to his use at any time as above directed for my oldest son.
Sons: Emmery Dent Prior & Paschal Brimajum Prior the remainder of my estate to be sold & equally divided between them.
Seal: Eleanor (her x mark) Prior
Exer: trusty friend John Moore
Wits: James Johnson (Jurat) William Moore Anne Moore

AN ANNOTATED DIGEST OF WILL BOOK A, GUILFORD COUNTY, NORTH CAROLINA

A:0293 p:294/295 SAMUEL PORTER 20 Oct. 1806 Nov. Ct. 1806
Father: [not named] $100.
Brother: John & his wife $10.
Sister: Margaret $500.
Cathren Qu----[?] $100. If she should die in non age it is to go to Isaiah McBride. [non age - minor before reaching age 21]
William Finley: who lives in the State of Caintucke $200.
Allemance Congregation: to be applyed as they judge best the sum of $100. The sum of $200 to be laid out in purchasing such books as shall be judged best for usefull knowldedge for the benefit of the Allmence Settlement & Congregation, the books to be under the care & direction of a Committee of Seven of whom Mr. Jedediah Cusick & my 3 Executors are to be 4 of the number.
The remainder of my estate if any is to be equally divided among all of my relations that are not in the above will & testament & none of them that are already mentioned only William Findley & John Porter are to be entitled to a share of this dividend.
Seal: Samuel Porter
Exrs: John Porter Isaiah McBride Walter McConel
Wits: Margaret McBride William McBride (Jurat)

A:0294 pp:295/296 JOSEPH PERKINS 1 Dec. 1806 Feb. Ct. 1807
Wife: Ann the best bed & furniture, 1 mare & colt, the Bell cow* & 1 heifer her choice, 1/2 of the money that shall be raised from the sale.
Son: Jared 2 pair of drawing chains, harrow, frow, chisels & augre.
Son: Jared's wife Nancy Perkins 1 cow.
Sons: Joseph, John, Isaac & Thomas each $1.
Grandson: Joseph s/o Joseph Perkins Jnr. $20.
The remainder of my property to be sold at publick sale at 12 months credit to wit: the next feather bed & rose blanket, my saddle, bridle & surcingle, 1 walnut dough table, 1 arm chair, 1 pair dressers, 1 corner cupboard, 1 large cast kettle, 1 large pot, a middle sized pot, a middle sized oven no lid, 1 small oven & lid, 1 large chest, & 1/2 the young cattle that remain after the 1 be taken.
Daus: Mary & Betty the remainder of the money after all charges is paid to be equally divided between them.
Seal: Joseph Perkins
Exr: esteemed friend Moses Mendenhall continued
Wits: Moses Mendenhall (Jurat) Mary Mendenhall (Jurat) & Charity Mendenhall (Jurat)
"revokes"
* note: the Bell cow was usually the leader of the herd and wore the said bell. JSH

A:0295 pp:296/297 JOHN PAISLEY 25 July 1811 Nov. Ct. 1811
Wife: Mary Ann all my estate real & personal now in my possession for her use & benefit during the term of her natural life.
Son: William Paisley 2 Negroes Milley & Aaron
Son: James Paisley 2 Negroes Gilbert & James.
Children of Dau: Nancy Hanner 2 Negroes Sophia & Teney.
Sons of Dau: Nancy Hanner all that part of the plantation on which I now live lying on the North of the present great road & Each of Burch Creek, also 85 acres on which my Dau. Nancy Hanner now lives.

Son: John Paisley 3 Negroes Peter, Cate & Dick, all their offspring from this date, also the plantation on which I now live, together with all the stock & household furniture &etc. at my wife's decease.
Dau: Elenor Paisley 2 Negroes Seventy & Sally & 50 acres of land it being part of a survey adj the NW corner of the plantation on which I now live.
Son: George Paisley 2 Negroes Emmy & Isaac.
Dau: Elizabeth Gibson 2 Negroes Rose & Mary.
Dau: Mary Ann Paisley 2 Negroes Jenny & Moses & other property simular & equal in value with that which my Dau. Elizabeth has received.
If any of the Negroes should die or become useless before they are received by my heirs then each legatee is to make up equal dividend to whom the Negro may belong, to make up for the loss, first deducting an equal part for the looser.
Seal: John Peasley[Paisley]
Exrs: sons John Paisley Moses Gibson
Wits: William Paisley (Jurat) George Paisley
"revokes"

A:0296 p:298 JAMES POE   9 Feb. 1812   Feb. Ct. 1812
" I, James Poe..."
Wife: Sarah Poe all my estate of what name nature soever as long as she remains my widow & no longer.
Children: Gabril, Nansy, Metildy, Betsey, Sandy, William, Reny, Hannah, James, Polly & John all property to be sold & divided equally among all them and including wife, if still living.
Seal: James (his x mark) Poe
Exrs: worthy friends William Poe & Josiah Unthank
Wits: Bethuel Coffin (affirmed in Court) John Unthank David McGready

A:0297 pp: 298/299 JAMES PORTER   24 Feb. 1812   Aug. Ct. 1812
Son: John the plantation I now live on containing 360 acres & all & every of the remainder of my estate whether real or personal.
Dau: Margaret Wiley alias Margaret Porter $300 in case all my outstanding debts can be collected, & in case of any deficiency 1/2 of the same shall be reduced of the sum before mentioned together with 2 cows, my cow lot [sic] & tea table & 1/2 the pewter of my property on or belonging to my Dresser.
Seal: James Porter
Exr: Son John Porter
Wits: Walter McConnell (Jurat) Joseph Hanner (Jurat)
"revokes"

A:0298 pp:299/300/301 JEHU PEEBLES   23 April 1813   Aug Ct. 1813
Wife: Caty to have during her natural life & for her use untill her death all that part of my plantation in Guilford County whereon I now live, which I shall not dispose of otherwise, 7 of my Negroes with their increase her choice, also all my household furniture & as many horses as she shall choose, 1 waggon with gears for 4 horses, her choice of plantation tools, & horned cattle, sheep & hogs.
Children: all horses, plantation tools, horned cattle, sheep & hogs not chosen by wife to be equally divided.
Son: Wyatt Peebles the plantation in Guilford County after the death of my wife & 68 acres of land whereon George McKinney formerly lived.

Son: Herbert Peebles that tract of land I purchased of Hugh Cummings after death of my wife, containing 150 acres.
Dau: Sally Jean $120 to be raised out of my estate after my wifes death.
Sons: & Daus: Drury, Herbert, Nathaniel, Wyatt, Sally Jean & Nancy McKinney all my Negroes not heretofor disposed of, to be valued by 2 indifferent persons for the most equitable distribution among them.
Son: Seth Peebles is deceased & no part of my estate is to revert to his wife or to her relations after my decease or the decease of my wife.
Seal: Jehu Peebles
Exrs: wife Caty sons Drury Peeples & Wyatt Peeples
Wits: Christian Wagoman (Jurat) C. F. Bagge (Jurat)
NB It is my will & desire that all monies paid by me for and on account of my daughter Nancy McKinney are to be deducted by my Executors out of her part of her legacy bequeathed to her by me in this will.
"revokes"

A:0299 p:301 WILLIAM PARSONS nuncupative will 13th of 5th mo 1814
My smith tools to my son George by paying little John at Baptis Clarks $10. Also the land to be divided equally between my son James & John, and James to have the gun & Mary $5 woth of property The still to remain on the place belonging to the orchard untill James & John comes of age & then to be divided equally between them and the balance of the property to be divded equally among all the rest of the girls and for my wife Eleanor to have a peacefull and reasonable living off of the place during her Widdowhood and at the end of that to have her Bead and furniture and 1 cow and for my accounts all to be collected and the balance over what pays my debts to be equally divided among all the Boys and the five Girls, Katharine, Ruth, Patience, Charity, and Eleanor -

State of North Carolina Guilford County George Parsons and John Parker came before me Jonathan Parker one of the Justices in and for the County of Guilford and after being duly sworn deposeth and sayeth that the above instrument of righting was committed to wrighting for a will for William Parsons Dec'd. and at his request in his Last Sickness and appeared to be in his sound mind and memory which was at his own house in Guilford County
Sworn and subscribed to before me this 10th of 5th mo 1814
Wits: George Parsons, Jr. (Jurat) John Parker (Jurat)
Jonathan Parker, J. P.

A:0300 pp:301/302 HENRY PORTER 6 Oct. 1813 Feb. Ct. 1816
George Griffins Children: allow the use of my plantation the term of 4 years, it to be taken care of by my Exrs: that the Limber & other things be not destroyed or damaged at the expiration of 4 years the plantation to be sold to the best advantage the money to be put to interest and last out for the Education of Orphant children at the descretion of my Exrs.
John Finley: my books I allow to be kept in his hands to be put into a Society Library if such should be instituted in the term of 4 years. If not my Exrs. to dispose of them as they may Judge.
My big Bible to be kept by my Exrs. until Henry Porter Griffin is 21 years of age then to be given to him.
Seal: Henry Porter
Exrs: Levi Huston John Finley
Wits: Elva (her x mark) Finley (Jurat) Wm. (his x mark) Mccurney (Jurat)

AN ANNOTATED DIGEST OF WILL BOOK A, GUILFORD COUNTY, NORTH CAROLINA

A:0301   pp:304/305   WILLIAM QUAIT/QUATE   25 July 1803   May Ct. 1805
Wife: Elizabeth Quait the plantation I now live on & all moveable property during her life or widowhood. Wife to pay all just debts, pay $44 to Neley Cirkman [Kirkman] for a colt which my son James Quait bought of her.
Son: Samuel Quait to have plantation at death or marriage of wife.
Son: Robert Quait 100 acres of land beginning at a post oak on my own line corner & Robert Hannar line run the East side of the original tract.
Son: James Quait 100 acres of land off the South side of the plantation as it now stands.
Dau: Isbel Quait 1 gray mare 5 years old & her colt & saddle, bed & furniture, 1 cow 4 years old of a pied color, 1 red year old heffer & two year old steer, her walnut chest, 6 pewter plates, 6 knives & 6 forks, 1 pewter dish, 1 pot, 2 chairs.
Dau: Margret Quait 1 two year old heffer, & a Cloke or $5 in money over and above what she has already received.
Son: William Quait 10 sh over & above what he has already.
Dau: Agnes Muehard [?] Morehead [?] 10 sh.
Dau: Mary Ridle 10 sh over what she has alredy recieved.
Son: David Quait 10 sh over what he has already received.
Granddaughter Ann Quait d/o Agnes Muchard [?] Morehead [?] the sum of £10 hard money or to the value of that same in property.
Seal: William Quait
Exrs: wife Elisabeth Quait   Daniel Gillaspie
Wits: Thomas Landreth   (Jurat)   James Hanner

A:0302   p:306   JAMES REEVES   [will undated, but note on original will's folder is 1781]   probated May Ct. 1805
Wife: Milissent Reeves my plantation I now live on to be hers during her natural lifetime, also all my beds & household furniture, her Saddle & bridle, my sorrel horse her choice of a cow & calf out of my stock, 1 Ram & a yew, [ewe] 1/3 of my stock of hogs & all my geese.
Son: Malachia Reeves 1 cow & calf.
Son: Jeremiah Reeves 1 yew & lambs.
Son: William Reeves my plantation I now live on to be his whole & sole property at the death of my beloved wife Malissent & not before.
Dau: Elizabeth Holmes 2 yews & Lambs.
Dau: Judith Moon 1 heifer.
Dau: Delilah Russel 1 heifer.
Dau: Rhode Parker 1 lamb.
Grandson: James Reeves my Roan horse, saddle & bridle.
Seal: James   (his \ mark) Reeves
Exrs: wife Melissent Reeves   son William Reeves
Wits: Jno. Campbill   Michel Reeves   Jeremiah Reeves [Jurat/s not given]

A:0303   pp:306/307   WILLIAM REA   23 Feb. 1789   May Ct. 1789
Wife: Margret Rea £50 & the benefit of the plantation & land I rented of Jean Blair.
All goods & chattels to be sold at publick vendue & the money arising therefrom after paying my just debts to be laid out for land on the western waters of this State at the descretion of my Exrs: & the sd land

to be equally divided agreeable to quantity & quality among all my children [not named] as they come to the age of maturity daughters as well as sons & also the lands I now claim on the waters of Cumberland River after satisfying the power of attorney given to James Billingsly the remainder to be divded in the same manner as above.
Seal: William Rea
Exrs: Henry Ross William Gowdy
Wits: James Billingsly (Jurat) William Gowdy Henry Ross
"revokes"

A:0304 pp:307/308 **HENRY REED**   13 April 1789   Aug. Ct. 1789
Wife: Agness Reed a childs part of all estate real & personal to be by her freely enjoyed for ever and also the benefit of the plantation while she remains a widow to raise & school my children, 1 horse & saddle.
Daus: & Sons: [not named] remaining part of estate real & personal equally divided among my children, share & share alike.
Negroe wench [not named] remain on the plantation to work & raise the children.
There is to be no sale of personal estate unless to pay debts the same to remain in the hands of my beloved wife to raise my children as above at the directon of my Exes: that the same be not embezzled.
Seal: Henry Reed
Exrs: William Gowdy William Scott
Wits: Wm. Graham (Jurat) Moses McCuiston William Reed (Jurat)
"revokes"

A:0305 pp:308/309   **JOHN RUDDUCK, SENIOR** 7th of 10th mo 1787
Feb. Ct. 1790
"farmer"
"Whereas, I ...John Rudduck"
Wife: Jane Rudduck use of dwelling house & other buildings, use of 1/2 the plantation her life time & all household goods & chattles to be at her disposal during her lifetime.
Children: Dinah Mendenhall, Phebe Mendenhall, John Rudduck Junr., Jemima Pendry, Jane Ruth, Willm. Rudduck & Sarah Sanders to divide the above at death of wife.
Son: William Rudduck all my plantation at his mothers decease, he having the use of 1/2 at present.
Children: William excepted, 20 sh each one.
Seal: John Rudduck Senior   [continued]
Exrs: sons John Rudduck William Rudduck William Tomlinson
Wits: Jno. Talbot (Jurat) Sam Pidgeon Thos Thornbrugh
"revokes"

A:0306 pp:309/310 **JOHN ROSS**   19 April 1791   May Ct. 1791
Dau: Rebecka 1 horse saddle & bridle, 2 cows & 1 bed & furniture, the horse to be worth £12.
Dau: Nancy 1 horse saddle & bridle, 2 cows & 1 bed & furniture.
Dau: Marget 1 horse, saddel & bridle, 2 cows, a bed & furniture.
Youngest Daus: Mary & Jean the same portion as their older sisters when they are come of age, equal in value with their oldest sister.
Son: Thomas 250 acres of my land lying next to John Tomlinsons, 1 horse, sadle & bridle, 2 cows, 2 calves, a plough, plough irons & others tacklins [tackle] belonging to the plough.

AN ANNOTATED DIGEST OF WILL BOOK A, GUILFORD COUNTY, NORTH CAROLINA

Son: John the land wereon dwelling house now stands, 200 acres reserving the priviledge of my wife living in the house & her maintenance during her life or widowhood.
James & Andrew: 350 acres to be divided between them. One to have 200 acres & the other is to have the remainder & a horse to make up the value of the 200 acres.
Wife: Mary her saddle & bridle, her bed & furniture, the dresser, & the household furniture, & the other things not expressly mentioned to be at her disposal.
It is to be remembered that after John Ross the within Testator signed & delivered the within that he made mention of some money that was in the house & said that the money should be divided between his 4 boys.
Seal: John Ross
Exrs: wife Mary   son Thomas Ross   Walter Denny
Wits: John Starrat (Jurat) Edward Green (Jurat)   Jean Flack (Jurat)

A:0307   pp:310/311   **JOHN RHODES**   5 Oct. 1791   Nov. Ct. 1792
"of Rockingham County"
Wife: Fortune Rhodes all the effects & land chattles of every kind of things that she bought at the vandue of the effects that did belong to the Estate of her former husband Malychia Reeves all things she bought at the vandue to have to her use.
Heirs of my first born Son: Hezekiah Rhodes 1 French Crown to their use.
Son: Joseph 1 French Crown to his use.
Dau: Sarah Rhodes 1 Negro named Phib, 1 feather bed & furniture to her use.
Son: Samuel 1 Negro man named Chance to his use.
Son: Absolom 1 Negro man named Bob to his use.
Sons: Samuel & Absolom the remainder of my estate to be equally divided betwixt them by my Exrs:
Seal: John Rhodes
Exrs: son John Rhodes   son-in-law [step-son?] William Reeves
Wits: Henry Work (Jurat) John Rhodes, Jr. Samuel Rhodes   William Reeves
"revokes"

A:0308   pp:311/312   **ADAM RITSEL[WRITSEL]** 3 June 1792 Nov. Ct. 1792
Wife: [not named] all my reale & personal estate during her widowhood for the support of herself & my children & their education. If she marry she to have an equal part with my children -
Children: Hennery, Christipher, Adam, John, Marget, Mikel & Gorge.
It is also my will that all my rale & personal estate should be valued by 2 honest men & a true inventory taken of the whold & to ay in the hands of John Long & John Morres [Morris or Moretz] to see the true performance of the whole & an equal divide after the marrige or death of my wife.
Seal: Adam Reitzel [signed in German]
Exrs: wife [not named]
Wits: John Long (Jurat) Phillip (his   mark) Kime (Jurat)

A:0309 pp:312/313 **JOHN RYAN**   17 Oct. 1794   Nov. 1794
Wife: [not named] for term of life 1/3 of all moveable property with her bed & furniture, 1 cow & calf & wheel & my plantation till my children comes of age, 1 young bay horse & all other beds to her to dispose of to the children as she sees cause.

126

Dau: Ellener 1 cow.
Son: Robert 1 sorrel colt & 1 cow.
Son: John 1 colt.
Dau: Margat 1 cow.
Dau: Mary Ann 1 cow.
Son: William £10 & 1 cow.
Dau: Ginna 1 cow.
2 Negroes: sall & Press to be sold & the money equally divided amongst my children sons & daughters that remains.
Sons: Robert, John, William equally divide 310 acres of land.
Seal: John Ryan also signed by wife Margaret Ryan
Exrs: sons Robert, John & William and trustees of my children
Wits: William Sillaven (Jurat) Eleanor (her x mark) Silleven (Jurat)

A:0310 pp:313/314 WILLIAM RAPER   16 July 1794   Feb. Ct. 1795
Wife: Elizabeth the use of my house with the East half of my orchard that lyeth North side of the road that passeth my house, the use of my garden, & a priviledge of cutting firewood North of her part of the orchard, & my corn cribs, the use of 1/2 of my barn & the equal half of my fenced meadow & the field that leyeth South of my meadow joining James Colwells line with the woodland that leyeth South of sd field for a privilege of Timber for repairing fences during her natural life. Also a feather bed, furniture & bedstead, a chest, a little wheel, a horse, bridle & saddle, 2 cows with the third part of the rest of my moveable estate, which said moveables I give to her forever as her right of Dowrey [dower] out of my Estate.
Son: William Raper the whole of homestead plantation whereon I now dwell containing 200 acres to him & his heirs forever - (only he is not to possess nor interrupt my wife on that part that I have given her during her Naturel life.)
Children of my Dau: Christian, deceased which was the wife of Richard Glovyer the sum of 15 sh, together with what I have already given them which is their share out of my Estate.
Son: Thomas Raper £10 together with what I have already given him as a barr to cut him off from ever inheriting or claiming any other part of my Estate.
Sons: Isaac Raper, & William & Dau: Elizabeth the wife of James Gray & Lydia the wife of Daniel Killey the remaining part of my moveable estate that is not above mentioned to be equally divided between them.
Seal: Wm (his   mark) Raper
Exrs: sons Jacob Raper William Raper
Wits: Nathaniel Moore   (Jurat) Stephan (his x mark) Ruke Henry Davis
"revokes"
Feb. Ct. 1795 Stephen Ruke proved the execution of the within will & that he saw Nathaneil Moore & Henry Davis sign as witnesses at the same time came in William Raper one of the Exrs. appointed (the other refusing) and qualified.

AN ANNOTATED DIGEST OF WILL BOOK A, GUILFORD COUNTY, NORTH CAROLINA

A:0311 pp:314/315 WILLIAM RUSSELL 19 June 1792 May Ct. 1795
"planter"
Wife: Elenore a full priviledge to hold all the land rights she was possessed with before I married her & to dispose of them to her Children according to her agreement with me before marriage & to be understood the same as if I never had married her & likewise all the moveable property that is now of what she brought with her when I was married to her & I also give her 1 cow & calf, her spinning wheel, saddle & cards, I give to my Beloved Elenore to have as her whole portion of my estate.
Eldest Son: Robert Russell all the land East of the Still house branch & North of the Big Branch at the NE corner of my tract of land whereon he lives & that to be his full part of my estate.
5 Sons: William & John & David & James & Alexander Russell all the remainder of my land equally divided amongst them.
2 Daus: Elisabeth Downey & Marthew Maxwell all my household furniture that I hold to be understood all which remaineth above my wife's part already mentioned.
2 Sons: James & Alexander Russell all the remainder of my moveable estate.
Seal: William Russell
Exrs: son-in-law James Maxwell John Gilchrist
Wits: Valentine Mileham William Fleming Rosey Daughtery (Jurat)

A:0312 pp:316/317 ROBERT RANKIN, SEN'R. 30 May 1795 Nov. Ct. 1795
"planter"
Son: George Rankin the land I enjoy on Buffalo be divided by my Exe: in the following manner Viz.-Beginning at a scaly barked hickory & poplar on the South side of Buffaloe being a corner of my original tract from thence East to the stump of a black jack oak from thence North until it strikes piney run there make a corner from thence a straight course to an ash standing in the forks of the branch that runs through the meadow below all the clear land marked with 2 notches for that purpose with a black oak sapling marked R from thence up along the North fork of sd branch following sd branch to be the line until it comes to the conditional line between Adam Mitchel & me from thence a NW course till it strikes the line of my original tract from thence a West course to the original corner thence South to the above mentioned scaly barked hickory & poplar all within these described lines together with my interest of land on the waters of Duck River (containing 1000 acres entered by James McCoy & in his name. [is this land located in Tennessee?]JSH
Grandsons: William Rankin Willson, Andrew Willson, Maxwel Willson sons of my daughter Mary Willson alias Rankin an equal share of the remainder of the land.
Dau: Isabel my Negro wench Rhoda & her bed cloths.
Son: George my desk when emptied of what may be in it together with my carpenters tools, my bigg Bible, my razor, my wearing cloths together with a fifth part of money if any.
Daus: now living 1/5 part of the remaining moveables & my books each & money if any.

Andrew Wilson, formerly my son-in-law to be Guardian for my 3 grandchildren above named.
Signed: Robert Rankin, Senr. [no seal on will]JSH
Exrs: John Donnell   William Scott
Wits: Wm Scott (Jurat) Walter Mileham John Rees (Jurat) **"revokes"**

   A:0313   p:317   ROBERT RAMSEY   nuncupative will 15 Oct. 1799
Nov. Ct. 1799
State of North Carolina Guilford County} This is the Last Will and testamony of Robert Ramsey was that his horse & saddle should be sold to pay his expences & his Clothes to be given to Thos. McCullock Jur. His shoe Boots to Charles Hardin & a Callico gown to be bought for Mary McCullock of her own choosing at the espence of his estate & the remainder of his estate to be conveyed to his wife & family. [not named] October the 15th day 1799.
State of North Carolina Guilford County} this day came Charles Hardin and Thomas McCullock before me one of the Justices of the county aforesaid and both made oath that the above will is the last will and Testamony of Robert Ramsey which is now Deceased   Sworn to and subscribed this 19th Day of October 1799.
Signatures: Thomas McCullough   Charles Hardin

   A:0314 p:318 JOHN ROSS   4 Dec. 1801   Feb. Ct. 1802
Wife: Mary Ross her bed & furniture, 1 cow, her saddle & bridle, 1 pot, 6 pewter plates, & her living upon the land as long as she remains my widow. The remainder of my estate to be sold & my wife Mary to get a childs part. [no others are named]
Seal: John Ross
Exrs: wife Mary brother Thomas Ross
Wits: John Welborn (Jurat) James Ross (Jurat)

   A:0315   pp:318/319 WILLIAM RANKIN   5 Dec. 1803   Feb. Ct. 1804
Wife: Jeane Rankin all the plantation I now live on with all the stock & farming utensils & household and kitchen furniture & cupboard furniture, with my Negro boy Leven except such parts thereof as specially disposes of hereafter that she may have the opportunity to raise & school the family. She to have the disposing of the property in her hand to my 3 sons to wit: Thomas   Robert & William when & as she pleases as may be most suitable for her as I expeck she will do them justice.
Negro boy Leven be set free at my wifes death or at my youngest sons being at full age, whichever is the longest term as it is my will he should not serve another master after me nor any masters save the present one he has now.
Son: John Rankin besides what he has already gotten all that track of Land which he now lives containing 210 acres on the waters of Reedy fork joining William Dennys line which is left entirely to my disposal by my father in law John Chabers [?] in his last will & testament which I give to him & his heirs forever.
Son: Thomas Rankin all that track of land on the Reedy branch joining William Donnels North line & Shumakers line containing 225 acres to him & to his heirs forever & 1 horse & saddle.
2 youngest Sons: Robert & William I give & bequeath all that track of land I now live on containing 268 acres to them & their heirs forever with 1 horse & saddle to each one.

AN ANNOTATED DIGEST OF WILL BOOK A, GUILFORD COUNTY, NORTH CAROLINA

3 oldest Daus: Elesabeth, Agness, & Sarah besides what they have already gotten £1 to each.
2 youngest Daus: Ann & Jena 1 horse & saddle, 2 cows, 1 bed & furniture to each of them with the devide of some of the kitchen furniture and cupboard furniture to each of them.
Seal: William Rankin
Exrs: wife Jenney Rankin   son John Rankin
Wits: John Rankin, Sr. (Jurat) Joseph Rankin Robert Rankin
"revokes"

    A:0316 p:320 **WILLIAM RUDDUCK** 17th of 7th mo 1797   Feb. Ct. 1804
"I, William Rudduck...
Wife: Mary & Dau: Jane all moveable property to be equally divided between them.
Wife: to have possession of it during her lifetime if she remains my widow, but if she marries then it is to fall to my Dau: Jane.
Seal: William Rudduck
Exrs: wife Mary   Isaac Mendenhall
Wits: none
State of North Carolina Guilford County} February Court 1804   The within will was admitted to record by the verdict of a Jury Impanneled on the Issue of a Caveate Tryed in Open Court   Then came in Mary Rudduck Widow &etc. of the deceased & Isaac Mendenhall and qualifyed as Executors to said will. John Hamilton Clerk of Court

    A:0317 p:320 **ROBERT RUSSELL**   12 March 1804 May Ct. 1804
Wife: Susanne Russell the hole of my estate to buy & sell as she sees proper her self while she remains a widow & if she should marry then the hole estate is to be put to Auction & she get the third part.
Negroe Woman: Cricey & her son Jeffery their freedom from all persons claiming or attempting to claim them forever.
John Donaldson: $50.
Robert Russell & Alexander Russell, sons of Robert Russell, dec'd $50 each.
Brother William's son William Russell, brother David's sons Thomas Russell & Robert Washington Russell the remainder to be equally divided amongst them.
Seal: Robert (his x mark) Russell
Exrs: wife Susanna   trusty friends Robert Thompson & John Gullett
Wits: Edward Weatherly (Jurat) Martin Weatherly William Weatherly
"revokes"

    A:0318 pp:321/322 **ANNANIAS RECORDS**   8 June 1806   Feb. Ct.07
Wife: Mary the sole use & management of the plantation during her widowhood with all the horses, cows, hogs & sheep, & all household furniture & all other property belonging thereunto & at the expiration of her time the plantation whereon I now live to my wife Mary's grandchild Elijah Leward.
At the expiration of her time all the personal property is to be sold & divided bewteen Elijah Lewark and Joseph Lewark, 1/3 to Elijah and 2/3 to Joseph Leward.
Seal: Annanias (his x mark) Records
Exrs: wife Mary Records   Jeremiah Forbis
Wit: Nehemiah Causey (Jurat)

AN ANNOTATED DIGEST OF WILL BOOK A, GUILFORD COUNTY, NORTH CAROLINA

A:0319   pp:322/323   WILLIAM RUSSELL   21 Aug. 1810   Nov. Ct. 1810
Wife: Margaret 50 acres of land including the dwelling house where I now live during her life or widowhood, 1 feather bed & furniture.
Daus: Susanna Ross, Sarah Chilcutt, Margarat Dillworth, & Martha Donnell each 5 sh current money.
Daus: Lucretia & Nancy 1 feather bed & furniture each.
Sons: Robert William & Jesse Russell lands be equally divided amongst them.
Wife: Margaret, Daus: Lucretia & Nancy, Sons: Robert, William, & Jesse Russell the balance of my estate divided between them.
NB I also will that there be a reasonable allowance of provisions given to my wife & family for one year.
Seal: William Russell
Exrs: wife Margaret Russell   trusty friend Thomas Ross
Wits: Howel Parker   James Ross   (Jurat)
"revokes"

A:0320   pp:323/324   JAMES RUSSELL   10 April 1811   May Ct. 1812
"planter"
Sons: William Russell & Robert Russell each 5 sh sterling.
Dau: Martha 5 sh sterling.
Son: David Russell 50 acres of land joining Sampson Stewart & Luke Dier [Dyer?].
Son: Alexander Russell 150 acres of land.
Son: David, if he does not come in 6 years, that 50 acres shall fall to my son Alexander Russell.
Son: Alexander Russell to receive all moveable property.
Seal: James (his x mark) Russell
Exrs: William Vowell   Alexander Russell
Wits: William Vowel (Jurat)   Wiley Stewart (Jurat)
NB if Alexander calls his oldest son James what I have left to my son Alexander shall fall to him.

A:0321   p:324/325   JOHN RANKIN   20 July 1812   May Ct. 1814
"I, John Rankin..."
Wife: Hannah 1/3 of the plantation I now live on during her life & a house to live in & 1 horse & saddle, 1 cow & 2 sheep all at her own her chusing & all the household furniture to dispose of as she sees fit.
Youngest Son: Robert all the land I now own & the waggon & gears & all other farming utensils.
Daus: Polly & Ann 1 bed to each one of them with good furniture, their loom & gears belonging to it. I allow Robert's family the use of it while it stands there & I allow all my stock of living creatures that I possess at that time to them & what cash I then have by me I allow to them & I allow them the privilege to live in the house with their mother 8 years or their mother's lifetime if longer if they still live unmarried.
Rest of Children [not named] that if married I allow 5 sh beside what they have got.
Seal: John Rankin
Exrs: oldest sons Samuel Rankin   Joseph Rankin
Wits: James Gray   Robert Rankin (Jurat)   William Rankin
"revokes"

AN ANNOTATED DIGEST OF WILL BOOK A, GUILFORD COUNTY, NORTH CAROLINA

A:0322   p:325   HANNAH RANKIN   30 April 1814   Aug. Ct. 1814
"I, Hannah Rankin..."
Son: Joseph my 2 sheep.
Son: Robert my cow & kettle pot.
Daus: Polly & Ann the balance of estate.
Children: all books to be divided equally.
Seal: Hannah Rankin
Exrs: 2 oldest sons: Samuel Rankin   Joseph Rankin
Wits: James Gray   (Jurat)   Robert Gray
"revokes"

A:0323   p:326   DAVID REYNOLDS   7th of 11th mo 1812   Aug. Ct. 1815
"Whereas I, David Reynolds..."
Grandson: David Benbo 1/2 the Note or the money arising therefrom that I have on William Dun & David Worth which is for the sum of $100 & it to be the first note that will become due to me from them.
Dau: Lydia Benbo to have the other 2 notes for $100 each that I have upon the sd William Dun & David Worth or the money arising on them.
Son-in-law: Benjamin Benbo to be paid $40 out of my Estate in consideration of my having some use of Black Bill.
Two Daus. & Niece: Elizabeth Davis & Lydia Benbo, & Susannah Reynolds, d/o my brother Jeremiah Reynolds all the remainder part of my Estate to be equally divded between the three.
Seal: David Reynolds
Exrs: friend Jonathan Parker   nephew David Reynolds
Wits: John Reynolds (Jurat)   Rezin Reynolds   (Jurat)

A:0324   p:327   SUCA ROBERTSON   15 Dec. 1796   Aug. Ct. 1797
Bro: James Robertson for my love & good will to have my featherbed I now lie on & furniture.
Bro: Nathaniel Robertson to have my cow.
Bro: Jas. [?] Robertson my horse colt.
Nancy J. Rose my hunting saddle & cardinel* at my mother's death.
All the rest of my wearing Clothes should be disposed of by my Mother as I have directed her heretofore.
Seal: Suca (her x mark) Robertson
Exrs: brother James Robertson
Wits: William Rose   Nathaniel (his x mark) Robertson
*cardinel: short hooded cloak worn by women. Think Little Red Riding Hood. [JSH]

A:0325 pp:327/328   JOSEPH RUCKMAN   13 April 1792   Nov. Ct. 1792
"Whereas I, Joseph Ruckman..."
Wife: Sarah 1 cow & all my beds & furniture & every article that belongs to the dresser & all pots & Cedar [?] ware forever, and all the rest of my free estate to be sold & let out at Interest   I also give my wife all the Interest of my free estate during her life & as much of principle as my Exrs. hereafter named may think she stands in need of to procure the necessaries of Life if the Interest is not sufficient to maintain her.

After the decease of my wife I give to New Garden Meeting 1/4 of my free estate, the rest to be equally divided between 3 Children: Hannah Dillon, Isaiah Ruckman & Sarah Lewis to them & their heirs forever.
Seal: Joseph Ruckman
Exrs: friends Enoch Macy Jesse Williams
Wits: Wm. Armfield (Jurat) Edward Thornbrough

A:0326   pp:328/329   WILLIAM BYFORD   8 July 1796   Aug. Ct. 1796
Beloved companion: Tabith Byford all my lands goods debts & moveable effects all & singular to her & her heirs forever to have and to hold free and clear.
Seal: William (his   mark) Byford
Exrs: wife Tabbetha Byford father-in-law Smith Heath
Wits: Hezekiah Wheeler (Jurat)   Mary (her   mark) Heath
"revokes"

A:0327   pp:329/330   SHUBAL STEARNS   24 Oct. 1771   Feb. Ct. 1772
Brother: Isaac Stearns all my wearing cloths of every sorts & kinds.
Wife Sarah Starns all & singular my lands goods of all kinds together with all my estate for her use while she liveth for her support & after her decease to be sold by my Exrs: and all the money arising from such sale to be equally divided between my Bretheren & Sisters as followeth: Peter Stearns, Isaac Stearns, Rebeka Polk, Elisabeth Simson & Martha Marsheal.
Seal: Shubal Stearns   Sarah (her   mark) Stearns
Exrs: Seymore York   Tidence Lane
Wits: Thomas Swift   Jeremiah York (Jurat)   Sarah (her x mark) Cunerod [Conrad]
"revokes"

A:0328   pp:330/331   ENOCH SPINKS   20 March 1772   May Ct. 1772
Wife: Amy Spinks a Negro man named Sampson, her horse & saddle, her bed & furniture.
Son: John Spinks 150 acres of land lying on Deep River & a Negro man named Adam.
Dau: Martha Spinks a lot of land with all conveniences thereon including the storehouse that Southerland is possessed with.
Son: Enoch Spinks a quantity of land lying on Fork Creek crossing at an old mill near the sd creek & running a North & South course crossing the sd creek to each line.
Son: Lewis Spinks the land & plantation I now live on with all the appertenances thereto from the sd old mill & the line of my son Enoch downwards for the compliment that shall remain in the survey.
Son: Dowley a 70 gallon still with all the conveniencies thereto.
Son: Garrett Spinks £40 to be raised out of my estate.
Dau: Sarah Spinks a bed & furniture with £8 to be levied out of my estate.
Seal: Enoch Spinks
Exrs: John Larrance   John Needham   wife, Amy Spinks
Wits: John Lawrence   William Comb, Junr.   Windsor Pearce (Jurat)
"revokes"

AN ANNOTATED DIGEST OF WILL BOOK A, GUILFORD COUNTY, NORTH CAROLINA

    A:0329   pp:332/333   JOHN SCOTT   5 Oct. 1774   Nov. Ct. 1774
[the writing in the original will apparently stumped the Clerk when he wrote it into the Will Book, for many of the words are unreadable or omitted; however we have done the best we could and I do believe all the heirs are included. Also, this will was written and probated in 1774 but not recorded until many years later. JSH]
Son: Thomas that part of the plantation that lies on the North side of Haw River, the young brown mare & saddle & bridle as .... of hogs when he take use [of?] house also my brown coat & brown ---- & white jacket.
Wife Margaret 6 bushels of corn & 1/2 a barrel of wheat yearly from my son Thomases part of the plantation while she lives, her living as formerly & to manage & order as she used to do so long as she lives.
Dau: Jinet her living here as she formerly had while she is single & at her marriage she to have what her mother sees cause to give her if she be living.
Dau: Jineot at her marriage the two parts of all the cow kind that may be on the place, 1 bed & furniture, saddle & bridle, & 1/3 of the dresser furniture.
Son: Samuel that part of the plantation lying on the South side of Haw river whereon I presently live, all the moveable estate after his mothers death after the above bequests are satisfied. My best store coat & blew Jacket & Britches.
Dau: Nancy privilege of house & firewood so long as she continues unmarried.
Son: William my great coat & 1 English shilling.
Dau: Martha 1 English crown.
I discharge any seale by vendue. [any sale by auction]
Seal: John Scott
Exrs: son Thomas Scott   Gabriel Scott
Wits: Nancey   (her x mark) Scott   Jinny [?] (her x mark) Scott
"revokes"

    A:0330   pp:333/334   WILLIAM SEARCEY   4 Feb. 1776   May Ct. 1776
Wife: Kezia her living out of my estate which she is to enjoy in peace & greatness during her natural breath.
Son: William at the death of his mother all lands & livings he is peaceably to enjoy except what is herein after mentioned.
Dau: Theron a certain neck of land called Mogans neck which she is safetly & peaceably to enjoy, 4 Welch cows out of stock, a feather bed & furniture & 1/3 part of the pewter, Delft, & china.
Dau: Mary Pearce 1 sh lawful money of great Briton.
Grand Dau: Mary Pearce a black heifer.
Seal: Wm. Searcey
Exr: son William Searcey
Wits: Arthur (his x mark) Smith   James Whittel (Jurat)   Adam Wornock [?]
[the name is found in the 1790 Census of Stokes County, NC]
"revokes"

AN ANNOTATED DIGEST OF WILL BOOK A, GUILFORD COUNTY, NORTH CAROLINA

A:0331 pp:334/335 BENJAMIN STARRATT 15 Nov. 1776 May Ct. 1778
Son: John Dobins 5 sh.
Son: William Flemen £5.
Son: James Starratt £5.
Dau: Mary a hors worth £15, her saddle & bridle, 2 cows & 2 calves, a bed & furniture.
Dau: Joanna a hors worth £15, saddle & bridle, 2 cows & calves, bed & furniture.
Granddaugter: Harriet Dobins £16.
Son: B------[covered in tape] the plantation I now live on.
Benjn., Hanna, & Hester remainder of estate sold & equally divided in 3 equal shares.
Seal: Benjn. Starratt
Exr: Ralph Goral [sic]
Wits: James McAdow (Jurat)
"revokes"

A:0332 p:335 JOHN SHARP 6 Mar. 1778 May Ct. 1778
Wife: Cathrin plantation whereon I now live, 1 Negro man named Isaiah, 1 man named Tom, 1 Negro boy named bob, 1 negro wench named Hagor, all stock, horses, cattle, hogs, sheep, all & every kind, my household furniture to enjoy during her natural life.
Sons: Richard Sharp & James Sharp the plantation at the decease of my wife.
Children: Richard, Sam'l., Elizabeth, Mary, Sary, Isham, Susannah & Agness remaining estate at the decease of my wife Catharine.
Son: James the above named Negroe boy named bob.
Seal: John (his   mark) Sharp
Exrs: none given
Wits: John Reagan (Jurat) James Pratt (Jurat)

A:0333 p:336 ROBERT SMITH 27 Nov. 1772 May Ct. 1778
"farmer"
Son: Robert Smith all that tract of land laying on North Bufalow with all the improvements that I now possess, he to sell or let this tract of land as he shall think proper after my decease.
Sons: Samuel Smith & Robert Smith to equally divide all the chattels & moveables now in my posession at my decease. They to choose honest neighbors to help them.
Sons: William Smith, Thomas Ledford & Hugh Neely, Sen. each 10 shillings proclamation money.
Seal: Robert (his + mark) Smith
Exrs: sons William Smith Thomas Ledford
Wits: Robert Breden Edward Gilbert (Jurat) Rees Porter (Jurat)
"revokes"

A:0334 pp:337/338 JOSEPH SCALES 17 Sept. 1773 May Ct. 1774
"planter"
Wife: Mary Scales all the land & plantation &etc. containing 200 acres, 1 Negro man named Samson, 1 Negro woman named Nell, 1 feather bed & furniture, 1 grey mare known by that name, 6 cows & calves, 1 gelding called black Jack, 1 side saddle & bridle, 1 still now on the aforesaid plantation, 6 head of sheep for her proper use during her natural life

provided she remain unmarried. After her marriage or death, that then (except the land before mentioned) all I have given to my said wife the use of be sold by my Exers. & ye [the] monies arising therefrom to be equally divided among part of my children, to wit:
Children: Henry Scales alias Henry Gibson, Joseph, James, Nathanael, Agness & Bettsey Scales & Sarah Davis & Hannah Owings.
Son: Henry Scales otherwise Henry Gibson 1 Negro man Sciaro & 1 Negro woman named Marma & a bond on John Glenn for a certain sum of money he has now in possession.
Son: Joseph Scales 775 acres of land in the upper end whereon he now lives, part of a tract containing 1075 acres lying & being on the great branch of Cascade Creek in Pittsylvania County, Virg'a. & 1 Negro woman named Bett.
Son: James Scales 500 acres of land in the North end of a tract of 693 acres lying on both sides of Beaver Island Creek in Guilford County [now Rockingham County]JSH in the province of North Carolina, 1 Negro man named David.
Son: Nathanael Scales the afsd. 200 acres of land after the marriage or death of his mother, 1 Negro man named Jacob, 1 mare called the sorrell mare.
Son: Robert Scales 300 acres of land the remaining part of the afsd. tract of 1075 acres on the great branch of Cascade Creek be the same more or less & 1 Negro boy named Harry.
Son-in-law: John Davis the remaining part of the afsd. tract of 693 acres on both sides of Beaver Island Creek. [now Rockingham County]JSH
Dau: Sarah w/o my said son-in-law 1 Negro woman named Silvess.
Dau: Hannah Owings 1 Negro girl named Sall, 1 side saddle now in her possession.
Dau: Agness Scales 1 Negro woman named Jude, & I also give to my last sd dau. 1 feather bed & furniture.
Dau: Bettsey 1 Negro boy named Isaac, 1 Negro girl named Lett, 1 feather bed & furniture.
Sons: John & Thomas Scales the sum of 5 sh Sterling money each to be paid to them by my Exrs.
Daus: Ann Hill & Mary Rice 5 sh Sterling money each to be paid to them by my Exrs.
Son: David Scales 5 sh Sterling money to be paid to him by my Exrs.
My will & desire is that my wife Mary afsd. clear nor cause to be cleared no more land on the tract I now live on which she is to have the use of after my decease & further my will is that all the residue or remainder of my stock, household goods, personal estate &etc. not herein before mentioned be sold & the money arising therefrom to be equally divided among my wife & part of my children to wit:
Henry Scales alias Gibson, Joseph, James, Nathanel & Robert Scales, Sarah Davis, Hannah Owings, & Agnes & Bettsey Scales & further my Exrs. are to get my tobacco carried down by my waggon & horses before they are sold to pay my debts.
Seal: Joseph Scales
Exrs: sons Henry Scales alias Gibson, Joseph & James Scales & Philemon Deatherage
Wits: John Morgan (Jurat)   Thomas Walker   Henry Jester (Jurat)

AN ANNOTATED DIGEST OF WILL BOOK A, GUILFORD COUNTY, NORTH CAROLINA

A:0335   p:339   JOHN SMITH   7 November 1776   Feb. Ct. 1777
Sarah Powel the tract of land & plantation, stock of every kind, household goods & all moveable estate together with my just debts. [no relationship given]
Son: Charles Smith 1 carpenters Tenant Saw now in my possession.
Son: Joshua Smith 5 sh.
Son: John Smith 5 sh.
Son: Abraham Smith 5 sh.
Dau: Rachel Goacher 5 sh.
Seal: John   (his   mark) Smith
Exrx: Sarah Powel
Trustees: loving friends Alexander Joyce   John Pratt   Philemon Deatherage
Wits: William Watson (Jurat)   Sarah (her x mark) Watson   John Fields   Ansyl (his x mark) Fields   [possibly present Rockingham County]
"revokes"

A:0336   p:340   JOHN SHELLY   17 Dec. 1788   n.p.d.
Memorandum of a will made by John Shelley is as follows:
1st that all my debts be paid & that my wife have 1 cow & I will to my son James the plantation that I now live on to wit: 500 akers of land & sd James to pay to Jeremiah my son 10 sh & likewise to my son Nathan £50 to be paid in 5 years from this Date in money or trade & my Daughter Mary 10 sh & likewise that £75 be equely divided betwixt my son John's 3 children [not named] as they come of age & my bed I leave to my gran son Jesy & all my moveable property I will to son James & the sd James is to pay all my debts & I dow constitute my son James my sole Exacutor.
Seal: John Shelly
Exr: son James
Wits: John Ryan

A:0337   pp:340/341   ROBERT SCOTT   24 April 1791   May Ct. 1791
Wife: Mary Scott house & lot whereon I now live in the town of Martinville, 1 Negro girl named Patience to her & her heirs for ever proveded she does not marry for 2 years after my decease, otherwise the house & lot to be sold immediately after her marriage & the Negro to remains hers with bolt of fine linen, her choice & clothing & all my house furniture.
Bro: Thomas Scott 150 acres of land lying in Rockingham County being part of the tract on which the sd Thomas Scott now lives, 1 stud hourse now in my possession to be delivered to him at my decease & all my body close.
Sister: Margaret Gooding £50.
Half-Sister Hannah Scott £10.
Thomas Moody £10 & saddle & bridle.
All cash on hand be furthered to Petersburg to go to my credit with Donaldson & Stol [?] and that all my moveable property to be sold at publick sale giving 1 year credit, & after my debts are paid & the before mentioned legacies discharged the resudue to be equall divided between my heirs.
Seal: Robert Scott
Exrs: James McMurry   Thomas Scott
Wits: David Barr   James McMurrey (Jurat) John Hamilton (Jurat) **"revokes"**

AN ANNOTATED DIGEST OF WILL BOOK A, GUILFORD COUNTY, NORTH CAROLINA

A:0338 pp:341/342 MATTHEW STEPHENSON 1 Mar. 1788 n.p.d.
Wife: Ann Stephenson 1 gray mair during her life & then to be given to Ann Stephenson, Junor d/o John Stephenson provided that she the sd Ann Stephenson will give to John Stephenson Juner the 1st colt that the mare shall rease & my Disire is that my beloved wife shall have 2 of the Best of my cows & all my household stuff & shelf furniture, also all my sheep to her & her heirs & assigns forever.
Sons: Hugh Stephenson, William Stephenson & Alexander Stephenson 20 sh each upon demand.
Son: Matthew Stephenson 20 sh paid upon demand & 1 blue Cloath coat.
Son: John Stephenson all plantation containing 100 acres more or less lying upon the watters pole catt & Allemance beg. at Shannons line thence East thence North to Neeleys line thence West to Shannon line, but he is to furnish his mother Ann Stephenson with provisions & fire wood sutable for her maintaniance & well being during her life & all my cattle that is not bequeathed & all my carpenters touels [sic] & all my farming utenchels [sic] & all my wearing aparel except 1 Blue Cloath Coat.
Seal: Matthew (his x mark) Stephenson
Exrs: John Stephenson   William Dickey
Wits: Soloman Shannon   George Johnson (Jurat)   William (his   mark) Shannon
"revokes"

A:0339 pp:342/343 LUDOVICK [LUDWICK] SWING 16 Oct. 1790   n.p.d.
"planter"
Wife: [not named] for the Tarm of her life this hous where in I now Dwele & plantation with all the Housen forniture & and all my stock of Evry Kind as Long She Reamance [remains] a Wedo [widow] if other Wice She is to have the third of all my Mufebels [moveables] and after Her Death said lands and tenements I give to my son George Swing and the mufebels I will and order what is left after my Wifes Death to be Equil devitet amongst my childern so that the [they] com Equil in Shere with thos that I have let have sum of my mufeble Estate alredy exapting what Laber My son George does with his Mohter after my Death and what stock he Rases is not to be divitet amongst the rist of his sisters & brothers.
Imprimis: I give to my grandson Ludovick Swing fifty acres of Land to him his heirs & asignes for Ever lying in said County ajoining George Cortners Line NW Side & Anthoney Cobels on the NE wich will more fully apere by a plot when it whos [was] survead whicht Datet the 3 Day of the 9th month 1790.
Imprimis: I geve to my son John Swing fifty acres of land to him & his Heirs asigns for ever Leyeng in Said County on the NW side of my ouldest tract wich will more fully apere by a plot when it was Surveyed wich datet the 3rd Day of the Ninth Month 1790.
Imprimis: I geve to my Son Matthew Swing to him his Heirs & Assigns for Ever fifty acres of Land lying in said County on the South & SW Side of my oldest Track of Land wich will more fully apere when surveyed by the plot - turnover [continue to reverse of paper] JSH wich datet the 3rd day of the 9th month 1790 & I do apint my Dere & beloved Wife & my beloved Nabuer [neighbor] Daniel May Exacoters of this my Last will and Tastament in witness whereof I have hereunto maid my mark and affixed my

seal this 16th day of October 1790 and aknowledget this to be his Last will and Tastamant
Seal: Ludovick (his X mark) Swing Seal
Exrs: wife and beloved neighbor Daniel May
Wits: Geo Cortner (Jurat) Mathew (his M mark) Swing George (his x mark) Swing} Jurat
[Reading this will phonetically will make it easier to understand, and may give a clue to the sound of their speech. JSH]

A:0340 pp:343/344 ELIJAH STACK 17 Sept. 1791 Nov. Ct. 1791
Wife: Lovey my plantation that I now live on to her during her widowhood or to my children comes of age & then the plantation to be equally diveded between Thomas and David & Elijah and Leven.
Wife: Lovey 1 bed & furniture, 1 cow.
Dau: Rachel £4
To the child that my wife is with £4 if it is a gerel & if it is a boy its shear of the land.
All children: the small remainder of my estate to be equally devided between [&] only 1/3 to my wife.
Seal: Elijah (his   mark) Stack
Executors & Trustees for wife and children John Ryan William Sillivan
Wits: George Pope (Jurat) J. McBride Levi Silliven (Jurat) Lovey (her x mark) Stack [why did wife Lovey sign as a witness?]JSH

A:0341 pp:344/345 JOHN SANDERS 4 March 1790 May Ct. 1793
"farmer"
"Be it remembered..."
Wife: [not named] all this I possess after my just debts be paid, during her life, and after her decease, I give unto my son Joel Sanders his heirs or assigns the land whereon I now live and all my moveable effects I desire and it is my will that [that the whole?] should be equally divided among all my children and Philip Ham's children to come in for their part equally as though their mother were living.
Seal: John Sanders
Exrs: sons John & Joel Sanders
Wits: Mathew Macy (Jurat) Amos Mills (Jurat)
"revokes"

A:0342 p:345 WILLIAM SHAW 9 Sept. 1793 Nov. Ct. 1793
"I, William Shaw..."
Two beloved brothers: Joseph Ross & Benjamin [sic] all my clothes to be equally divided between them.
Mother [not named] & 2 young sisters Jean Ross & Sussana [no surname] £3 each.
2 older sisters: Sarah Shaw & Grizzald [Griselda] and Girzzalds youngest boy Thomas Ross, the rest of my estate to be equally divided between those three equally.
Seal: Wm. Shaw [no Seal]
Exrs: Thomas Wiley Robert Shaw
Wits: William Matthews (Jurat)

AN ANNOTATED DIGEST OF WILL BOOK A, GUILFORD COUNTY, NORTH CAROLINA

A:0343 p:346   SHADRACH STANLEY   1 Aug. 1792   Nov. Ct. 1793
"I, Shadrach Stanley ..."
"planter"
Son: Robert Stanley a tract of land joining on the East side of the land wheare I now live that I have partly paid for, provided he fullfils the payment according to my agreement with John Rankin the former owner of the Land.
Son: Jessa Stanley the use & profit of all my Estate both real & personal to have the care of and bringing up my Children untill they come to be of age, but if any of my daughters shuld marry in the time, my will is they shuld have a bed, cow & calf if they can be spaired.
Four Sons: Jessa, Edward, Richard Henry, & Shadrach when all children come of age all my real estate to be equally devided between them not prefering one before the other.
Three Sons [sic]: Edward, Richard Henry, & Shadrach each a horse & saddle.
Son: Jasson Stanley a debt dew me from William Duval in Virginia to use in the family as he thinks best.
Four Daus: Mary, Judith, Elizabeth, & Agness all my personal estate not herein disposed of to be equally divided.
Seal: Shadrach Stanley
Exrs: son Jessa Stanley   friend Joel Sanders
Wits: Hezekiah Starbuck   Elazer (his   mark) Hunt (Jurat, affirmed)
Phebe Stanely (Jurat, affirmed)

A:0344 pp:347/348 RICHARD SIMPSON, SENIOR   24 Dec. 1793   May Ct. 1795
Son: Thomas Simpson 1 breeding sow & a chair.
Son: Richard Simpson all the Land on which I now live & also the 20 acres on which Elizabeth Carrol lives & the 20 acres on which he my said son Richard now lives.
Son: Natthaniel Simpson my white mare.
Daus: Elizabeth Knight & Jane Marcillot my feather bed & what feathers I have. The feathers to be equally divided between but the tyke [tick] to be Elizabeth Knights. Elizabeth also received 1 3-quart bason & a chair.
Dau: Jane Marcillot 1 small trunk & 1 pewter dish.
Dau: Eleanor Hicks 1 large pewter beson & 1 stone Quart mug.
Stepdau: Elizabeth Carrol 1 spinning wheel, 1 Quart pewter bason, my chaff [mattress probably filled with wheat or corn chaff] bed, a sheet, & washing tub & 1 piggin [a small wooden pail or tub with a handle formed by continuing one of the staves above the rim.]
Granddau: Elizabeth Ross Hicks a 3 year old heiffer.
Granddau: Elizabeth Simpson d/o my son Thomas, my chest.
Grandson: Natthaniel Simpson s/o my son Thomas my young cow named Rock.
Four Grandsons: Richard s/o Thomas, Peter Ryan Simpson & William Simpson s/o Richard Simpson & Richard Simpson s/o Richard Simpson all the rest of my estate not mentioned in this will to be sold by my Exrs: & the product equally divided between the four grandsons.
Seal: Richard Simpson
Exrs: sons Thomas & Richard Simpson
Wits: Jn [John] Campbell (Jurat) Mary Campbell   Edward Edwards
"revokes"

AN ANNOTATED DIGEST OF WILL BOOK A, GUILFORD COUNTY, NORTH CAROLINA

A:0345 p:348 **ANN STEVENSON**   3 Oct. 1796   Feb. Ct. 1797
Granddau: Ann Stevenson 2 cows & all the remaining part of my goods and chattels & money & all debts, notes & demands that is due to me or to become due.
Seal: Ann (her   mark) Stevenson
Exrs: trusty friend William Dickey
Wits: John Coe (Jurat) John Stephenson (Jurat)
"revokes"

A:0346 p:349 **JAMES SHELLEY**   21 Sept. 1797   Nov. Ct. 1798
Wife: Mary dureing her widowhud 1 bed & furniture, 1 cow, 1 sadle, 1 case of drawers & 1 flax wheel, 1 Bay mair, 1 young Bay horse, all my plows, harrows, hoes axes & gears, 1 Bef cow, all hogs for provision this year & all the remainder of my Stock, 100 acres of land joining Josep Eadins Willima [William?] Garner is to be sold & all just debts paid out of same, the plantation whereon I now live.
Three sons: John, Francis, & William the plantation to be equally divided among them at wife's death.
Daus: Elonnor, Betsy, Mary at wife's death or marag the above articles to be equally divided amongst them except the bed & that only to Mary.
Dau: Elonner 1 bed & furniture & 1 flax wheel
Dau: Betsy 1 bed & furniture & 1 flax wheel.
Three sons: John, Francis, & William at wife's death or marage what remains of Said property to be sold & equally divided among them. The remain if any with all my Book Debts & Notes of Hand to be Equally devided among them.
Seal: James Shelly
Exrs: wife Mary Shelly William Ryan
Wits: J. Henley Wm Stanfield Margaret (her x mark) Ryan (Jurat)

A:0347 pp:350/351 **GEORGE STALKER** 9th of 8th mo 1797   May Ct. 1798
"I, George Stalker..."
"planter"
Wife: Rachel Stalker 1 horse, saddle & bridle & a comfortable Peacible living off of my Homestead during her widowhood for her & our children under age.
Dau: Alice Davis 5 sh she heving had her part given to her before now.
Son: Thomas Stalker 5 sh he having received his part of my Estate already.
Dau: Rachel Stanfield 5 sh she having received her part before now.
Dau: Grace Stanfield 5 sh she having had her part Dowery already given her.
Dau: Rebecca Stalker 1 cow, & 3 head of sheep more then already given her.
Sarah Bradley (my wifes Daughter) 1 cow & 3 head of sheep.
Son: Jonathan Stalker tract of land called the Schoolhouse Tract containing 124 acres ground & 1 cow.
Son: John Stalker 100 acres of land to be measured off of the East land of a Tract I own Leying in Randolph County on the waters of Back Creek.
Son: George Stalker 100 acres of land being the improvement part of the Tract that my son John Stalker is to be measured off. If son John does not live to heir the same that it shall fall to his Mother to dispose of as she may think best to her use & her Children.

AN ANNOTATED DIGEST OF WILL BOOK A, GUILFORD COUNTY, NORTH CAROLINA

Son: Nathan Stalker Homestead Tract of land of 200 acres with all the Improvements & benefits reserving my wifes comfortable living during her Widowhood & small children, 1 horse & saddle & bridle. If son Nathan should not live to lawfully heir my said Homestead Lands it is my will that son Jonathan Stalker should have the same.
Wife: Rachel & under age Children: Lydia, Hannah, Elizabeth, George, Deborah, & "one my wife is big with" [my stress] all residue that remains of my personal or moveable estate unto them share and share alike.
Seal: George Stalker
Exrs: wife, Rachal Stalker son, Jonathan Stalker
Wits: William Gifford (Jurat) James Caldwell (Jurat)
"revokes"

A:0348 pp:351/352 JOSEPH SHARBROUGH no date May Ct. 1799
"Be it remembered..."
Sister: Barbra Smithson £25 to be paid her by my Exrs: as soon after my deceas as they may find convenient but not be compeled thereto for the space of 5 years.
Son: Malakia Sharborough 20 sh.
Wife: Perthena Sharbrough all the reminader part of my Estate both real & personal whatsoever kind it may be of.
Seal: Joseph Sharbrough
Exrs: wife Perthena Sharbrough friend John McDaniel
Wits: Jno. Ruddick (Jurat) Nancy Jennings (Jurat) Miriam Jennings
"revokes"

A:0349 pp:352/353/354 WILLIAM SCOTT, SENIOR 8 Nov. 1798 Feb. Ct. 1801
Wife: Rebekah Scott her bed & furniture with such things & other furniture she got by her mothers will to be at her direction as she please, all her other body apparel & her chest of drawers, a good horse, sadle & bridle, 2 cows & calves, 4 head of sheep, her choice, 1/2 a bushel of flaxseed to be sown for her either on this place or on the Old Plantation yearly or every year as best suits without cost to her during her natural life, also full free & uncontroulable [sic] privilege of Mansion house, Kitchen Spring house & Smoak house or what may be necessary for her use of them, also a comfortable maintainence of living & diet free of cost, & every year she remaining a Widow she shall have $5 to purchase such necessaries as she may think fit.
Son: Samuel Scott £30 hard money to be paid to him by my son Adam Scott out of that £50 which his is owing to me & this to be a full part of my estate.
Son: Adam Scott $1.
Son: William Scott a tract of land beginning on a South line with Joseph McDonals line & my own line 30 rods South of where the Court House Road Crosses it & to corner on sd line thence with a direct course to the uper South corner of the field where my son Samuel Scott once lived so as not to take in said field and for the said upper South corner of the field to the Reedy fork where Andrew Wilsons line & mine crosses the creek & there to corner on sd line & to have all the land that lies between the before mentioned lines & Adam Scotts land & a good, horse with his sadles he now has, also a plough & gears for 2 horses.

Son: Thomas my Mill place & Mills with the land lying on both sides of Reedy fork as described to his Brother William joining Joseph McDonells East & West line & Andrew Wilsons down the creek with 25 acres on the East side of the Big Run where it empties into the Reedy fork, thence down the Reedy fork so as to conclude that compliment of low grounds but to the foot of the hill for the use & benefit of the Mill place & a good horse & sadle, to have full possession when he is of age of all that I have hereby given but not so as to injure his Mother or to deprive her of any priviledges that I have given her above while she remains my widow.

Four Daus: Mary, Margaret, Rebekah, Nansey £50 hard money each, a good horse, sadle & bridle, a good bed & furniture, 1 cow & calf each, & to live with their Mother under her tuition, clothing both wearing apparel & outgoing suitable to their rank or condition in life & that without cost & to have kitchen & dresser furniture suitable.

The land lying East of the Big Run over to James Staffords line & James Bass line except the 25 acres researved for the use of the mill of Low grounds joining the Big Run & Reedy fork to be sold by my Exrs: to pay off any debts & any remaininig to be divided equally amongst my Daus.

Further my bargain with John Rees I allow to remain good.

Sons: Adam & William to have the use of the Wagon when they stand in need of it but so as to help keep her in repair I reserve for the use of the family from my son William all the meadow ground that is cleared & fit for mowing in the old field & on the North side of Richland Creek adjoining the Road to the Mill from Adam Scotts until such time as there is Meadow cleared on the mill place.

Son: William the Meadow that I reserved from my son Adam as before said and £25 out of the £50 which my son Adam Scott is owning to me.

Son: Adam Scott the following researve made with Adam when a title was made to his land & is as follows 2 good poplar trees of his own choosing & logs for a Double Barn to be got on the land joining where Andrew Owings now liveth when wanted & likewise 1 Repair Rail of timber on the South side of Richland Creek to repair the old field fence on the North side oppisite to it when wanted.

Seal: William Scott, Senior

Exrs: wife Rebekah Scott Hance McKain, Esqr. "If wife should marry, she is to discontinue as Executrix & son William Scott to succeed in her place".

Wits: John Gilchrist (Jurat) John Rees (Jurat)
"revokes"

A:0350 pp:354/355 JACOB SOUTZ [SOOTS/SUITS] 7 May 1793 Aug. Ct. 1800
Three Sons: Christian Sutz, Adam Sutz, Frederick Sutz 1 English shilling each.

Daughter: Margret Sutz 100 acres of land lying & being in the County afsd on the waders of Allamence a joining my son Jacob Sutz land on the SW side.

Son: Tobias Sutz 200 acres lying in the county afsd on said waders a jining [joining] my son Jacob Sutz land on the North side, & my carpenters tools.

Yungest [sic] Dau: Mary 1 English shilling out of my Estate & there with she is to be condent [content].

AN ANNOTATED DIGEST OF WILL BOOK A, GUILFORD COUNTY, NORTH CAROLINA

Wife: [not named] all moveables excepting my Carbenters tools, 100 acres of land lying & being in sd county joining my son Jacob on the South & Jacob Clapp & John Swing on the North side.
Sons: Jacob & Tobias Sutz after death of wife if there is aney thing left of my Estate that it shall be equally devidet & Managed by them.
Seal: Jacob Soutz
Exrs: wife [not named] & after her death sons Jacob & Tobias
Wits: George Cortner (Jurat) David Lau/Low Jacob Sutz (Jurat)

A:0351 pp:355/356 WILLIAM SHAVER 17 July 1801 Nov. Ct. 1801
"I, William Shaver ...a citizen of one of the United States of Amarica called North Carilinia"
Wife: Catherine the privilage of living in my House, her bed & furniture, 1/3 of all the table & Citchen furniture wit her chest & all her clothing, her choice of 2 of the best cows & calfs, 1 horse, sadle & bridle, her choice to be at her disposal at her death to any of my children. 1/3 of all cleared land including orchard & meddy [meadow] & every year all full priviledge of getting timber on the residue of the tract for fuell & other nessary repairs.
Son: Jacob Shaver 1/2 of that tract of land I purchased of Adam Larance as it now stated devided betwixt him & his brother William estemated at 160 acres.
Son: Wm. Shaver the other 1/2 of sd tract of land with his brother Jacob as it now stands devided by Brattens line.
Son: Conrod Shaver 160 acres of land where he now lives to be divided off my other land by a North & South line in such a maner as will take a good spring near a large poplar tree & to include his improvement.
Son: Lasch [?] Shaver my youngest son the other part of my House with my wife & the residue of all my land not above given away & at his mothers decease to enjoy all & singular the land whereon I now reside except that given to his brother Conrod, to pay to his sister Eliabeth Shaver $150 in 2 payments the first 1 year after my decease, the second year after that together with all the stock & furniture that she may have at my decease, & the free privilege of living in the House with her Mother should she choose it.
Oldest Dau: Cathrine Long $3, she having received her proportion of my estate heretofore.
Seal : William Shaver
Exrs: son Jacob Shaver wife Cathrine Shaver
Wits: William Patterson (Jurat) Ralph Gorrell
"revokes"
[note: the given names of the family are similar to those used by other 18th century Germans, & Shaver is also seen as Shaffer. The signature of the Devisor, on the original will, appears to have been written in the German Scrip.JSH]

A:0352 p:357 PATRICK SHAW 1 Jan. 1802 Feb. Ct. 1802
Oldest Son: John Shaw 5 shillings.
Second Son: William Shaw 5 shillings.
Son: Hugh 5 shillings.
Residue of estate to be divided into 5 shares, which shares are to be diveded in the following manner:
Wife: Nancy 1 share.

AN ANNOTATED DIGEST OF WILL BOOK A, GUILFORD COUNTY, NORTH CAROLINA

Eldest Dau: Betsy Shaw 2 shares.
Dau: Polly Aydelotte 1 share.
Dau: Nancy Shaw 1 share.
Seal: Patrick (his x mark) Shaw
Exrs: wife Nancy Shaw worthy friend James S. Gillaspie
Wits: David Price (Jurat) James Holland (Jurat)

A:0353 pp:357/358 HENERICK SICKFRET* 22nd of 4th mo 1801 Feb. Ct. 1802

"I, Henry Sickfret..."
"I do give all my pasinal [personal] astate to my Daughters [not named] an Equel Devide Except Cathorine to have my Bed and Bed Close more then the rest my two Daugters Mary & Neomi that is Deceast there Shear is to be Devided Equally amongst there Children [not named].
My Son John to have my Land what layes along his line the rest to be Solde and the money Devided as the other property.
I do constitute and ordain William & John Hodgson Executors of this my Last Will and Testement"
Seal: Henerick Sigfret [signed in German]
Exrs: William & John Hodgson
Wits: Isaac Frazer (Jurat) Rebekah Frazer (Jurat)
*[His given name is spelled Henry, Henerick, Hendrick; his surname is spelled Sigfred, Sickfret, and is possibly the origin of the present name Saferight,. JSH]

A:0354 pp:358/359 WILLIAM SMITH 15 June 1801 Nov. Ct. 1802

Wife: Elizabeth the house & plantation I now live on during her life, her bed & furniture & household furniture sufficient for her use, 2 horses, 4 cows, 6 sheep, 10 hogs, my Negro man named Dick, & a woman named Sall. My moveable property to be equally divided betwixt my sons Joseph, William & Robert and the plantation together with 100 acres of land joining to the West end of it is to fall to my son William.
Son: Joseph the plantation where the saw mill is on, a Negro woman named Elcy & her child named Richard & a boy named Andra & a boy named Jeorge.
Son: William a Negro boy named John & a boy named Tom.
Son: Robert a Negro girl named Nance.
Sons: Joseph & William all the balance of my Estate to be equally divided betwixt them.
Seal: William (his W mark) Smith
Exrs: sons Joseph & William Smith
Wits: John Nelson (Jurat) [there may have been another witness, but it is not included in the clerk's copy and is too faint to read on the original]JSH

A:0355 pp:359/360 JAMES STARRAT 30 Aug. 1803 Aug. Ct. 1804

Grandson: William Starrat 1/2 of stock of horned cattle, 1/2 my hogs, 1/2 of my household furniture & 1/2 of farming tools, his gray mare & all her Breeds, 250 acres of Land, he has a deed of gift.
Son: John Starrat the remaining Stock of cattle, hogs, Household furniture, farming tools,& 100 acres of land he has a deed of gift, also 100 acres of Land on the West Branch of Buckhan [?] joining Nelsons & Flack lands.
Dau: Mary Hall £5.
Dau: Isbell Telford £5.

AN ANNOTATED DIGEST OF WILL BOOK A, GUILFORD COUNTY, NORTH CAROLINA

"What money I may leave in my chest or elsewhere after paying my 2 Daus: afsd each the said sum of £5 & other contingent expenses to be equally divided between my son John Starret & my Grandson William Starrat.
Let it be remembered that the $40 I lent to James Hall Starrat be added to the whole amount & to be counted as so much of my Grandson William Starrats part.
Seal: James (his x mark) Starrat
Wits: Edward Green (Jurat) Benjamine Wilson

A:0356 pp:360/361 REBECCAH SCOTT 1 Jan. 1806 May Ct. 1806
Daus: Nancy Scott, Mary & Margarot Rankin to have an equal share of Household furniure & clothing.
Dau: Nancy Scott $10 to make her equal with the others, 1 hefer, her choice of 2 that is now of the stock on hand beside the Cattle allowed her in her fathers Will.
Son: Thomas Scott a bed & furniture commonly called his including a stand of curtains. [bed curtains]
Granddau: Hannah Rankin my bed tick & curtains.
Elizabeth Henderson now living with me 1 heffer which I got from James Russell.
Remaining Estate sold and divided amongst my 3 daus: now living, & my Grand Daughter Rebeccah Meek Scott, d/o my son Sammuel Scott now living in the State of Tennessee.
Seal: Rebeccah Scott
Exrs: son-in-law Samuel Rankin Hance McCain
Wits: Asa Brasher, Jr. John Rankin (Jurat)
"revokes"

A:0357 pp:361/362 WILLIAM SHANNON 12 Aug. 1803 n.p.d.
"Know all men by these presents..."
"planter"
Plantation & all stock & goods be put to sale at one years Credit.
Dau: Margret Gossett w/o Elijah Gossett; two Granddaus: Ann & Isabbella Shannon, ds/of/ Solomon Shannon, Dec'd., Dau: Ann Wiley; Dau: Jane Wilson & Dau: Isabella Wilson each 1/5th part of the money that shall be raised from the aforenamed sale.
Seal: William (his   mark) Shannon
Exrs: Daniel Sheerwood [Shearwood/Sherwood] Gorge [sic] Johnson
Wits: John Stephnson (Jurat) John Stephnson, Junior

A:0358 pp:362/363 WILLIAM SPRUCE 10 Aug. 1808 Nov. Ct. 1808
Wife: Sarah Spruce all personal Estate except 2 horses which I shall hereafter mention, also the use & enjoyment of the Land I now live on during her widowhood, all but 2 acres which I shall hereafter mention, but in case she should marry I allow her henceforth 1/3 part of said Land.
Son: George Spruce 2 acres of land to be laid off as followeth; beginning at the SE Corner of his own tract thence North with his own line 65 rods thence East thence South thence West to beginning.
Dau: Elizabeth Spruce 1 horse called Cooper.
Sons & Dau: John Spruce, William Spruce, Quinton Spruce, Joseph Spruce, & Sarah Strain 10 shillings to be paid to each of them 6 months after my decease.

AN ANNOTATED DIGEST OF WILL BOOK A, GUILFORD COUNTY, NORTH CAROLINA

Son: Thomas Spruce the tract of land whereon I now live he paying my
Dau: Elizabeth Spruce 6 months after his mothers decease $50, also 1 colt that sucks, [a foal not yet weaned] a Mare called Fly bait & if my son Thomas Spruce should die before his mother having no legitimate issue my will is that my wife Sarah Spruce have the sole disposal of said land.
Seal: William Spruce [continued]
Exrs: wife Sarah Spruce trusty friend George Nicks, Sen'r.
Wits: James Denny (Jurat) Robert Hatrick George Donnell
"revokes"

A:0359 pp:363/364 **FINLEY STEWART** 12 June 1807 Feb. Ct. 1809
"Know all men by these presents..."
Wife: Prudence 2 Negros Jean & Rose, 1 mare named Phenix & whatever of my property she many choose, 1/2 of all the black cattle my property, 1/2 of the sheep, 2 beds, bedsteads & furniture, whatever of the Kitchen furniture she may choose & the Bowfat [buffet] with all thereto belonging, the whole authority over 2 Negro boys Will & Obed, the whole of their Labour to be applied as she may choose or direct with as much of the plantation I now live on, to be Laboured as she may think proper dureing her lifetime.
Son: Robert Stewart $50.
Grandson: Finley Stuart $50.
Grandson: Finley G. Stuart $50.
Dau: Susannna $100.
Dau: Jennet $50 with 1 Negro girl named Becky, sd Negro girl & offspring if any, to fall to her heirs at her decease each entitled to an Equal dividend.
Grandson: Finley Stuart Forbis $50.
Dau: Euphance $100 & 1 Negro boy named George.
GrandDau: Sarah Hannah*, alias McAdow 1 Negro boy named Billy.
Son: John Stuart remainder of my Estate after the aforesaid bequests are settled, excepting such farming utensils as my wife may stand in need of together with what money may be left, Negro boys Will & Obed after wifes decease.
Grandson: Finley Shaw Stewart 1 Negro girl named Hanna.
Dau: Susannah must likewise be excepted out of the whole mentioned to John.
Seal: Finley Stewart
Exrs: son John Steward son-in-law David Gorrell
Wits: Roddy Hannah, Esq. (Jurat) Isaiah McBride (Jurat)
"revokes"
* it is unclear if Hannah if her given name or her married name. There were many families named Hanna/Hanner/Hannah in Guilford County, i.e. the witness, Roddy Hannah, Esq. JSH

AN ANNOTATED DIGEST OF WILL BOOK A, GUILFORD COUNTY, NORTH CAROLINA

A:0360 pp:364/365 JOHN SANDERS 8th of 4th mo 1809 May Ct. 1809
"I, John Sanders..."
Heirs of son Jesse Sanders, dec'd.: Forrest, Jermima [Jemima?] John, Jane, Susanna & Jesse 1/4th part of Estate to be equally divided among them or their Heirs.
Dau: Martha Hubbard, dec'd. Daus: Susanna, Elizabeth, Jane, Martha, Judith & Sarah 1/4th part or portion of Estate to be equally divided.
Son: James or his heirs 1/4th part or portion of estate.
Son: Joseph or his heirs 1/4th part of estate provided he doth pay $60 to his Brother's (namely Jesse & James Sanders) Children to be equelly divided among them parts & parts alike.
Seal: John Sanders
Exrs: son Joseph Sanders esteemed friend Barnabas Coffin
Wits: David Sanders (Jurat) Valentine Pegg Charles Gordon (Jurat)
"revokes"

A:0361 pp: 365/366 JOHN SULLEN 8th & 3rd 1802 Aug. Ct. 1809
"I, John Sullen...being well stricken in years, and somewhat troubled with the infirmities of ould age..."
"planter"
Wife: Barbary Sullen the whole of my Estate both real & personal during her Natural life.
Dau: Elizabeth the wife of William Spikeman 5 sh.
Dau: Catherine the wife of James Sulgrave 5 sh.
Dau: Mary or her heirs the widow of Andrew Lowery 5 sh.
Dau: Ann or Nancy 5 sh. [sic] [Nancy was a nickname for Ann]
Dau: Margaret 5 sh.
Son: John Sullen after the Decease of my said wife Barbary all the residue of my said Estate both real & personal, Excepting a reasonable maintenance out of the same for my son Jacob during his Natural life.
Seal: John Sullen
Exrs: trusty friend James Mendenhall son John Sullen
Wits: Daniel Mendenhall (Jurat) Enos Hiatt Isaac Hiatt
James Sulgrave, Jr.
"revokes"

A:0362 pp:366/367 DANIEL SULLEVAN 1 Feb. 1805 Nov. Ct. 1809
Sons: William, Daniel, Edward 1 shilling Sterling.
Daus: Maryan Sillivan, Sarah Shepherd 1 shilling Sterling.
Heir of Son Florence [sic]: Caleb Sillevan 1 shilling Sterling.
Son: John Sillevan 1 horse beast named Kill Devil.
Dau: Nancy Sillevan 1 cow & calf named white face, a loom & a linen wheel.
Dau: Henney Sillevan 1 cow & calf, 1 feather bed & furniture, & 1 linen wheel.
Wife: Marget Sillevan: land & the rest of stock, farmers utensils, working tools & household furniture during her widowhood, at her death or marriage all to go to Son: Joel Sillivan.
Seal: Daniel (his X mark) Sullivan
Exrs: Andrew Williams Andrew Russel
Wits: Obed Aydelotte John Ozment Winsmore Howren (Jurat)
"revokes"

AN ANNOTATED DIGEST OF WILL BOOK A, GUILFORD COUNTY, NORTH CAROLINA

A:0363 p:368 ROBERT SAPP 28 Dec. 1809 May Ct. 1810
"I, Robert Sapp..."
Wife: Sarah Sapp after just debts are paid the whole of my estate both real & personal during her natural life or widowhood.
Sons: Samuel Sapp & James Sapp (after the intermarriage of my above named wife Sarah Sapp) my land & plantation whereon I now live to them & their heirs forever to be equally divided between them.
Dau: Dorothy Sapp 1 cow & calf, 1 new womans Saddle, & 1 feather bed & furniture to her & her heirs forever.
Son Robert Sapp 10 shillings as his part of my estate.
Son: Benjamin Sapp the sum of 10 shillings as his part of my estate.
Sons: & Dau: Samuel Sapp, James Sapp & Dorothy Sapp all the rest of the estate after the death or marriage of my wife Sarah Sapp be sold & equally diveded between the three children.
Seal: Robert Sapp
Exrs: wife Sarah Sapp   son Samuel Sapp
Wits: Annuel (his x mark) Edwards   Joshua Edwards (Jurat)
"revokes"

A:0364 p:369 JOHN STONE 7th of 6th mo 1808 Feb. Ct. 1812
"Know all men by these presents..."
"Beloved & only Son: Sallathiel Stone all my carpenters tools & all my wearing apperel."
Grandson: Sallathiel Stone a tract of Land lying on the East side of Polecat Creek whereon I now live at the day of my death to him and his Heirs & assigns forever.
My three children: Sallathial Stone, Hulda Phillips, Christian Russell all the residue of my estate to be equally divided among them.
Seal: John (his   mark) Stone
Exrs: son Sallathiel Stone   friend Daniel Worth
Wits: William Dicks (Jurat)   Job Worth (Jurat)
"revokes"

A:0365 pp:369/370 SUSANA SHOEMAKER 15 Oct. 1808 Feb. Ct. 1813
Daus: Barbara & Elizabeth my Negro woman named Charlot & 1 Negro boy named Abner to be their right & property.
Dau: Barbara to have 1 cow, 1 bed & all the furniture to it belonging.
Dau: Elizabeth to have 1 cow, her choice of all my hors criters to take one, & 1 bed with all the furniture belonging thereto, 1 jest [chest], 1 iron pot, 1 Dutch oven, & one 5 or 6 gallon iron pot.
Dau: Caty to have 50 Silver dollars.
Dau: Susana 50 Silver dollars.
Dau: Marry 50 Silver dollars.
Five Daus: Caty, Barbara, Susana, Mary & Elizabeth shall have all the puttor [pewter] belonging to my Treasure to be equally divided among them.
Sons: George Shoemaker, Jacob Shr.[Shr. is the abbreviation used here for Shoemaker. The writer saved time and paper by not writing the name each time]JSH   Conrad Sh.[sic], Adam Shr[sic], John Shr.[sic],Daniel Shr.[sic] & Christian Shoemaker "now remember that my each and every of this above mentioned sons has received out of my estate each one hundred Dollars in my life time and all what is over and above all my sons and

149

AN ANNOTATED DIGEST OF WILL BOOK A, GUILFORD COUNTY, NORTH CAROLINA

Daughters or children shall be come in as Equil shear whom I likewise constitute make & ordain to this my last will & testament" [sic]
Seal: Sussana   (her   mark) Shoomaker
Exrs: trusty friend John Coble   John Crisman
Wits: Caty Coble d/o John Coble(Jurat)   Adam ---   2 names signed in Dutch [sic].
"Revokes"

A:0366 p:371 JOSEPH SMITH   5 Feb. 1813   Feb. Ct. 1813
Dau: Sally a Negro girl named Jane [?] Lane [?] & her children which she now has in her possession.
Son: Nathaniel a tract of land lying on Ritchland whereon he now lives containinig 176 acres, a Negro boy named Jim & a girl named Edd, on his paying into the Estate $100 for the use of my other heirs.
Son: Larkin a Negro girl named Lile, a Negro boy named Peter, 1 bed & furniture.
Son: John the tract of land whereon he now lives, a Negro girl named Nan, & a Negro boy named Howard.
Mrs. Polly Banner [no relationship given] to have my Negro man Pompey so long as she remains a widow, at her marriage or death Pompey to return unto my Estate for the use of my Heirs.
Residue of my property to be sold, all just debts paid & the balance if any equally divided between my sons Larkin and John.
Seal: Joseph Smith
Exrs: George Nix, Jr.   John Smith
Wits: Robert Lindsay   (Jurat)   James Johnson

A:0367 pp:371/372/373 PETER SMITH   11 Sept. 1813 Nov. Ct. 1813
Sons: Nicholas & Adam 500 acres of land on Pleasant Mountain Creek bought of Nathen Aldridge or all the land I own on sd creek; land rated at $542.
Son: John 172 1/2 acres of land conveyed to me from Nicholas Smith rated at $387.
Son: David 100 acres where he now lives bought of James Wire rated at $350 also off the tract I live on all on the West side of the Fayetteville Road as far North as the corner of my fence NW of my barn then North until it strikes the old line, rated at $2 per acre.
Son: Jacob all the land that I own North & West of my sons John & David 150 acres rated at $290.
Son: Philip all the tract of land I now live on East of the line above mentioned for my son David Rated at $500, excepting the priviledges hereafter given to my Daughter Molly.
Dau: Molly the dwelling house, half the garden, 1 acre of meadow to be her choice out of my meadow & the spring we now use, 3 acres of land in the field toward Wrightsels as we go in said field from the house as long as she sees cause to stay, after she moves off then to fall to Philip, and Molly must have firewood off the place while she stays, $60 "for the trouble she has had with me", 20 bushels of wheat, 200 weight of pork & 3 barrels of corn, & the priviledge of fruit for to dry and for house use as long as she stays.
All Children: all my moveable estate shall be sold at publick sale & divided among them equally "those that have received heretofore to be deducted out of their share & those that have land to be deducted out of their shares at the rates aforementioned."

Seal: Peter Smith
Exrs: trusty friends Henry Wrightsel & Jonathan Hadley "with full power to act on my behalf and to sell my share of my Brother Adam's land and divide it equally among all my children."
Seal: Peter Smith
Exrs: trusty friends Henry Wrightsel Jonathan Hadley
Wits: George Coble (Jurat) Philip Kime (Jurat)
[note: are there unnamed children, possibly daughters, here who have already received their portion of Peter's estate?]

A:0368 pp:373/374 GAYER STARBUCK 5th of 3rd mo 1813 May Ct. 1814
"Know all men by these presents..."
Wife: Rachel Starbuck the use profit & income of all my Estate both real & personal while she remains my widow, & at her decease or marriage.
Dau: Eunice Starbuck my Clock, large Walnut table, Loom & weaving utensils, the Cookpots, puter basons, dishes, knives & forks, shuvel & Tongs, & all the hand Irons in the House forever & a comfortable living in the House & on the plantation as long as she remains single.
Son: Reuben Starbuck at the decease of my wife the plantation where I now live with all the buildings & appurtenances thereunto belonging, also my waggon & Tackle, all my farming utensils of Every kind, also my large Chest that was my Sea Chest.
Grandson: Daniel Starbuck, son of Peter deceased, 1 midling good Horse & Saddle, also 1 feather bed, bolster & 2 pillows, 2 sheats 1 blanket & Coverlet.
Children: Pamely, Elizabeth, Rachel, Thomas, Ruth, Lydia, Dorcas, Reuben, Eunice Starbuck, and Grandson Daniel Starbuck, s/o Peter, deceased all the remaining part of my Estate of whatsoever name or nature not herein before disposed of to be Equally devided among them, but if either of them decease without leaving Lawful Issue that his her or their part or parts be Equally divided among the Survivors.
Seal: Gayer Starbuck
Exrs: brother Hezekiah Starbuck son Thomas Starbuck
Wits: Paul Macy (Jurat) Latham Starbuck Jemima Macy

A:0369 pp:374/375 JOEL SANDERS 2nd of 3rd mo 1814 May Ct. 1814
"Know all men by these presents..."
Wife: Mary Sanders the use, profit, & income of Mills & all the Land & Buildings on the South side of the Mill pond & creek, also all the fields adjoining the creek on the North side during her natural life. At her decease -
Son: Jesse Sanders all the above mentioned premises extending from a Hickry in the Field neer the North end a West course to Charles Benbo's line thence along his line & Nathan Dillons line to Solomon Deans land, also 2 Beds & Furniture.
Colloured Man: Tony all the land bought of Jesse Dillon except 1/2 of the meadow ground & Timber sufficient to fence it.
Dau: Priscilla Beason 1/3 part of the meadow ground I bought of Edward Bullocks estate to be laid off at the North end of Bullocks land neer Haw River.
Son: Joel Sanders 1/3 of the meadow ground I bought of the above said Edward Bullocks Estate, also the plantation where he now lives begining at NW end of the dividing fence thence a strait line to the Bold Branch

then NW along Archalus Bowmans line to the Claim bought of John Stuart thence a Strait line to the SE end of the above said fence.
Son: Thomas Sanders the balance of the Bullock Tract of Land not herein disposed of also all my Land on the waters of Deep River adjoining the Land belonging to Hezekiah Ham & John Goardin [Gordon?] being about 110 acres.
Son: John all that tract of land where he now lives.
Son: Hezekiah Sanders all that tract of Land on the North side of the Reedy Fork adjoining William Bunch's Land where he used to live & the Land he bought of William Ogbourn.
Sons: John & Joel my cotton machenary.
Dau: Mary Benbo 1/2 of the meadow ground I bought of Jesse Dillon, also 1/3 part of all my household furniture.
Daus: Priscilla Beason & Jean Groose all the remainder of my household furniture to be equally divided between them.
Granddau: Martha Smith Sanders $200 in cash, also a good horse & saddle, a cow & Calf, & a good bed & furniture.
5 Sons & 3 Daus: namely Jesse, John, Hezekiah, Thomas, & Joel Sanders, Priscilla Beason, Jean Groose, and Mary Benbow all the remainaing part of my Estate not herein disposed to be equally divided among them.
Seal: Joel Sanders
Exrs: sons John & Jesse Sanders
Wits: Barnabas Coffin John Hubbard John Stuart (Jurat)

A:0370   pp:375/376/377/378   MATHEW STARBUCK   14th of 1st mo 1815   n.p.d.
"I, Mathew Starbuck..."
Wife: Dinah Starbuck the use & profit of 1/3 part of my plantation & 1/3 part of my dwelling house with every priviledge thereto belonging during her widowhood. She to have all the wearing cloths, beds & furniture, & every article she had when I marray her that is now in being, 2 pair of sheets of common sort, 1 good pair of homemade blankets, the use of my State Waggon. The 1/3 part of the income of any plantation does not afford a sufficeincy for my wife's support that my Executors furnish her with what they may think best, out of my Estate.
Son: Reuben Starbuck $20 with what I have heretofore given him.
Four Sons: John, George, Charles, & Benjamin Starbuck all the land I own in Guilford County, No. Carolina to be equelly divided between them provided they pay $20 to my son Reuben as above mentioned.
Dau: Eunice Gardner 5 shillings with what I have heretofore given her.
Dau: Mary Starbuck $50.
Dau: Elisabeth Gardner $50.
Dau: Sallay Coffin $50.
Dau: Lydia Wheeler $50.
Dau: Avice* Starbuck $50 & a large green bedquilt bought at Nantucket.
Son: Charles my desk & the horse coalt that is now called his.
Son: Benjamin my watch.
Four Sons: Seth, George, Charles & Benjamin Starbuck all farming utensils to be equally divided.
Sons: George, Charles, & Benjamin to have each of them a silver spoon, each spoon mark'd in the two Letters of their Names, that is GS CS & BS.
Six Daus: Eunice, Mary, Elisabeth, Sallay, Lydia & Avice all the residue of my personal Estate.
Seal: Matthew Starbuck

AN ANNOTATED DIGEST OF WILL BOOK A, GUILFORD COUNTY, NORTH CAROLINA

Exrs: sons Seth & George Starbuck
Wits: Barnabas Coffin William Starbuck (Jurat affirmed) Paul Starbuck
"revokes"
*Avice is an old English name. JSH
Codicil: 21st of 6th mo 1815
Wife: while she remains on my plantation & continues my widow the use of 2 of my horses to go in the State Waggon when it appears convenient for her to ride from home, the use of 2 cows & if she should marray she to have 1 of them & the other to go into the residue of my Estate. It is also my will for her to have the use of 1 spare bed & furniture while she continues at my house.
Sons: George, Charles, & Benjamin Starbuck 1 bed & common furniture or value thereof to be Equelly divided between them.
Dau: Avice Starbuck 1 cow with what I have heretofore given her.
Son: Benjamin the use of my mare call'd Cate that he has now put to the horse till he can raise a coalt from her and after the coalt is weaned for sd Mare Cate to go into the residue of my estate.
"It is my will and meaning and I want it to be so understood that all the above articles mentioned in this Codicil for the use of my beloved wife Dinah, be at her command & for her use during her continuance at my house as my widow, but if she should move to some other place for her home, for the above mentioned Articles to go into the Residue of my Estate."
Seal: Mathew Starbuck
Exrs: sons Seth & George Starbuck
Wits: Barnabas Coffin William Starbuck (Jurat affirmed) Paul Starbuck

A:0371 pp:378/379 HEZEKIAH SANDERS 13th of 5th mo 1789 n.p.d.
"I, Hezekiah Sanders..."
"carpenter"
Wife: Martha use & profits of the plantation that I now live on and the grist mill during my wife's widowhood and my daus. unmarried state, & if my wife should incline to merray, my will is before she doth that all my daughters that remains in an unmarr'd state shall have the use & profits of the plantation I now live on. Also 2 mares the old Sorrel mare, the black mare, 1 feather bed with furniture, 1 sadle with a legacy left to us in Virginia by my wife's father all of which I give unto my beloved wife Martha Sanders forever if she should marry.
Son: John Sanders the plantation that he now lives on & the remainder of my Carpender tooles except 1 hand saw, auger & 2 shissles [chisels] for the use of the plantation, and the Black Stone Colt.
Son: David Sanders the plantation that he now lives on and that plantation I bought of Micajah ------ [the will was torn or had ink spilled on it at this point, and the Clerk could not make out the name; neither can I. JSH] during the time my wife & daus. hold possession, also the grist mill with the priviledge thereunto belonging with his paying each of my daus. £25 of good and lawful money.
Six Daus: Mary, Elisabeth, Martha, Sarah, Rebekah, & Jemimah all the residue of my Estate to be equally divided between them.
Seal: Hezekiah Sanders
Exts: my brothers John Sanders & Joel Sanders
Wits: Barn'a Coffin Samuel Coffin (Jurat) Matthew Macy (Jurat)

AN ANNOTATED DIGEST OF WILL BOOK A, GUILFORD COUNTY, NORTH CAROLINA

A:0372   pp:379/380 RICHARD SIMPSON, SENIOR 20 Nov. 1803   Feb. Ct. 1804
Wife: Selah Simpson 1/3 of all my Lands during her lifetime & 1/3 of all my other Estate her lifetime.
Son: William 50 acres of Land at the upper end of my land where my Brother Thomas Simpson formerly lived.
3 Other Sons: Peter, Richard & James the remainder of my Land to be equally divided amongst them & Selah's part of the Land at her decease to be equally divided among them.
Nephew: Thomas Knight my young Sorrel mare.
All Children: Peter, Pheraby, William, Richard, Elenner, Anna & James all the rest of my Estate to be equally divided amongst them & likewise at Selahs decease her part of the moveable Estate to be equally divided amongst them.
Seal: Richard (his X mark) Simpson
Exrs: two eldest sons Peter and William Simpson
Wits: Tho. Kirkman   Peter Simpson
"revokes"
Feb. Court 1804 The within will was admitted to record by the verdict of a Jury impanneled on the issue of a caveat tryed in Open Court then came in Peter Simpson and William Simpson & qualifyed as Executors to the will. [my underline, JSH]

A:0373   p:380   HENRY THOMSON   22 July 1771   Nov. Ct. 1771
"Residence - Second Creek"
Wife: [not named] all household goods and all personal Estate to hold in her owen hands during her widow hood & if Shee should mary again the Executor to take offe 2/3 of what there is to be fore [for] the yuce [use] of my children [not named]
Seal: Henry Thomson
Exrs: Wife & brother John Thomson
Wits: Thomas Millsaps (Jurat)   William Drapar

A:0374   p:381   SIMEON TAYLOR   12th of 7th mo 1773   May Ct. 1774
"Whereas I, Simeon Taylor, being far advanced in years..."
All the remainder of my estate after paying just debts & funeral charges to be lodged in the hands of my executors & that my wife [not named] shall have a sufficient maintenance out of the same during her life. Anything remaining at her decease to be at her disposal to divide the same among my children: Thomas Taylor, Rachal Lamb, Cathran Eldredge, Ann Parry & John Taylor.
Seal: Simeon Taylor
Exrs: son-in-law Robert Lamb   Brother-in-law Zacharias Dicks
Wits: William Williams (Jurat)   Jain (her 0 mark) Williams
"revokes"

A:0375 p:382   THOMAS THORNBRUGH   21st of 4th mo 1796   May Court 1797
"Whereas I Thomas Thornbrugh..."
Son-in-Law John Farrington 32 acres of land in the SW corner of my tract of land whereon I now live, to begin on the EW line, on the South side of the afsd. tract & to run from thence to McGrady's Branch, to be of an Equal width, from the beginning, to the afsd. branch so as to contain 32 acres.
Wife: Martha Thornbrugh the use of my dwelling house, garden & pasture, 1/3 part of my orchard & horsecart while she remains the widow of my

body, 1 horse, 1 cow & calf, all Sheep, & all household furniture, the wherewithall to support a Cow & Horse with grass & hay & a sufficient maintenance for to live upon while she remains the Widow of my Body.
Dau: Prudence Hunt 1 feather bed & Large iron pot.
Dau-in-law: Mary Thornbrugh my Sewels History.
Son: James all the remaining part of the land & plantation at wife's death or marriage, & to enter into the use of my land & plantation at my death provided he supplies my wife with the afsd necessities, but if he fails in this my wife to rent out the plantation for her support during her widowhood. James to have all my Carpenters, farming and all other tools of all kinds, & my wearing cloths & all the remaining Estate of whatever kind.
Son: Joseph 1 new Cloath Coat.
Dau: Elizabeth Farrington 1 cow & $5 for her use.
Daus: Susanna Stuert & Judith Horne $1 each.
Seal: Thomas Thornbrugh
Exrs: son James Thornbrugh friend William Starbuck
Wits: Strangeman Stanley (Jurat) Micajah (his U mark) Stanley Temple Stuart

A:0376   pp:383/384   THOMAS THORNBRUGH, JUNIOR   1st of 9th mo 1787
Feb. Ct. 1788
"Whereas I..."
"farmer"
Wife: Martha Thornbrugh the use & profits of the plantation whereon I now Live during her Widowhood or until my youngest son William comes to the age of 21 years, & after that for her to have 1/3 of said profits. I give her her riding mare & saddle, feather bead & furniture, 1 cow & calf & 1/3 of the remainder of my household stuf.
Son: Thomas 55 acres of land that I bought of my brother Joseph Thornburgh, 1 horse & the Bible with my name printed in it.
Two Sons: Henry & William all the remainder of my Land to be equally divided as to value & for my youngest son William to have the homestead, each a horse & my farming tools equally divided.
Three Sons: all wearing clothes, all carpenters tools equally divided.
Sophia Ballanger [no relationship stated] 1 feather bed & furniture, 1 cow & 1 Ewe Sheep.
Three Daus: Ruth, Hannah, & Mary Thornbrugh 1 feather bed & furniture each, & 1 sheep each & any remainder of estate.
Dau: Ruth my small pocket Bible.
Offspring: [children] the use of my New Translation.
Wife: Martha all the remainder of my Estate of what name soever (except my Shear [share] of a Sawmill lately built on the land of John Thomas) to bring up my Children & Schooled.
If either of my sons should die in their minority or without heir that his Legacy should be equally divided between the 2 survivors, same for my 3 daughters.
Seal: Thomas Thornbrugh, Juner
Exrs: son Thomas Thornbrugh friend Jacob Hunt
Wits: Jesse Williams (Jurat) Hannah Ballinger Jemima (her mark) Stanly
"revokes"

AN ANNOTATED DIGEST OF WILL BOOK A, GUILFORD COUNTY, NORTH CAROLINA

    A:0377 pp:384/385 JAMES THOMAS   16th of 9th mo 1788   n.p.d.
"Whereas I, ..."
Wife: Milly my House, plantation & piece of Land which I live on, with the Horse, Cattle & Hogs, plantation utensils & house furniture during her life or widowhood.
Son: Benjamin the sd piece of Land after the death or marriage of his mother.
Son: John a certain piece of Land lying on Bare Creek in Richmond County & state affsd with 1 horse bridle & saddle, 1 cow & calf.
3 of John Thomas children: namely Elijah, Stephen, & Francis if either of my sons should die without Heir the above to Descend and belong to his Brother & if they should both decease without heirs, then for both their portions to descend and belong to Elijah, Stephen, & Francis for to be theirs Equal as though they were my own children.
Seal: James Thomas
Exrs: friends John Thomas & his son Isaac Thomas
Wits: Aaron Mendenhall   Thomas Willents   Laban Tharp
"revokes"

    A:0378 pp:385/386 JOHN THOMPSON
State N. Carolina, Guilford County. *Nuncupative Will*
"This day came Col. John Gillespie of his own free will & accord befor me Ralph Gorrell one of the Justices of the Peace for the County afforesaid and after being duly sworn deposed and said that on or about the 13th of this instant [present month] at your Deponants own House in sd County a certain John Thompson, was there and it appeared wished to communicate his Mind to your Deponent respecting the Deviding his Estate among his three sons, namely Wm. F. Thompson, James & John younger sons that the afsd John Thompson in his life time the day and place afsd pronounce these words to your Deponant (as he had at sundrie times before words nearly to the same Substance) and required him to take notice as he in all probability would not live long, namely that he had made his oldest son Wm. F. a deed for a piece of the land he lives on and allowed his son James to bring his brother Wm F. through his schooling and supporting his family and afterward that his son Wm. F. Thompson was to return the Deed of the Land to his son James that is the whole of the tract of land that the deceased John Thompson then lived on and all the goods and chattles that he owned when living and on the premises to be left to the afsd James and to his Mother namely Jane Thompson your Deponet saith that the afsd John Thompson Directed his son James to pay £40 to Majer Donnell for land his two sons had purchased namely James & John F. Thompson and allowed his younger son John to get that land upon paying up the Majer the balance and allowed that your Deponet would endeavour to see it settled accordingly and further your Deponeth saith not".
Sworn to before me 28th of November 1793.
Signed: John Gillaspie
State of North Carolina Guilford County} February Court 1793 the execution of the Words of the within will was proven before the subscribing Justice & admitted to record and the Administration granted to Col. John Gillaspie & James Thompson who gave Bond & qualifyed as such agreeable to Law &etc.
Test. John Hamilton C.C.

A:0379 p:386 NICHOLAS TALLEY   7 Mar. 1795   May Ct. 1795
"being advanced in years..."
Wife: Mary all estate both real & personal during her Natural Life & after her decease to be divided as follows:
Son: John Talley 200 acres of land where I now live including the plantation & dwelling house to him & his heirs lawfully begotten of his body forever.
Grandson: Nicholas Talley, s/o John 100 acres of land to be laid off convenant to the Rock Spring.
Aggay & her increase shall be sold & the money arising from the sale, together with all my personal Estate to be equally divided amongst my 8 children. [Not named]
Seal: Nicholas Talley
Exrs: Josua Haines   wife Mary Talley
Wits: Phebe Rich   Joseph Haines (Jurat)

A:0380 p:387 JOSEPH THORNBURG 27 Jan. 1793 Aug. Ct. 1800
"Whereas, I ... & being far gone in years".
Wife: Ann Thornburg 1 mare, 2 Cows, all the household furnuture forever, 6 apple trees & a sufficient maintainance of my land during her widowhood.
Son: Joseph Thornburg 100 acres of land laid of[f] of where he now lives.
Sons: Edward & Isaac Thornburg all the rest of my land to be equally divided between them.
Daus: Ann Hoggatt, Mary Hodgson, Margret Hoggatt, & Elisabeth Hodgson 5 shillings each.
Son: Isaac Thornburg all the rest of free estate.
Seal: Joseph (his X mark) Thornburg
Exrs: sons Edward & Joseph Thornburg
Wits: Wm. Armfield, Esq. (Jurat) Jos. Thornburg

A:0381 p:388 GEORGE TILLEY Nuncupative Will
"We John Gunn & Joseph Gunn both of Guilford County do state on oath that on the 23rd day of July last we were called upon by George Tilley dec'd. at the House of Solomon Jones in said County where he usually resided, and was desired to commit to memory his will and desire to making his property which is as follows - He said he had some little money of which he intended his daughter Nancy should have $30 and his Daughter Betsy Jones should have the rest, the residue of his property to be dieved among his said Daughters & his working tools to be Solomon Jones'.
Seal: John (his x mark) Gunn Joseph (his x mark) Gunn
 Guilford County, NC} August Court 1801   The within will was proven in Open Court by the oaths of John Gunn & Joseph Gunn and ordered to be recorded. Test. John Hamilton C.C.

A:0382 pp:388/389 THOMAS TAYLOR 6th of 7th mo 1802 Aug. Ct. 1802
"Know all men by these presents..."
Wife: Mary Taylor the use, profits, & income of all my Estate both Real & Personal during her Widowhood, but in case she marries again my will is she shall have but only the use of 1/3 thereof.

AN ANNOTATED DIGEST OF WILL BOOK A, GUILFORD COUNTY, NORTH CAROLINA

Sons: Thomas & Alexander all the land where I now live with all the priviledges thereunto belonging to my sons be equally divided between them not preferring one before the other but in case one of them die without lawful issue my will is the Survivor shall have his part provided they pay their Brothers & Sisters [not named] 5 shillings each.
Seal: Thomas (his T mark) Taylor
Exrs: son-in-law William Starbuck   friend Hezekiah Starbuck
Wits: Hezekiah Starbuck (Jurat)   John Kellam (Jurat)   Thomas Bingerman

A:0383   pp:389/390   MARY TAYLOR   25th of 2nd mo 1806   May Ct. 1806
"Know all men by these presents..."
4 Sons: Nathan, Simeon, Thomas & Elexander 5 shillngs each.
Son: John, <u>deceased</u>, 5 shillings [that's what it says! JSH]
2 Daus: Ruth & Lydia [Rose or Ross] 5 shillings each.
4 Daus: Jean Starbuck, Phebe Fulps, Ester Bingerman & Anna Ferrington all the remaining part of my estate of whatsoever name or nature to be equally divided between them.
Seal: Mary (her + mark) Taylor
Exrs. Son-in-law William Starbuck   friend Hezikiah Starbuck
Wits: Zacharias Coffin (Jurat)   Wm. Starbuck   Hannah Dillon

A:0384   pp:390/391   EDWARD TATUM   24 Sept. 1805   Feb. Ct. 1811
Wife: Suckey Tatum during her natural life all personal Estate with my Negro Slaves Suck, Dick, & Sarah at her decease to be appropriated to the payments of the several legacies herein after devised, the residue to be equally divided among all my children or their heirs.
Son: Harbert $70 current money of the U. S. with 1 pewter dish & 1/2 dozen plates.
Son: Sihon the plantation & improvement whereon John Pyatt formerly dwelt & also that part of the tract of land purchased from his heirs which lyes situate on the upper side of Pyatts branch, $40 current money of the U. S., 1 new pewter dish & 1/2 a dozen plates.
Son: Edward all my land lying betwixt the lands of Harbert Tatum & that now devised to Sihon Tatum, $40 current money of the U. S., 1 new pewter dish, & 6 plates.
Dau: Patsey Tatum in addition to what I have heretofore bestowed on her $25 current money of the U. S. States.
N. B. Son: Henry Tatum all the plantation & tract of land where Devisor lives, 1 new pewter dish, 1 bason, 1/2 dozen plates.
Seal: Edward Tatum
Exrs: wife Suckey Tatum   sons, Harbert & Sihon Tatum
Wits: William Ogburn (Jurat)   Kinchin Vaughan (Jurat)   Tabitha Vaughan   Charles Bruce (Jurat)
"revokes"

A:0385 pp:391/392   JAMES THORNBURG   18th of 4th mo 1813   Aug. CT. 1814
"I, James Thornburg..."
Wife: Mary Thornburg the use & profits of my plantation as long as she remains my widow, the use & service of as much stock & plantation tools as my Exrs. shall think proper for her support, the sorrel mare that she commonly rides, 1 cow, her choice of 1 feather bed & its furniture that is now in the house, 1/2 the kitchen furniture, 1 years provision out of the crop.

Sons & Daus: Thomas Thornburgh, Richard Thornburgh, Rachal Mendenhall, Susannah Royl, Abigal Stanley, Ann Jackson each 10 shillings.
Son: Benjamin Thornburgh 50 acres of land off the SE corner of this tract that I now live on with all priviledges.
Son: Thomas Thornburgh 1 acre of land off the afsd. Tract including the Spring of water that he makes use of.
Dau: Mary Clark 1 ewe lamb.
Dau: Martha Thornburgh all the remainder part of household & kitchen furniture except that given to wife's use, 1 cow & calf, 2 sheep & use and priviledge of my dwelling house for a home while she remains single.
Son-in-law: Edward Stanley that tract of land lying the West side of Brush Creek that was formerly my fathers with all the Priviledges to him & his heirs forever with his providing & supplying my Step Mother Martha Thornbrugh with a Decent & Comfortable living while she remains my fathers widow.
Children: this plantation that I now live on to be sold at private or public sale and remaining Stock & Devided among all my children.
Seal: James Thornburgh
Exrs: son Thomas Thornbrugh Bethuel Coffin
Wits: Paul Macy (Jurat) Hannah (her x mark) Coffin Esther (her x mark) Connly

A:0386 pp:392/393/394 JONAS TOUCHSTONE 23 Mar. 1815 May Ct. 1815
Wife: Sarah as much of my lands & Estate as she shall think proper to cultivate or occupy during her natural life with tools & farming utensils, 2 horses, 2 milch cows, my stock of Hogs my cupboard dresser & furniture, 2 beds & their furniture.
Dau: Jean Delay 100 acres of land in Guilford County on the waters of Haw River beginning at a Black gum standing on the North bank of said Asa Brashears corner on Jesse Brashears line, & a line of James Hays, dec'd. Thence running with sd line South 164 poles to a small hicory saplin Jacob Walker's corner then East 115 poles crossing a branch to a small hicory Bush, sd Jacob Walkers other corner on William McKemies line thence running with McKemies line North 48 poles to a stone sd McKemies corner near to a branch thence running West crossing sd branch 24 poles to a sassafrass saplin then North 116 poles to a grub on Gasper Stutts line then with his line and a line of Asa Brashers West up the River 21 poles to the first beginning.
Dau: Mary Ross the balance of my landed estate, 1 mare, 1 cow, 1 bed & furniture.
The balance of my property not herein described or mentioned should remain in the possession of my wife Sarah Touchstone during her natural life & then to be sold on a credit of 9 or 12 months by my Exrs. & the moneys arising be equally divided between my 2 Daus: Jean Delay & Mary Ross.
Grandson: Jonas Ross $100 to be put to interest until he arrives to the age of 21 & then be applied to giving my Grandson Jonas Ross a liberal education.
Seal: Jonas Touchstone
Exrs: worthy friends Thomas McCuiston of Buffaloe & Samuel Hunter
Wits: U. D. Brasher (Jurat) Thos. McMichael Noel Parrish (Jurat)
"revokes"

AN ANNOTATED DIGEST OF WILL BOOK A, GUILFORD COUNTY, NORTH CAROLINA

A:0387 pp:394/395 SAMUEL THOMPSON 29 June 1801   Aug. Ct. 1801
"I, Samuel Thompson..."
My whole estate real & personal be appraised by William McAlhatton, James Finley & Thomas Dick.
Son: John a sorrel 5-year old colt called Flincho & $500.
Brother: Robert Thompson an Island in the Reedy fork of 10 acres.
Wife: Margerie and 6 Daus: Letice, Isabel, Rebecca, Margarit, Levina & Nancy the remainder of my estate, equally among them.
Exrs: to raise & educate my children.
Seal: Samuel Thompson
Exrs: wife Margerite   son John Thompson
Wits: Alexander Pritchett, (Jurat) Henery Huffin Thos. Dick (Jurat)

A:0388 pp:395/396 LEVI TUCKER   4 Mar. 1816   May Ct. 1816
Wife: Peggy Tucker 1 feather bed, 2 cows, 8 head of Hogs, her riding saddle & 1 horse Beast, 2 sheep all of her own choosing from my Estate, & the plantation whereon I now live as long as she remains my wife, that is South of the Fayetteville Road.
Son: Zadok my Still house & all my Stills & all utensils thereunto belonging, also my Wheat Fan, but it to remain in the barn where it stands for the use of his Mother & him while she remains in possession of sd land, that above mentioned land at the decease or marriage of his Mother, & my house clock.
Son: Anderton Tucker that tract of land of 150 acres on which he now lives.
Son: John Tucker that tract he now has in possession called the Neelley Tract containing 200 acres as soon as he pays his sister Mary Tucker $100 & Interest from January 1818, but if John dies before he has any children by lawful marriage, land to be sold & the price equally divided between his sisters.
Son: Abbit Tucker my Silver Watch & all the land I now possess North of the Fayetteville road & NE till it comes to the original corner once belonging to Andrew Gambl to run a SE course until it strikes Frederick Tyers line & this to be a division betwixt Zadoc & Abbit Tucker.
Dau: Nancy, wife of Charles Causey, $100 to be paid out of my estate.
Dau: Mary 1 feather bed & furniture, 1 cow & calf, 1 horse beast worth $50, her side saddle, & $100 to be paid out of my Estate.
Dau: Dianna 1 good feather bed & furniture, 1 horse & saddle, 1 cow & calf, $200 out of my estate.
Dau: Leah Tucker 1 good feather bed & furniture, 1 cow & calf, & $250 from 1 year after my decease untill she arrives at the age of 18.
Two Youngest Daus: Sarah & Elisabeth, $300 each & the interest of it from they arrive to the age of 10 years until 18 years & their money to be made & raised out of my Land in the Western Country & that Land to be sold in the year 1820 & after all expenses are paid & sd money raised to be divided among my 3 youngest children. [not named]
Remaining property to remain in the hands of my Executors until the death or marriage of my wife Peggy Tucker, then to be sold & equally divided betwext all my daughters & my son Abbit, except 30 acres of land lying to the SE of the land on which Anderton Tucker lives, which land was entered by John Core, which land I give & bequeath to Anderton Tucker's daughter Patty when she arrives to the age of 18 years.
Seal: Levi Tucker

Exrs: wife Peggy   sons Anderton Tucker   Zadoc Tucker   [continued]
Wits: McCullock [sic] (Jurat)   Frederick Tyer (Jurat)
"revokes"

A:0389   pp:397/398   **JOSEPH UNTHANK**   5th of 4th mo 1780   n.p.d.
"In the fear of God..."
"yeoman"
Son: Josiah all the tract of land whereon I now live, 39 acres adj. the meadows over the Creek being part of the 900 acre tract; my right of a tract of Land I bought of James Whitly near where Robert Lindsly [sic] now lives; my wagon, harrow, carpenters tools, 1/3 of all my Books, the Great Bible, a rifle gun & my Clock, a young horse colt, my best bed & bedstead & furniture, Desk, oval table, large iron pot, brass kettle & saucepan; except two tracts of 17 acres & 129 acres adj my son Allen's land.
Son: John Unthank 1/2 of the remaining part of the 900 acre tract laying upon the waters of Bruss [Brush ?] Creek & Horsepen Creek, my best Hat, Setoak [?] coat, warming pan, a tin of paint, 1/3 part of all my Books, a large iron shovel, a Brasscock, a large Bale Box & my pocket Book of Memorandums.
Son: Allen Unthank the 1/2 of the remaining part of the 900 acre tract afsd, also 17 acres & 129 rods of the NW corner of the tract where I now live, run out for him by Enoch Macy beginning at the NE corner of his land running North 45° West 104 rods to a hickory saplin on my North & South line joining Allen's land, my best Coat & Jaciett, a tin of paint, a small iron shovel, 1/3 part of all my Books, my common wearing hat, a Brasscock & a large Bale Box.
Grandson: Joseph Unthank: a smoothe bored gun, a young Bay horse, my best pair of Breeches, a cotton Jackett, a pair of Brown Worsted Stockings.
Grandson: Jonathan Unthank a smoothe bored Gun that was in the hand of William White, & a young mare.
Wife: Judith Unthank the use & profits of the plantation whereon I now live with all household goods not already disposed of & 1/3 part of my other parsonal Estate that is not already disposed of, 2 roan horses & the old mare (if the old mare should have colts that my son Josiah should have the first one)   6 cows, 1 large steer, 3 yearlings, 2 calves, 9 Ewe sheep, 1 ram & 2 lambs; all the cloth I have now at the fulling Mill & as much hard money as will pay for the dressing of it also all the Wool that comes off all my Sheep this year. All to her use as my widow & maintain and educate my son Josiah until he arrives to the age of 18 years.
Sons: John, Allen, Josiah all the residue of my estate to be divided equally among them.
If son Josiah should die before he arrive to the age of 18 years or without leaving any Heir of his Body, then all that was intended for him be equally divided between my other two sons John & Allen.
Seal: Joseph Unthank
Exrs: sons John & Allen Unthank
Wits: Tho. Thornburgh (Jurat)   William Coffin (Jurat)   Richard Williams

AN ANNOTATED DIGEST OF WILL BOOK A, GUILFORD COUNTY, NORTH CAROLINA

A:0390   pp:398/399   JOHN UNTHANK   8 of 10th mo 1780   Aug. Ct. 1782
"I, John Unthank..."
"yeoman"
Brother: Allen Unthank a small tract of land adj. his land.
Bro-in-law: Jacob Hunt 30 acres of land of the right I bought of Hugh Foster adj the land he now lives on.
Bro-in-law: William Hunt 100 acres of the best part of the remainder of the afsd claims.
2 Daus: Mary & Hannah 100 acres of deeded Land of that [part] of my land that adj John Hussey's nigh the Salisbury Road, also a claim that is adj the afsd land also 1/3 part of household goods to be equally divided between them to each one half.
Wife: Sarah Unthank the use & profits of all my estate both real & personal during her widdowhood or untill my son Joseph arrive to the age of 21 years & then for her to have the use of not more than 1/3 of my estate & if she should marry before my sons are of age for her to have the use of but 1/3 of my estate from that time.
2 Sons: Joseph & John all the residue of my Estate of what name or Nature soever to be equally divided between them.
Seal: John Unthank
Exrs: brother Allen Unthank   brother-in-law William Robinson
Wits: William Coffin (Jurat)   David Brooks   Strangeman Stanley

A:0391 pp:399/400   MICHAEL WITT   26 Mar. 1790   Nov. Ct. 1795
Wife: Mary 1/3 of all estate both real & personal & at her death is to leave all her said 1/3 part to the chidlren to be divided among them equally.
Daus: Mary, Catherin, Elesabeth, Esther, Jean, Margaret, Rosanah £12 & 1 cow each.
Son: John all my plantation & if it should or doe be a boy that my wife is big with when it is born I order & allow him & John to have the Land equally divided between them, & if it should be a girl she is to have an equal share with the rest above. If any of the above named children should die in their none age [minority] I order that the part of such child under age or before marriage is to be equally divided among all the rest.
Seal: Michael Witt
Exrs: wife Mary Witt
Wits: Andrew Smith   (Jurat)   Jacob [Werick? He is the only person of that name who shows near Michal Witt in the 1790 census.   JSH]
"revokes"

A:0392   pp: 400/401   THOMAS WELBORN   2 April 1778   May Ct. 1778
"I, Thomas Welborn..."
Wife: [not named] her bed & clothing, horse & sadle, a Negro wench called Dinah to work for her, free privileges to live on the plantation & enjoy the dwelling house & stock to raise the children till the youngest comes of age, then 2/3 of the land to be sold at Public sale & the same divided as I shall appoint in this will if she remains a widow. If she marries I bequeath her only her horse & Saddle & wearing cloths, & to quit the plantation for the use of the Children & the whole of the land to be sold & divided as before mentioned when the youngest child comes of age if She either dies or mareys before sd term.

Eldest Son: John £50 currency to be raised out of my estate in 18 months after my decease.
Dau: Ruth her choice of any 2 mares a black one & a gray, her saddle, Bridle, wearing cloths, a fether bed & furniture, 1 cow & calf as soon as she is married.
Son: Joshua his horse, sadle, bridle, & wearing clothes now in his possession, any doler bills in my possession.
Children: Cealep [Caleb?], Thomas, Ephreim, Elijah, Ezekiel, William, & Emy [Amy?] as they come of age 1 horse, sadle, bridle & sute of clothes each & to be schooled at the majority of youngest child, land to be sold & my Negroes with their increase sold to the highest bidder, except the old wench for the use of my wife, all other estate not devised herein to be sold & the money to be divided in the following manner: Cealep, Thomas, Ephram, Elisha, Ezekiel, William & Amy unless it should amount to more in proportion than I have left to the three Eldest, if so the over plus to be divided evenly amongst my 10 children.
All stock & Emplyments belonging to the plantation be kept thereon toward raising & schooling the Children.
Seal: Thos. Welborn
Exrs: son John wife (if wife should die or marry, son Joshua to take her room [room = place]
Wits: James Hunter Semore York Sarah Engleson (Jurat)
"revokes"

A:0393 p:402 JOHN WRIGHT   19 Feb. 1783   May Ct. 1783
"Know all Men by these presents..."
Son: James my land, 3 cows, 4 sheep, 4 horses, a Negro wench named Eal, a Child named Fan/Fern[?], 1/2 of all other moveables.
Son: John a Negro boy named Tom, a cow & yearling, & the half of all other moveables not disposed of above.
Son: James to make a deed to son John for 126 acres of land.
Seal: none
Exrs: none
Administration with the will annexed is granted to James Wright in the amount of £200 for the faithful discharge of his duty
Wits: Robert Wright William McMurrey
[Because John Wright did not sign his name or make his mark, and because he named no executors, his estate was treated as an intestate estate with Administrators appointed by the Court. However, the provisions of the will were usually followed]JSH

A:0394 p:403 JAMES WRIGHT, JUNIOR 28 June 1784   Feb. Ct. 1785
Wife: Prudence 100 acres of the land whereon I now live during her life & such part of my moveable estate as shall be thought proper, 2 work creatures & a plough, all horses, cattle, hogs for her & her family's sustenance during her life.
Seven Children: Alex'r, Elizah, Wm., Micajah, Dianna, Jane & Lyda Wright "and as for the remaining 300 acres whereon I now live, together with the land my Father James Wright, Sen'r. now lives on (after my father & mothers deceased) tis my Will that it should be equally divided among my

AN ANNOTATED DIGEST OF WILL BOOK A, GUILFORD COUNTY, NORTH CAROLINA

above named children & likewise that the part Willed to my wife should after her decease be equally divided among my above named children."
Seal: James Wright, Jrn.
Exrs: wife Prudence Wright
Wits: Michael Henderson   Lucy (her x mark) Wright   James Reagan
"revokes"

A:0395   pp:403/404   JOHN WHITE   5 Feb. 1787   May Ct. 1787
Wife: Jean [or Jane] 1/3 part of all my Land that She may sell & convey or dispose by Will, all household furniture, house, barn, her choice of 2 of my cattle, 1/2 of all my stock of Horses, cattle sheep & hogs, 1/3 part of the grain, all firewood to be hauled to her door, 1/3 part of all my money in hand or arising from Bonds, notes or out Standing Debts.
Son-in-Law: Joseph McDowell 2/3 of all my Lands & the remaining part of personal Estate not disposed of as above.
Seal: John White
Exrs: wife Jean White   Joseph McDowall, Jr.   Robert Peasly[Paisley]
Wits: W. Gowdy (Jurat)   Steven (his x mark) Goss   Robt. McCann (Jurat)
"revokes"

A:0396   p:405   ALSE WALTON   30 June 1791   Aug. Ct. 1791
"this day I have made my Will and I have left to my youngest son Nathaniel Walton the track of Land which he doth now Live on which is two hundred and forty acres"
Seal: Alse Walton
Exrs: none
Wits: John Walton

A:0397   p:405   ALLEN/ALLON WILSON   9 April 1792   May Ct. 1792
"Know all men by these presents..."
"planter"
Cousin: Allon Wilson son of James & Jain Wilson "all my rail & parsonal astate after my just debts is paid to him and his heirs forever when he comes of age"
Seal: Allon (his   mark) Wilson
Exrs: James Wilson
Wits: John (his   mark) Canady (Jurat)   John Wilson (Jurat)

A:0398   p:406   EDWARD W. WILLEY   5 July 1793   Aug. Ct. 1793
"of Dorchester County Maryland"
Brothers: John & Thomas W. Willey "all my right, title, & claim to all the land willed to me by my father, Prichard Willey, dec'd., lying, & being in & near the town of Cunna [?] on the Eastern Shore of Maryland to be equally divided between them.
Jno. Willey all my wearing apparel.
Sister: Emelia Willey what ever sum or sums of money may remain after my just debts are paid the same to be delivered her at the discretion of my Aunt Sarah White, residing on Great Choptank River or in case of her death by my friend R. Stanford"
Seal: Edward W. Willey
Exrs: Aunt Sarah White   R. Stanford
Wits: R. Stanford (Jurat)   John Van Storre (Jurat)   Catheron (her x mark) Van Storre

AN ANNOTATED DIGEST OF WILL BOOK A, GUILFORD COUNTY, NORTH CAROLINA

A:0399 pp:406/407 **JAMES WADDLE** 2 June 1786 Nov. Ct. 1796
"being exceedingly ille and for aught I know, near my departure from this world".
Wife: Elizabeth Wadell, all I have and possess of every kind both Land and moveable property during the term of time she lives single.
If she should marry or decease before the children comes of age, I desire & request Lavin Minor to take them into his care and see them right.
At her decease or Marriage that my Children [not named] have all the property & land devided amongst them directed by sd Lavin Minor.
Seal: James (his x mark) Waddle
Exrs: Lavin Minor
Wits: Levin Minner Joshua Holland (Jurat)

A:0400 pp:407/408 **JOHN WOODSIDE** 24 Feb. 1796 Nov. Ct. 1801
Wife: Hannah 1/3 part of my land and a child's part of all personal property during her natural life.
Sons: William, Samuel, John, James, & Robert Woodside all lands to be equally divided among them.
All Children: respectively my personal property to be equally divided among them. [not named]
Seal: John Woodside
Exrs: son William Woodside friend Charles Breed
Wits: John Endsley Jane (her mark) Nelson [also seen as Jean](Jurat) Alexander (his + mark) Nelson
"revokes"

A:0401 p:408 **RICHARD WALKER** 16 April 1802 May Ct. 1802
Wife: Eliner all estate during her widowhood if not married during her natural life. She to make sale of such property as she shall see fit to pay just Debts, except the land.
Son: James Walker, land at death of wife.
Beloved: John Walker all my wearing apparel. [The word "son" does not appear in the original or in the clerk's copy].
Seal: Richard (his x mark) Walker
Exrs: wife Eliner Walker son James Walker
Wits: Wm. Harris Wm. Hogson (Jurat) Joseph Hogson (Jurat) [Hodgson?]

A:0402 p:409 **JOHN WORK** 2 Aug. 1781 n.p.d.
"being sick in body"
Wife: Margaret Work to have the charge of all my Estate during her widowhood, 1 childs part with my 3 children: Jean, Sarah, & Elizabeth of any estate sold as they shall be of age by Law.
Child yet unborn, if a boy he is to have my Land & 1 equal part same as my daughters. All children to be schooled & raised on the Expense of my Estate, to be taught to Reed & Write & if a son to be taught Arithmetick as far as the rule of three.
Uncles of Children: John Cunningham & Henry Work to value and make division of my estate as the children come of age.
Seal: John Work
Exrs: wife Margaret Work John Cunningham Henry Work
Wits: Henry Work Frances McBride [Francis?]
"revokes"

AN ANNOTATED DIGEST OF WILL BOOK A, GUILFORD COUNTY, NORTH CAROLINA

A:0403 pp:410/411 JONATHAN WILLSON 13 May 1805 May Ct. 1805
"be it remembered..."
"being weak in body..."
Three Sons: land shall be divided equally when they come of age; plantation rented until my sons are of age and the rent equally divided between them.
Children under age, except Nancy, shall be Bound out to good places where they shall have good schooling & my sons get trades.
Son: Jonathan to be a Black Smith.
Son: William to be a joiner.
Son: Robert a taylor [sic]
Smith tools shall be rented out & put in good repair, & given to my son Jonathan in good order together with the rent when he comes of age.
Two youngest sons: Waggon shall be sold and the money equally divided between them when they come of age.
6 Daughters: [not named] all the remainder of Estate shall be sold, the money put out at Interest for them when they come of age to be equally divided between my 6 daughters.
Seal: Jonathan (his x mark) Willson
Exrs: Mathew Coffin James Dunning
Wits: Silas Peace (Jurat) Edward Ricks

A:0404 pp:411/412 WILLIAM WEATHERLY 16 Sept. 1805 Nov. Ct. 1805
"being sick and weak in body..."
Wife: Elizabeth Weatherly land & premises bought of Jeremiah Pritchett containing 133 acres lying on the waters of Haw River for her use and benefit during her natural life; all household goods, furniture, farming tools, 2 horses, all cattle & hogs for her support, "dureing hir life & also 1 bed & furniture that was hers before we ware Married."
Son: Levi Weatherly after death of my wife Elizabeth the land above described, and the remainder of my estate left over from support of wife.
Grandson: Noah Weatherly when he shall come of age 1 horse worth $40 & a suit of clothes.
Dau: Mary Weatherly (the Mother of Said Noah) after the death of my said Wife 1 cow, 1 puter Dish & 3 plates.
Seal: William (his x mark) Weatherly
Exrs: son Levi Weatherly trusty friend William Brown
Wits: John Coe (Jurat) Wm. King
"revokes"

A:0405 pp:412/413 WILLIAM WHITE 29 March 1806 Nov. Term 1806
"I, William White..."
Wife: Susanna all lands and tenements, goods & chattels & personal estate whatsoever for her own proper use & maintenance during her natural life.
After decease: Land & all other estate be Sold to the best Advantage & the money raised to be distributed in the following manner:
Sons: Thomas, John, William, James, Joel, & Isaac White (whom I have already provided for - $1.00.
Daus: Elizabeth Thornbury, Hannah Walker, Mary Carney, Alice Gosset, & Sarah Walker be paid the Remainder of sd Estate (after their brothers above, mentioned being paid off as above directed) & to be divided in such a manner the Elizabeth Thornbrough and Hannah Walker receive $16.00

more that their other Sisters, who have already received part of their quota hereto fore.
Seal: William White
Exrs: sons Thomas & Joseph White
Wits: John Underhill, Leonard Mash (Jurat)

A:0406 pp:413/414 FRANCIS WORTH 10th of 6th mo 1804 Aug. Court 1807
"Whereas I Francis Worth,..."
Wife: Mary Worth all estate both real & personal during her Life for her Comfortable maintainance & after her Decease to be Divided as follows:
Dau: Phebe Wooten £5
Dau: Mary Worth 50 acres of land she shall chuse, but that shall be discharged by my son Wm. Worth paying her $100.00, 1/2 of household furniture & all cattle & 1 horse creature that she shall chuse.
Dau: Anna Davis the other half of my household furniture.
Son: Wm. Worth all the rest of the Estate both Real & Personal.
Seal: Francis Worth
Exr: Friend, Wm. Starbuck
Witnesses: George Rayl,Jr. (Jurat) George Hubbard
"revokes"

A:0407 pp:414/415 WILLIAM WOODBURN 18 Oct. 1806 Nov. Court 1806
"Blacksmith & Planter"
Wife: Thankful Woodburn all the land I die possessed of during her natural life & to be disposed of by her at her death as she may think proper, household furniture (except what may be otherwise willed), 300 bu corn; 20 bu wheat, all my farming utentials, & 1/2 of the mony that remains after all debts & legacies are paid, my black horse, 2 cows & calves, 1 steer, 1 sow & 5 Barrows [farrows?/piglets?] out of my stock. Except should she marry again it is my will that all my lands fall to my beloved daughter Ann Woodburn.
Dau: Ann Woodburn my black Mare colt, 1 bed & furniture, the other half of the money that remains after all debts & legacies are paid to be held in the hands of my Executors untill she is of age.
The rest of my property to be Sold and out of the money arising therefrom all my just and lawfull debts to be paid.
Bryan Peirce, my Apprentice $15.
Seal: William Woodburn
Exrs: Brother and trusty friends Jedidia Cusick Arthur Woodburn
Wits: James Denny, Sr. James Denny, Jr. (Jurat)
"revokes"

A:0408 pp:415/416 EDWARD WEATHERLY 12 Sept. 1810 Nov. Court 1810
Wife: Henrietta Weatherly that part of my plantation whereon I now live to be at her Disposal, all my houses, all the Property thereon to be hers During her natural Life or Widowhood only such Exceptions as may be hereafter made.
Eldest Son: Mark Weatherly the whole of that tract of Land whereon he now lives.
Son: Edward Weatherly 160 acres of land whereon he now lives that is to a conditional line formerly made.
Son: William Weatherly the land whereon he now lives & also the land whereon I now live at his Mother's decease.
Son: Martin Weatherly $40 to be paid unto at Widows decease.

AN ANNOTATED DIGEST OF WILL BOOK A, GUILFORD COUNTY, NORTH CAROLINA

Dau: Sally McClintock $1.
Dau: Elisabeth Fulton $1.
Dau: Mary Weatherly 1 Negroe boy named Abraham at her Mothers decease, 1 horse & sadale, her Bed & furniture.
Dau: Henrietta Stafford $1.
Deborah Shelcott $1.
[Note: no relationship is given for Deborah in either the original will or the Clerk's copy]JSH
Seal: Edward Weatherly
Exrs: sons Mark Weatherly Edward Weatherly
Wits: William Lucas (Jurat) John Walker Leven Walker John Gilchrist (Jurat)

A:0409 pp:416/417 ISAAC WHITE 16 Sept. 1803 Nov. Court 1811

"Whereas I Isaac White of Guilford County & State Of No. Carolina do think proper to Leave the following Lines as my Last Will and Testament..."
First It is my will that all my just debts be paid.
2nd I Leave & bequeath to my Son Stanton White all that Track of Land where he now Lives with the farming Utentials, to him his heirs and assigns for Ever.
3rd I give and bequeath the Remander of my Movable property to be Equally divided amongst my Seven Daughters [not named] Except money if there should be any at my Decease it is my will that it should be equally divided amongst all my Children son & Daughters.
And Lastly I constitute and appoint my Friends Thomas White and Stanton White whole & sole Executors of this my Last will & Testament in witness where of I have here unto set my hand & affixed my seal this sixteenth day of the Ninth month in the year of our Lord one thousand eight hundred and three."
Seal: Isaac White
Exrs: friends Thomas White Stanton White
Signed Seald & acknowledged in the presence of Richard Williams (Jurat) Ruth Stanton

A:0410 pp:417/418 THOMAS WILEY 31 May 1812 Aug. Court 1812

[this will is a transcription of the original because it was just too confusing to attempt to digest it correctly. JSH]
1st I give & bequeath to my two sons David & Ely Wiley my land that is to be Equally to be divided between them by an East & West line by the Remark that will be made hereafter that is I give & bequeath to my daughter Ann the house I now live in together with 3 acres about the house or on the premises during the time she lives unmarried in peaceable possession with wood & water sufficient & if Ann should Marry or alter her way of living then which ever side of the above mentioned line the said house falls into will belong to that side.
I also give & bequeath to my daughter Ann her Choice of two horse creaters and also her Choice of 2 cows.
I also give & bequeath to my grand daughter Mary Matthews the other hors cretor & one cow, and I do alow the Stock of Sheep to be Equally divided Between Ann & David Wiley & Mary Matthews
I also allow David Wiley 1 cow & the Stock of hogs to go to the use of the house, the farming tools together with the wagon to be equally divided Between David & Eli Wiley

I do allow Eli Wiley My house Bible & David Wiley one Volume of Flavel and Ann Wiley the other Volume of Flavel then the other Books to be Equally divided Between Ann David & Eli Wiley & Mary Matthews
I do further alow Ann & David Wiley 1 bed & furniture each also Mary Matthews one bed & furniture
I do further alow my daughter Ann at her own discretion When Mary Matthews leaves her to divide the household furniture with her in a decent manner.
I also give & alow my Son William Wiley My Wearing clothes.
I also do alow my son John Wiley $1.
I also allow my daughter Elizabeth Forbis $1.
I do also allow my daughter Mary Matthews $1.
I do also alow Hugh Matthews $1.
And if my son Hugh Wiley is living and Ever comes to this Country I do allow him & it is my will that he shall pay $50 to the four legatees that is now at home to wit: Ann David Eli Wiley & Mary Matthews.
I Now Ratify & Confirm this to be my Last will & Testament in Witness Whereof I have set my hand & fixed my Seal this 31st Day of May 1812
N.B and in Hugh Wiley's Complying with this his note shall be given up to him   and I apoint David & Eli to Execute this my Last Will & Testament.
Seal: Thomas Wiley
Exrs. David Wiley Eli Wiley
Test. Signed Before us
Robert Wiley   James Wiley (Jurat) [witnesses]
August Court 1812 James Wiley one of the witnesses came into Open Court & proved the Execution of the Within Will and on motion was ordered to be Recorded. Then came in David & Eli Wiley Executors appointed in Said Will & Qualifyed as such accordingly. Jos. Davis, Deputy Clerk

A:0411 pp:418/419 JOHN WHITE 10th of 8th mo 1812 Aug. Court 1812
"I, John White...being in a low state of health"
Nephews: John and Benjamin White land & stock to be equally divided with all my household & chichen [kitchen] furniture, my farming & working tools.
Nephew: John 1/3 of my part of the Crop now in the ground.
Nephew: Benjamin the balance of the crop of wheat now raised.
Seal: John (his   mark) White
Exrs: Beloved friends Abraham Cook Benajah Hiatt
Wits: Joel Willis Wm. Hiatt

A:0412 pp:419/420 WATSON WHARTON 6 Dec. 1812 Nov. Court 1813
Four Sons: Elam & Elisha & John & Gidion hath had Deeds given to them for Lands I shall say no more about them In this place til hear after..
Dau: Tabitha Rankin my Negro Man Steevan & My Negro Woman his wife Susee & my Negro Boye Noah & my Negro Garl [girl] Abogal & hanay [Hannah] & also my clock & case to be holden by Hir [her] & hir hars [heirs] forever.
Dau: Martha Woodborn $550 to Bee payed with hir one Note as fare as tha will goe & the Rest to Bee pad in cash & also my Negro Garls Sall & Rath & My Deske & Book case and my Righten [writing] Desk to be held by her and her hars for ever.
Son: Evans Wharton upon sarton conditions as will hear after mentioned that is to say that if my wife Angolata & Evans Both doe Well & truly

stand & abide by this my Last Will I Revoke & Disannull all their Gifts that hear after Will be mentened [mentioned] & the same to Be Sold at Publick Sale Borth [both] Land & other property the Money arisen from the sale to be Divided a mong all my Seven children Namely Elam Elisah John Gidion Evans Tabitha Martha But if Evans & his Mother complies with the above conditions then their Gifts to be conformed [confirmed] to them & thir hars its My Will & Desier the Land & Plantation whare on I now Live his mothers thirds on Excepted Being Land I bought of Robert Smith & Andra Wilson & Elam Wharton the bounds to be known by the Deeds thar of & My Blaxsmith tuls [tools] & my 2 wagens & my Duch farm & all my farmen tuls such as plows & harrow hoes and exes [axes] my han saw & turner tuels three aughers & three former [sic] chisels & its my Will & Desire he shal have a twelve Month to pay what part he chuses to pay in cash for the stock that is in his hands by way of an artickel of an agreement & this to be all his part of my estate

Wife: Angalata: one reasonable Bed & furniture & one Chest hir sadel hir flax wheel 3 chers [chairs] & 1 tabel & 1/4 part of all my cichen [kitchen] furneaty [furniture] & cobard [cupboard] furnetur Borth puter & Iron earthen & wooden vesals to Be holden by hir & hir Hars for Ever

Negro Woman Abogal: have hir one [own] Free Chois to Live with whomsoever She Chues [chooses] of all my hars Wife or Children.

Now as to all the Resadue & Remandr part of all my Estate It is my Will & Desier that it should Be sold a publick oction [auction] at the Discresion of my Exacuters of this My Last will & Testament & the mony A Ressen [arising] from the Sale to appropiated as folows.

Elam Wharten to have $100 given out of his Note which I have on him for 350 Doler.

Soon [Son]: Gidion Wharton have 100 Dolers out of this Last Sail.

All the Remandur of my Estate Be Equall Divided a mong My Six Children namly Elam Elisha John Gidion Tabitha and Martha to be holden by them & thir hars for ever.

Seal: Watson Wharton
Exrs: sons Elam & Elisha Wharton
Wits: Robert Rankin (Jurat) Martha Rankin

A:0413 pp:421/422   JOHN WORK   25 Dec. 1801   Aug. Court 1802
[this will needed to be transcribed in its entirety. JSH]
"being in a low state of helth"
Wife Polley 1 Nigro garl [girl] Jude 1 Good Horse 2 cows & calfs Fifty Dollars in Cash & all the Household furniture she brought to my House after we was married, to her and at her disposial. Also, I lend to my beloved wife Polley Work during her being my widow, or such term of time as is here after mentioned, the Plantation whereon I now live & Land all the nigroes, to wit; Ned. Abb. Isaac. Dick & Jin with all the stock of Horses, Cattle, hogs & sheep & House hold & Kitching furniture to be governed in manner and form hereafter mentioned by my Executors

Whereas my wife now being with child, if she Shood have a son I give unto him & his Heirs for ever the Land & Plantation whereon I now live on & all my Nigros lent to my wife to wit; Ned, Abb, Isaac, Dick & Jin & all Stock of Horses, cattle Hogs sheep & hogs with all the household & Kitching furniture that is lent to my wife to him and his heirs for ever If my wife shood have a Daughter I give and bequeath unto her all my Negroes to wit Ned Abb Isaac Dick & Jin with all the stock of all kinds & house hold & Kitching furniture to her and her Heirs forever.

If my Wife shood have two Children in that case it is my will that there shall be an Equal Devition between them.

If my wife shood have a Daughter it is my Desire that John Massey shood have the land & Plantation where on I now live (son of Nathan Massey) him & his heirs forever to have Posession at the time my wife ceases to be my Widow & my Daugher if such comes to the age of 21 years & if she shood have a Son and Dye without lawfull heir in that case said John Massey is to have & Injoy Land, Negroes, stock and all other articles lent to my said wife for ever or if she shood have a Daugher & dye without Lawful heir then in that case Said John Massey is to enjoy her right forever.

I give unto Thos. Masey & John Massey sons of Nathan Massey $20 and it is my Desire that all my Just Debts shood be truly paid for which their is a Sum Sufficient due to pay all I owe if it can be Collected & if Not with a Sum Sufficient to be made out of the Stock, and it is my desire that my child or Children Shood be Raised & Schooled without cost further then can be Raised on the place & it is further my will that my Executors shood conduct all the Plantions Business for the Support of my Widow (during her being my widow) & heir or heirs and if my heir or heirs of my body shood come to the age to be thought necessary for a Devision before my wife ceases to be my widow in that case my Executors by order of court is to allot such part of the Nigroes & Stock as belongs to them, & if a son & he comes to the age of 21 years & wants to work the place he is to have the priviledge of 1/2 of the land not to tuch [touch] the Dwelling House where I now live if my wife shood then reamin my widow & it is my will that this legeses left in money shood be paid as soon as they convenianly can of the produce of the plantation.
Seal: John Work
Exrs: John Cunningham Abraham Peeples
Wits: Hubbard Peeples (Jurat) John (his x mark Work James (his x mark) Davis
August Court 1802 Then came in Polley Work Widow & relict of the deceasd and entered Her Disent to said Will
(vide docket) or (wide Docket) [Court Minutes of the appropriate time may shed more light on this. JSH]

A:0414 pp:422/423/424 DAVID WILEY, SR. 9 March 1816 May Court 1816
"being weak of body"
Wife: Peggey Wiley £100 in cash, 2 beds & furniture at her choise, 1 chest of Drawers & as much of the Clothing that She Brought hear as Will Sellisgy [satisfy] her, 2 Cows & Calves, 2 Sheep, a horse or mare at her Chois & Saddle & Bridle, 1/2 Of my Dresser & Cichen [kitchen] furneture, 1 table, 1 Negro Woman named Sall to Wait on her and at her Decess the Negro Woman is to be Set free.
Her command of the house I live in & the meaddow Below the Barn & the 1/4 part of the orchard & 2 fields of Land at her Choise & firewood with gearden & truck patch, 1 stable during life or Widdow hood. NB Her spinning wheel.
Son-in-law: Robert McKnight a Negro women Named Easter with him paying to my son-in-law William Tome the half price that the Said Negro being valued at.
Son: Thomas Wiley $100.
Son: James Wiley 1 Negro Gairl named Beeck with Reserve hereafter menssoned.

AN ANNOTATED DIGEST OF WILL BOOK A, GUILFORD COUNTY, NORTH CAROLINA

Son: Hugh Wiley a Negro Gairl named Nice [?] now in his possion.
Son: David Wiley the tract of Land I now live on containing 378 acres With Reserve of What I leve to my Wife Peggy & Likewise the Whole of the farming utencials only What my Wife Peggy has need of & a Negro man named Isaac with Reserve hear after mensioned I allow my [sic] to keep my wife Peggy in fier wood and to keep her field in good repair errors excepted for me.
Son-in-law: Harper Tome $100.
Polley Perter Tome: my cubert [cupboard]
NB I allow my 2 sons James and David Wiley to pey to my son Thomas $60 each in behalf of the negroes I gave them.
Daniel Tome son of Harper and Catron Tome $25 to be paid to him when he is of age free from Intrest to be paid By my executers David Wiley Jr. and William Tome.
Should there be any more than before mensioned I allow it to be devided between my wife Peggy Wiley and my ---- [sic] children Mary McKnight Nancy Tome Thomas Wiley James Wiley Hugh Wiley David Wiley
Seal: David Wiley Sr.
Exrs: wife Peggy Wiley son David Wiley William Tome
Wtis: Andrew McGee (Jurat) Eli (his x mark) Wiley

A:0415   p:424   THOMAS WRIGHT   15 of 4th mo 1815   May Court 1816
"I, Thomas Wright...
Wife: Rebekah Write the use & prophits of my Estate as long as she remains my widow Except my Black People Namely one Nigro Woman Peg, 1 Negro Lot, a young man almost grown named Jime, 1 younger named Sam, 1 Negro girl named Hannah, & 1 Negro child named Daniel which I give and bequesth unto the Society of Friends of New Garden Monthly Meeting or their agents and their successors.
Wife: Rebekah It is my will that my wife She have all my land at her disposal.
Black People: All the personal property of my Estate to the above Named Black peole to be sold and Equaly divided among them except what I give unto Whiley Wright and his Son Thomas.
I also Give and Bequeath unto my supposed Son Whiley Wright Ten shillings.
I also give and bequesth unto Whiley Writes Son Thomas $50 to him and his heirs for ever.
Seal: Thomas (his x mark) Wright
Exrs: Worthy Friends Bethuel Coffin Joshua Dicks William Hunt
Wits: Seth Dicks (Jurat) Ann Dicks (Jurat) Deborah Evans (Jurat) "Jurats affirmed"

A:0416 pp:425/426 ARTHUR WOODBURN 26 Apr. 1816 May Court 1816
Wife: Patsey Woodburn my waggon & gears, her choice of 2 of my work horses, 1st choice of 8 head of cattle, 1st choice 8 Ewes & Lambs, also 1st choice of all my household & kitchen furniure to be Disposed of among the Children as she may think fit, also all the profits arising from my two plantations until the heirs of the Land comes to the age of 21 years, 10 head of hogs also 1st choice to gether with 2 sows & their pits [piglets ?] which Choice is to be made in the faul after the crop is gathered, also the Riding Chair & harness & a sufficient quantity of Grain to Support the family & stock for 1 year. When my children come

of full age she is to take Choice of the Negros which Negro is to be her own property.
Sons: Watson and William my buffelow plantation to be Equally divided between them. If not otherwise Disposed of hereafter.
Dau: Tabitha Woodburn $250
Wife: may choose to sell the above plantations & Lay out the price in the purchase of other Land which shall be conveyed to the boys at the Same time as mentioned above. She having her Living & Land for Lifetime.
When all my Children comes of full age the Negros not before mentioned are to be Equally Divided among my five Children - Except the Coult of my pll [?] mare to be given to Watson.
The ballance of my property not mentioned to be sold at Publick sail my accounts Collected and my debt that are Lawful paid and the money so arising to be Equally Devided among my wife and Children Except fifty Dollars which I leave to Jonathan Wilson on Condition that he keeps and takes Care of my Stud horse till the season is Expired agreeable to advertisement and if he should not chose to keep the horse the afore mentioned fifty Dollars to be Devided.
Also the sail not to take place till the Crop is gathered this faul.
Seal: Arthur Woodburn
Exrs: wife Patsey Woodburn
Wits: Obed Aydelotte (Jurat) John Landirth (Jurat)

A:0417 pp:426/427 GEORGE ZIMMERMAN 15 Oct. 1800 Aug. Court 1812
Son: George Zimmerman all the Land & plantation which I possess & live on now according to the Deed for said Land Providing that he shall pay to his three sisters 20 Silver Dollars;
The 1st year after my Death he shall pay the said $20 to his sister Mary Margret.
The 2nd year he shall pay the same Sum to his sister Hanna.
The 3rd year he shall pay the sd $20 to his Sister Mary Dorothy, or if she is then under age to her guardian.
Son: George shall maintain his Mother during her Life & provide for her all the Nessities of Life so that she does not suffer for want of them and she is to live on the plantation with my Son George during her Life.
Son: George & Three Daus. & Wife [not named] after just debts are paid, everything shall be sold at private Sale between them so that the 5 shall divide all my moveable property into five equal parts among themselves so that my Wife Mary Margret shall draw an equal share with my 4 children, & after my Wifes Death the property she possesseth shall be divided into equal parts among the children.
Seal: George (his x mark) Zimmerman
Exrs: son George Zimmerman John Boon Senior
Wits: George Shoemaker (Jurat) John Boon
"revokes"

A:0418 pp:428/429 ROBERT LINDSAY 5 Feb. 1801 May Court 1801
Wife: Nancy all Stock of houses, cattle, hogs & sheep & all the utenceals of husbandry that has been in use on the plantation and all my household furniture that has been in use, also $1000 she allowed to have the use of one half of said tract of land Including the Improvements so longe as She continues my widow.
Son: John $250

AN ANNOTATED DIGEST OF WILL BOOK A, GUILFORD COUNTY, NORTH CAROLINA

John's Children: Samuel, Easter, Mary, Robert, ----- [?], Sarah, each $50.
Son: Robert 1 tract of land No. 4 as discribed in the paper plot anexed to this will, also $250.
Son: William 1 tract of land No. 3 as Described in the peaper before mantioned also $2000.
Son: Andrew 1 tract of Land whereon I now live No. 5 as described in the peaper before mantioned.
Son: David 1 tract of Land No. 1 described in the before mentioned peaper & $1500.
Dau: Jenne 1 tract of land No. 2 as Described in the peaper before mantioned & $2000.
Dau: Elizabeth 1 tract of land No. 6 as described in the before mantioned peaper &$2000.
Dau: Susannah $2,500.
All the remander of my Estate I allow to be Equaley Devided betwixt my Wife and children, my son John excepted.
Seal: Robert Lindsay
Exrx: wife Nancy Lindsay
Wits: Jane Lindsay Elizabeth Lindsay
The handwriting proven by Samuel Hartgrove (Jurat) Paris Chipman (Jurat) Moses McGrady (Jurat)
on the Clerk's copy of this will- "note The original will is slightly torn & the blanks cannot be supplied" [2 sets of initials accompany this note but they are too small to decipher. For some reason this will is out of the alphabetical sequence. JSH]

Thus endth Guilford County Will Book A as found on microfilm reel C.046.80001. Filmed by the North Carolina State Archives, Raleigh, NC. [Supplemented with photocopies of the originals as needed]

**Jane Smith Hill
2003**

AN ANNOTATED DIGEST OF WILL BOOK A, GUILFORD COUNTY, NORTH CAROLINA

GUILFORD COUNTY UNRECORDED WILLS

For reasons not known, the following wills, which fit into the time frame of Will Book A, were not recorded by the Clerk/s. However, the originals are now in the North Carolina State Archives for researchers to use.

The following digest has been made from the microfilmed wills, except for instances in which the film was unreadable.

THE UNRECORDED WILLS

ZEBULON CAUSEY   13 MARCH 1809   MAY COURT 1809
"very weak in body...
Wife: Diana Causey peacable possession of the House I now live in & plentiful maintainance of the plantation I now live on with all household furniture, 1 sorrell horse called brit, 1 cow & calf, 1 sow & pigs, 1 ewe during her widowhood.
Son: Zebulon Causey my plantation at death or marriage of his mother.
Sons: John Causey Solomon Causey & Dau: Peggy Tucker the remainder part of the stock to be divided equally among them and the household furniture after the death or marriage of their mother.
Granddaughter: Pegga Causey 10 pounds of good goose feathers.
Seal: Zebulon (his x mark) Causey
Exr: son Zebulon Causey
Wits: Hugh Sherwood William (his x mark) Fitzgerald

PETER COBLE 8 DEC. 1815   MAY COURT 1816
My will is that my Negro man named Augustine, my smiths tools, my still, my rifle gun, and my watch, and whatsoever other things my beloved wife Elizabeth Coble thinks she can conveniently spare to be sold after my decease at publick sale the money arising therefrom I give and bequeath to:
Dau: Mary Coble $100, & her bed & bedstead that she claims.
Son: Peter Coble $100, 1 colt got by the horse called the Prospect.
Two youngest Daus: Sally Coble and Nelly Coble to heir each the value of $100, in cash or property to make them equal with those of my children that has been married and left me.
Wife: Elizabeth the balance of my movable property and money and all my land and all my Debts I leave in the hands of my beloved wife for her to make use of for herself and for the use of my family untill her Death or marriage.
All the property both real and personal be sold at publick sale the money arising therefrom with all the money in hand and Debts on hand to be equally divided amongst all my children & that my son David's children Sally and David shall heir his share equally the same as he would if he was living.
If any of my children should die before my wife it is my will that their children should have their part the same as if they had a lived.

AN ANNOTATED DIGEST OF WILL BOOK A, GUILFORD COUNTY, NORTH CAROLINA

At the Death or marriage of my beloved wife Elizabeth that my Children shall appoint whosoever they think proper to administer to this my last will and testament.
Seal: Peter Coble
Exrs. None appointed
Wits: Richard Proctor (Jurat) Andrew (his A s) mark Shatterly
Note: Andrew Shatterly and John Black qualified as Administrators with the Will annexed.

ROBERT COLE*   5 MARCH 1813   MAY COURT 1816

I give and bequeath to Clarisey McCain, formerly Clarisey Beavil, now wife of Wm. McCain, 1 Negro boy named onden being six or seven years of age to belong to her and her heirs for ever, 1 cow & calf, one loom; I also allow her keep in her own right 1 mare, 1 cow & calf & 2 feather bed and other property that I have given her.
Wife: Dicy Coal keep her choice of my 2 stills. And all the still tubes. 2 head of horse creatures, her choice, her choice of 5 head of cattle, & my yoke of oxen, 1/2 of the monies. Wife to have at her disposal the whole estate as long as she remains my widow, and at her death to son James.
Son: James Coal the 2 stills and tubes at death of wife Dicy & 1/2 of the monys.
Seal: Robert (his x mark) Cole
Exrs: wife Dicy   son James
Wits: Hance McCain (Jurat) Wm. Bevil   James Tomlinson
"revokes"
* The name is spelled Coal in the body of the will]

MARGARET COOK   NUNCUPATIVE WILL   JANUARY COURT 1817

Rebecca Davey: 1 pot & tea Kittle, 6 pewter plates, 1 pewter dish, 2 tin cups, 1 coffee pot, 1 cotton sheet.
David Stack: 1 large pot & Dutch oven.
Isaac Anderson: her bed.
Richard Ozment as certified to James, J.P.

JAMES COOTS   27 July 1816   May Court 1820

Wife: Mary Coots the hole [sic] use of the plantation where I live, & all the household furniture & 1 hors named Dick & 1 Neger gerl named Heger [Hagar ?]
Grandson: John Spens 1 Negro boy named Jo.
Eldest Dau: Jiny Dilling 1 Negro girl named Elsy.
Third Dau: Levine Eyedolot [also seen as Aydelot] $50 to be paid 6 months after my decease.
Granddau: Minervy Eydlot my boy named Pery of Dow'alow [do allow?] to live with my wife during her life and then become the property of Minervy.
5 Grandchildren: John Spens, Elves Spens, William Spens, Betsy Spens, and menervy Eydolot.
Seal: James Coots
Exrs: wife Mary
Wits: none

May Court 1820 A Jury being impallelled & Sworm say they find the written Instrument of writing to be the last Will & Testament of James Coots, dec'd. Whereupon it was admitted to probate. Test: JnoHanner, CCC

RACHEL CUMMINS   8 NOV. 1815   FEB. COURT 1816
Sister: Mary Ann Cummins the East end of my land beginning for west of an old road leading from Shedrach Loftins to Samuel Cummons as a South line will take in all the Improved land & likewise my part of the hogs & sheep, 1 cow & calf, all my household furniture, except my bed and furniture.
Niece: Mary Ann McKnight my other cow.
Niece: Rachel McCaley my bed & furniture.
Nephews: John & James McCaley my remaining land.
Brother-in-Law: William McKnight my Negro boy named Austin.
Seal: Rachel (her   mark) Cummins
Exrs: trusty friends Elisha Wharton, Esqr. William Denton, Esqr.
Wits: James Denny (Jurat)
"revokes"

ROBERT DONNELL   22 SEPT. 1806   MAY COURT 1816
Wife: Elizabeth Donnell 1 horse & sadle, 1 C--- bed & furniture, her living off the Land during widowhood; all house-hold furniture not mentioned in this my last will and testament which I alow to be equally divided amongst the Lagetees at my wifes death.
Son: Edmond Donnell the tract of land on which I now live as well as a part of the tract of land on which Elihu my son-in-law now lives on, Beginning at a pesimmon [persimmon tree] on the North side of a branch known by the name of Brusshy Branch on Andrew Donnells line running up the sd branch ontill it strikes the direct road Betwixt -- thence West till Leckeys Line thence North to the beginning corner a white oak thence East to the above mentioned pissimon, together with my smith tools & farming utensils, Waggon and Geer with all my horses Cows Sheep and hogs not mentioned to other Legatees & bed and furniture.
Dau: Margaret Donnell 1 horse satle bridle, 2 cows 2 sheep 6 puter plates a bed and furnatirue and one Case of Drawers at my wife's death two puter dishes 5 cups half douzen of knives and forks and two pots.
Dau: Mary Jean $5.
Son: Thomas Donnell $5.
Seal: Robert Donnell
Exrs: wife Elizabeth son Edmond
Wits: Leathom [Latham] Donnell (Jurat) Thomas Donnell
"revokes"

HUGH FORBUS   4 APRIL 1816   MAY COURT 1816
Wife: Elizabeth Forbus all the tract of Land on which I now live, containing 194 acres together with all right and previledge free and clear from all incumbrances for her to occupy and injoy during her natural life.
4 Youngest Sons: Eli, David, Abner Robert Forbus all the Land on which I now live and the plantation joining it Which I bought of Hendrix to be equally Devided among them, Eli & David to have their portion in the Hendrix place and Abner and Robert to have the Ballence to them their heirs and assigns for Ever.

AN ANNOTATED DIGEST OF WILL BOOK A, GUILFORD COUNTY, NORTH CAROLINA

Son: John Forbus a tract of land lying on the waters of the Big Allemance which I bought of Porter containing 150 acres to him his heirs or assigns for Ever provided that he shall pay to my three Daughter: Mary Willy, Nancy and Ann Forbus the sum of $15 to each of them.
Son: Ralph Forbus a tract of land lying on the waters of the Bufelow containing 120 acres to him, his heirs and assigns.
Three Daus: Mary Willy, Nancy and Ann Forbus one tract of land lying on the waters of the Bufelow near Wilsons Mill to be Devided among them so as to give to each an equal share to them there heirs or assigns for Ever.
My Still I will to be Sold and the price thereof be applied to the payment of my Debts.
Wife: Elizabeth my Smith tools for her and the Children at home to make use of and injoy also one Clock also 5 feather beds and ferneture, also one mare named Nell for her leisure also 5 horse beasts to her for the use of the Plantation and by her to be given to the Children at home and all the shepe to be apropreated in the same way also all my farming tools and the Ballence of the house Hoale [hold] furneture that is not before mentioned for her and the use of the family apart of which she is to give to the Children at her descretion.
Son: John Forbus 1 mare named Juel to him his heirs or assigns forever.
After death of wife Elizabdth that all my Estate then remaining shall be sold and equely devided among all my Children giveing to Each an Equal share.
Seal: Hugh Forbus
Exrs: trusty friends Andrew McGee   John Coe
Wits: Solomon Linthicum   (Jurat)   Caty Gilbreath
"revokes"

JOHN HAMILTON   14 OCTOBER 1818   NOV. COURT 1819
I give and bequeath to my 4 grand Children three sons and one Daughter, children of my Daughter Mary McNairy Deceast and of James McNairy (namely) John H. McNairy, Boyd McNairy, James McNairy, & Amanda McNairy $250 each to be paid them when they arrive at the age of 21 years or marriage, with intrust thereon from 2 years after the probate of this my last will and if either of them should die before they come to maturity or marriage that the survivors equally devide the money.
2 Granddaughters: Harriet H. Davis and Betsey Ann Davis, Daughters of my Daughter Sarah Davis my Boffett [buffet] with all its usual contents.
Grandson: Hamilton Davis my riding horse saddle bridle, [the will was torn at this place, the word sadle is repeated, and the remaining words written on the tear may be bed and furniture. JSH]
Grandson: Nathaniel Davis all my printed Books, and the young mare generaly called his.
Grandson: John H. Davis my Sword with all my milliterry [orders?].
Wearing apparrel be equally divdided between the Sons of my 2 Daughters Anne McNairy and Sarah Davis.
GreatGrandson: John H. Dickson, son of Joseph Dickson, $50.
GreatGranddaughter: Betsey H. Dickson daughter of David Dickson $50 to be paid to Robert McNairy as their guardian for their use and be paid to them at mature age & if either of them should die in their minority then their part to return to my estate.
All residue of my Estate of what Ever kind or nature soever to be sold Except my bank Stock and with the rest of my estate be Equally divided

between my two Daughters Namely Ann McNairy and Sarah Davis during their natural life without intrust, provided they secure the principle sum so as not to be diminished, by giving Bond and sufficient Security to the Coart, and on failing to doe to receive only the annual interest and in either case that part allotted to Each of them to be Equally divided between the Heirs of their own Body.
Seal: John Hamilton
Exrs: worthy friends Hance McCain Senr. William Ryan, Esqr.
Wits: Robt. Lindsay Wm. McCain (Jurat) Robert Burney (Jurat)

JOHN HARDEMAN 29 Aug. 1774 no probate date
Son: Thomas a negro woman & [marked through and not completed]
Wife: Dority estate both real and personal...
Children: Esther, Elizabeth, Judith, Dority, Jane, John, Eddy, Susannah, estate to be equally divided after the decease or marriage of wife; Ester's to be for her lifetime and then heirs... [sic]
Seal:
Exrs: wife Dority Hardeman Peter Perkins
Wits: Robert Crockett Salley Crockett Elizabeth Bostick

HENRY MACY 2 AUGUST 1812 MAY COURT 1816
"Whereas I,..."
Wife: Elizabeth Macy my 2 East Rooms with the Chamber above the Long Room of the House where I now live with all my houshold furneture with a good mentanance of my Land Encluding the yearly payment which is cuming to my wife Elizabeth Macy from her Son Aaron Coffin to be provided by my two Sons Henry Macy & Thomas Macy, also the use of one cow to be at her disposal for and during the time she remains the widdo of my Body.
2 Sons: Henry Macy & Thomas Macy all my tract of lalnd whereon I now live to be equally Devided between them in Quantity and Quality, provided thay Supply my Wife with a good mantainance as before Directed, to them and there Heirs for Ever.
4 Daus: Sarah Anthony, Love Davis, Deberah Swain & Mary Jenkins and
Grand Son: Henry Swain, son of my Daugher Susana Swain Deceased, each of them above five Sixths parts of my household furniture and my Deceased
Dau: Phebe Leonards heirs the other Sixth at my wifes death or marriage to be Equally Devided between them.
Sons: Henry Macy & Thomas Macy 2/3 of the remainder part of my Esate to be Equally devided between them and my
Son: Joseph Macy, Decest Children the other part to be equally devided between them. [not named]
My will also is that my Cclok [sic] remain with my wife Elizabeth Macy while she remains my widdo and at her deces or marey it to be Equally belonging to my two sons Henry and Thomas Macy.
Seal: Henry Macy
Exrs: sons Henry Macy son Thomas Macy
Upon reflection on the above will my Desire is that after the Deces or mary of my Widdo my Case of Drawers Shal go to my Granddaugher Sary Macy Daughter of Henry Macy
Wits: Jonathan Parker (Jurat) Henry Davis

AN ANNOTATED DIGEST OF WILL BOOK A, GUILFORD COUNTY, NORTH CAROLINA

ARCHIBALD McMICHEAL   23 Sept. 1818   Nov. Court 1818
Wife: Charitee all my property both real & personal during her life to be disposed of at her death as she may think proper.
Seal: [none found]
Exrs: wife Charotee McMicheal
Wits: Edward Lloyd   James McNairy

JOSIAH TROTTER   25 Feb 1792   May Court 1792
Wife: Jane 300 acres plantation, household goods, stock, negro women Nancy Beck & girl Nancy Alse, during her widowhood
5 Daus: Nancy, Rachel, Jane, Betsy & Mary household goods, cows, sheep & hogs at wife's decease or marriage.
Dau: Betsy negro woman Beck at wife's decease, by paying one fifth of her appraisal to her sisters.
Dau: Hannah Crannor negro Nancy Alce at decease of wife.
Youngest sons: Joseph, Edward, & Oldom plantation   100 acres each
Son: Epharim [sic] 150 acres where he lives on waters of S. Buffalo
Son: Benjamin 150 acres on waters of S. Buffalow I bought from Benjamin Thompson.
Son: George 100 acres on the Rocky Branch adj. my line, Frances [sic] Cummins & the New Garden Road.
Seal:
Exrs: son Benjamin Trotter
Wits: Benja. Thompson   John Hignutt

ISAIAH WEATHERLY   5 Sept. 1817 [?]   Aug. Court 1818
[this will is faded and illegible in parts]
Daus: Rebecca ------- & Peggy ----- each five shillings
Son: Isaiah the tract of land he now lives on. If he dies without heirs, land to be divided between sons Abner & William.
Dau: Polly five shillings.
Dau: Lena Weatherly   [?]
Dau: Betsy Weatherly $4.00
Dau: Rachel Lovett 5 shillings.
Son: Isaac the two tracts of land he now has.
Son: Henry tract of land I purchased from Vincent Russum, also negro boy Eli.
Son: Abner tract purchased of Dennis ------, $200, bed & furniture.
Son: William all remaining part of lands & tenements, 2 beds & furniture, $50 & half my smith tools.
Dau: Any Weatherly $60 in cash.
Wife Nancy: dower or until William becomes of age, negro man Bob, also feather bed & furniture, 2 milch cows, team of horses & farming tools.
Children: Isaiah, Henry, Abner, William, Betsy Weatherly, Lena Weatherly, Rachel Lovett & Ana Weatherly residue of estate.
Seal:
Exrs: sons Isaac & Henry Weatherly
Wits: William C. Chapman   Thomas Ozment   William Maben

AN ANNOTATED DIGEST OF WILL BOOK A, GUILFORD COUNTY, NORTH CAROLINA

ROBERT WILSON　　13 May 1821　　**Aug. Court 1821**
Wife: Sarah all the stock, household furniture, farming tools during her life to do with as she pleases after debts are paid.
2 Children: David Wilson & Nancy Wilson 2 notes; one $35 & the other $5 on Samuel Guyer in Washington County, Indiana in the hands of Nicholas Hubbard.
Seal:
Exrs: wife Sarah Wilson　Nathan Johnson
Wits: John Davis　James Henderson

[Copies of the above original wills are housed in the North Carolina State Archives, Raleigh, North Carolina]

Jane Smith Hill

SLAVES NAMED IN THE WILLS

"A"

Aaron, 121
ABB. 170
Abner, 149
Abogal, 169, 170
Abraham, 168
Adam, 133
Aggay, 157
Agnis, 83
Ails, 32, 110 [Alice?]
Alex, 63
Alice, 32
Allie, 15
Amey, 27
Amy, 82
Andra, 145
Anne, 110
Anthony, 111
Augustine, 175
Auston, 26

"B"

Benn, 10
Beck, 53, 180
Becky, 147
Beech, 171
Bett, 136
Betty, 19
Bill, 28, 60
Billey, 113
Billy, 147
Bob, 59, 92, 109, 126, 135, 180
Bobb, 10

"C"

Buck, 114
Care mine, 26
Cate, 63, 82, 122
Ceasar, 82
Chance, 126
Charles, 15, 63, 85, 113
Charlot, 149
Charity, 118
China, 120
Cisley, 63
Cleria, 15
Cricey, 130

Creese, 92
Cug, 2

"D"

Daniel, 86, 172
Darcus, 59, 60
David, 68, 136
Dick, 1, 28, 82, 92, 107, 108, 122 145, 158, 170, 172
Dina, 35
Dinah, 53, 82, 92, 110, 162
Dorcas, 63
Draper, 56

"E"

Eal, 163
Eals, 88
Easter, 56, 118, 171
Edd, 150
Elcy, 145
Eli, 180
Elsy, 176
Emmy, 122

"F"

Fame, 63
Fan, 163
Fanny, 63
Fern, 163
Fil, 111
Filllis, 63, 91
Fob, 111
Franck, 22
Frank, 28

"G"

George, 147
George Ellick, 114
Gilbert, 121
Gilet, 88
Gillet, 88
Grace, 56, 58

"H"

Hagar, 82, 176
Hagor, 135
Hanna, 68, 147

Hannah, 2, 60, 109, 114, 169, 172
Hanay, 169
Hanney, 10
Hary, 60
Harry, 76, 82, 136
Heber, 110
Heger, 176
Henry, 118
Howard, 150

"I"

Isaac, 18, 26, 86, 109, 122, 136, 170
Isaiah, 135
Isham, 63
Ishmael, 59
Ishmel, 27

"J"

Jack, 1
Jacob, 1, 76, 83, 92, 110, 136
Jam, 41
James, 121
Jams, 114
Jane [?] 150
Jean, 147
Jeffrey, 11, 130
Jenny, 1, 22, 63, 82, 122
Jeorge, 145
Jerepta, 63
Jerry, 110
Jim, 109, 150
Jime, 172
Jin, 170
Jo, 176
Joe, 10
Joe Phib Tappley Silvey, [sic] 114
John, 145
Jonas, 41
Josh, 112
Juba, 63
Jude, 1, 82, 136, 170
Judith, 110
Judy, 63

"L"

Lane, [?] 150
Lea, 60

Leah, 53
Lett, 136
Leven, 129
Lier, 2
Lile, 150
Linch, 89
Lot, 172
Luce, 56
Lucy, 58, 63, 114
Luse, 41, 68
Lydia, 22

"M"

Mall, 118
Marma, 136
Martha, 120
Martin, 3
Mary, 76, 110, 122
Mill, 56
Milley, 121
Mol, 41
Moll, 63
Moses, 122

"N"

Nan, 82, 150
Nance, 56, 145
Nancey, 22
Nancy, 48, 110, 180
Nancy Alse, 180
Nat, 110
Nathan, 63, 118
Ned, 41, 76, 82, 170
Nell, 10, 21, 135
Nelley, 28
Nice, 53, 172
Noah, 169

"O"

Obed, 147
Onden, 176

"P"

Pat, 56
Patce, 56
Patience, 109, 137
Pats, 53
Patt, 114
Peg, 172
Pegg, 82
Penny, 92

Pery, 176
Peter, 1, 60, 92, 106, 110, 122, 150
Peter Amey, Ellis, [sic] 114
Pheby, 63
Phib, 126
Phill, 44
Phillis, 1
Poll, 52
Pomp, 61
Pompey, 5, 56, 150

"R"

Rath, 169
Rhoda, 128
Richard, 145
Rose, 60, 122, 147
Ross, 63
Rous, 88

"S"

Sal, 88
Sali, 56
Sall, 86, 106, 136, 145, 169, 171
Sally, 26, 122
Sam, 3, 10, 76, 82, 92, 172
Sampson, 133
Samson, 135
Sarah, 2, 158
Sciaro, 136
Selah, 92
Senah, 86
Sesar, 63
Seventy, 122
Silve, 110
Silvess, 136
Sisley, 40
Smith, 59, 60
Sophia, 121
Steevan, 169
Suck, 158
Sue, 82, 114
Suikey, 120
Sukey, 63
Susee, 169

"T"

Tamor, 5
Tena, 59

Teney, 121
Thankful, 26
Tom, 10, 35, 59, 60, 63, 106, 135, 145, 163
Tony, 151
Toney Kitt, 114

"V"

Venis, 5
Violet, 44, 106

"W"

Walker, 3
Will, 82, 106, 110, 147

"Z"

Zilph, 110

INDEX

Adams, William 86
Adear, Charles 2
Adear, Elsabeth 2
Adear, Jane 2
Adear, John 2
Adear, Margaret 2
Adear, Mary 2
Adear, Sarah 2
Adear, William 2
Ades, John 14
Agnew, Robt. 82
Aken, John 4
Aken, Robert 4
Albertson, Phenias 75
Albright, Christina 22
Albright, Phillip 22
Alcorn, John 42, 43
Aldridge, Nathen 150
Alexander, Agnes 84
Alexander, Ann 71
Alexander, Martha 3
Allen, Ann 4
Allen, Benjamin 4
Allen, Daniel 3, 4
Allen, Jemima 4
Allen, John 4
Allen, John, Jr. 3
Allen, John Sr. 3
Allen, Joseph 4
Allen, Keziah 4
Allen, Mary 4
Allen, Sarah 3, 4
Allison, Elisabeth 3
Allison, Isiah 3
Allison, Jain 3
Allison, James 3
Allison, John 3
Allison, Martha 3
Allison, Mary 3
Allison, Samuel 3, 11
Alton, James 104
Anderson, Archibald 57
Anderson, Isaac 6, 176
Anderson, James 5, 6
Anderson, Jean 95
Anderson, Jno. 32, 49
Anderson, John 6
Anderson, Robert 42
Anderson, Sarah 5, 6, 57
Anderson, William 6
Andrews, Benet 4
Andrews, Jeremiah 4
Andrews, Mary 4
Anthony, Charlotta 2
Anthony, James 1, 2
Anthony, Jonathan 1
Anthony, Judah 2
Anthony, Lyda 2
Anthony, Mary 1
Anthony, Merab 2

Anthony, Obed 1, 2
Anthony, Phebe 2, 99
Anthony, Ruth 2
Anthony, Sarah 179
Anthony, William 32
Archer, Catherine 1
Archer, David 1
Archer, James 1
Archer, John 1
Archer, Sarah 1
Archer, Thomas 1, 78
Archibald, Robert 82
Armfield, Ann 2
Armfield, David 5
Armfield, Elizabeth 2
Armfield, Isaac 2, 83
Armfield, Jacob 2
Armfield, John 2, 43, 83
Armfield, Jonathan 2
Armfield, Joseph 2, 5
Armfield, Lidia 5
Armfield, Mary 43
Armfield, Nathan 2, 5, 53, 83
Armfield, Sarah 2
Armfield, Solomon 2, 5
Armfield, William 2, 53, 83
Armfield, William, Sr. 5
Armfield, Wm. 2nd 78
Armfield, Wm. 5, 78, 109, 133
Armfield, Wm. Esquire 157
Armfield, Wm. Senior 78
Arnett, Isbel 51
Ashley, Mary 114
Avery, Waightstill, Esquire 82
Aydelet, Mary 31
Aydelot, Levine 176
Aydelott, Benjamin 5
Aydelott, Leven 5
Aydelott, Lucy 5
Aydelott, Parker 5
Aydelott, Sarah 5
Aydelott, Shadrach 5
Aydelotte, Obed 148, 173
Aydelotte, Polly 145
Aydelotte, Tabithy 5
Ayers, Gallant 99

Ba---, Libni 94
Bagge, C. F. 123
Bailey, Elizabeth 95
Baldwin, Daniel 13, 15, 24, 105
Baldwin, Elisabeth 72

Baldwin, Elizabeth 15
Baldwin, Jane 15
Baldwin, Jesse 15
Baldwin, John 15
Baldwin, Sarah 15
Baldwin, Uriah 13
Baldwin, William 15
Ballenger, Sophia 155
Ballinger, Hannah 155
Ballinger, Nansey 111
Banner, Mrs. Polly 150
Barham, Benjamin 33
Barham, Charles 33
Barham, James 69
Barham, Nathan 33
Bark, ----- 72
Barnard, Benjamin 7
Barnard, Elisha 7
Barnard, Elizabeth 20
Barnard, Eunice 7
Barnard, Frederick 7
Barnard, Libni 7
Barnard, Lusinda 7
Barnard, Lyda 7
Barnard, Mary 7
Barnard, Matilda 7
Barnard, Shubal 7
Barnard, Timothy 7
Barnes, Elisabeth 14
Barnes, Jesse 14, 15
Barnes, John 14
Barnes, Sophia 18
Barnet, Margaret 8
Barnett, Anne 8
Barnett, Elizabeth 8
Barnett, Jas. 8
Barnett, Jean 15
Barnett, John 8, 9
Barnett, Joseph 9
Barnett, Joseph D. 85
Barnett, William 9
Barnhill, Robert 9
Barnhill, Sarah 9
Barnhill, William 9
Barr, David 137
Barrom, James 141
Bartley, Rachel 73
Bass, Ann 39
Bass, James 143
Battlesey, Mr. 64
Bayr, Agnes, 106
Bayr, James 106
Beach, Sarah 18
Beadey, William 119
Beales, Eleazer 7, 8
Beals, Ann 8
Beals, Caleb 7, 8
Beals, Jesse 7, 8
Beals, John, 7, 8, 40, 85
Beals, John Jr. 66
Beals, Susanna 85
Beals, Susannah 7, 8

Beals, William 7, 8
Beard, David 9
Beard, Lydia 10
Beard, Margarett 84
Beard, Paul 79
Beard, Rachel 9
Beard, Reuben 85
Beard, William 9, 10, 71
Beason, Isaac 77, 101
Beason, Priscilla 151, 152
Beathel, Capt. William 118
Beavil, Clarisey 176
Beavill, John 116
Beavill, William 116
Beeson, Benjamin 14, 37, 55, 114
Beeson, Charity 14
Beason, Edward 14
Beeson, Isaac 14, 65
Beeson Isaac Juner 114
Beeson, John 55
Beeson, Martha 14
Beeson, Mary 14, 96
Beeson, Nathaniel 14
Beeson, Phebe 14
Beeson, Richard 14, 114
Beeson, Samuel 14, 54
Beeson, William 14
Bell, Betsy 26
Bell, Nancy 18
Bell, Robert 107, 116
Bell, Robt. 116
Benbo, Benjamin 132
Benbo, Charles 151
Benbo, David 132
Benbo, Lydia 132
Benbo, Mary 152
Benbo, Thos. 72
Bennett, Elisha 35
Bennett, Ruth 76
Benson, John 10
Benson, John Jr. 10
Bevil, Wm. 176
Bevill, Hezekiah 114
Billing, James 57
Billingsley, Bazel 12
Billingsley, Betsy 57
Billingsley, Clarenca 12
Billingsley, Elizabeth 12, 54
Billingsley, Henry 57
Billingsley, James 12, 57, 125
Billingsley, John J. 12
Billingsley, Martha 12
Billingsley, Samuel 12
Billingsley, Walter 1

Billingsley, William 12, 57
Bingerman, Ester 158
Bingerman, Thomas 158
Bishop, Marey 113
Black, John 176
Black, Thomas 20, 57
Blair, Agnes 12
Blair, Andrew 6
Blair, Eleanor 45
Blair, Hugh 6
Blair, James 12
Blair, Jean 6, 124
Blair, John 6, 12
Blair, Jonathan 6
Blair, Martha 6
Blair, Mary 12, 13, 106
Blair, Thomas 6, 17, 45, 108
Blair, Thos. 6
Blaise, Margaret 9
Blayr, Mary 106
Blear, John 12
Blear, Martha 12
Bleckley, Robert 43
Blizard, Purnel 68
Boak, Robert 11
Boon, Ann 11
Boon, Catherine 11
Boon, Daniel 11
Boon, Jacob 11
Boon, John 11, 173
Boon, John Senior 173
Boon, Martin 11
Borton, Richard 28
Borton, Richard, Sr. 10
Bostick, Elizsbeth 179
Bouldin, Margate 93
Bourland, William 54
Bourton, Dorcas 10
Bourton, Richard, 10, 11
Bourton, William 10, 11
Bowen, Abner 21
Bowman, Archalus 152
Bowman, Edmond 39
Bowman, Richard 40
Boyd, Andrew 11
Boyd, Ann 110
Boyd, Catherine 11
Boyd, Catrine 11
Bradley, Sarah 141
Braley, Joseph 80
Brannock, Henry 51
Brannock, William 51
Brasheares, Jesse 159
Brashears, Asa 159
Brashers, Asa Jr. 146
Brasher, U. D. 159
Brassel, Jacob, 117

Brattain, Robert 85
Brazell, Jacob 117
Breden, Alexander 6, 8
Breden, Charles 8
Breden, Margaret 8
Breden, Mary 7
Breden, Robert, 7, 8, 135
Breden, William 6
Bredon, Alexander 36
Breed, Charles 165
Bridges, William 118
Briggance, Davis 74
Bright, James 103
Bright, Margret 103
Brittain, Anne 13
Brittain, Cath 13
Brittain, Henery 13
Brittain, Joseph 13, 74
Brittain, Rebekah 13
Brittain, Ruth 13
Brittain, William 13
Brittain, Wm. 74
Britton, Jane 3
Britton, William 22
Brogden, Kesia 15
Brogden, Patience 15
Brogdon, Anne 15
Brogdon, James 15
Brooks, David 162
Browder, Isham 117
Brown, Adam 22
Brown, Agnes 88
Brown, Catharine 22
Brown, Elias 13
Brown, George 13
Brown, George L. 55, 71
Brown, James 13
Brown, John 10, 13, 76
Brown, Joseph 2, 117
Brown, Margaret 105
Brown, Mary 5, 8, 55
Brown, Matt'w. 41
Brown, Matthew 13, 14, 45
Brown, Nancy 13
Brown, Nathaniel 10
Brown, Rebekah 13
Brown, Robert 13
Brown, Thomas 10, 40, 41, 86, 88
Brown, William 10, 13, 14, 45, 55, 166
Brown, Williamson 107
Brown, Wm. 14, 15
Bruce, Charles 17, 18, 68, 158
Bruce, George 44
Buchanan, Frances 95
Buckner, Aylett 55
Buckner, Thomas 55

Bullar, Anna 114
Bullard, William 55
Bullock, Ann dogged 15, 16
Bullock, David 15
Bullock, Edmund 13
Bullock, Edward 15, 31, 151, 152
Bullock, George 15
Bullock, James 15
Bullock, John 15
Bullock, Len 15
Bullock, William 15
Bullock, Winneford 15
Bunch, William 43, 152
Burke, Michael 48
Burney, Adam Lackey 91
Burney, Catherine 11, 12
Burney, Elizabeth 11, 18
Burney, John 11, 91
Burney, Mary 91, 92
Burney, Rebekah 11
Burney, Robert 11, 12, 179
Burney, Samuel 92
Burney, William 11, 80, 91
Burrow, Ephraim 22
Burrow, Eve 22
Byford, Tabbetha 133
Byford, Tabitha 133
Byford, William 133
Byfords, Quillar 89
Byfords, William 89

Caffee, John 18, 93
Caffee, Lucy 18
Caffee, Margaret 18
Caffee, Michael, 18, 93
Caldwell, ---- 103
Caldwell, Alex'r. 95
Caldwell, Alexander 36, 104
Caldwell, David, Rev. 6, 53, 54, 105
Caldwell, James 10, 142
Calhoon, Ann 21
Calhoon, Easter 33
Calhoon, Eleanor 20, 21
Calhoon, Elizabeth 21
Calhoon, James 20, 21, 32, 69
Calhoon, Jean 32
Calhoon, Jeney 33
Calhoon, Jinnet 20
Calhoon, John 33
Calhoon, John j. 20

Calhoon, John Jonstone 20, 21
Calhoon, Mary 21
Calhoon, Robert 21, 33, 69
Calhoon, Samuel 20, 21, 33
Calhoon, Sarah 21
Calloway, Jonathan 41
Callaway, Obediah 41
Campbell, Archibald 28
Campbell, James 17, 28
Campbell, Jn. 140
Campbell, Jno. 124
Campbell, Moses 13, 17
Campbell, Polley 28
Campbell, Rebecca 17
Campbell, William 17
Camplin, Annetta 27
Camplin, Henry 27
Camplin, Hooper 27
Camplin, James 27
Camplin, Rebekah 27
Camplin, Sally 27
Canada, John 164
Canaday, Nathan 74
Cannaday, Henery 100
Carney, Mary 166
Carr, Betsy 105
Carrington, Col. George 64
Carrol, Elizabeth 140
Carson, Agnes 105
Carter, Giles 64
Carter, John 7
Carter, Sarah 7
Carter, Walker 34
Casey, Larkin More 103
Causey, Aaron 53
Causey, Charles 160
Causey, Diana 175
Causey, John 175
Causey, Nancy 31, 160
Causey, Nehemiah 50, 131
Causey, Pegga 175
Causey, Zebulon 175
Cessency, Sally 73
Cessency, Stephen 66
Chabers, John 129
Chadwick, Joshua 54
Chambers, Elenor 17
Chambers, Elizabeth 32
Chambers, John 32
Chambers, Thomas 17
Chamness, Joseph 65
Chance, Purnell 14
Chapman, William C. 180
Charles, Anna 21
Charles, Elijah 21
Charles, Gean 19
Charles, Isaac 21

Charles, Leah 21
Charles, Leven C. 69
Charles, Mary 21
Charles, Michael 11
Charles, Ruben 21
Charles, Sarah 21
Charles, Solomon 21
Charles, William 21
Chilcutt, James 93
Chilcutt, Sarah 131
Chipman, John 30
Chipman, Margaret 30
Chipman, Paris 174
Chipman, Peres 30
Christman, Abraham, 17
Christman, Anna Maria 17
Christman, Balthaser 17
Christman, Barbara 17
Christman, Catherina 17
Christman, Daniel 17
Christman, David 17
Christman, Elisabeth 17
Christman, Henrich 17
Christman, Jacob 17, 71
Christman, John 17, 27
Christman, John George 17
Christman, Joseph 17
Christopher, Garett 34
Christopher, Simon 34
Cirkman, Neley 124
[see also Kirkman]
Clap, Mary 26, 58
Clap, Tobias 28, 59
Clap, Tobies 58
Clapp, Adam 21
Clapp, Barbary 22, 28
Clapp, Christina 27
Clapp, Daniel 27
Clapp, Elizabeth 28
Clapp, George 28
Clapp, Isaac 28
Clapp, Jacob 90, 144
Clapp, John 21, 81
Clapp, John Phillip 21, 22
Clapp, Luddowick 21, 22
Clapp, Magdalena 28
Clapp, Margeret 28
Clapp, Mary 81
Clapp, Philip 27
Clapp, Tobias 22. 28
Clapp, Tobias, Sen'r. 27
Clapp, Valentine 21, 27
Clark, Ann 26

Clark, Baptis 123
Clark, Charles 24
Clark, John 24
Clark, John Sen'r. 27
Clark, Margaret 85
Clark, Mary 24, 159
Clark, Nathaniel 26
Clark, Rebecca 4
Clark, Ruth 116
Clark, William 4
Clark, Wm. 4
Clarke, Ann 21
Clarke, Catherine 21
Clarke, Hance 21
Clarke, Hans 21
Clarke, Jean 21
Clarke, Mary 21
Clayton, Bennoni 91
Clerk, Jacob 81
Cleyton, Bennoni 91
Clifton, Margaret 55
Clos, Thomas 104
Close, Joseph 110
Close, Thomas 104
Closs, Jos. 110
Closse, Joseph 110
Cluts, John 68
Coal, Dicy 176
Coal, James 176
Coaling, Robert 34
Cobb, Felty 35
Cobb, Henry 35
Cobb, Henry, Sener 35
Cobb, John 35
Cobb, Valentine 35
Cobble, George 26
Cobel, Anthoncy 138
Coble, Anne 26
Coble, Anthony 19
Coble, Catren 58
Coble, Caty 150
Coble, David 19, 26, 175
Coble, Eli 26
Coble, Elizabeth 175, 176
Coble, Eve 26
Coble, George 19, 151
Coble, Jacob 19, 22, 58, 63
Coble, Jacob, Sr. 81
Coble, John 19, 26, 150
Coble, Ludwick 19, 26
Coble, Mary 26, 35, 175
Coble, Nelly 175
Coble, Peter 175, 176
Coble, Sally 175
Coble, Sarah 26
Coble, Sophia 26
Cochrain, Martha 105

Cochran, Robert Sr. 105
Coe, Avery 31
Coe, Every 31
Coe, Hannah 73
Coe, Hulda 31
Coe, John 31, 115, 141, 166, 178
Coe, John Gamble 31
Coe, John Sen'r. 53, 73
Coe, Coe, Joseph 31
Coe, Sarah 31, 115
Coffee, Elizabeth 25
Coffee, John 25
Coffee, Joshua 25, 26
Coffin, Aaron 20, 179
Coffin, Abel 25, 33, 34
Coffin, Abigail 98
Coffin, Abijah 20, 30
Coffin, Achsa 23
Coffin, Adam 20
Coffin, Barn'a 153
Coffin, Barna 10
Coffin, Barnabas 20, 23, 25, 29, 30, 31, 33, 54, 72, 77, 148, 152, 153
Coffin, Barnabs 33, 34
Coffin, Barnabus, 15
Coffin, Benjamin 20
Coffin, Bethuel 7, 8, 20, 23, 30, 34, 96, 100, 122, 159, 172
Coffin, David 25
Coffin, Elihu 22, 23
Coffin, Elizabeth 20, 22, 98
Coffin, Esther 23
Coffin, Hannah 99, 159
Coffin, James 101
Coffin, Jethro 25
Coffin, Job 23
Coffin, John 25
Coffin, Joseph 33, 34
Coffin, Levi 20, 30, 99
Coffin, Libni 20, 30
Coffin, Lydia 25
Coffin, Mary 20, 24, 25
Coffin, Mathew 30, 75, 99
Coffin, Matthew 20, 21, 25, 30, 31, 101, 166
Coffin, Nathan 23
Coffin, Phebe 20, 33, 54
Coffin, Priscilla 20, 25, 30, 31, 33, 34
Coffin, Rachel 20

Coffin, Sallay 152
Coffin, Sam'l. 23
Coffin, Samuel, 20, 24, 25, 30, 153
Coffin, Stephen 33
Coffin, Thomas 25
Coffin, Vestal 23
Coffin, William 13, 20, 22, 23, 161, 162
Coffin, Wm. 37
Coffin, Zacharias 158
Coffins, 40
Cole, Robert 176
Coleman, John, Jun'r. 93
Colston, Hannery 104
Colwell, James 127
Comb, William, Jun'r. 133
Comer, Elizabeth 65
Comer, Joseph 65
Connly, Esther 159
Conrad, Sarah 133
Cook, Abraham, 24, 55, 169
Cook, Elizabeth 29
Cook, Isaac 7, 24, 29
Cook, Jacob 29
Cook, James 36
Cook, John 24, 29
Cook, John, Capt. 118
Cook, Joseph 28, 29
Cook, Margaret 176
Cook, Mary 28
Cook, Nathan 29
Cook, Ruth 24
Cook, Sarah 24
Cook, Thomas 28, 29
Cook, William 29
Cook, Zimri 29
Cooper, Ann 21
Cooper, David 21
Cooper, John 21, 22
Cooper, Thomas, 21
Cooper, William 21
Coots, Hannah 68
Coots, James 15, 176, 177
Coots, John 68
Coots, Mary 176
Copp, Barbara 35
Coop, Catranina 35
Copp, Dorely 35
Copp, Dorothea 35
Copp, Elanor 35
Copp, Elizabeth 35
Copp, Hana 35
Coop, Hany 35
Copp, Henry 35
Copp, Jacob 35
Copp, Magdalena 35
Copp, Margaretha 35
Copp, Margret 35

Core, John 160
Corsbee, W. 113
Corsbie, W. 26
Corsby, William 111
Cortner, Catarena 19
Cortner, Geo. 90, 139
Cortner, George, 19, 90, 115, 138, 144
Cortner, Peter 90
Cotner, David, Jr. 22
Couch, Samuel 32
Covey, Leven 28
Covey, Mary 32
Covey, Noble 42
Covey, Sarah 28
Cowan, Samuel 88
Cox, Abner 16
Cox, Daniel 16
Cox, Joshua 16
Cox, Martha 16, 82
Cox, Mary, 51
Cox, Naomy 65
Cox, Sarah 16
Cox, Solomon 16, 65
Cox, Thomas 16
Craft, Charlotte 19
Craft, Gean Charles 19
Craft, John Charles 19
Craft, Lydia 19
Craft, Marry 19
Craft, Nelle 19
Craft, Rebecka 19
Craft, Sarah 19
Craft, Thomas Charles 19
Crannor, Hannah 180
Cranor, Hannah 23
Cranor, Joseph 23, 29
Cranor, Joshua 29
Cranor, Moses 23
Cranor, Sarah 29
Cranor, Thomas 23, 29
Crawley, Frances 16
Crawley, John 16
Crawley, Thomas 16
Crisman, John 150
Criswell, James 29, 78
Criswell, Jean 29
Criswell, Mary 29
Criswell, William 29
Crockett, Robert 179
Crockett, Salley 179
Crouch, Thomas 57
Crowder, Elizabeth 18
Crowder, Fanny Wilson 18
Crowder, Isaac 18
Crowder, Jeremiah 18
Crowder, Marthy 18
Crowder, Pleasant 18
Cumming, Elizabeth 34
Cummings, Hugh 123
Cummings, John 108

Cummins, Ann 30
Cummins, Anna 30
Cummins, Charles 32
Cummins, Elija 30
Cummins, Elisabeth 32
Cummins, Frances 180
Cummins, Francis 29
Cummins, Frs. 30
Cummins, George, 31, 32
Cummins, James 32
Cummins, Jean 30
Cummins, Jeane 30
Cummins, John 32
Cummins, Joseph 31
Cummins, Martha 30, 32
Cummins, Mary Ann 177
Cummins, Mathew 32
Cummins, Rachel 177
Cummins, Sarah 31, 32
Cummins, Thomas 30, 31, 32, 34, 109
Cummons, Anny 26
Cummons, Any 26, 27
Cummons, Betsy 26
Cummons, Hugh 31, 32
Cumons, Jane 26
Cummons, John 27
Cummons, Margareth 26
Cummons, Mary 26
Cummons, Rachel 26, 27
Cummons, Robert 27
Cummons, Samuel, 27, 177
Cummons, Thankful 30
Cummons, Thomas 26, 27
Cummons, Thos. 30
Cumpton, Elisabeth 90
Cunerod, Sarah 133
Cunningham, Isabel 18
Cunningham, James 12, 18
Cunningham, Jeremiah 18, 47, 90
Cunningham, John 53, 56, 109, 116, 165, 171
Cunningham, Mathew 18
Cunningham, William 18
Curtis, Charles 18
Curtis, Claiborn 83
Curtis, Claiborne 31, 51
Curtis, Margery 18
Curtis, Peter 18
Curtis, Sarah 31
Cusick, Jedediah 121
Cusick, Jedidia 167

Dabney, John 66, 67
Daugherty, Betsy 42
Daugherty, Daniel 37, 38

Daugherty, Elizabeth 37
Daugherty, Hannah 37; 38
Daugherty, James 38
Daugherty, Jean 42
Daugherty, Jenny 51
Daugherty, John 37, 38, 42, 51
Daugherty, Polly 51
Daugherty, Robert 42
Daugherty, Rosey 128
Daugherty, Samuel 42, 51
Daugherty, William 37, 38, 42
Davey, Rebecca 176
Davis, Alice 141
Davis, Anna 167
Davis, Betsy Ann 178
Davis, Deborah 37
Davis, Elisabeth 37, 132
Davis, Hamilton 178
Davis, Harriet H. 178
Davis, Henry 127, 179
Davis, Hepzibah 37
Davis, J. 34
Davis, Jacob William 63
Davis, James 171
Davis, John 36, 36, 136, 181
Davis, John H. 178
Davis, Jos. 169
Davis, Joseph 61, 62
Davis, Love 179
Davis, Lydia 37
Davis, Nathaniel 178
Davis Peter 37
Davis, Sarah 136, 178, 179
Davis, Thomas 37
Davis, Tristram 37
Davis, 40
Dean, Charity 39
Dean, Elizabeth 39
Dean, Fanna 39
Dean, Frances 39
Dean, Fredrick 39, 40
Dean, Isaac 39
Dean, Jean 39
Dean, Mary 39
Dean, Nansa 39
Dean, Rebeckah 39
Dean, Sarah 39
Dean, Solomon 38
Dean, Thomas 39
Deatherage, Bird 36
Deatherage, Elizabeth 36
Deatherage, George 36
Deatherage, James 36

Deatherage, Mary 36
Deatherage, Philemon 36, 136, 137
Deatheage, Sarah 36
Deatherage, Schiles 36
Deatherage, Solomon 36, 151
Deer, Bradley 44, 45
Deer, Catherine 44
Deer, Charles 44, 45
Deer, Elisabeth 44
Deer, Reuben 44, 45
Delay, Burgess 4
Delay, Jean 159
Dell, Joseph 17
Dell, Mary 17
Denney, Alvin 46
Denney, George 12, 46
Denney, Hannah 24
Denney, James 44, 46
Denney, Peggy 46
Denney, Rebecca 46
Denney, Thomas 46
Denney, William 39, 46

Dennis, Daniel 41
Dennis, Edward 37
Dennis, John 37
Dennis, Leah 41
Dennis, Levinah 41
Dennis, Matthias 41
Dennis, Sarah 37
Dennis, Thomas 37
Dennis, William 41
Dennis, Wm. 41
Denny, Dorcas 69
Denny, Geo. 46
Denny, George 39
Denny, Hannah 39
Denny, James 35, 36, 39, 44, 95, 104, 109, 147, 177
Denny, James, Jr. 167
Denny, James, Sr. 167
Denny, Mary 35, 36
Denny, Thomas 44
Denny, Walter 126
Denny, William 35, 36, 39 46, 129
Denton, William, Esqr. 177
Deviney, James 84
Dewese, Enckial 93
Dewess, Ezchiel 99
Deyhill, Tos. 45
Diamond, John 42
Diamond, Mary 42
Diamond, Patrick 42
Diamond, Sarah 42
Diamond, Stuard 42
Diamond, William 42
Dick, Isabell 111

Dick, James 45, 111, 112
Dick, John 45
Dick, Obediah 45, 100
Dick, Polly 45
Dick, Rebecca 45
Dick, Samuel 45
Dick, Thomas 45, 77, 160
Dick, Thos. 160
Dick, William 45, 86, 118
Dickey, William 115, 138, 141
Dicks, Ann 172
Dicks, Elizabeth 40
Dicks, James 20, 40
Dicks, Joshua 7, 13, 68,
Dicks, Nathan 7, 64, 68
Dicks, Peter 40
Dicks, Ruth 78
Dicks, Seth 172
Dicks, William 40, 149
Dicks, Zacharias 40, 154
Dickson, Betsey H. 178
Dickson, David 178
Dickson, John H. 178
Dickson, Joseph 178
Dickson, Major 118
Dier, Luke 131
Dilling, Jiny 176
Dilling, L. 15
Dillon, Charity 40, 46
Dillon, Daniel 43
Dillon, Daniel Jr. 38, 40
Dillon, Hannah 133, 150
Dillon, Isaac 43
Dillon, Jesse 43, 151, 152
Dillon, Martha 43
Dillon, Nathan 43, 151
Dillon, Patience 43
Dillon, Peter 40, 43, 46
Dillon, Susannah 50
Dillon, William 43
Dillworth, Margaret 131
Dimon, Mary 18
Dinkins, John 15, 57
Dix, Joshua 13
Dixon, Benjamin 14
Doak, Ann 43
Doak, Anne 41
Doak, Daniel 41
Doak, Elizabeth 41
Doak, Hannah 40, 41
Doak, James 41, 45, 73

Doak, James W. 45
Doak, Jean 45
Doak, John 3, 41, 42, 45, 60, 61, 91
Doak, Jonathan 42
Doak, Josiah 42
Doak, Martha 42, 45
Doak, Mary 41, 42, 45
Doak, Robert 40, 41, 42, 45
Doak, Roddy 42
Doak, William 41, 42, 43
Doak, William P. 45
Doak, William, Jr. 73
Doak, Wm. 41
Doake, John 41
Dobins, Harriett 135
Dobins, John 135
Dobson, Will'm 39
Doggett, --- 15
Donaldson, John 130
Donaldson, Stol [?] 137
Donnal, George 88
Donnal, Isabella 88
Donnal, Robert 104
Donnel, Daniel 5
Donnel, James 8, 104
Donnel, Jno. 32
Donnel, John 8, 39
Donnel, Robert 19
Donnel, Thos. 8
Donnel, William 129
Donnell, Agness 39
Donnell, Andrew 177
Donnell, Edmond 177
Donnell, Elizabeth 39, 44, 177
Donnell, George 86, 87, 147
Donnell, Hannah 44
Donnell, Harry 44
Donnell, Jean 44
Donnell, Jno. 44
Donnell, John 6, 129
Donnell, Latham 177
Donnell, Leathum 177
Donnell, Lydia 49
Donnell, Majer 156
Donnell, Margaret 177
Donnell, Martha 131
Donnell, Mary 44
Donnell, Robert 44, 177
Donnell, Robt. 46
Donnell, Samuel 44
Donnell, Thomas 44, 177
Dougherty, John 42, 93
Downey, Elisabeth 128
Draper, William 154
Drift, Margaret 14

Drog, Jacob 17
Duck, Mary 39
Duff, Abram 40
Duff, Elizabeth 106
Duff, James 40
Duff, John 40
Duff, Mary 4-
Duff, Robert 40
Duff, Samuel 40
Duff, William 40
Dun, William 132
Dunlap, John 43
Dunlap, Margaret 43
Dunlap, Robert 43
Dunning, James 84, 166
Duval, William 140
Dwigans, John 94
Dwigans, Mary, 94
Dwigens, John Jr. 30
Dwiggins, Ann 38
Dwiggins, Daniel 38
Dwiggins, Elizabeth 38, 39
Dwiggins, James 38
Dwiggins, John 38
Dwiggins, Joseph 38
Dwiggins, Lydia 38, 39
Dwiggins, Mary 38
Dwiggins, Robert 38, 39
Dwiggins, Sarah 38, 39
Dwigins, Samuel 38
Dwigons, James 38
Dwigons, John Jr. 3
Dwigons, Samuel 38
Dyer, Luke 131

Eadins, Josep 141
Eddins, Sarah 78
Edwards, Abel 98, 99
Edwards, Annuel 149
Edwards, Edward 28, 140
Edwards, Haniwel 102
Edwards, Joshua 149
Edwards, Thomas 98, 99
Eken, William 119
Elder, Jean 106
Eldredge, Cathran 154
Elette, John 91
Ellet, John 91
Elliot, --- 37
Elliott, John 75
Elliott, Joseph 62
Elliott, Joseph 62
Elliott, Priscilla 62
Ellis, Levina 17
Endsley, Abraham 46, 47, 90, 116
Endsley, Elizabeth 47
Endsley, John 13, 46, 47, 165

Endsley, Mahala 47
Endsley, Mahaly 47
Endsley, Samuel 46
Endsley, Samuel V. 46
Engelson, Sarah 163
Erwin, George 46
Erwin, James 46
Erwin, Mary 46
Erwin, Robert 46
Erwin, Robt. 46
Erwin, Samuel 46
Esterig, Henry 74
Eubanks, Catharine 47
Eubanks, Elizabeth 47
Eubanks, Frances 47
Eubanks, George 47
Eubanks, John 47
Eubanks, Katharine 47
Eubanks, Philip 47
Eubanks, Polly 47
Eubanks, Rachel 47
Eubanks, Richard, 47
Evans, Deborah 172
Evans, Jesse 70, 72, 77
Eydlot, Minervy 176
Eyedolot, Levine 176

Fairbanks, David 49
Fairbanks, Mary 49, 50
Fairbanks, Susannah 49
Fairbanks, William 49, 50
Farrington, Elizabeth 155
Farrington, John
Ferguson, Hannah 106
Ferrington, Anna 158
Field, Ann 5, 48, 49
Field, David 49
Field, Elisabeth 48, 49
Field, Hester 49
Field, Jeremiah 49, 53
Field, Jesse 49
Field, John 48, 49
Field, Jonathan 53
Field, Joseph 49
Field, Lideah 49
Field, Mary 48, 49
Field, Nancy 53
Field, Robert 49
Field, Thomas 49
Field, William 48, 49, 53
Fields, Ansyl 137
Fields, John 137
Findley, George 52
Findley, William 121
Finely, Elva 123
Finley, Abigal 52

Finley, Alsey 52, 53
Finley, Betsy, 52, 53
Finley, Elizabeth 6
Finley, George 52, 53
Finley, Isabella 3
Finley, James 52, 53, 160
Finley, John 3, 6, 91, 123
Finley, Josiah 52, 53
Finley, Lettis 52, 53
Finley, Polly 52
Finley, Rachel 52
Finley, William 121
Fipps, Aaron 81
Fipps, Christina 81
Fisher, Daniel 50
Fisher, David 50
Fisher, Hanner 50
Fisher, Henry 61
Fisher, John 50
Fisher, Jonathan 50
Fisher, Mary 50
Fisher, Molloston 50
Fisher, Nathan 50
Fisher, Sarah 50
Fisher, Theodoris 50
Fisher, Thomas 50
Fitzgerald, William 175
Flack, --- 145
Flack, Andrew 51
Flack, Dorcas 51
Flack, Dorcus 51
Flack, Elijah 51
Flack, Elisha 51
Flack, Hannah 51
Flack, James 51
Flack, Jane 51
Flack, Jean 126
Flack, Jenny 51
Flack, Susan 42
Flack, Thomas 51
Fleming, Alexander 51
Fleming, Beniah 51
Fleming, Betsy 51
Fleming, Elizabeth 32
Fleming, Robert, 51
Fleming, Sarah 51
Fleming, Silas 51
Fleming, William 128
Flemon, Elizabeth 32
Flere, Jan 48
Flere, Jane 48
Flere, Jean 48
Flere, Judith 48
Flere, Thomas 48
Flere, Thos. 48
Fogleman, George 115
Fogleman, Malkia 115
Forbes, 49
Forbes, Anne 49

Forbes, Elizabeth 49, 60
Forbes, George 119
Forbes, Ralph 61
Forbis, 49
Forbis, Ann 47, 48 52
Forbis, Anne 49
Forbis, Arthur 47, 48, 49
Forbis, Eli 51, 52
Forbis, Elizabeth 48, 49, 169
Forbis, Finley Stuart 147
Forbis, George 9
Forbis, Hugh 52
Forbis, Jeremiah 131
Forbis, Jeremiah, Major 3
Forbis, Jeremy 51, 52 103
Forbis, Jessy 51, 52
Forbis, John 47, 48, 51, 52, 86, 92
Forbis, John Sr. 48
Forbis, Liddy 51
Forbis, Marthy 48
Forbis, Mary 3, 48, 51
Forbis, Poley 52
Forbis, Rebeckah 52
Forbis, William 47, 51, 52
Forbus, Abner 177
Forbus, Alise 49
Forbus, Ann 178
Forbus, David 177
Forbus, Eli 177
Forbus, Elizabeth 177, 178
Forbus, Hugh 177, 178
Forbus, John 178
Forbus, Nancy 178
Forbus, Ralph 178
Forbus, Robert 177
Forbush, --- 49
Ford, Elizabeth 29
Ford, Henry 23, 29
Ford, Moses, 29
Ford, Prudence 29
Ford, Sarah 29
Ford, Thomas 29
Ford, William 29
Ferguson, John 69
Foster, Hugh 162
Foster, John 30
Fourhand, David 50
Fourhand, Garesies [?] 50
Fourhand, Gordin 50
Fourhand, John 50
Fourhand, Molley 50
Fourhand, Molly 50
Fourhand, Owing 50

Fourhand, Prudence 50
Fourhand, Thomas 50
Frazer, Isaac 145
Frazer, Rebekah 145
Frazier, James 85, 113
Freer, Isaac 89
Frees, Isaac 89
Fryar, William [?] 92
Fulkerson, Abram 17
Fulkerson, Frederick 17
Fulkerson, Mary 17
Fulps, Phebe 158
Fulton, Elisabeth 168
Fulton, Sols 51

Galbreath, James 31
Galbreath, Robert 3
Gallaway, Charles 36
Callaway, James 36
Gambl, Andrew
Gamble, Hannah 31
Gannon, Nancy 62
Gardner, --- 103
Gardner, Abigail, 2, 7
Gardner, Eliab 71
Gardner, Elisabeth 152
Gardner, Eunice 152
Gardner, Hezekiah 71
Gardner, Isaac 100
Gardner, Silvanus 32
Gardner, Stephen 2, 7, 10
Gardner, Stephen, Jr. 2
Garner, William 141
Garner, Wm. 16
Garratt, William 117
Gates, Charles 83
Geren, S. 61
Geren, Simeon 62
Gesford, Rebekah 78
Gibson, Andrew 11, 81
Gibson, Elizabeth 122
Gibson, Henry 136
Gibson, Jos. 85
Gibson, Moses 122
Gibson, Widow 45
Gifford, Eunice 54
Gifford, Hannah 54
Gifford, Jonathan 54
Gifford, Mary 54
Gifford, Sarah 54
Gifford, William 54, 142
Gilbert, Edward 53, 135
Gilbert, Josiah 75
Gilbreath, Caty 178
Gilchrist, John 12, 29, 57, 62, 63, 80,

81, 95, 96, 111, 128, 143, 168
Gilchrist, Moses 80, 111
Gilchrist, Patrick Davidson 63
Gilchrist, Robert 63, 78. 96
Gilchrist, Samuel 63, 78, 96
Gilchrist, Wm. 63
Gillaspie, --- 59
Gillaspie, Charles Joseph 57
Gillaspie, Daniel 56, 57
Gillaspie, Daniel, Col. 109
Gillaspie, Elizabeth 56
Gillaspie, James S. 56, 57, 145
Gillaspie, James S. Esqr. 57
Gillaspie, Jno., Jr. 43
Gillaspie, John 56, 57
Gillaspie, John, Rev. 57
Gillaspie, Margaret 57, 109
Gillespie, Daniel, Sr. 43, 85, 124
Gillespie, Daniel, Col. 30, 43, 85, 91
Gillespie, Daniel, Sr. 6
Gillespie, John 41, 156
Gillespie, John, Col. 43, 156
Gillespie, Robert 80
Gilliam, David 18
Gilmer, David 18
Gilmer, Robt. C. 3
Gladson, Ann 57
Gladson, Daniel 57
Gladson, John 57
Gladson, Joshua 57
Gladson, Leven 57
Gladson, Nathan
Glas, Barbra 19
Glas, Eve 19
Glass, Crisley 63
Glass, Philip 58
Glassgow, 8
Glenn, John 136
Glenn, Joseph 14
Gles, Christen 58
Gles, George 58
Gles, Mary 59
Gless, Barbrey 58
Gless, Crisley 63

Gless, George 58, 63
Gless, Paul 58
Gless, Philip 58, 59
Gless, Philpenah 58
Gless, Powel 58
Glover, Richard 9, 10, 127
Glovyer, Christian 127
Goacher, Rachel 137
Goardin, John 26
Gobel, George 26
Gobel, Jacob 59
Goble, Jacob 22
Gooding, Margaret 137
Goral, Ralph 135
Gordin, John 152
Gordon, Charles 148
Gordy, Eunice 62
Gordy, Isaac 62
Gordy, Moses 62
Gordy, Nansey [Stewart?] 62
Gordy, Polly 62
Gorral, Kettren 88
Gorral, Marey 88
Gorral, Ralph 88
Gorrell, Catherine 59, 60
Gorrell, David 59, 60, 61, 62, 147
Gorrell, James 59, 60
Gorrell, John 61
Gorrell, Margaret 59, 60
Gorrell, Mary 59
Gorrell, Ralph 40, 59, 60, 61, 62, 86, 87, 88, 91, 106, 144, 156
Gorrell, Robert 41, 59, 61
Goss, Steven 164
Gosset, Alice 166
Gossett, Elijah 146
Gossett, Margret 146
Gough, Daniel 56
Gough, James 56
Gough, Jean 56
Gough, Nancy 56
Gough, Polly 56
Gough, Samuel 56
Gowdy, James 53, 54, 57
Gowdy, John 54, 57
Gowdy, Robert 54, 57
Gowdy, Sarah 54
Gowdy, W. 6, 105, 164
Gowdy, William 6, 12, 36, 49, 53, 54, 105, 125
Graham, Wm. 125
Graves, Mary 19
Graves, Thorely [Dorothea] 19

Gray, Elizabeth 127
Gray, Isaac 55, 107
Gray, James 54, 131, 132
Gray, Jesse 55
Gray, John 55
Gray, Joseph 55
Gray, Lydia 55
Gray, Robert 132
Gray, Samuel 55
Gray, Thomas 55
Gray, William 13, 40, 54, 55, 107
Greear, Thomas 112
Green, Charles 55
Green, Edward 126, 146
Green, Jehu 55
Green, John 55
Greer, Thomas 62
Greeson, Dorothea 81
Greeson, George 28
Greeson, Isaac 81
Greeson, Turley [Dorothea] 81
Grier, Eleanor 62
Grier, Joanna 68
Grier, Mary 62
Grier, Matthew 62
Grier, Rebecca 68
Grier, Thomas 62
Griffin, Alex. 69
Griffin, George 123
Griffin, Henry Porter 123
Grimes, Esther 3
Grimes, William 75
Groose, Jean 152
Gulbirt, Edward 53
Gulbirt, Elizabeth 53
Guilbirt, John 53
Guilbirt, William 53
Guilbreath, Robert 23
Gullet, Ezkel 119
Gullet, George 55
Gullet, John 55
Gullett, John 130
Gullett, Joshua 14
Gullett, Minte 57
Gunn, John 157
Gunn, Joseph 157
Guyer, Samuel 181
Gwin, Isabella 58
Gwin, James 58
Gwin, Martha 58
Gwin, Robert 58
Gwyn, Isabel 58
Gwyn, Isbel 56
Gwyn, John 56
Gwyn, Nelly 56
Gwyn, Pollyley 56
Gwyn, Rachel 56

Hacket, Elizabeth 57
Hadley, Jon'n. 35
Hadley, Jonathan 35, 151
Hagey, Conrod 22
Hagey, Molly 22
Haines, Joseph 157
Haines Josua 14, 157
Hains, Hannah 78
Hains, Joshua 78
Haith, Elisabeth 78
Haith, John 77, 78
Haith, Samuel 77, 78
Haith, Smith 77, 78
Haith, Tabitha 77, 78
Haith, William 78
Haitt, George 78
Hall, --- 105
Hall, Agnes 79, 80
Hall, Becky 79, 80
Hall, Benjamin 93
Hall, Eli 80
Hall, James 79, 80, 105
Hall, John 79, 80
Hall, Mary 145
Hallum, John 11
Hallum, John, Esqr. 11
Hallum, William 11
Ham, Hezekiah 77, 152
Ham, John 77
Ham, Philip 77, 139
Hamilton, Elizabeth 1
Hamilton, Gawin 68
Hamilton, George 68
Hamilton, Jane 39
Hamilton, John 130, 137, 156, 178, 179
Hamilton, John, Clerk of Court 34
Hamilton, Joseph 68
Hamilton, Mary, 1, 68
Hamilton, Thomas 62, 68
Hamilton, William 68
Hampton, George 97
Hancock, John 5
Hand, John 36
Hanes, Elizabeth 78
Hanes, Hannah 78
Hanes, Jacob 78
Hanes, Jeremiah 78
Hanes, Jobe 78
Hanes, John 78
Hanes, Joseph 78
Hanes, Joshua 78
Hanna, Robert 86
Hanna/Hannah/Hanner 147
Hannah, Alfred 57
Hannah, Anna 56
Hannah, Bille 43
Hannah, John 57

Hannah, Mr. 61
Hannah, Robert 9
Hannah, Robert, Sr. 43
Hannah, Robt. Sr. 3
Hannah, Roddy, 43, 50
Hannah, Roddy, Esqr. 147
Hannah, Sarah 147
Hannar, Robert 124
Hanner, J. 62
Hanner, James 124
Hanner, Jane 53
Hanner, Jesse 53
Hanner, Jno. 177
Hanner, John 61
Hanner, Joseph 122
Hanner, Nancy 121
Hanner, Robert 91
Hardeman, Dority 179
Hardeman, Eddy 179
Hardeman, Elizabeth 179
Hardeman, Esther 179
Hardeman, Jane 179
Hardeman, John 179
Hardeman, Judith 179
Hardeman, Susannah 179
Hardeman, Thommas 179
Hardin, Catherine 74
Hardin, Charles 73, 74, 129
Hardin, Elisabeth 113
Hardin, Jean 74
Hardin, John 74
Hardin, Rebecca 74
Hardin, Stewart 74
Hargrave, Jesse 71
Hargrave, Martha 71
Hargrave, Naomi 71
Hargrave, Samuel 71
Harper, ---72
Harrell, David 93
Harrell, Elizabeth 92, 93
Harrington, Ann 88
Harris, Christopher 65
Harris, David 72
Harris, Elizabeth 72
Harris, Hanna 69
Harris, Hannah 65
Harris, James 74
Harris, Joel 92, 116
Harris, John 65
Harris, Mr. 25
Harris, Nelley 69
Harris, Obadiah 30, 54, 72
Harris, Peter 69
Harris, Polly 25
Harris, Robert 65
Harris, Thompson 65
Harris, Wm. 165
Hart, Henry 47

Hartgrove, Samuel 174
Hartley, Francis 68
Hartley, Sarah 68
Harvey, William 6, 79
Harvy, John 75
Harvy, Nanney 75
Hatrick, Robert 147
Haworth, Elizabeth 73
Haworth, George 73
Haworth, Hannah 73
Haworth, Jane 73
Haworth, Mary 73
Haworth, Micajah 73
Haworth, Phebe 73
Haworth, Rachel 73
Haworth, Richard, 73
Haworth, Solomon 73
Haworth, Stephanus 73, 98
Hays, Isaac 9
Hays, James 159
Hays, John 69
Hays, Patrick 69
Hays, Rebekah 69
Healey, Hugh 76
Healey, Jesse 76
Healy, John 76
Healy, Mary 76
Healy, Patrick 76
Healy, Phebe 76
Healy, Pheobe 76
Heath, Charlotte 80, 103
Heath, Delilah 63, 78, 80, 81
Heath, Elizabeth 80
Heath, Henry 77
Heath, Jacob 80
Heath, Jestin 80
Heath, John 80
Heath, Kesiah 80
Heath, Levina 80
Heath, Mary 80, 133
Heath, Nancy 80
Heath, Ralph 80
Heath, Rebekah 80
Heath, Robert 80
Heath, Samuel 80
Heath, Sarah 63, 80
Heath, Smith 77, 133
Heath, William, Senior 78
Heirs, Robert 118
Heirs, Thompson 118
Hellon, James 105
Henderson, Daniel 72
Henderson, Elizabeth 146
Henderson, J. 54
Henderson, James 181
Henderson, John 72
Henderson, Michael 164
Henderson, Rebeca 72

Henderson, Thomas 48, 72
Henderson, Thos. 48
Henderson, William 72
Hendricks, Hendnay 86
Hendricks, James 86
Hendricks, Mary 86
Hendrix, --- 177
Hendrix, Mary 86
Hendrix, Samuel 65
Henley, J. 141
Heth, Jestin 80
Hiatt, Aaron, 76
Hiatt, Amos 70
Hiatt, Asher 68, 69
Hiatt, Bennajah 77, 169
Hiatt, Christopher 68, 69, 70
Hiatt, Enos 148
Hiatt, Esther 70
Hiatt, Isaac 148
Hiatt, Isom 77
Hiatt, Jehu 70
Hiatt, Joel 77, 88
Hiatt, John 69, 70, 78
Hiatt, Lydia 69, 70
Hiatt, Martha 78
Hiatt, Mary 68, 85
Hiatt, Mordicai 70
Hiatt, Nathan 68
Hiatt, Rebecca 77
Hiatt, Silas 77
Hiatt, Susannah 78
Hiatt, William 68, 70, 76, 77
Hiatt, Wm. 78, 169
Hicks, Eleanor 140
Hicks, Elizabeth Ross 140
Hiett, Jno. 64
Hiett, Sarah 64
Hiett, Susannah 64
Hiett, William 64
Hignutt, John 180
Hill, Ann 136
Hill, Elizabeth 66
Hill, Isaac 66, 67
Hill, Richard 66
Hill, Sarah 66
Hilom, John 11
Hilton, Abraham 71
Hilton, Elaxander 71
Hilton, Hannah 71
Hilton, James 71
Hilton, John 71
Hilton, Mary 71
Hilton, Peter 71
Hilton, Priscilla 71
Hilton, Stephen 71
Hilton, William 71
Hinds, John 64
Hines, Joseph 64, 65

Hines, Levi 64
Hines, Simon 64
Hines, Susannah 64, 65
Hitchcock, Hannah 75
Hitchcock, William, Senior 75
Hodge, John 117
Hodgens, Jonathan 108
Hodgins, Anne 65
Hodgins, Robert, Srn'r. 65
Hodgson, Ann 31
Hodgson, Elisabeth 157
Hodgson, George 31, 64, 73
Hodgson, Hur 46
Hodgson, John 64, 73, 145
Hodgson, Jonathan 43, 46, 108
Hodgson, Joseph, 64, 73
Hodgson, Mary 73, 157
Hodgson, Robert 64
Hodgson, William 145
Hodson, Achsa 79
Hodson, Axey 79
Hodson, Charity 79
Hodson, David 79
Hodson, Deborah 76
Hodson, Elizabeth 79
Hodson, Ester 93
Hodson, George 76
Hodson, Hester 79
Hodson, Hur 79
Hodson, Isaac 76
Hodson, Jesse 79
Hodson, Jonathan 79
Hodson, Margaret 79
Hodson, Martha 79
Hodson, Mary 79
Hodson, Rachel 76, 79
Hodson, Rebecca 79
Hodson, Richard, 46, 79
Hodson, Robert 79
Hodson, Ruth 102
Hodson, Sarah 79
Hodson, Simmeon 79
Hodson, Susannah 76
Hodson, Thomas 79
Hodson, William 76
Hodson, Zachariah 76
Hofhains, Barbara 70
Hofhains, Christian 70
Hofhains, Christina 70
Hofhains, Daniel 70, 71
Hofhains, David, 70
Hofhains, Elisabeth 70
Hofhains, Jacob 70, 71
Hofhains, Mallena 70

Hofhains, Mary Elizabeth 70, 71
Hofhains, Philip 70
Hofman, James 47
Hoggatt, Agnes 64
Hoggatt, Ann 157
Hoggatt, Anthony 67, 68
Hoggatt, David, 67, 101
Hoggatt, Hannah 65
Hoggatt, Isaiah 77
Hoggatt, Jean 67
Hoggatt, John 66, 67
Hoggatt, Joseph 66, 67, 68, 77
Hoggatt, Mahlon 77
Hoggatt, Margaret 66
Hoggatt, Margret 157
Hoggatt, Mary 67
Hoggatt, Nathan 77
Hoggatt, Phebe 77
Hoggatt, Philip 67, 68, 77
Hoggatt, Sarah 77
Hoggatt, Stephanus 77
Hoggatt, Stephen 66
Hoggatt, William 65, 66, 67, 68, 77
Hoggatt, Zimri 77
Hoggett, Deborah 93
Hogson, Joseph 165
Hogson, Wm. 165
Holderness, James 83
Holker, Adam 38
Holland, James 145
Holland, Joshua 165
Holliday, Ann 32
Holmes, Elizabeth 124
Holton, Dinah 73
Holton, Lewis 73
Homes, John 119
Homes, Meryann 119
Hood, John 119
Horne, Judith 155
Horner, William 12
Horney, Hannah 30
Horney, Manlove 76
Horney, Mary 30
Horney, Philip 71
Horney, Samuel 76
Hoskins, Ann 72
Hoskins, Arnold 72
Hoskins, Eli 72
Hoskins, Elisabeeth 71, 72
Hoskins, Ellie 72
Hoskins, Hannah 71, 72
Hoskins, Jean 72
Hoskins, John 8, 72
Hoskins, Joseph 71, 72
Hoskins, Mary 72
Hoskins, Neley 72

Houlston, Solomon 69
Houlston, Thomas 69
Houe, Mary 83
Howel, John 20
Howell, Hannah 85
Howell, John 73, 75, 85, 98
Howlet, Ann 117
Howlet, Harmon 117
Howlet, J. H. 117
Howren Finsmore 23
Howren, Sarah 29
Howren, Winsmore 29, 148
Hubbard, Elizabeth 148
Hubbard, George 167
Hubbard, Jane 148
Hubbard, John 152
Hubbard, Judith 148
Hubbard, Martha 148
Hubbard, Nicholas 181
Hubbard, Sarah 148
Hubbard, Susanna 148
Huddleston, Stephen 55
Huddlestone, Elizabeth 71
Huddlestone, Hannah 71
Huddlestone, Jonathan 71, 101
Huddlestone, Levinah 71
Huddlestone, Lydia 71
Huddlestone, Mary 71
Huddlestone, Rachel 71
Huddlestone, Sarah 71
Huddlestone, Seth 71
Hiffin, Henery 160
Huffman, Catherine 81
Huffman, John 81
Hughes, Sally 93
Hunt, Barnabas 33
Hunt, Elazer 140
Hunt, Eleazer, 77
Hunt, Elisabeth 33, 34
Hunt, Hannah 13, 74
Hunt, Jabez 75
Hunt, Jacob 74, 155, 162
Hunt, Joel 16
Hunt, John 22, 74
Hunt, Libni 30
Hunt, Miriam 31
Hunt, Nathan 75
Hunt, Phebe 33, 34
Hunt, Polly 74
Hunt, Priscilla 75
Hunt, Prudence 155
Hunt, Sally 74
Hunt, Samuel 77
Hunt, Semira 75
Hunt, Stuard 74
Hunt, Thomas 23

Hunt, William 74, 88, 162, 172
Hunt, Zebulon 75
Hunter, Alexander 63
Hunter, Edward 63, 64
Hunter, James 59, 64, 118, 163
Hunter, John 63, 64
Hunter, Samuel 103, 159
Hussey, Anne 65
Hussey, Bathalder, 20
Hussey, Christopher 65
Hussey, John 162
Hussey, Stephen, 16, 65
Huston, John 108
Huston, Levi 123
Hutchinson, Widow 45
Hutton, Arnold 74, 75
Hutton, Elizabeth 74
Hutton, George 74, 75
Hutton, James 74
Hutton, Jemima 74
Hutton, Lydia 74
Hutton, Mary 74
Hutton, Ruthy 74
Hutton, Sarah 14
Hutton, William 74

Iddings, Joseph 97, 98
Ingle, Adam 81
Ingle, Barnabas, 81
Ingle, George 81
Ingle, George, Senior 81
Ingle, Jacob 81
Ingle, John 81
Ingle, Lovena 81
Ingle, Ludwick 81
Ingle, Margaret 81
Ingle, Matlena 81
Ingle, Philpena 81
Ingle, Sophia 81
Insley, David 75
Isley, Christian 81
Isley, Elizabeth 81
Isley, Lodweek 81
Isley, Lodwick, Junior 81
Isley, Palliser 81

Jackson, Andrew 83
Jackson, Ann 159
Jackson, David 83, 84
Jackson, Gabril 84
Jackson, James, 83, 84
Jackson, James, Jr. 16
Jackson, James, Sr. 16
Jackson, John 85
Jackson, Joseph 84, 85

Jackson, Margaret 83
Jackson, Sarah 85
Jackson, W. 86
Jackson, William 83, 85
James, -----, J. P. 176
Jamison, Elisabeth 84
Jamison, George 84
Janson, Jane 49
Jarrell, Nancy 34
Jean, Edmund 94
Jean, Mary 177
Jean, Sally 123
Jean, William 120
Jenkins, David, 82
Jenkins, Ephraim 85
Jenkins, John 82
Jenkins, Lettis 81
Jenkins, Mary 179
Jenkins, Thomas 81, 82
Jenkins, William 9, 85
Jennings, Miriam 142
Jennings, Nancy 142
Jessop, Rachel 24
Jester, Henry 136
Jester, Isack 55
Job, John 21
Job, John, Jr, 22
Johnson, --- 118
Johnson, Alexander 83, 84
Johnson, Ann 77
Johnson, Caleb 85
Johnson, Elenor 98
Johnson, Elizabeth 77, 83, 84
Johnson, Esbell 84
Johnson, Esebell 84
Johnson, 18, 84, 138, 146
Johnson, Isabel, 84
Johnson, James 85, 120, 150
Johnson, Jane 49
Johnson, Jennett 84
Johnson, Joel 83
Johnson, John 83
Johnson, Joshua 85
Johnson, Mary 84
Johnson, Nancy 18
Johnson, Nathan 18
Johnson, Pleasant 83
Johnson, Robert 107
Johnson, Sarah 84
Johnson, Solomon 85
Johnson, Talton 76
Johnson, Tarleton 21
Johnson, Thomas 19, 84
Johnson, William 77
Johnston, George 18
Jones, Betsy, 157
Jones, John 118

Jones, Mary 102
Jones, Solomon 157
Jones, Thomas 115
Jones, Travis 120
Jonson, Caleb 13
Jordan, Elizabeth 17
Jordan, Mary 82
Jordan, Michael 82
Jordan, Nottey 17
Joy, Dinna 95
Joyce, Alexander 82 83, 137
Joyce, Andrew 82, 83
Joyce, Elijah 82, 83
Joyce, Elisha 82, 83
Joyce, Elizabeth 82, 83
Joyce, Esther, 82
Joyce, James 36, 82, 93
Joyce, Jane 82, 83
Joyce, John 82, 83
Joyce, Joseph 82
Joyce, Margarett 82, 83
Joyce, Mary 83
Joyce, Robert 82, 83
Joyce, Sarah 82
Joyce, Thomas 82, 83
Judkins, Carolus 1
Judkins, Joel 1
Julian, Peter 63

Keok, Henry 28
Kellam, John 87, 158
Kellam, Joshuway 87
Kelley, Rebecca 27
Kellum, John Purnel 87
Kellum, Samuel 77
Ke-ney, Mary 29
Kennedy, William 48
Kenworthy, John 16
Kerr, Ann 40
Kerr, Catherine 86, 87, 88
Kerr, David 86, 76, 88
Kerr, Elizabeth 87
Kerr, Isbell 87
Kerr, James 87
Kerr, Jean 88
Kerr, John 60, 88
Kerr, Kettren 88
Kerr, Margaret 87
Kerr, William
Kersey, Aleazer 34
Kersey, Amos 77
Killan, Custus 87
Killam, Elisabeth 87
Killam, Ester 87
Killam, Henry 87
Killan, John Tumbleston 87

Killam, John, Senior 87
Killam, Samuel 87
Killam, Shadrick 87
Killey, Daniel 127
Killey, Lydia 127
Killingsworth, William 57
Kime, Philip 126, 151
King, Abigail 92, 93
King, Peter, Sr. 17
King, William 93
King, Wm. 166
Kirkman, Eleanor 86
Kirkman, Elijah 85
Kirkman, Elisha 86
Kirkman, George 85, 86
Kirkman, James 85, 86
Kirkman, John 86
Kirkman, Mary 86
Kirkman, Neley 124
Kirkman, Peter 86
Kirkman, Rodger 86
Kirkman, Rodjer 50
Kirkman, Sarah 86
Kirkman, Tho. 154
Kirkman, Thomas 56
Kirkman, Thomas Sherwood 86
Kirkman, William 85, 86
Klutts, John 68
Knight, Abel 32, 87, 88
Knight, Andrew 88
Knight, Elizabeth 140
Knight, Jonathan 88
Knight, Samuel 87
Knight, Thomas 87, 88, 154
Knott, Justain 26, 32, 113, 116
Knott, Nancy 26

Lackey, Adam 91
Lackey, Alexander 91
Lackey, Martha 91
Lackey, Samuel 91
Lackey, William 89
Lacy, Anne 100
Lakey, John 89
Lakey, Rachel 89
Lakey, William 89
Lamb, Isaac 75
Lamb, John 93
Lamb, Rachal 154
Lamb, Robert 64, 75, 93, 154
Lamb, Samuel 75, 93, 97, 154
Lamb, Simeon 93
Lamb's, --- 40

Land, James 66
Land, Rubin 69
Landirth, John 173
Landreth, Asa 91
Landreth, Francis 91
Landreth, Jedidiah 91
Landreth, John 91
Landreth, Martha 91
Landreth, Simon 91
Landreth, Thomas 3, 9, 91, 124
Lane, Tidance 12, 133
Lane, William 101
Larance, Aam 144
Larkins, John 29
Larrance, John 29
Lau, David [Low] 115, 144
Laurence, Ann 92
Laurence, Caleb 92
Laurence, John Sen'r. 92
Law, Andrew 92
Law, Elizabeth 92
Law, James 92
Law, Margaret 92
Law, Rachel 92
Law, Robert 27, 92
Lawrence, John 133
Leacky, Adam 106
Leacky, Martha 106
Leckey, --- 177
Lecky, Adam 91
Ledford, Thomas 135
Lee, Frances 63
Lee, Henry 92, 93
Lee, Henry King 92
Lee, John 92
Lee, Joshua 92, 93
Lee, Sarah 92
Leekey, Martha 91
Leeky, Adam 91
Leger, Daniel 117
Leonard, James 103
Leonard, Phebe 179
Lester, Mary 29
Leward, Elijah 130
Lewis, Barbary 89
Lewis, Mary Elizabeth 89
Lewis, Phillip 89
Lewis, Sarah 133
Lights, Christian 58
Lillard, Moses 18
Lindsay, Andrew 174
Lindsay, David 174
Lindsay, Easter 174
Lindsay, Elizabeth 174
Lindsay, Jane 174
Lindsay, Jenne 174
Lindsay, John 173, 174
Lindsay, John son'r. 105

Lindsay, Mary 174
Lindsay, Nancy 173, 174
Lindsay, Robert 105, 150, 173, 174, 179
Lindsay, Sam 75
Lindsay, Sam'l. 81
Lindsay, Samuel 22, 174
Lindsay, Samuel, Esqr.
Lindsay, Sarah 174
Lindsay, Susannah 174
Lindsay, William 174
Lindsly, Robert 161
Linthicum, Solomon 178
Linzy, Robert 1
Littall, Jonas 105
Lloyd, Edward 180
Lockman, Christian 90
Lockman, Christopher 90
Loftin, Shedrach 177
Loman, Adam, Senior 93
Loman, Elisabeth 93
Loman, George 93
Lomax, Ann 88
Lomax, Anne 88
Lomax, Elizabeth 88
Lomax, James 88
Lomax, Robert 88
Lomax, Terrence 88
Lomax, William 88
Loney, Edward 90
Loney, James 90
Loney, John 47, 90
Loney, Mary 90
Loney, Sarah 90
Loney, Susanna 15
Long, Cathrine 144
Long, Edw. 19
Long, John 126
Lorimer, Hugh 89
Lorimer, James 89
Lorimer, Mary 89
Lorimer, Sam'l. 89
Love, John 69
Love, Sarah 32
Love, W. 117
Lovet, Sarah 73
Lovett, Rachel 180
Lovil, Wm. 18
Low, Cunrod [Conrad] 90
Low, David 89, 90
Low, Eve 89, 90
Low, Greenbury, 44
Low, Lesabeth 89
Low, Samuel 89
Lowe, Thomas 11
Lowery, Andrew 148
Lowery, Mary 148
Lowman, Andrew 93
Lucas, William 15, 168

Ludenum, Catherene 86

Maben, William 180
McCane, Jennet [?]
MacNeely, Thomas 63
MacClintock, Isabells 111
MacClintock, John 111
MacClintock, Robert 111
MacClintock, Samuel 111
MacClintock, William 111
AcAden, Wm. 105
McAdow, Darcus 107
McAdow, David 107, 110, 111
McAdow, Ezrah 197
McAdow, James 107, 108, 110, 111, 135
McAdow, Jean 111
McAdow, John 107, 108
McAdow, Margaret, 111
McAdow, Margret 107, 108
McAdow, Martha 107
McAdow, Mary 107
McAdow, Samuel 110, 111
McAdow, Sarah 107, 147
McAdow, William 107, 108, 111
McAdow, Wm. 108
McAlhatton, William 160
McBride, Elisabeth 111
McBride, Francis 13, 106, 165
McBride, Isaiah 98, 112, 121, 147
McBride, J. 139
McBride, James 21, 111
McBride, Jean 111
McBride, John 2, 111
McBride, John Sen'r. 111
McBride, Joseph 3
McBride, Leawell [Seawell?] 106
McBride, Linvell 106
McBride, Margaret 121
McBride, Margarett 106
McBride, Martha 106
McBride, Sarah 111
McBride, William 121
McCain, Clairsey 176
McCain, Joseph 47
McCain, Wm. 176, 179
McCain, Hamilton Hance 109

McCain, Hance 45, 49, 57, 100, 106, 146, 176
McCain, Hance, Sen'r. 179
McCaley, James 177
McCaley, John 177
McCaley, Rachel 177
McCaly, Timothy 104
McCall, John 105
McCall, Mathey 105
McCall, Matthew 105
McCall, Robert 105
McCall, Timothy 104
McCann, John 113
McCann, Robt. 164
McCann, Thomas 113
McClean, Dorcus 112
McClean, Elizabeth 112
McClean, Elizabeth 112
McClean, Jean 111, 112
McClean, John 47, 111, 112
McClean, Joseph 112
McClean, Joseph Sr. 112
McClean, Margaret 111
McClean, Marshell 111, 112
McClean, Mary 104
McClean, Moses 104
McClean, Nancy 112
McClean, Nelly 111
McClean, Polly, 111, 112
McClean, Robert 111, 112
McClean, Thomas 111
McClellan, Samuel 105
McClennan, Samuel 105
McClintock, Sally 168
McCollans, John 118
McConel, Walter, 121
McConel, Ann 64
McConnel, Walter 91
McConnell, John 106
McConnell, Mary 106
McConnell, Walter 122
McConnell, Wm. 106
McCoy, James 128
McCracken, Samuel 88
McCuiston, Ann 48
McCuiston, Elizabeth 108
McCuiston, James 41
McCuiston, James, Jun'r. 48
McCuiston, John 108
McCuiston, Moses 108, 125
McCuiston, Robert 45, 106, 108
McCuiston, Thomas 48, 159

McCuiston, Thos. 48
McCuiston, Walter 45
McCuiston, William 108
McCulhatton, Polly 15
McCulhatton, William 15
McCullock, Mary 129
McCullock, Thomas, 129
McCullock, Thomas Jun'r. 74
McCullock, Thomas, Sen't. 129
McCurney, Wm. 123
McDaniel, John 142
McDarman, Charles 107
McDarman, Hannah 107
McDarman, James 107
McDarmon, Michal 107
McDorman, Charles 107
McDill, Betsy, 113
McDill, Isaiah 3, 113
McDill, Jane 3
McDill, Jean 113
McDill, Samuel 111, 113
McDonals, Joseph 142, 134
McDowell, James 106
McDowell, John 106
McDowell, Joseph 164
McDowell, Joseph Junior 106, 164
McDowell, Joseph, Senior 106
McDowell, Mary 106
McElhatton, --- 15
McElhatton, Abraham 36
McGahey, Joseph 112
McGaughy, David 111
McGaughy, James 111
McGaughy, Joseph 39
McGaughy, Margaret 111
McGee, Andrew 3, 31, 172, 178
McGee, Harmon 92
McGeem, Sarah 47
McGibboney, David 109
McGibboney, Patrick 56, 109
McGibbony, Patrick, Maj. 85
McGiboney, Isbel 109
McGiboney, Jean 109
McGiboney, Martha
McGlamery, Edward 62, 95
McGrady, Moses 174
McGready, Aaron 108
McGready, David 108, 122
McGready, Hannah 108
McGready, James 108
McGready, Jean 108

McGready, Judah 108
McGready, Moses 108
McGready, Samuel 108
McGready, Samuel R. 108
McGready, Samuel Rutherford 108
McKaige, John 113
McKain, Hance 143
McKean, Hance 106
McKeen, Alexander 45
McKeen, Alex'd. 89
McKeen, Mary 45
McKemies, William 159
McKemma, Charity 113
McKemma, Gideon 113
McKemma, James 113
McKemma, Shadrach 113
McKemma, William 113
McKeney, Catey 113
McKeney, Demsey 113
McKeney, Elisabeth 113
McKeney, Fanny 113
McKeney, George 113
McKeney, Jarrat 113
McKeney, Lettes 113
McKeney, Lettice 113
McKeney, Polly 113
McKinney, George 122
McLane, Marshall 98
McLosses, --- 109
McMicheal, Charitee 180
McMichael, Archibald 180
McMichael, Thos. 159
McMin, Daniel 52
McMuir, Daniel 86
McMurrey, Elizabeth 110
McMurrey, Hanna 110
McMurrey, James 109, 110
McMurrey, Ophelia 110
McMurry, Elizabeth 10
McMurry, James 10. 69, 105, 137
McMurry, Jean 105
McMurry, John 105
McMurry, John, Senior 105
McMurry, Robert 105, 106
McMurry, William 105
McMury, Mary 106, 107
McNaught, William 104
McNairy, Amanda 178
McNairy, Anne 178, 179
McNairy, Boyd 178
McNairy, James 178, 180
McNairy, John H. 178
McNairy, Mary 178

McNairy, Robert 178
McNaught, Will 104
McNeary, Nathaniel 10
McNeight, Hugh 104
McNeight, William 104
McNery, Francis 118
McKnight, Alexander 104
McKnight, Catrine 103, 104
McKnight, Elizabeth 103
McKnight, Hannah 95, 103, 104
McKnight, Jean 104
McKnight, John 103, 104
McKnight, Mary 172
McKnight, Mary Ann 177
McKnight, Robert 103, 104, 171
McKnight, William 103, 177

Mackie, Jane 63
Macy, Abigail 98
Macy, Anna 94, 95, 100
Macy, David 95
Macy, Dinah 94, 95, 100
Macy, Elizabeth 179
Macy, Enoch 2, 24, 95, 100, 133, 161
Macy, George 98
Macy, Hannah 94
Macy, Henery 100
Macy, Henry 179
Macy, Isaac 95
Macy, Jemima 151
Macy, John 101
Macy, Joseph 179
Macy, Matthew (Junior) 23
Macy, Matthew 94, 98, 139, 153
Macy, Miriam 100
Macy, Nathaniel 37, 97, 98
Macy, Paul 37, 97, 98, 151, 159
Macy, Paul, Junior 98
Macy, Sarah, 95, 100
Macy, Sary 179
Macy, Stephen 100
Macy, Thaddeus 94, 95, 100
Macy, Thomas, 179
Macy, Zaccheus 98
Majer, Jenne 105
Major, Margaret 98
Major, Thomas 98
Manship, Elijah 85

Marcillot, Jane 140
Mares, Zadok 97
Marley, Robert 53
Marris, John 99
Marsheal, Martha 133
Martin, Alexander 36, 63, 64
Martin, Alexander, Col. 118
Martin, Frances 96
Martin, Francis 96
Martin, Henry 96
Martin, James, 64, 96, 97
Martin, John 96
Martin, Lucretia 3
Martin, Mary 96
Masey, Thos. 171
Mash, Leonard 167
Mason, Abraham 102
Mason, Michal 30
Mason, Rachel 102
Mason, Reuben, 102
Massey, John 171
Massey, Nathan 171
Matthews, David 113
Matthews, Hugh 169
Matthews, James 60
Matthews, Mary 60, 61
Matthews, William 139
Maxwell, James 128
Maxwell, John 44
Maxwell, Matthew 128
Maxwell, Mary 60, 61
Maxwell, Ralph 61
May, Daniel 138, 139
May, Sarah 63
Mayben, Ann 34
Mayben, David 34
Mears, Elizabeth 97
Mears, Zedock 97 [see also Mares]
Mebane, Ann 34
Medaris, John 120
Medearies, Charles 94
Medearies, Elizabeth 94
Medearies, John 94
Medearies, Malchi 94
Medearies, Stephan 94
Medearies, William 94
Medearis, John 31, 113
Medearis, Massey C[hristmas] 120
Medearis, Thomas 94
Medlen, Sarah 42
Meiner, Henry 67
Meiner, Jean 67
Meining, Ludwig 17
Mendenhall, Aaron, 41, 96, 99, 102, 119, 156
Mendenhall, Abigail 101

Mendenhall, Ailee 10
Mendenhall, Ann 102
Mendenhall, Asenath 97
Mendenhall, Betty 102
Mendenhall, Beulah 97
Mendenhall, Charity 96, 121
Mendenhall, Daniel 148
Mendenhall, Dinah 96, 125
Mendenhall, Enos 97
Mendenhall, George 14, 71, 100, 101
Mendenhall, Hannah 101
Mendenhall, Isaac 97, 99, 130
Mendenhall, James 96, 101, 102, 148
Mendenhall, Jemima 101
Mendenhall, John 97, 08, 102
Mendenhall, Judith 101
Mendenhall, Mary 98, 101, 102, 121
Mendenhall, Mary Jane 97
Mendenhall, Miriam 96, 98, 102
Mendenhall, Mordecai 97, 99
Mendenhall, 96, 97, 98, 99, 102, 121
Mendenhall, Moses, Sen'r. 102
Mendenhall, Nathan 100, 101
Mendenhall, Phebe 97, 125
Mendenhall, Richard 99, 101
Mendenhall, Richard 2nd 102
Mendenhall, Ruth 97
Mendenhall, Seth 97
Mendenhall, Stephen, 99
Mendenhall, Susannah 102
Mendenhall, Thomas 97, 99
Mendenhall, William 101
Meroney, Elezebeth 97
Meroney, Isaac 97
Meroney, John 97
Meroney, Lyda 97
Meroney, Nathan 97
Meroney, Rachel 97
Meroney, Ruth 97
Meroney, William 97
Michals, Adam 118
Mileham, --- 129
Mileham, Ann 99
Mileham, Ebenezer 93
Mileham, Elizabeth 93
Mileham, Jacob 99
Mileham, John 93
Mileham, Mary 10
Mileham, Nancy 93
Mileham, Samuel 93, 99
Mileham, Sarah 93, 99
Mileham, Valentine 42, 99, 128
Mileham, Walter, 99
Mileham, William 42
Milford, Elizabeth 18
Mill, Joseph 33
Miller, Jonathan 78
Millia, Nickoson 85
Millican, Samuel M. 72
Millikan, Benjamin, 7
Millikan, Margaret 7
Millis, N. 79
Mills, Amos 139
Mills, Benoney 46
Mills, Benoni 40
Mills, Catherine 100
Mills, Charity 46, 99
Mills, Hannah 72
Mills, J. 34
Mills, James 97, 119
Mills, Jonathan 29
Mills, Joseph 15, 72
Mills, Margaret 100
Mills, William 100
Mills, Wm., Jr. 109
Minner, Lein 165
Minor, Lavin 165
Mire, Philip 63
Mitchal, Adam 95
Mitchal, Margarate 95
Mitchel, Adam 128
Mitchel, Rebecca 95
Mitchel, Robert 95
Mitchell, Henry 69
Mitchell, John 106
Mongomary, George 103
Mongomary, Irwin 103
Mongomary, James 103
Mongomary, Levi 103
Mongomary, Mary 103
Mongomary, Rebekah 102, 103
Mongomary, Robert 102, 103
Mongomary, William 102, 103
Mongomery, Charlotte 94
Mongomery, Elizabeth 94
Mongomery, James 94
Mongomery, Jane 94
Mongomery, John 94
Mongomery, Lydia 94
Mongomery, Margret 94
Mongomery, Mary 94
Mongomery, Rebekah 46
Mongomery, Samuel 103
Mongomery, William 94
Montgomery, --- 46
Mood, Alexander 104
Moody, Thomas 137
Moon, Judith 124
Moore, Anne 120
Moore, J. 28
Moore, John 45, 100, 120
Moore, Joshua 76
Moore, Nathaniel 97, 127
Moore, Smith 45
Moore, Thomas 77, 137
Moore, Thos. 101
Moore, William 120
Morehead, Agnes 124
Moreland, Elizabeth 114
Moreland, Francis 114
Moreland, Jane 114
Moreland, Thomas 114
Moreland, William 114
Moretz, John 126
Morgan, Habikuk 103
Morgan, James 103
Morgan, John 103, 136
Morgan, Nancy 103
Morgan, Thos. 47
Morres, John 126
Morris, Curtis 18
Morris, George 18
Morris, John 99, 126
Morris, Judy 18
Morrison, Nary 100
Morrow, David 58
Morrow, Samuel 104
Morton, John 18
Moss, William 67
Mount, Elenor 17
Mount, John 65
Mountgomery, David 95, 96
Mountgomery, Hannah 95, 96
Mountgomery, Jean 95
Mountgomery, Jean 95
Mountgomery, John 95, 96
Mountgomery, Rebekah, 95
Mountgomery, William 95, 96
Mückseh, John Matthew 17
Muehard, Agnes 124
Mulloy, Daniel 99
Mulloy, Edward 98, 99
Mulloy, James 99
Mulloy, Jane 99

Mulloy, Jeremiah 99
Mulloy, Ruth 99
Mumgummery, William 46
Murdock, John 72
Murphy, A. 62
Murry, Jean 57
Murry, Joel 57
Murry, Rebekah 57

Nation, Bethia 114
Nation, Christopher 114
Nation, John, Senior 114
Nation, Joseph 114
Needham, John 133
Neeley, --- 138
Neeley, Elizabeth 115
Neeley, James 115
Neelley, --- 160
Neelley, Marthy 115
Neelley, Robert 115
Nelly, Hugh, Senior 135
Nelson, --- 145
Nelson, Alexander 115, 116, 165
Nelson, Alice 47
Nelson, Ayls 47
Nelson, Betsy 116
Nelson, Elizabeth 115
Nelson, Ezebell 115
Nelson, George 116
Nelson, George, Senior 116
Nelson, Isabell 115
Nelson, James 115
Nelson, Jane 165
Nelson, Jean 115, 116
Nelson, Jessay 116
Nelson, John 89, 145
Nelson, Joseph 116
Nelson, Marget 116
Nelson, Nansy 116
Nelson, Olleyjan 116
Nelson, Prudence 116
Nelson, Robert 115
Nelson, Ruth 115
Nelson, Sally 116
Nelson, Susanny 116
Netherly, Jean 38
Newby, Pheby 77
Newlin, Thomas 2
Newnom, Edward 116
Newnom, Mary 116
Newnum, Ann 116
Newnum, Benjamin 116
Newnum, Mary 116
Newnum, Sarah 116
Nicks, George, Sen'r. 147
Nix, George, Jr. 150

Norman, Charles Deer 44
Norman, Fanny 44, 45
Norman, Hiram 44
Norman, John 44, 45
Norman, Joseph 44
Norman, Rebecca 18
Norris, Thomas 117
Norton, Edward 65
Nots, Barbra 114
Nots, Catrena 114
Notts, John 114, 115
Notz, Johannes 115
Notz, John 114
Nutter, Benjamin 14

Oaks, Sary 87
Ogbourn, William 152
Ogburn, William 158
Oliphants, Elizabeth 62
Oneal, James 120
Ordhooks, --- 24
Orr, John 6
Osbon, Ad 27, 28
Osborn, Anna 100
Osborne, Adlai 27
Owen, Judith 117
Owen, Mary 117
Owen, Samuel 117
Owings, Andrew 143
Owings, Hannah 136
Ozborn, Phebe 76
Ozbun, Anna 94
Ozbun, Joseph 82
Ozbun, Samuel 82
Ozbun, William 64
Ozeas, John 71
Ozment, James 60, 61
Ozment, Jane 34
Ozment, John 148
Ozment, Richard 176
Ozment, Thomas 180

Paisley, Eleanor 122
Paisley, George 122
Paisley, James 121
Paisley, John 121, 122
Paisley, Mary Ann 121, 122
Paisley, Robert 119, 164
Paisley, William 119, 121, 122
Parker, Howel 131
Parker, John 123
Parker, Jonathan 103, 123, 132, 179
Parker, Rhode 124
Parkhill, John 119
Parkhill, Martha 119

Parkhill, Meriann 119
Parkhill, Nancy 119
Parkhill, William 119
Parrish, Noel 92, 159
Parrott, Ben 66, 67
Parry, Ann 154
Parsons, Charity 123
Parsons, Eleanor 123
Parsons, George 123
Parsons, George, Jr. 123
Parsons, James, 123
Parsons, John 123
Parsons, Katharine 123
Parsons, Mary 123
Parsons, Patience 123
Parsons, Ruth 123
Parsons, William 103, 123
Patterson, William 144
Payne, Anny 102
Payne, Benjamin 102
Payne, Roda 102
Peace, Silas 166
Pearce, Joseph 184
Pearce, Mary 134
Pearce, Silas 84
Pearce, Windsor 133
Peasely, John, Col. 14, 98
Peasly, Thomas 98
Peasley, John 122
Peasly, Mary Ann 39
Peasly, Robert 98, 164
Peay, Geo. 64
Peay, George 18
Peebles, Caty, 122, 123
Peebles, Drury 123
Peebles, Herbert 123
Peebles, Jehu 122, 123
Peebles, Nathaniel 123
Peebles, Seth 123
Peebles, Wyatt 47, 122, 123
Peeples, Abraham, 28, 171
Peeples, Drury 19, 116
Peeples, Frederick 116
Pegg, Martin 32
Pegg, Valentine 32, 148
Pegram, Edward 120
Pegram, Patsy 113
Pegram, Patty 120
Peirce, Bryan 167
Pendry, Jemima 125
Pennington, Isaac 98
Peoples, David 18
Peoples, Hubbard, 18
Perking, Isaac 108, 119, 121
Perkins, Ann 121

Perkins, Betty 212
Perkins, Caleb 119
Perkins, Jared 119, 121
Perkins, John 119, 121
Perkins, Joseph 121
Perkins, Joseph, Jr. 119, 121
Perkins, Mary 119, 121
Perkins, Nancy 121
Perkins, P. Col. 66
Perkins, Peter 179
Perkins, Pheriah 108
Perkins, Thomas 119, 121
Petersen, Hans 85
Peterson, Hance 85
Phillips, Hulda 149
Philpott, Charles 118
Philpott, David 117, 118
Philpott, Edward 118
Philpott, Elezebeth 118
Philpott, John 118
Philpott, Mary 118
Philpott, Maryann 117, 118
Pidgeon, Sam 125
Piggott, William 75
Pilkington, Ede 80
Plunket, Catharine 120
Plunket, William 9
Plunkett, Caty, 120
Plunkett, Is 120
Plunkett, Thomas 120
Plunkett, William 120
Poe, Betsey 122
Poe, Gabril 122
Poe, Hannah 122
Poe, James 122
Poe, John 122
Poe, Metildy 122
Poe, Nansy 122
Poe, Polly 122
Poe, Reny 122
Poe, Sandy 122
Poe, Sarah 122
Poe, William 122
Polk, Rebeka 133
Pope, George 139
Porter, --- 178
Porter, Ann 117
Porter, Henry 106, 123
Porter, Hugh 117
Porter, James 117, 122
Porter, Jane 91
Portr, John 121, 122
Porter, Margaret 121, 122
Porter, Rees 135
Porter, Robert Gynn 59
Porter, Samuel 121
Porter, Vilet 117
Porter, Violet 117
Porter, William 58
Potter, Abraham 117
Potter, Alice 117
Potter, Ephraim 117
Potter, Henry 87
Potter, Joseph 117
Potter, Martha 117
Potter, Mary 87
Potter, Sarah 117
Potter, Zadock 87
Powel, Sarah 137
Powell, Elisabeth 49
Pratt, James 135
Pratt, John 137
Price, David 100, 145
Price, Molly, Mrs. 100
Priden, James 78
Prior, Eleanor 120
Prior, Emmery Dent 120
Prior, Paschel Brimajum 120
Pritcher, Elizabeth 119
Pritcher, Ezekel 119
Pritcher, Zebulon 119
Pritchet, David 74
Pritchet, Ekel 119
Pritchet, Isaac 119
Pritchet, Unity 119
Pritchet, Zachariah, 119
Pritchett, Alexander 160
Pritchett, Ezekiel 119
Pritchett, Hesse 119
Pritchett, Jeremiah 166
Pritchett, John 80
Pritchett, Joseph 18
Pritchett, Sarah 119
Pritchett, Sary 18
Pritchett, William 42
Proctor, Richard 176
Pulliam, Drury 66, 67
Putall, Fill 104
Pyatt, John 158

Qu---, Cathren 121
Quait, Ann 124
Quait, David 124
Quait, Elizabeth 124
Quait, Isbel 124
Quait, James 124
Quait, Margret 124
Quait, Robert 124
Quait, Sameul 124
Quait, William 124
Quate, William 124

Ragsdale, Wm. 31
Rail, Jean 14
Rain, Jean 14
Rainey, Benja. 11
Rainey, Wm. 11
Ralph, Elizabeth 15
Ramsey, Robert 129
Rankin, Agness 130
Rankin, Ann 130, 131, 132
Rankin, Elesabeth 130
Rankin, George 128
Rankin, Hannah 131, 146
Rankin, Isabel 128
Rankin, Jeane 129
Rankin, Jena 130
Rankin, Jennet 32
Rankin, Jenney 130
Rankin, John 8, 39, 49, 118, 129, 131, 140, 146
Rankin, John, Sr. 130
Rankin, Joseph 130, 131, 132
Rankin, Margaret 146
Rankin, Martha 170
Rankin, Mary 128, 146
Rankin, Polly, 131, 132
Rankin, Robert 95, 104, 129, 131, 132, 170
Rankin, Robert, Juner 118
Rankin, Robert Sen'r. 128, 129
Rankin, Samuel 131, 132, 146
Rankin, Sarah 130
Rankin, Tabitha 169, 170
Rankin, Thomas 129
Rankin, William 32, 129, 130, 131
Rannolds, Lewis 73
Rannolds, Nancy 73
Raper, Christian 127
Raper, Elizabeth 55, 127
Raper, Isaac 127
Raper, Jacob 127
Raper, Solomon 102
Raper, Thomas 127
Raper, William 102, 127
Rawley, Elijah 14
Ray, William 85
Rayl, George 69, 96
Rayl, George, Jr. 167
Rayle, William 41
Rea, Margret 124
Rea, William 124, 125

Read, Nancy 32
Reagan James 164
Reagan, John 135
Reaves, --- 114
Reaves, Martha 10
Reaves, Richard 10
Reaves, Thomas 10, 114
Records, Annanias 130
Records, Mary 130
Reed, Agness 125
Reed, Henery 118
Reed, Henry 125
Reed, William 118, 125
Rees, John 129, 143
Reeves, James 124
Reeves, Jeremiah 124
Reeves, Malachia 124
Reeves, Malissent 124
Reeves, Melissent 124
Reeves, Michel 124
Reeves, Milissent 124
Reeves, William 124, 126
Reynolds, Ann 93
Reynolds, David 132
Reynolds, Jeremiah 37, 65, 132
Reynolds, Joash 79
Reynolds, John 132
Reynolds, Lewis 73
Reynolds, Rezin 132
Reynolds, Susannah 132
Rhodes, Absolom 126
Rhodes, Fortune 126
Rhodes, Hezekiah 126
Rhodes, John 126
Rhodes, John, Jr. 126
Rhodes, Joseph 126
Rhodes, Samuel 126
Rhodes, Sarah 126
Rice, Mary 136
Rich, Aaron 76
Rich, Phebe 157
Ricks, Edward 166
Ridle, Mary 124
Ried, Sarah 24
Right, Deborah 103
Ritsel, Adam 126
Ritsel, Christopher 126
Ritsel, Gorge 126
Ritsel, Hennery 126
Ritsel, John 126
Ritsel, Marget 126
Ritsel, Mikel 126
Roberts, Prudence 64
Robertson, James 132
Robertson, Jas. 132
Robertson, Nathaniel 132
Robertson, Suca 132
Robins, Bethis 114
Robins, Frances 114

Robinson, Elinor 9
Robinson, James 9
Robinson, Naomy 13
Robinson, Nicholas 98
Robinson, Rebekah 13
Robinson, William 162
Roger, Jacob 20, 23
Ros, John 57
Ros, Rebekah 57
Rose, Lydia 158
Rose, Nancy J. 132
Rose, William 120, 132
Rosier, John 2
Ross, Andrew 126
Ross, Benjamin, 139
Ross, Francis 99
Ross, Francnai 99
Ross, Girzzald 139
Ross, Griselda 139
Ross, Grizzald 139
Ross, Henry 49, 53, 54, 105, 107, 125
Ross, James 126, 129, 131
Ross, Jean 139
Ross, John 57, 97, 125, 126, 129
Ross, Jonas 159
Ross, Joseph 139
Ross, Levi 99
Ross, Lydia 158
Ross, Marget 125
Ross, Mary 83, 87, 95, 97, 125, 126, 129, 159
Ross, Nancy 125
Ross, Rebecka 125
Ross, Rebekah 57
Ross, Susanna 131
Ross, Susannah 99
Ross, Thomas 51, 125, 126, 129, 131, 139
Royl, Susannah 159
Ruckman, Isaiah 133
Ruckman, Joseph 132, 133
Ruckman, Sarah 132
Ruddick, Jno. 142
Ruddock, John 2, 72
Ruddock, John, Jr. 2
Rudduck, Jane 125, 130
Rudduck, John, Jun'r. 125
Rudduck, John, Senior 125
Rudduck, Mary 130
Rudduck, William 125
Rudduck, Willm. 125
Ruke, Stephan 127
Russel, Andrew 148
Russel, Delilah 124
Russell, Alexander 128, 130,, 131
Russell, Christian 149

Russell, David 128, 130, 131
Russell, Elnore 128
Russell, Hepzabah 95
Russell, James 128, 131, 146
Russell, Jesse, 131
Russell, John 128
Russell, Lucretia 131
Russell, Margaret 131
Russell, Martha 131
Russell, Matthew 48
Russell, Nancy 131
Russell, Robert, 128, 130, 131
Russell, Robert Washington 130
Russell, Susanne 130
Russell, Thomas 130
Russell, William 128, 130, 131
Russum, Vincent 180
Ruth, Jane 125
Ryan, Ellener 127
Ryan, Ginna 127
Ryan, John 126, 127, 137, 139
Ryan, Margaret 127, 141
Ryan, Margat 127
Ryan, Mary Ann 127
Ryan, Robert 108, 127
Ryan, W. 108
Ryan, William 127, 141
Ryan, William, Esqr. 179

Saferight, --- 145
Sanders, Jane 148
Sanders, David 148, 153
Sanders, Elisabeth 153
Sanders, Forrest 148
Sanders, Hezekiah 152, 153
Sanders, James 55, 148
Sanders, Jemima [?] 148
Sanders, Jemimah 153
Sanders, Jermima 148
Sanders, Jesse 148, 151
Sanders, Joel 139, 140, 151, 152, 153
Sanders, John 15, 65, 139, 148, 152, 153
Sanders, Joseph 148
Sanders, Martha 153
Sanders, Martha Smith 152
Sanders, Mary 151, 153
Sanders, Rebekah 153

Sanders, Sarah 125, 153
Sanders, Susanna 148
Sanders, Thomas 152
Sapp, Benjamin 149
Sapp, Dorothy 149
Sapp, J., Jr. 13
Sapp, James 149
Sapp, Nowel 32
Sapp, Robert 149
Sapp, Samuel 149
Sapp, Sarah 32, 149
Scales, Agness 136
Scales, Bettsy 136
Scales, David, 136
Scales, Henry 136
Scales, James 136
Scales, John 136
Scales, Joseph 135, 136
Scales, Mary 135, 136
Scales, Nathanael 136
Scales, Robert 136
Scales, Thomas 136
Scott, Adam 142, 143
Scott, Cabrell 104
Scott, Gabriel 134
Scott, Hannah 137
Scott, Jineot 134
Scott, Jinet 134
Scott, Jinny 134
Scott, John 134
Scott, Margaret 134, 143
Scott, Martha 134
Scott, Mary 137, 143
Scott, Matthew 104
Scott, Nancey 134
Scott, Nancy 134, 146
Scott, Nansey 143
Scott, Rebecca 146
Scott, Rebecca Meek 146
Scott, Rebekah 142, 143
Scott, Robert 137
Scott, Samuel 134, 142, 146
Scott, Thomas 134, 137, 143, 146
Scott, William 24, 32, 53, 54, 96, 104, 118, 125, 129, 134, 142, 143
Scott, William, Senior 142, 143
Scott, Wm. 134
Searcey, Keziah 134
Searcey, Theron 134
Searcey, William 134
Searcey, Wm. 134
Searsbuck, Peter 55
Seprall, Jane 68

Settle, Josiah 4
Sh., Conrad 149
Shannon, --- 138
Shannon, Ann 146
Shannon, Isabella 146
Shannon, Solomon 138, 146
Shannon, William 138, 146
Sharborough, Malakia 142
Sharbrough, Joseph 142
Sharbrough, Perthena 142
Shard, Ann 3
Sharp, Agness 135
Sharp, Catharine 135
Sharp, Cathrin 135
Sharp, Elizabeth 135
Sharp, Isham 135
Sharp, James 135
Sharp, John 135
Sharp, Mary 135
Sharp, Richard 135
Sharp, Sam'l. 135
Sharp, Sary 135
Sharp, Susannah 135
Shatterling, Molly 19
Shatterly, Andrew 35, 176
Shaver, Catherine 144
Shaver, Conrod 144
Shaver, Eliabeth 144
Shaver, Jacob 22, 144
Shaver, Lasch 144
Shaver, Mary 22
Shaver, William 144
Shaver, Wm. 144
Shaw, Benjamin 139
Shaw, Betsy 145
Shaw, Hugh 106, 144
Shaw, John 144
Shaw, Nancy 144, 145
Shaw, Patrick 144, 145
Shaw, Robert 118, 139
Shaw, Sarah 139
Shaw, Sussana 139
Shaw, William 139, 144
Shaw, Wm. 139
Shearwood, Daniel 146
Sheerwood, Daniel 146
Shelcott, Deborah 168
Shelley, --- 101
Shelley, Betsy 141
Shelley, Elonnor 141
Shelley, William 141
Shelly, Francis 141
Shelly, James 137, 141
Shelly, Jane 10
Shelly, Jeremiah 69, 119, 137
Shelly, Jese 137
Shelly, John 137, 141

Shelly, Mary 137, 141
Shelly, Nathan 137
Shepherd, Sarah 148
Sherman, Benjamin 51
Sherman, Samuel 84
Sherwood, Daniel 84, 146
Sherwood, Hugh 50, 175
Shoemaker, Barbara 149
Shoemaker, Caty 149
Shoemaker, Christian 149
Shoemaker, Elizabeth 149
Shoemaker, George 149, 173
Shoemaker, Marry 149
Shoemaker, Susana 149
Shoffner, George 120
Shofner, Anna Margaretha 120
Shoomaker, Sussana 150
Short, Andrew 14
Shr., Adam 149
Shr., Daniel 149
Shr., Jacob 149
Shr., John 149
Shumaker, --- 129
Sickfret, Cathorine 145
Sickfret, Henerick 145
Sickfret, John 145
Sickfret, Mary 145
Sickfret, Neomi 145
Sigfred, Henerick 145
Sillaven, William 127
Sillevan, Caleb 148
Sillevan, Florence 148
Sillevan, Henney 148
Sillevan, John 148
Sillevan, Marget 148
Sillevan, Nancy 148
Silliven, Hannah 96
Sillivan, Joel 148
Sillivan Maryan 148
Sillivan, William 139
Silliven, Levi 139
Simmons, Wm. 55
Simons, Elizabeth 10
Simpson, Anna 154
Simpson, Elenner 154
Simpson, Elizabeth 140
Simpson, James 154
Simpson, Nathaniel 99, 140
Simpson, Peter 154
Simpson, Peter Ryan 140
Simpson, Pheraby 154
Simpson, Richard 140, 154
Simpson, Richard, Senior 140, 154

Simpson, Selah 154
Simpson, Thomas 140, 154
Simpson, William 93, 114, 154
Simson, Elisabeth 133
Sisney, Sally 73
Sisney, Stephen 66
Sloan, James 4
Smith, Abraham 137
Smith Adam 150, 151
Smith, Alexander 36, 83
Smith, Andrew 162
Smith, Ann 82
Smith, Arthur 143
Smith, Bryan 101
Smith, Charles 137
Smith, David, 150
Smith, Elizabeth 145
Smith, Jacob 150
Smith, James 31, 72
Smith, John 47, 92, 93, 110, 137, 150
Smith, Joseph 145, 150
Smith, Joshua 36, 137
Smith, Larkin 150
Smith, Lidia 102
Smith, Lisabeth, 19
Smith, Mary 31
Smith, Molly 150
Smith, Nancy 55
Smith, Nathaniel 150
Smith, Nicholas 83, 150
Smith, Peter 150, 151
Smith, Philip 150
Smith, Robert 135, 145, 170
Smith, Sally 150
Smith, Samuel 135
Smith, William 110, 135, 145
Smithson, Barbra 142
Soots, Jacob 143
Southerland, --- 133
Soutz, Jacob 143, 144
Soutz, Mary 143
Spence, Charles 56
Spence, John 49
Spence, Nathan 50
Spence, Shaday 5
Spence, Sidney 49
Spens, Betsy 176
Spens, Elves 176
Spens, John 176
Spens, William 176
Spikeman, Elizabeth 148
Spikeman, William 148
Spinks, Amy 133
Spinks, Bowley 133
Spinks, Enoch 133

Spinks, Enoch 133
Spinks, Garrett 133
Spinks, John 133
Spinks, Lewis 133
Spinks, Martha 133
Spinks, Sarah 133
Springer, Sarah 98
Spruce, Elizabeth 146, 147
Spruce, George 146
Spruce, John 146
Spruce, Joseph 146
Spruce, Quinton 146
Spruce, Sarah 146, 147
Spruce, Thomas 147
Spruce, William 146, 147
Stack, David 139, 176
Stack, Elijah 139
Stack, Leven 139
Stack, Lovey 139
Stack, Rachel 139
Stack, Thomas 139
Stafford, Henrietta 168
Stafford, James 143
Stafford, Sarah 15
Stalker, Deborah 142
Stalker, Elizabeth 142
Stalker, George 141, 142
Stalker, Hannah 142
Stalker, John 141
Stalker, Jonathan 141, 142
Stalker, Lydia 142
Stalker, Nathan 142
Stalker, Rachel 141, 142
Stalker, Thomas 141
Standley, Jesse 25
Standley, Jonathan 2
Standley, Strangeman 40, 46, 50, 155, 162
Stanely, Edward 140, 159
Stanely, Robert 140
Stanfield, Grace 141
Stanfield, Rachel 141
Stanfield, Wm. 141
Stanford, Jenney 113
Stanford, R. 164
Stanley, Abigail 159
Stanley, Agness 140
Stanley, Barnabus 33
Standley, Elizabeth 140
Stanley, Hulda 33, 34
Stanley, Jasson 140
Stanley, Jessa 140
Stanley, Jesse 25, 33, 46
Stanley, Judith 140

Stanley, Mary 140
Stanley, Micajah 155
Stanley, Michel 50
Stanley, Phebe 72, 140
Stanley, Richard Henry 140
Stanley, Sarah 2, 102
Stanley, Shadrach 140
Stanley, Thom 102
Stanley, Zachariah 98
Stanly, Jemima 155
Stanly, Jesse 25
Stanton, Abigail 94, 95
Stanton, Ruth 168
Starbuck, Avice 152, 153
Starbuck, Benjamin 152, 153
Starbuck, Charles 152, 153
Starbuck, Daniel 151
Starbuck, Deborah 25
Starbuck, Dinah 152, 153
Starbuck, Dorcas 151
Starbuck, Elizabeth 151
Starbuck, Eunice 151
Starbuck, Gayer 151
Starbuck, George 152, 153
Starbuck, Hezekiah 14, 16, 40, 50, 78, 117, 140, 151, 158
Starbuck, Jean 158
Starbuck, John 152
Starbuck, Latham 16
Starbuck, Lydia 151
Starbuck, Mary 152
Starbuck, Mathew 152, 153
Starbuck, Matthew 34
Starbuck, Pamely 151
Starbuck, Paul 153
Starbuck, Peter 151
Starbuck, Rachel 151
Starbuck, Reuben 151, 152
Starbuck, Ruth 151
Starbuck, Seth 152, 153
Starbuck, Thomas 151
Starbuck, William 16, 23, 50, 152, 153, 155, 158
Starbucks, Wm. 158, 167
Starbucks, Peter [?] 55
Starns, Sarah 133
Starr, Adam 28, 90
Starr, John 89

Starrat, Benjamin 135
Starrat, Jacob 42
Starrat, James 145, 146
Starrat, James Hall 146
Starrat, John 126, 145, 146
Starrat, William 145, 146
Starratt, B---- 135
Starratt, Benj'n. 135
Starratt, Hannah 135
Starratt, Harriett Dobins 135
Starratt, Hester 153
Starratt, James 135
Starratt, Joanna 135
Starratt, John Dobins 135
Starratt, Mary 135
Starratt, William Flemen 135
Starret, John 26
Starrett, Betsy 56
Starrett, J. H. 61
Stearns, Isaac 133
Stearns, Peter 133
Stearns, Shubal 133
Stephens, Mary 24
Stephens, Ursley [Ursula] 78
Stephenson, Alexander 138
Stephenson, Ann 138
Stephenson, Ann, junor [Junior] 138
Stephenson, Hugh 138
Stephenson, John 84, 138, 141, 146
Stephenson, John, junor 138, 146
Stephenson, Matthew 138
Stephenson, William 138
Stevens, John 1
Stevenson, Ann 141
Steward, John 147
Steward, Agnes 60, 61
Stewart, Euphance [Euphemia ?] 147
Stewart, Finley 147
Stewart, Finley Shaw 147
Stewart, Jennet 147
Stewart, John 62
Stewart, Mary 61
Stewart, Prudence 147
Stewart, Ralph 61
Stewart, Robert 147
Stewart, S. 62

Stewart, Sampson 14, 131
Stewart, Susanna 147
Stewart, Wiley 131
Stewart, [?] Nancey Gordy 62
Stone, John 149
Stone, Salathiel 40
Stone, Sallathial 149
Strain, Sarah 146
Stuard, Jehugh 74
Stuart, Adam Lackey 91
Stuart, Finley 147
Stuart, Finley G. 147
Stuart, George 98
Stuart, Henry 2
Stuart, John 21, 25, 62, 69, 147, 152
Stuart, John, Jr. 29
Stuart, Jonathan 69
Stuart, Mary 9
Stuart, Moses 69
Stuart, Robert 91
Stuart, Samuel 42
Stuart, Sarah 17, 29
Stuart, Temple 155
Stuarts, --- 43
Stuert, Susanna 155
Stutts, Gaspar 159
Suits, Jacob 143, 144
Sulgrave, James 148
Sullen, Ann 148
Sullen, Barbary 148
Sullen, Jacob 148
Sullen, John 148
Sullen, Margaret 148
Sullen, Nancy 148
Sullevan, Daniel 148
Sullevan, Edward 148
Sullevan, William 148
Sullivan, Joel 43
Sullivan, Sarah 6
Summers, Joseph 83
Summers, Peter 81
Sumner, Hollom/Holon 67
Sutz, Adam 143
Sutz, Christian 143
Sutz, Frederick 143
Sutz, Jacob 144
Sutz, Margret 143
Sutz, Tobias 143, 144
Swaim, Michael 66
Swaim, Susana 179
Swain, Deberah 179
Swain, George 27
Swain, Henry 179
Swain, Mariam 95
Swain, Thomas 79
Sweet, John 101
Swift, David 50
Swift, Thomas 133

Swiggitt, Rodey 14, 15
Swigitt, Aney 14
Swigitt, Ellisebeth 14
Swing, Barbary 22, 81
Swing, Eve 81
Swing, George 81, 138, 139
Swing, John 138, 144
Swing, Ludovick 138, 139
Swing, Ludwick 138
Swing, Mathew 139
Swing, Mathias 22
Swing, Matthew 138
Swisher, Jacob 89
Swisher, John 89

Talbert, John 101
Talbot, Jno. 10, 125
Talley, John 157
Talley, Nary 157
Talley, Nicholas 157
Talor, Edw. Tatum 92
Tarrell, Deborah 34
Tate, Allay 63
Tate, John 64
Tatum, Edw. [?] 92
Tatum, Edward 158
Tatum, Habert 158
Tatum, Henry 158
Tatum, Jonathan 56
Tatum, Patsey 158
Tatum, Sihon 158
Tatum, Sukey 158
Taylor, Alexander 158
Taylor, Elexander 158
Taylor, John 154, 158
Taylor, Mary 157, 158
Taylor, Nathan 158
Taylor, Ruth 150
Taylor, Simeon 154, 158
Taylor, Thomas 154, 157, 158
Teas, William 45
Tease, William 100
Telford, Isbell 145
Terrel, Deborah 30
Terrell, Deborah 25, 34
Terry, Thomas 13
Tharp, Elizabeth 32
Tharp, James 72
Tharpe, Laban 156
Tharpe, Alse 32
Thom, Ellenor 88
Thom, John 4, 88
Thom, Samuel 62
Thomas, Benjamin 156
Thomas, Elijah 156
Thomas, Francis 156

Thomas, Isaac 156
Thomas, James 156
Thomas, John 96, 119, 155, 156
Thomas, Milly 156
Thomas, Molley 96
Thomas, Stephen 156
Thommeson, John 42
Thompson, --- 65
Thompson, Benja. 180
Thompson, Benjamin 180
Thompson, Isabel 160
Thompson, James 156
Thompson, John 57, 156, 160
Thompson, John F. 156
Thompson, Letice 160
Thompson, Levina 160
Thompson, Margarit 160
Thompson, Margerie 160
Thompson, Margerite 160
Thompson, Nancy 160
Thompson, Rebecca 160
Thompson, Robert 108, 130, 160
Thompson, Wm. F. 156
Thomson, Henry 154
Thomson, John 154
Thornborough, James 8
Thornbrough, Edward 133
Thornbrough, Elizabeth 166
Thornbrough, Joseph, Juner 38
Thornbrugh, Hannah 155
Thornbrugh, Henry 155
Thornbrugh, James 155
Thornbrugh, Joseph 68, 73, 155
Thornbrugh, Martha 154, 155
Thornbrugh, Mary 155
Thornbrugh, Ruth 155
Thornbrugh, Thomas, Junior 155
Thornbrugh, Thomas 154, 155
Thornbrugh, Thos. 125
Thornbrugh, William 73, 155
Thornburg, Ann 157
Thornburg, Caleb 8
Thornburg, Edward 157
Thornburg, Isaac 157
Thornburg, James 8, 24, 158, 159
Thornburg, Jos. 157
Thornburg, Mary 158
Thornburgh, Benjamin 159
Thornburgh, James 102

Thornburgh, Martha 159
Thornburgh, Richard 159
Thornburgh, Tho. 161
Thornburgh, Thomas 102, 159
Thornburgh, Wlater 68
Thornbury, Elizabeth 166
Thorp, Aaron 28
Thorpe, John 28
Thrift, Abraham 66
Thrift, Susanah 66
Tilley, George 157
Tilley, Nancy 172
Tom, Ann 60, 61
Tom, John 86, 87
Tome, Catron 172
Tome, Daniel 172
Tome, Harper 172
Tome, Polley Perter 172
Tome, William 171, 172
Tomlinson, James 176
Tomlinson, John 99, 125
Tomlinson, John, Sen'r. 93
Tomlinson, William 125
Tompson, Sameul 160
Touchstone, Jonas 4, 159
Touchstone, Sarah 159
Trotter, Benja. 23
Trotter, Benjamin 180
Trotter, Betsy 180
Trotter, Edward 180
Trotter, Ephraim 180
Trotter, George 180
Trotter, Jane 180
Trotter, Joseph 180
Trotter, Josiah 180
Trotter, Mary 180
Trotter, Nancy 180
Trotter, Oldom 180
Trotter, Rachel 180
Tryon, William 92
Tucker, Abbit 160
Tucker, Anderton 160, 161
Tucker, Dianna 160
Tucker, John 160
Tucker, Leah 160
Tucker, Levi 160
Tucker, Mary 160
Tucker, Nancy 160
Tucker, Patty 160
Tucker, Peggy 160, 161, 175
Tucker, Zadoc 160, 161
Tumbleston, John 87
Turner, TGR 118

Tyer, Frederick 160, 161

Underhill, John 167
Underwood, Joshua 31
Unthank, Allen 20, 85, 161, 162
Unthank, Hannah 162
Unthank, John 122, 161, 162
Unthank, Jonathan 161
Unthank, Joseph 13, 161, 162
Unthank, Josiah 122, 161
Unthank, Judith 161
Unthank, Mary 162
Unthank, Sarah 162

Van Storre, Catheron 164
Van Storre, John 164
Vaughan, Kinchin 158
Vaughan, Tabitha 158
Vaughon, George 65
Vaughon, Mary 65
Vernon, Alexander [Joyce] sic 83
Vernon, James 83
Vickrey, Elizabeth 114
Vowell, William 131

Waddell, James 165
Wadell, Elizabeth 165
Waggoner, Felty 35
Wagnor, George 93
Wagoman, Christian 123
Walker, David 63
Walker, Eliner 165
Walker, Elizabeth 63, 105
Walker, Hannah 166
Walker, Jacob 159
Walker, James 165
Walker, Joel 63
Walker, John 15, 63, 165, 168
Walker, John Hunter 63
Walker, John, Jr. 15
Walker, John Sen'r. 63
Walker, Leven 168
Walker, Richard 165
Walker, Sarah 166
Walker, Thomas 136
Walker, William 63
Wallace, Elisabeth 43
Wallace, Sarah 43
Wallace, William 58
Walton, Alse 164
Walton, John 94, 164

Walton, Nathaniel 94, 164
Ward, Mary 76
Warren, Solomon 26
Wason, Margaret 11
Watson [?], Margaret 11
Watson, Sarah 137
Watson, William 137
Weatherby, Abner 180
Weatherford, Thomas 118
Weatherly, --- 59
Weatherly, Abner 180
Weatherly, Andy 87
Weatherly, Any 180
Weatherly, Betsy 180
Weatherly, Edward 57, 130, 167, 168
Weatherly, Elizabeth 166
Weatherly, Henrietta 167
Weatherly, Henry 180
Weatherly, Isaac 180
Weatherly, Isaiah 91, 180
Weatherly, James 19
Weatherly, Jessie 57
Weatherly, Joab 60
Weatherly, Lena 180
Weatherly, Levi 166
Weatherly, Mark 167, 168
Weatherly, Martin 130, 167
Weatherly, Mary 166, 168,
Weatherly, Nancy 180
Weatherly, Noah 166
Weatherly, Peggy 180
Weatherly, Polly 180
Weatherly, Rebecca 180
Weatherly, William 93, 130, 166, 167, 180
Webb, Thomas 31
Weirman, Will 65
Welborn, Amy 163
Welborn, Coalep/Caleb 163
Welborn, Elijah 163
Welborn, Elisha 163
Welborn, Emy 163
Welborn, Ephraim/Ephreim 163
Welborn, Ezekiel 163
Welborn, John 129, 163
Welborn, Joshua 163
Welborn, Ruth 163
Welborn, Thomas 162, 163
Welborn, Willaum/William 163

Wells, James 44
Werick, Jacob 162
West, Siphence 66
Wharten Watson 115
Wharton, Angolata [Welsh feminine name] 169, 170
Wharton, Elam, 169, 170
Wharton, Elisha 169, 170
Wharton, Elisha, Esqr. 177
Wharton, Evans, 169, 170
Wharton, Gidion 169, 170
Wharton, John 87, 169, 170
Wharton, Watson, 169, 170
Wheatly, Mary 32
Wheeler, Charles 39
Wheeler, Henry 30
Wheeler, Hezekiah 89, 92, 133
Wheeler, Lydia 152
Wheeler, Manlove 30
Whicker, James 40
White, Aunt Sarah 164
White, Benjamin 169
White, Elizabeth 93
White, Isaac 166, 168
White, James 166
White, Jane 164
White, Jean 164
White, Joel 166
White, John 164, 166, 169
White, Joseph, 167
White, Stanton 168
White, Susanna 166
White, Thomas 33, 72, 166, 167, 168
White, William 161, 166, 167
Whitesel, David 35
Whitesell, Adam 11
Whitesell, Margaret 11
Whitly, James 161
Whittel, James 134
Wickersham, Sarah 85
Widows, Jn. 78
Wierman, William 16
Wiley, Ann 146, 168, 169
Wiley, David 86, 168, 169
Wiley, David, Jr. 172
Wiley, David Sr. 171, 172
Wiley, Eli 172
Wiley, Ely 168, 169

Wiley, Hugh 52, 169, 172
Wiley, James 169, 171, 172
Wiley, John 169
Wiley, Margaret 122
Wiley, Peggy 171, 182
Wiley, Robert 169
Wiley, Thomas 4, 47, 48, 87, 139, 168, 169, 171, 172
Wiley, William 86, 87, 88, 169
Wilkerson, Thomas/Thos. 66
Wilkey James 3
Wilky, Martha 3
Will---, Jacob 65
Willents, Thomas 156
Willey, Ann 88
Willey, David 88
Willey, Edward W. 164
Willey, Emelia 164
Willey, James 113
Willey, Jno. 164
Willey, John 164
Willey, Prichard 164
Willey, William 88
Williams, Bartholomew 69
Williams, Andrew 85, 148
Williams, Catherine 99
Williams, Dolly 27
Williams, Eleanor 85
Williams, Isaac 101
Williams, Jain 154
Williams, Jesse 68, 72, 133, 155
Williams, John 76
Williams, Margaret 64
Williams, Richard 20, 77, 161, 168
Williams, Sophia 27
Williams, William 114, 154
Williamson, Stephen 67
Willis, John 169
Willis, Mary 4
Willis, Roger 4
Willson, Andrew 128
Willson, James 83
Willson, Jonathan 166
Willson, Mary 105, 128
Willson, Maxwell 128
Willson, Nancy 166
Willson, Robert 166
Willson, William 166
Willson, William Rankin 128
Willy, Mary 178
Wilson, Alice 32

Wilson, Allen/Allon 164
Wilson, Andra 170
Wilson, Andrew 24, 32, 129, 142, 143
Wilson, Archer 57
Wilson, Augness [Agness?] 32
Wilson, Benjamin 42
Wilson, Benjamine 146
Wilson, Daniel 32
Wilson, David 181
Wilson, Fanny 18
Wilson, George 83
Wilson, Isabella 146
Wilson, Jain 164
Wilson, James 27, 32, 36, 78, 164
Wilson, Jane 146
Wilson, Jeane 64
Wilson, John 1, 164
Wilson, Jonathan 173
Wilson, Marry Ann 46
Wilson, Michael/Michel 71
Wilson, Nancy 181
Wilson, Robert 32, 181
Wilson, Thomas, 57, 64
Winegardner, Joseph 89
Wire, James 150
Wire, Philip 63
Wirtburgar, John Henry 17
Witt, Catherin 162
Witt, Elesabeth 162
Witt, Esther 162
Witt, Jean 162
Witt, John 162
Witt, Margaret 162
Witt, Mary 162
Witt, Michael 162
Witt, Rosahan 162
Witty, Mary 13
Wood, John 65
Woodborn, Martha 169, 170
Woodburn Ann 167
Woodburn Arthur 167, 172, 173
Woodburn, Patsey 172
Woodburn, Tabitha 173
Woodburn, Thankful 167
Woodburn, Watson 173
Woodburn, William 167, 173
Woodside, Hannah 165
Woodside, James 165
Woodside, John 165
Woodside, Robert 165
Woodside, William 165
Woollen, John 81
Woollen, Levin 81
Wooten, Phebe 167
Work, Elizabeth 165
Work, Henry 58, 126, 165
Work, Jean 165
Work, John 165, 170, 171
Work, Margaret 29, 165
Work, Polley 170, 171
Work, Sarah 165
Wornock, Adam 134
Worth, Daniel 20, 93, 149
Worth, David 76, 132
Worth, Francis 167
Worth, Job 20, 76, 149
Worth, Mary 167
Worth, Wm. 167
Worth, Zeno 93
Wright, Alex'r. 163
Wright, Dianna 163
Wright, Elizah 163
Wright, James 163
Wright, James, Junior 163, 164
Wright, James, Sen'r. 163
Wright, Jane 163
Wright, John 163
Wright, Levin 50
Wright, Lucy 164
Wright, Lyda 163
Wright, Micajah 163
Wright, Prudence 163, 154
Wright, Thomas 172
Wright, Wm. 163
Wrightsel, --- 150
Wrightsel Henry 151
Write, Rebakah 172
Write, Whiley 172
Writsel, Adam 126

Yarbrough, Arch'd. 66, 67
York, Jeremiah 133
York, Semore 163
York, Seymore 133

Zimmerman, George 173
Zimmerman, Hanna 173
Zimmerman, Mary Dorothy 173
Zimmerman, Mary Margaret 173

LOCATIONS MENTIONED IN THESE WILLS

Alamance 41
Alamance Congregation 98
Alamance Presbyterian Church 98
Alamance Settlement 62
Albemarle County, VA 67
Allamance Creek 111, 112
Allamence 143
Allemance, Waters of 138
Allemence Congregation 121
Allemence Settlement 121
Allimance Meeting House 115
Allimance, headwaters of 115
Back Creek 141
Bare Creek 156
Beaver Crick 43
Beaver Island Creek 136
Bever Creek 19
Bever Krick 90
Big Branch 128
Big run 143
Bold Branch 151
Bruch [Brush?] Creek 22
Bruss [Brush?] Creek 161
Buchan, West branch of 145
Bufelow 178
Buffalo 128
buffelow plantation 173
Bullock Tract 152
Burch Creek 48, 121
Caintuck 107
Cascade Creek 136
Caswell County 118
Commonwealth of VA 18
County Donegall 59
Court House Road 142
Crannock freehold 60
Cumberland 31, 68
Cumberland River 125
Cunna 164
Dann river 18
Davis Creek 40
Deep River 7, 24, 67, 77, 133, 152
Delewer [Delaware] State 99
Duck River 128
Eastern Shore of Maryland 164
Fayetteville Road 150, 160
Franklin County, VA 34
Grate Road 43, 87
Great Bird 67
Great Choptank River 164
Half Gone Creek 31
Haw River 31, 134, 159

Hogains Creek 117
Hogans Creek 118
Homestead Tract 142
Horsepen Creek 161
Ireland 24, 105
Island in the Reedy Fork 160
Kingdom of Ireland 59
Lancaster County 105
Louck Swolly 59
Lows Lutheran Church 89
Lurgy Brack Drown Hazel & Corouch Lea 60
Martinville 137
Maryland 115
Maxwell's Branch 44
McGrady's Branch 154
Meadow Branch 91
Mears Fork 41
Meeting House 89
Mogans neck 134
Muddy Branch 57
Murfries Branch 13
Nantucket 20
Nelson's Ferry 105
New England 20
New Garden Meeting 133
New Garden Monthly Meeting 172
New Garden Road 180
North Bufalow 135
Orange County 47
Pennsylvania 106
Petersburg, [VA] 137
Phils Creek 67
Piney Fork 117
Piney Run 128
Pittsylvania County, VA 82, 136
Pleasant Mountain Creek 150
Pole Catt, waters of 138
Polecat Creek 40, 76, 149
Randolph County, 141
Redy Fork 108
Reedy Creek 17
Reedy Fork 129, 142, 143, 152
Reedy Fork Creek 13, 43
Richland 150
Richland Creek 143
Richmond County 156
River Reedy Fork 93
Rock Branch 97
Rock Creek 109
Rock Spring 157
Rockingham County 18, 98, 99, 126, 137
Rocky Branch 180
Rowan County, NC 32

Russels Branch 54
S. Buffalo 180
S. Buffaloe 109
Salisbury Road 162
Sandy River 82
Schockles [Schockless] Creek 19
School house 112
Schoolhouse Tract 141
Second Creek 154
Spotsylvania County 18
Spring Creek 42
Stinking Quarter Creek 89
Stokes County 134
Tennessee 109, 128
Town Creek 117
Virginia 140
West Fork of Stones River, TN 45
Wilmington, NC 48, 82
Wilson County, TN 42
Wilson's Mill 178
Winter Harbour 20
Yourk [York] County, PA 105

www.ingramcontent.com/pod-product-compliance
Lightning Source LLC
Chambersburg PA
CBHW080429230426
43662CB00015B/2227